# NATO ASI Series

## Advanced Science Institutes Series

*A series presenting the results of activities*
*Committee, which aims at the disseminatic*
*technological knowledge, with a view to st*
*scientific communities.*

The Series is published by an international board of publishers in conjunction with the NATO Scientific Affairs Division

| | |
|---|---|
| A Life Sciences | Plenum Publishing Corporation |
| B Physics | London and New York |
| C Mathematical and Physical Sciences | Kluwer Academic Publishers Dordrecht, Boston and London |
| D Behavioural and Social Sciences | |
| E Applied Sciences | |
| F Computer and Systems Sciences | Springer-Verlag Berlin Heidelberg New York |
| G Ecological Sciences | London Paris Tokyo Hong Kong |
| H Cell Biology | Barcelona Budapest |
| I Global Environmental Change | |

## NATO-PCO DATABASE

The electronic index to the NATO ASI Series provides full bibliographical references (with keywords and/or abstracts) to more than 30 000 contributions from international scientists published in all sections of the NATO ASI Series. Access to the NATO-PCO DATABASE compiled by the NATO Publication Coordination Office is possible in two ways:

- via online FILE 128 (NATO-PCO DATABASE) hosted by ESRIN, Via Galileo Galilei, I-00044 Frascati, Italy.

- via CD-ROM "NATO Science & Technology Disk" with user-friendly retrieval software in English, French and German (© WTV GmbH and DATAWARE Technologies Inc. 1992).

The CD-ROM can be ordered through any member of the Board of Publishers or through NATO-PCO, Overijse, Belgium.

Series F: Computer and Systems Sciences Vol. 125

The ASI Series F Books Published as a Result of
Activities of the Special Programme on
ADVANCED EDUCATIONAL TECHNOLOGY

This book contains the proceedings of a NATO Advanced Research Workshop held within the activities of the NATO Special Programme on Advanced Educational Technology, running from 1988 to 1993 under the auspices of the NATO Science Committee.

The volumes published so far in the Special Programme are as follows (further details are given at the end of this volume):

67: Designing Hypermedia for Learning. 1990.
76: Multimedia Interface Design in Education. 1992.
78: Integrating Advanced Technology into Technology Education. 1991.
80: Intelligent Tutoring Systems for Foreign Language Learning. 1992.
81: Cognitive Tools for Learning. 1992.
84: Computer-Based Learning Environments and Problem Solving. 1992.
85: Adaptive Learning Environments: Foundations and Frontiers. 1992.
86: Intelligent Learning Environments and Knowledge Acquisition in Physics. 1992.
87: Cognitive Modelling and Interactive Environments in Language Learning. 1992.
89: Mathematical Problem Solving and New Information Technologies. 1992.
90: Collaborative Learning Through Computer Conferencing. 1992.
91: New Directions for Intelligent Tutoring Systems. 1992.
92: Hypermedia Courseware: Structures of Communication and Intelligent Help. 1992.
93: Interactive Multimedia Learning Environments. 1992.
95: Comprehensive System Design: A New Educational Technology. 1993.
96: New Directions in Educational Technology. 1992.
97: Advanced Models of Cognition for Medical Training and Practice. 1992.
104: Instructional Models in Computer-Based Learning Environments. 1992.
105: Designing Environments for Constructive Learning. 1993.
107: Advanced Educational Technology for Mathematics and Science. 1993.
109: Advanced Educational Technology in Technology Education. 1993.
111: Cognitive Models and Intelligent Environments for Learning Programming. 1993.
112: Item Banking: Interactive Testing and Self-Assessment. 1993.
113: Interactive Learning Technology for the Deaf. 1993.
115: Learning Electricity and Electronics with Advanced Educational Technology. 1993.
116: Control Technology in Elementary Education. 1993.
117: Intelligent Learning Environments: The Case of Geometry. 1993.
119: Automating Instructional Design, Development, and Delivery. 1993.
121: Learning from Computers: Mathematics Education and Technology. 1993.
122: Simulation-Based Experiential Learning. 1993.
125: Student Modelling: The Key to Individualized Knowledge-Based Instruction. 1994.

# Student Modelling: The Key to Individualized Knowledge-Based Instruction

Edited by

## Jim E. Greer

## Gordon I. McCalla

Department of Computational Science
1C101 Engineering Building
University of Saskatchewan
Saskatoon, Saskatchewan
Canada S7N 0W0

Springer-Verlag
Berlin Heidelberg New York London Paris Tokyo
Hong Kong Barcelona Budapest
Published in cooperation with NATO Scientific Affairs Division

Proceedings of the NATO Advanced Research Workshop on "Student Modelling: The Key to Individualized Knowledge-Based Instruction", held in Ste. Adele, Quebec, Canada, May 4–8, 1991

CR Subject Classification (1991): K.3, I.2

ISBN 978-3-642-08186-6

CIP data applied for.

© Springer-Verlag Berlin Heidelberg 2010
Printed in Germany

# Preface

This book is the result of a NATO sponsored workshop entitled "Student Modelling: The Key to Individualized Knowledge-Based Instruction" which was held May 4-8, 1991 at Ste. Adele, Quebec, Canada. The workshop was co-directed by Gordon McCalla and Jim Greer of the ARIES Laboratory at the University of Saskatchewan.

The workshop focused on the problem of student modelling in intelligent tutoring systems. An intelligent tutoring system (ITS) is a computer program that is aimed at providing knowledgeable, individualized instruction in a one-on-one interaction with a learner. In order to individualize this interaction, the ITS must keep track of many aspects of the learner: how much and what he or she has learned to date; what learning styles seem to be successful for the student and what seem to be less successful; what deeper mental models the student may have; motivational and affective dimensions impacting the learner; and so on. Student modelling is the problem of keeping track of all of these aspects of a learner's learning.

Student modelling is a centrally important issue in ITS research. Without a student model, an ITS would be doomed to follow a preset sequence of steps regardless of the impact of its actions on a student's learning. Unfortunately, student modelling is also a very difficult problem. It touches on many of the great issues of artificial intelligence and cognitive science: diagnosis, belief revision and truth maintenance, qualitative reasoning, mental modelling, temporal reasoning, non-monotonic and probabilistic reasoning, testing and evaluation, etc. It provides both a focus for the exploration of these issues, as well as an original twist on many of them. The original twist arises due to two main factors that are central to student modelling but are often not important in other applications. The first of these is the impossibility of keeping a completely accurate model of the learner, which forces the student model to deal with inherent uncertainty. The second factor is the constant revision the learner undergoes in his or her perceptions of the domain of study as the instructional interaction proceeds, a feature that presents a constantly moving target for the student modelling subsystem.

The workshop had the aim of bringing together researchers from a variety of perspectives with the goal that progress could be made in solving some of the difficult student modelling issues. It was also hoped that a new synthesis of ideas could be achieved among the different sub-disciplines represented at the workshop. To this end there were invited talks from researchers taking a formal artificial intelligence approach to the problem of student modelling, those with a more engineering-oriented perspective, and those with a psychological point of view. The audience for these talks consisted of established researchers and younger researchers from academe and industry who had a wide variety of backgrounds, perspectives, and goals. In the general discussion that followed each invited talk, input was encouraged from the entire audience, but for each talk there was also a subgroup of the audience who were on a panel with an explicit mandate to raise issues and stir up discussion. Panel members had been given the opportunity to read documents prepared in advance by the invited speaker associated with their panels.

It is our belief that the workshop format worked well, the sought for mutual understanding was beginning to happen, and that new syntheses leading to real progress in student modelling may be on the horizon. Such progress, of course, will only become fully evident after much additional research has been carried out. An immediate concrete result, however, was a special issue of the *Journal of Artificial Intelligence and Education* that grew out of the workshop. This issue appeared as Volume 3, Number 4 of the journal in November of 1992. Now a year later, this book is the second publication resulting from the workshop. It contains a total of thirteen papers, five of which appeared in whole or in part in the journal special issue and eight of which are new.

The thirteen chapters in the book have been categorized into five sections. Section 1, the background section, contains a single chapter by Holt, Dubs, Jones, and Greer. This chapter is a review of the field of student modelling, covering the basic concepts of overlay models, bug models, and various more recent student modelling representations. The function of student modelling is analyzed within the context of the intelligent tutoring system architectures.

Section 2 consists of five chapters that look at a variety of artificial intelligence techniques for student modelling. The first paper in this section, Chapter 2 by McCalla and Greer, discusses two research topics central to student modelling: how to represent knowledge about a learner at various grain sizes and reason with this knowledge to enhance the capabilities of an intelligent tutoring system, and how to maintain a consistent view of a learner's knowledge as the system-learner interaction evolves. The next paper is Chapter 3, by Bredeweg and Winkels. It explores the potential for using qualitative simulation models as the basis for student models. The authors present an integrated qualitative reasoning approach that can be used to build both domain models and student models. The modelling language appears to map directly on that of human reasoning about the domain. The third paper in this section (Chapter 4 in the book) is by Katz, Lesgold, Eggan, and Gordin. They investigate the potential for a fuzzy-logic-based student modelling and diagnosis approach in the avionics troubleshooting tutor, Sherlock II. The next paper (Chapter 5), by Woolf and Murray, explores several machine learning mechanisms which might enhance the functionality of a student model. Human learning experiments are described demonstrating the spontaneous nature of learning, for which action-oriented machine learning-based student model components are needed. Finally, Felisa Verdejo, in Chapter 6, concludes this section by discussing an approach to constructing a complete and practical student modelling environment in an intelligent tutoring system that teaches novice students about program specification. Her approach to building the student model relies on unobtrusively gathering a great deal of information about student behavior via a problem solving environment and a natural language interface.

Section 3 examines student modelling from a more psychological perspective, specifically investigating the relationship between what we know about human cognition and student modelling. There are three chapters in this part of the book. The first is Chapter 7, by Stellan Ohlsson, who describes a new approach to student modeling based on representing subject matter knowledge as sets of constraints. Constraint violations on the part of the learner indicate incomplete or incorrect knowledge and can therefore be used to guide system responses. In Chapter 8, Frasson and Kaltenbach assess the Cascade model of skill acquisition put forward by VanLehn to account for the "self-explanation" effect. They show how an alternative interpretation of the psychological evidence can explain the effects of self-explanation as well as explain the evolution from novice to expert. The last chapter in this section (Chapter 9) is by Möbus, Schröder, and Thole. Their chapter describes an approach to model learners' knowledge growth from novice to expert within the framework of the ABSYNT help system. The model is continuously updated based on the learner's actions, distinguishing between newly acquired knowledge, modelled by rule addition, and improved knowledge, modelled by rule composition.

Section 4 contains three chapters which take a formal approach to student modelling. The first paper in this part is Chapter 10 by Xueming Huang, who proposes a formal model for representing inconsistent beliefs. It is assumed that a learner can recognize inconsistencies in the beliefs under attention, so a tutor can lead the learner to remove the inconsistencies and the misconceptions behind them by bringing the inconsistent subset of beliefs to the learner's attention. A logic of attention is presented to formally describe the process of removing possibly inconsistent beliefs. In Chapter 11 Costa, Gaspar, and Coelho, show one possible way to formalize the notion of an Interactive Learning Environment, based on a modification of the idea of deductive structures. These deductive structures, accompanied by heuristic principles and criteria that define different types of societies and agents, can be used to model various distinct educational scenarios. The final paper in this part is Chapter 12. In this chapter, John Self considers at length student modelling from the perspective of the formal modelling techniques that are involved. He sets out to provide a theoretical, computational basis for student modelling which is psychologically neutral and independent of applications. The intrinsic difficulty of the student modelling problem becomes evident through its analysis in terms of formal artificial intelligence research.

The final section of the book, Section 5, is a single-chapter epilogue by Sack, Soloway, and Weingrad. Chapter 13 takes a more philosophical look at student models, past and present. Sack, Soloway, and Weingrad explain how their research into student modelling has moved away from mainstream objectivist formulations towards a more community-responsive, constructivist understanding of learners. Starting with two issues, "bugs" and "transfer" they explain how their theories about learner knowledge and learning have been forced to change and how this has resulted in a change in understanding of "bugs", "transfer", and student models. This chapter offers much food for thought through its philosophical discussions detailing a shift in position from objectivist to constructivist.

Overall, this book is a gold mine of ideas about student modelling. It is also a demonstration of how complex and multi-faceted the student modelling problem is. In fact, so difficult is the task, that it is tempting to conclude that maybe it would be better to try to avoid student modelling all together, to search for some magical "end run" around the need to understand the learner at all. Unfortunately, whether the tutoring system is an "old fashioned" present-and-test frame-based tutor, a deeply knowledgeable AI-based expert advisor, or a scaffolding environment situated in the learner's world, it must adapt to the learner or be forever condemned to rigidity, inflexibility, and unresponsiveness. If the learning is to be learner-centred, then the system that is meant to help this learning must be sensitive to nuances and changes in the learner's perceptions of his or her world. The problem of modelling the learner thus cannot be shrugged off, whatever the perspective of those building the learning environment, however hard the problem may seem.

For better or for worse, student modelling will remain a key problem to be resolved in the quest for truly supportive learning environments. And since student modelling is just a particularly interesting form of user modelling, which in turn is the key to adaptive and responsive human-computer interaction, it is a central problem in making computer technology of any sort accessible to human use. We as editors hope that this volume will shed light on student modelling, and will form a landmark on the road to better understanding of this critical problem.

We would like to acknowledge the support of NATO who funded the workshop from which this volume evolved and who helped to offset the costs of book production. Canada's Natural Sciences and Engineering Research Council also helped to fund the book through research grants to both of the editors. Of course, we are grateful to all of the workshop participants, to those who helped us organize the workshop, and to those who contributed papers to both the journal special issue and this book. Finally, we would like to express our heartfelt gratitude to Sharolynn Woodward who acted as an editorial assistant and a driving force to get this volume completed, if not with dispatch, at least within our lifetimes! Thank you all.

Jim Greer and Gord McCalla
October 1993

# Table of Contents

x

**Part 5. Epilogue**

Part 1

Background

# The State of Student Modelling

Peter Holt[1], Shelli Dubs[2], Marlene Jones[2], and Jim Greer[3]

[1]Computer Science and Information Systems, Athabasca University, Athabasca, Canada
[2]Advanced Computing and Engineering, Alberta Research Council, Calgary, Canada
[3]Department of Computational Science, University of Saskatchewan, Saskatoon, Canada

**Abstract:** This review of the field of student modelling covers the basic concepts of overlays, bugs, and various more recent modelling representations. The function of student modelling is analyzed within the context of the original intelligent tutoring system architectures and more recent elaborations of that architecture such as intelligent learning environments and case-based tutorial systems. The authors explore issues surrounding cognitive modelling and model building. The contributions to student modelling from various research areas are outlined. It is concluded that student modelling is a vital research area underpinning future developments in intelligent learning environments and tutoring systems.

**Keywords:** student modelling, diagnosis, bugs, learning environment, mental models

## 1 Introduction

During the last two decades, researchers have tackled the challenge of developing effective instructional systems that tailor interactions to an individual learner. One of the fundamental approaches employed concerns modelling the individual learner and exploiting the captured information to modify system interaction to best facilitate that person's learning. A variety of approaches have been employed to accomplish this task including the applications of techniques of artificial intelligence, cognitive psychology, and instructional science.

In this chapter we examine the past accomplishments in student modelling, describing the more common techniques employed in student modelling, the difficulties encountered, and the potential alternative approaches. The next section tackles the problem of "What is a student model?". Section 3 surveys the types of student models that have been employed in various instructional systems. This includes an examination of the kinds of knowledge captured in the model and how that knowledge is represented. Section 4 addresses the challenge of building a student model including eliciting the necessary information, model tracing, differential modelling, implementation techniques, and maintenance of the student model. Section 5 is a discussion of how to make use of a student model. This includes a survey of applications in a variety of learning approaches and corresponding instructional systems. Related issues, including mental modelling, qualitative reasoning, metacognition skills, and psychological validity, are discussed in Section 6. Section 7 includes concluding remarks.

## 2  What is a Student Model?

While a model of a learner can be described as an abstract representation of the learner, and thus could be a teacher's conceptualization of a learner, the term student model is typically used in connection with applications of computer-based intelligent instructional systems. In this context the student model is a representation of the computer system's beliefs about the learner and is, therefore, an abstract representation of the learner in the system.

It seems important to capture a learner's understanding and misunderstanding of the content domain. In the most general sense, a student model is the system's beliefs about the learner's knowledge. Assuming that knowledge is belief, a student model is also the system's beliefs about the learner's beliefs. There are various ways to reason about the learner's knowledge. If one keeps a simple history of learner behaviour as a data source, drawing inferences about the learner's knowledge is difficult. If one first makes interpretations of the learner's behaviour, subsequent inference is easier. Thus one could construct explanations of behaviour in light of prior explanations and save the new explanation.

There is no consensus as to what should be included in a student model or whether a student model is necessary for effective and efficient instruction (see Section 4 for further discussion of alternative approaches). A comprehensive student model would include all the learner's prior relevant learning, the learner's progress within the curriculum, the learner's preferred learning style, as well as other types of learner-related information. Implementing such a model would be a formidable if not impossible task; thus a large number of systems attempt to model the learner only in relation to the subject matter representation.

McCalla [66] makes a useful distinction between explicit and implicit student models. An explicit student model is a representation of the learner in the learning system that is used to drive instructional decisions. An implicit student model is reflected in design decisions that have been derived from the system designer's view of the learner. For example, the particular metaphor and icons used in the human interface reflect the system designer's beliefs about the learner. It is an explicit student model that is generally of interest to artificial intelligence researchers.

In order to make a system adaptable to individual learners, an explicit student model is highly desirable. Without an explicit student model, decisions about adaptation of the environment can be made only on the basis of observed learner behaviour snapshots. An explicit student model permits the system to store relevant knowledge about the learner and to use this accumulated knowledge as the basis for system adaptation to learner needs. Furthermore, an explicit student model, accumulating knowledge about the learner by studying patterns of behaviour, is the fundamental ingredient for an intelligent, individualized computer-based learning environment.

There are various barriers to student modelling which result from the problem of inferring knowledge from learner's behaviour. These barriers are:

- the environment contains a large amount of uncertainty and noise,
- the learner's inference may be unsound and may be based on inconsistent knowledge,
- constructing explanations from behaviour is computationally intractable, and
- learners are creative and inventive and frequently engage in unanticipated, novel behaviour that requires much sophistication to interpret (Self's "intractable problem" [81]).

## 3 Knowledge Representation in Student Models

In the past, student models have represented various types of information. Traditional computer-assisted learning systems store simple quantitative scores from domain tests. Most Intelligent Tutoring Systems (ITSs) store domain knowledge as an overlay [24] or mal-rules (BUGGY, [21]). Some represent the learner as a subset of a cognitive model for the domain (eg. the LISP Tutor, [3]). Little work has been done on representing individual learner characteristics such as learning style, affective state, specific idiosyncratic knowledge, or various individual learner attributes. Work has been limited by the lack of standardized means of easily determining the learner's state for individual characteristics beyond expert domain knowledge and common misconceptions.

In traditional computer-assisted learning the learner is represented by relatively unprocessed or unstructured data such as quantitativescores on tests or binary judgements of responses. These data can be used by the program to decide upon possible pre-programmed branches or loops. The data would not support any complex inferencing about the learner's current state without considerable additional processing by a tutorial component. Traditional computer assisted learning does not struggle with the student modelling problem and concentrates on having the instructional design hard-wired into the domain content material as simple branches and loops.

## 3.1 Overlay Models

As previously mentioned, a large number of systems attempt to model the learner only in relation to the subject matter representation. In such systems, the learner's knowledge at any point is treated as a subset of an expert's knowledge; the objective of instruction is to establish the closest possible correspondence between the two. A student model based on such a comparison is called an overlay model.

In an overlay :model, the student model is conceptualized by comparing the learner's behaviour with that of an expert. This approach assumes that all differences between the learner's behaviour and that of the expert model can be explained as the learner's lack of skill. Therefore, the knowledge of the learner is simply a subset of the expert's knowledge (see Figure 1).

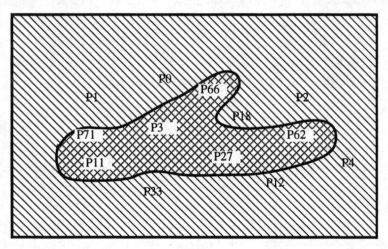

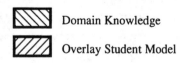

Domain Knowledge

Overlay Student Model

Figure 1: An overlay student model [57]

The following systems (and many others) use the general overlay model in their approach to student modelling: SCHOLAR, a geography tutor for South America [23], BIP, a problem-solving laboratory for introductory programming [6], and GUIDON [27].

In an overlay model the learner is represented by a relatively simple mechanism which supports inferencing about the learner's cognitive state relative to the ideal domain expert. The overlay model works well for systems where the goal is to strictly impart the knowledge of the expert to the learner. The main problem with the overlay model is that it assumes that a learner's knowledge can be merely a subset of that of an expert, which may not be the case. Although it is hoped that learners will learn the domain and gain knowledge through aspiring to become experts, they might possess certain knowledge (possibly misconceived) that experts do not. Novice learners often do not approach the task of problem solving in the same manner as experts. Novice learners will often rely on surface analogies between problems, while experts will tend to use deeper functional analogies [26].

The overlay model does not typically provide for any knowledge or beliefs the learner might have that differ from those of the expert. For example in WUSOR [24], if the learner has an alternative strategy for hunting the Wumpus that works well, the tutor will not recognize it and may actually try to correct the learner. These weaknesses have led to a variety of extensions to the overlay model.

The differential model is a modification of the overlay model. This model divides the learner's knowledge into two categories: knowledge that the learner should know and knowledge the learner could not be expected to know. Thus unlike the overlay model, the differential model does not assume that all gaps in the student model are equally undesirable. The differential model acknowledges and tries to explicitly represent both learner knowledge and learner-expert differences. This approach can be thought of as an overlay on the expected knowledge, which is essentially a subset of the expert general model (see Figure 2).

The following systems use a differential model in their approach to student modelling: WEST, an electronic board game to teach arithmetic [21] and GUIDON2, a tutor built on the medical diagnostic system MYCIN [29]. In WEST, the expert model simulates playing the game from the learner's viewpoint. At early stages of the game, the learner should know about "shortcuts" but might not be expected to know about "bumping". If the learner consistently forgets to take shortcuts when the expert would, the tutor would conclude that the learner lacks important knowledge about short cuts. On the other hand, if the learner does not "bump" the opponent, the expert also avoids the "bump" and no conclusion is yet drawn about the learner's knowledge of "bumping" opponents. Although the differential model is not so strict or presumptuous about the knowledge of the learner, it still suffers from most of the same difficulties as the standard overlay model. Since it still assumes that the student model is essentially a subset of the expert, the student model remains incomplete.

An elaboration of the overlay model uses a "genetic graph" a type of semantic network, which contains assumptions about the ways in which the learner develops various aspects of expertise [45]. The learner's knowledge is described in terms of the nodes of the graph and learning behaviour is described in terms of the edges. The learner's progress is shown by the possible paths through the graph and it is assumed that the learner will progress through a particular learning path in a general sequence corresponding to the graph's partial ordering. The necessary learning mechanism (eg. generalization, discrimination, etc.) for moving from one node to the next also becomes part of the student model (eg. [15]). It appears intuitive that some such elaborations would enhance the standard overlay model and support more sophisticated views of the learner with little additional computational overhead. Progress in delineating genetic graphs for student learning processes and sequences for particular domains has been slow.

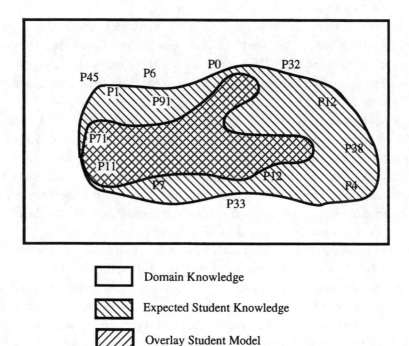

Domain Knowledge

Expected Student Knowledge

Overlay Student Model

Figure 2: A differential student model [57]

## 3.2 Perturbation Models and Bug Models

While the overlay model represents the learner only in terms of "correct" knowledge, a "perturbation" model [57] normally combines the standard overlay mode with a representation of faulty knowledge. In perturbation models the learner is not considered a mere subset of the expert, rather the learner will possess knowledge potentially different in quantity and in quality from expert knowledge. The common technique for implementing a perturbation model is to represent the expert knowledge and then augment this representation with explicit knowledge of likely misconceptions. The student model is then an overlay on the augmented general model (see Figure 3). The perturbation model maintains a close link between the learner and expert models but can also represent the learner's knowledge and beliefs beyond the range of the expert model.

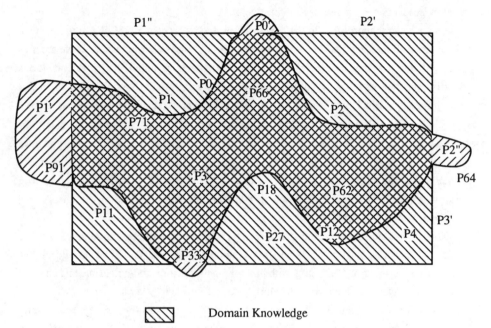

Domain Knowledge

Perturbation Student Model

Figure 3: A perturbation model [57]

When a learner demonstrates a more or less consistent but incorrect general model, this is commonly called a misconception. A "bug", on the other hand, refers to some structural flaw in a procedure that often manifests itself in faulty behaviour. Despite these definitions, the terms "bug" and "misconception" are frequently used indiscriminately. A fixed collection of bugs and misconceptions is generally referred to as a "bug library" or "bug catalogue". As the learner progresses, the perturbation model can be updated in regard to the presence or absence of bugs known in the bug library. The inclusion of the bugs in the perturbation model allows more sophisticated understanding of the learner than can be accomplished with a simple overlay on the expert model.

The following systems use a perturbation model in their approach to student modelling: DEBUGGY, a system to evaluate a learner's subtraction performance [20], LMS, a system for testing algebra skills [87], and PROUST, a system for PASCAL programming [88]. DEBUGGY uses a set of procedures which represent common mistakes made by learners performing subtraction. These possible mistakes represent perturbations to the expert model. LMS uses production rules to represent the correct methods of algebra and mal-rules for the common misconceptions learners have about algebra.

There are several approaches to the development and representation of bug libraries. One may enumerate all the bugs based on empirical analysis of learners' errors (enumerative theories of bugs) or one may try to generate bugs based on a set of underlying misconceptions (generative theories of bugs). Proust's bug library is an enumerative collection of Pascal programming bugs, which were discovered through careful protocol analysis of human tutoring sessions. Generative theories of bugs offer plausible mechanisms for explaining bugs in terms of their generation from an underlying cognitive model. Generative theories not only possess a language for expressing surface manifestations of bugs, but they include a performance model which provides the context for interpreting the observed errors. Generative theories can generate bugs on- or off-line. An example of this approach is VanLehn's "repair" theory [89] and his later work with Sierra [90].

Various approaches have been taken in recognizing bugs using generative theories. One approach is to generate bugs systematically in reaction to all possible variations on a generative model (as in repair theory). A difficulty with this approach is that many implausible bugs may be generated. The effort to include a plausibility check for each generated bug is excessive. Another approach is to reconstruct bugs on the basis of observed errors, possibly using a form of explanation-based generalization. This involves answering the question "What sort of known deeper misconception might have led to the observed error?". Generative approaches can support a more sophisticated perturbation model of the learner than can a simple bug library, provided the generative model is accurate. An accurate generative model of bugs that achieves good domain coverage but produces few implausible bugs is extremely difficult to create. VanLehn indicates that this is the principle drawback of repair theory [89].

Figure 4 presents a classification of some existing examples of theories of bugs. Since actual systems often combine characteristics from more than one type, the classification is done in two passes: the main classification (rows) is refined with additional distinctions (columns) along the same dimensions. Hence, pure examples of each type are on the diagonal. ([91], p. 348)

At the same time, a big hurdle in developing an enumerative bug library is the effort required to assemble and to maintain it. The approach typically entails the analysis of a large database of learner-tutor interactions. For example, see the developmental work undertaken for DEBUGGY [20]. It seems that the effort required to craft an accurate generative model is not much different from that of cataloguing instances of bugs from empirical observation.

The task of inferring bugs from learners' interactions with a computer system also poses problems. Misdiagnosis may still result, particularly if the existing bug is neither within the library nor is a combination of elements thereof. Whether using an enumerative or generative approach, coverage of the resulting bug library is a problem. Furthermore, differentiating random slips from instances of "buggy" rules and diagnosing higher order interactions between different bugs is difficult.

| | enumerative | reconstructive | generative |
|---|---|---|---|
| *enumerative* | ACTP: extensionally defined list of observable errors | DEBUGGY, LMS: combination of enumerated bugs that reconstruct observed errors | MENO-II: enumerated errors recognized and attributed to enumerated misconceptions |
| *reconstructive* | PROUST: reconstructs design intentions using a library of buggy plans | ACM, PIXIE, ADVISOR: reconstruct bugs from a language of neutral primitives | Young & O'Shea [95]: incorrect procedures reconstructed with manipulations that explain the nature of bugs |
| *generative* | Bonar & Soloway [12]: library of abstract bug generators to explain the origins of observed errors | REPAIR: generates bugs by replaying the inventive handling of impasses | REPAIR/STEP, Matz [65]: reduction of the occurrence of bugs to mislearning |

Figure 4: Types of theories of bugs [91]

Another concern with some of the perturbation models, such as DEBUGGY, is that although they may uncover what mistakes the learner has made, they do not explain why the mistakes have occurred. As with the overlay model, the enumerative bug model can be criticized as having no deep underlying representation of domain knowledge [11]. On the other hand, in generative theories, diagnosis may entail many competing hypotheses and hence, the knowledge gained by a particular diagnosis may not be particularly useful.

It must be emphasized that a bug library is not synonymous with a student model. A bug library alone will be useful to help recognize particular causes of errors and specific misconceptions. However, a bug library represents only a snapshot of the learner's knowledge state. A perturbation model adds an interpretation to evolving patterns of bug use and bug avoidance by a particular learner. It can also make use of a bug library to help define the space of plausible misconceptions at some point in the student's learning. In this way a perturbation model can utilize a bug library to extend the overlay beyond expert knowledge.

Although the additional information in perturbation modelling expands the ways to explain learner behaviour, it also poses new problems. Since the search space that must be dealt with in constructing and maintaining the student model is greatly expanded, heuristic search techniques are normally required to prune the search space.

Sleeman, Kelly, Martinak and Moore [86] questioned the usefulness of a "bug-based" student model for remediation when they found that for tutoring algebra, reteaching was as effective as remediating specific errors. Other studies have found that even within a select domain the bugs diagnosed vary greatly over schools, classes studied, etc., greatly limiting the generality of any system [74]. What is more, error patterns and learning styles that exist in one subject area have not been shown to apply to all or indeed any other subject areas; in other words, "transfer of training (or mistaking)", is not proven to exist. In summary, the bug aspect of perturbation modelling requires further research before its external validity for diagnosis and remediation is clearly established.

## 3.3 Other Approaches to Knowledge Representation

Elsom-Cook [37] claims that a tutor does not need to know exactly what state the learner's knowledge is in at any one time. He suggests that a system can maintain a confidence interval around the lower and upper bounds of the learner's knowledge. Elsom-Cook describes a simple implementation of this approach in a system for LISP tutoring, using standard machine learning techniques. The way the model is implemented could be considered a variation on an overlay model.

From learner behaviour, the system induces lower and upper bounds to what the learner knows. Then, on the basis of the system's domain knowledge, it uses deduction to generate predictions and generates problems to test these predictions. Admittedly, the learner may be producing behaviour that matches the tutor's prediction using idiosyncratic methods, and the deductions used in the system are not necessarily adequate models of the learner's reasoning processes. These bounded models can be more tractable to build than exact models because of the requirement for less precise remediation.

A constraint-based model represents the learner as the constraints upon the correct knowledge representation. This extends the standard overlay approach by permitting much more sophisticated reasoning about domain concepts beyond whether they are known or not. A violation of those constraints by the learner indicates that the model needs to be updated. The model is computationally simple and does not prescribe a particular tutorial strategy. It is unclear how this approach will generalize across domains and tutorial strategies but later in this volume Ohlsson elaborates upon this approach with examples from two domains (Ohlsson, this volume).

Katz and Lesgold (this volume) propose fuzzy diagnostic student models. In such a model statistical procedures are used to propagate changes from observable actions to local variables (eg. ability to measure test results) to more global variables (eg. ability to use equipment). The presence or absence of the knowledge variables (eg. ability to use test equipment) are represented by a probability distribution on five levels of the knowledge variable ranging from "no knowledge" to "fully developed knowledge". This elaboration in the representation of the knowledge allows finer grained tutorial actions based on a particular set of knowledge variables. The model is based on the concept of fuzzy sets and instantiated in an idiosyncratic fashion for one particular domain.

Gilmore and Self [44] explored other machine learning techniques as ways of representing the learner. One system for concept learning has a student model based on an ID3 [77] type classification system. Its shortcomings include requiring all the examples to be tested at one time and using an artificial metric in determining the most discriminating features. Shortcomings of a discrimination-tree approach are that it learns only conjunctive concepts and uses unrealistic search constraints.

Gilmore and Self [44] also looked at schemata learning as a method to acquire student models for learners reading stories. However, the learning mechanisms were found to be arbitrary with no psychological support. Overall there has been little success in directly importing machine learning techniques as mechanisms for student modelling. Woolf (this volume) more optimistically suggests that there are numerous ways in which machine learning can be usefully applied to student modelling.

## 3.4  State versus Process Models

Clancey [28] believes that one should classify knowledge bases, including student models, according to the different ways they describe processes. By doing this, one can then identify and study types of qualitative representations. The student model, then, can be viewed as capable of simulating the process by which the learner solves a problem. The model explains the learner's behaviour in terms of both a general (domain) model and an inference procedure (how the learner interprets observations and the general model). A simulation model of a learner should be able to predict what the learner will do next, as well as work backwards from learner behaviour to generate an explanation. Thus, such a model would be an executable process model. Relatively few existing systems employ executable process student models.

Many instructional systems, including SOPHIE, a laboratory for troubleshooting electronic circuits [20] and many of the systems described above, contain only state information. These systems may check if the final outcome or result of the learner's behaviour is consistent with an expert's result, but it will not explain the sequence of behaviour nor the rationale for the Fsequence of inferences that the learner made. PROUST [88] constructs a situation-specific task model that accounts for the learner's behaviour and hypothesizes how it might have been derived, but it does not verify that the inference procedure is the same as that used by the learner. MACSYMA ADVISOR, an advisor for the mathematical package MACSYMA [43], gets slightly closer as it relates intermediate steps in the problem-solving process to an idealized inference procedure.

Systems such as the LISP Tutor [38] are considered process models, as they attempt to explain learner behaviour through the order of inferences that are utilized for modifying the situation-specific model [28]. This notion of providing explanations for processes that occur over time, is one of the defining features of simulation models, in contrast to the snapshot nature of state models.

Within Clancey's category of simulation models he makes a further distinction between behavioural and functional simulation models. He distinguishes between a behavioural description of actions (what the learner is observed doing) and a functional description of beliefs and goals (what the learner knows and is trying to do). The LISP Tutor simulates the programming process through situation-action patterns but only captures behavioural information about the learner. A behavioural model may articulate the goals behind problem-solving steps, but these are strictly domain specific.

A functional model tries to represent the intended purpose of the instructional interaction. For instance in PROUST, the learner's code is analyzed in terms of its resulting behaviour rather than through static analysis alone. This provides the potential for generating explanations of learner behaviour at the plan level or intention level. The advantages of the functional model over behavioural models are due to its potential for generalizing the explanation of reasoning, the modelling misconceptions, and the anticipation of situations across domains. The explanations from behavioural models can only be behavioural. That is, the explanations cannot distinguish the difference between factual errors and errors in the underlying goals and plans and errors in translating plans into actions.

Figure 5 [28] illustrates the possible combinations of student models of the general model (domain model) and the inference procedure (model of reasoning). This figure illustrates that the inference procedure and the general model need not be the same type of process model. The process model is a more complete model of the learner since it not only represents the learner's behaviour in terms of the general model but also the inference mechanisms used to solve the problem. The advantage is increased ability to explain the learner's behaviour, particularly in the case of functional process models. The generality of the process model has the advantage of being less domain specific, lending itself to the goal of execution by standard inference engines.

Model of Reasoning

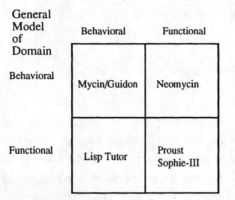

| General Model of Domain | Behavioral | Functional |
|---|---|---|
| Behavioral | Mycin/Guidon | Neomycin |
| Functional | Lisp Tutor | Proust Sophie-III |

Figure 5: Comparison of programs in terms of model of the domain and model of reasoning [28]

# 4  How to Build a Student Model

A range of issues arise in building student models. These can be described in terms of four aspects: who is being modeled, what is being modeled, how the model is acquired and maintained, and how the model might be used [40]. Some of these issues are described below.

- Who is being modelled?

  There are two specific issues we need to consider in evaluating who is being modelled: the degree of specialization, and temporal extent. The degree of specialization refers to whether we are modelling individuals or classes of learners. Temporal extent refers to the extent to which we maintain the knowledge of the learner over time (learner history).

- What is being modelled?

  The content of the student model will vary from application to application. In building a model one must determine what components are needed in order to maintain an appropriate model of the learner. The components represented could be learner goals and plans, capabilities, attitudes and/or knowledge or beliefs.

- How is the model to be acquired and maintained?

  In acquisition one is concerned about the techniques required to learn new facts about the learner. In maintenance one is concerned about the ability to incorporate new information into the existing model as well as dealing with any discrepancies.

- Why is the model there?

  The student model can be used in various ways, though the use is often dependent on the particular application. For instance the model may: (1) elicit information from the learner,

(2) provide the learner with help or advice, (3) provide feedback to the learner, or (4) interpret the behaviour of the learner.

## 4.1 Eliciting a Student Model

Eliciting a particular student model is closely tied to the student modelling approach. If it is simply an overlay model, the first step in defining a student model is the cognitive :modelling and knowledge acquisition for the expert model.  In GUIDON [27], the student modelling begins with the modelling of how expert practitioners think about, diagnose, and prescribe medication for bacterial infections.  It involves a long and difficult set of interviews and follow-ups with a number of experts.  Anderson's LISP Tutor [2] is based on a more comprehensive model of human cognition (ACT*) applied to the domain of LISP programming. The ACT* theory has been built and modified over years of protocol analysis, psychological experimentation, and computer modelling. Experts are modelled as set of correct production rules for creating LISP programs. Learners are modelled as a subset of these correct production rules along with common incorrect production rules.  Moebus, Schroeder and Thole (this volume) provide an elaborate cognitive model of functional programming consisting of over 600 rules.  This cognitive model is used to build an offline process model of a generic learner (external model) as well as a static online model which is used to determine tutoring actions (internal model).

Currently tools are being developed to assist in the area of acquiring expert domain models, such as tools for knowledge elicitation and structuring and tools enabling designers to categorize and describe users of a system. Breuker and Wielinga [17] use an expert systems tool (KADS) for helping elicit the expert representation for an ITS.  A survey on techniques for eliciting mental models has been prepared by Jones and Dubs [55].  Woolf (eg. [94]) has developed an entire language for describing knowledge units and learners' relative understanding of those units.  Anderson and Pelletier [4] outline a system for developing model-tracing tutors.  Such tools are not yet commercially available.  Katz and Lesgold (this volume) have considered the application of social science techniques such as multidimensional scaling, factor analysis, and cluster analysis in discovering and representing learners' domain knowledge.  While limited by a linear model, such tools could provide a means of explaining a large number of learner raw data points by a few underlying dimensions or factors in a student model, or cluster learners by their particular level in a model. More work needs to be done in that area.

Once a system is running, it must construct an individualized student model for each new learner. An early decision is how and what to represent about the learner.  For example: Is the knowledge to be included in the model procedural or declarative? Are the student's learning goals to be represented, and if so, how? In the related area of user modelling, Kobsa and Wahlster [60] detail various ways that a system can build up a model of a particular user. The construction is dependent upon default assumptions about all users, about the initial individual model, about the user input, and about the system input. Methods of initializing the user model include:

- users outlining their own learning goals,
- users providing a self-description (eg. personality, knowledge),
- users being given a pre-test on the subject area.

The system may compare the observations obtained from these inputs against the expert module, or may use machine learning techniques to integrate these observations to individualize an initial default user model. While this puts some burden on the user, using all available information to "seed" the student model should reduce the number of mis-diagnoses.

Differential modelling systems try to infer reasons for differences between correct or expert behaviour patterns and observed learner behaviour. Systems like GUIDON [27] rely on abductive rule-based inference to ascribe reasons to deviations between observed and expected behaviour. Since expert reasoning (the domain model) in GUIDON is also rule-based, the student modelling system essentially reasons about the application or mis-application of rules. GUIDON was originally conceived as an instructional shell that could be placed on top of expert systems.

A very similar "differential modelling" approach is taken in WEST [21]. The learner's move is compared to a list of all possible moves. If the move does not match the expert's move, the learner's move is evaluated in regard to a set of issues that determine move strategies. The learner's current state, in regard to knowledge of those issues and move strategies, is thus inferred and a response to the learner is generated. WEST takes a conservative approach in updating the student model recognizing that inconsistencies could be due to the "noise" of random slips and inattention.

In systems utilizing bug libraries, the challenge is to anticipate the range of possible learner errors. Learners seem to be infinitely creative in finding new ways to incorrectly solve a problem. In systems such as DEBUGGY, much of the original work involves arduous reviews of learners' mistakes followed by human reasoning about the underlying bugs. IDEBUGGY [20] includes procedures for generating hypotheses from learner input about the relevant bugs which are then followed up by producing tests to discriminate among candidate bugs. The search space is kept manageable by keeping only a small set of hypotheses active at one time. Ordering by commonality is one heuristic to reduce the set size. Recent work by Cerri, Cheli and McIntyre [25] also concerns the development of knowledge acquisition tools for semi-automatically extending bug libraries.

Generative models of bugs, such as repair theory, have automated the generation of feasible bugs [89]. This requires a runnable model for generating all the ways in which bugs can arise. In repair theory, a set of rules is constructed to alter or delete correct procedures when impasses are encountered. Simulating impasses thus triggers the generation of a number of possible new bugs.

## 4.2 Implementation Techniques

It is not our intent within this chapter to provide a comprehensive survey of implementation techniques. We settle for a very brief overview of common techniques, and mention specific issues to exemplify the field. The issues discussed here include model tracing, stereotypic knowledge, granularity of representation, and implementation tools.

A variety of approaches has been used to implement all or portions of a student model. The genetic graph is one approach for representing and implementing overlay models [14, 45]. Another common approach is the use of production:rules, both ideal and mal-rules. Logic :programming has been used as an alternative as it offers a simpler approach to implementing the inference procedure and knowledge representation [54]. Machine learning:techniques can be incorporated for representing how the knowledge of a learner changes. Another implementation approach is the use of confluence equations from qualitative physics, specifically for models which include physical devices [5]. Neural networks have been used for basic classification of learners [7].

In developing a student model, one typically starts by making some assumptions about the learner and then updates those assumptions as one proceeds. Hence, a common approach is the initial use of stereotypic knowledge which is then updated based on the learner's behaviour/interactions. The amount of individualization, of course, varies across systems. For example, WEST's student model is individualized to a further extent than the student model of the LISP Tutor which is more stereotypic. For related work regarding stereotypic user models, see [79].

One particularly interesting implementation of an overlay model is Anderson's LISP Tutor [3], which is based on a comprehensive psychological theory, ACT* [1] and uses a technique called models:tracing. The tutor defines an optimal solution path for a particular problem and guides the learner along the path minimizing deviations from that path [78]. The learner's ability to trace the model(s) of problem solving defined in the system indicates the knowledge that the learner has acquired. In the LISP Tutor, the measure of learner knowledge is the number of domain production rules apparently known by the learner. If the learner is able to trace a model for which the system fires production rules X, Y, and Z, then the learner is presumed to know those production rules. The tutor provides feedback as soon as there is a deviation from the correct model for LISP programming. Thus, the learner is compared on a rule by rule basis to the expert programmer and the student model is updated in that fashion. An inferencing mechanism compares erroneous "buggy rules" of the learner with the correct rules in formulating a response. Anderson and Pelletier [4] outline a standardized method and tools for implementing model tracing tutors.

One key issue throughout student modelling is the detail of representation and hence the specificity of diagnosis. The specificity required depends upon both the domain and the learner. A human tutor can recognize and diagnose a learner's solution at various levels or grain sizes, as well as focus on a range of general to specific strategies. Recent work in this area includes that of Greer and McCalla [47] based on the granularity theory developed by Hobbs [50]. Greer and colleagues have used this approach for student modelling by representing the learner's knowledge at an appropriately coarse or fine grain size depending on the information being represented. During interactions with the learner there can be shifts in the grain size, articulating to finer grain sizes or simplifying to coarser grain size. Jones and Poole [54] also apply this concept within the context of educational diagnosis; diagnosis proceeds to finer specificity based on the diagnostic information available. Eggert, Middlecamp, and Jacobi [35] extend the use of a granularity concept to a chemistry tutor. They maintain that one should be able to use one student model across different areas. Thus, the initial model might be sparse across the whole domain (large grained); then the system will detail a particular area as the learner progresses.

Very few student models are developed with commercial tools, such as an expert system shell or a courseware development environment. One reason may be that many ITSs are developed within a research environment for research purposes. At the same time, however, instructional systems are being produced for commercial purposes, often employing commercial tools in the development process. Within many of these systems, the student model is minimized or non-existent. There are ITSs which are built via development tools, but it appears that the use of the tools is typically limited to the development of simulations, the development of the expert model (eg. the use of KADS by Breuker et al [17]), and instructional interactions, rather than the development and maintenance of the student model. On the other hand some research systems such as Woolf's TUPITS [94], and shells for model tracing tutors [4], provide basic tools for beginning to implement student models.

## 4.3  Maintaining the Student Model

There has been recent interest in extending standard Truth Maintenance Systems (TMS's) to handle student model maintenance. Ongoing investigations include the work of Huang et al [53]. For a discussion of the issues involved, see [67]. Standard truth maintenance systems are able to spot how new information conflicts with existing information in some model of the world. The actual changes to the student model are then carried out not by the TMS itself but by a separate domain-specific reasoning system, which will resolve conflicts according to rules relevant to the domain. Huang et al [53] have investigated how to represent propositional knowledge about a learner so that the knowledge can change both monotonically and non-monotonically and when finding conflicts, revise a minimal set of beliefs in the model to attain consistency. Huang and McCalla [52] have extended that work so that the system focuses only on the student model beliefs that are relevant to the instructional task at hand, and for student modelling is considerably more efficient than traditional truth maintenance systems.

With traditional truth maintenance systems, all beliefs must be consistent with the new beliefs; however in student modelling this may be invalid. Errors in diagnosis and inaccurate observations are both common, leading to difficulty in assessing the learner. Learners may even have inherently inconsistent sets of beliefs. Huang (this volume) demonstrates how this apparent inconsistency can be dealt with by partitioning the student model.

## 4.4   Pragmatic Constraints

The tasks of eliciting, building, and maintaining a student model are extremely difficult and labourious. There are theoretical as well as practical challenges in most of these areas. Some of the problems are so severe that some believe that the task of constructing a useful student model is intractable. Self [79, 82] has made specific recommendations on making student modelling more tractable:

- design the student-computer interactions such that information needed to build a student model is provided by the learner rather than being inferred by the system,
- link the proposed content of the student model with specific instructional actions,
- make the content of the student model accessible to the learner, in order to encourage reflection on the part of the learner,
- assume a collaborative role for the ITS (the fidelity of the student model is of less importance), and
- view the contents of student models as representing the learner's beliefs about the world; the role of the ITS is then to assist the learner in elaborating those beliefs.

## 4.5   Conclusions

Student modelling is still an infant enterprise. The current tools used for building models are research tools and could soon be surpassed as the field progresses. Nevertheless they serve a function both in building systems and helping understand the nuances of student modelling. The guidelines and constraints for building student models should also be superseded as the field progresses. Nevertheless, understanding these constraints will facilitate elicitation, implementation, and maintenance of student models.

## 5  How to Make Use of a Student Model

In most systems the raison d'etre for a student model is to allow instruction to be designed specifically for an individual learner. Without the student model component, an ITS would be like a human tutor who knows nothing about the individual learner, and therefore is unable to adjust instruction to changes in the learner's behaviour. With knowledge about the learner, the tutor can control the order and difficulty of the material presented to the learner, as well as provide appropriate remediation. Thus the student model is used to assist in selecting the content, selecting the tutorial strategy, and confirming diagnoses.

Diagnosis is the process of inferring a student model; the student model and the diagnostic model are tightly interwoven. One can think of the student model as the data structure representing the learner's knowledge and diagnosis as the process that manipulates this knowledge. Designing these two components together represents the student modelling problem. The choice of student model significantly effects what can be accomplished in terms of diagnosis. VanLehn [90] outlines several common uses of a student model:

- Advancement: The student model can represent the learner's level of mastery. Periodically the system examines the student model for the level of mastery of the current concept or topic, weighs the results, and decides whether or not to advance the learner to the next concept or topic.
- Offering unsolicited advice: By knowing the learner's state of knowledge, the system can decide to offer advice to the learner when deemed appropriate.
- Problem generation: In order to generate appropriate problems or tasks, ie. those just beyond the learner's current abilities, the problem generation module consults the student model to determine the learner's current capabilities.
- Adapting explanations: In order for a system to issue instructive explanations to the learner, it consults the student model to determine what the learner already knows. Thus the system will restrict its explanations to those involving concepts the learner already understands.

Some of the constraints in regard to building student models suggested by Self [81, 83] and outlined in the previous section apply to using the student model. In particular the content of the model should be linked to specific actions and the system should not diagnose what it cannot remediate. More generally, Self [84] notes a move away from using the student model in remediation of specific domain specific errors, and toward managing the learning activities in regard to the learner's goals and metacognitive abilities.

## 5.1 Student Models in Various Instructional Paradigms

The original work in artificial intelligence and education led to a fairly standard architecture for an instructional system utilizing the principles of AI, an intelligent tutoring system (ITS). An ITS is a computer-based instructional system that teaches the learner in an interactive way, using the concepts of AI. One of the earliest ITSs was based on the MYCIN expert system [85]. Researchers reasoned that if they could capture the expertise required to perform a specific task, they could use this knowledge representation as a basis for instruction ("This is how I do it; follow my example"). This ITS, called GUIDON, [27] had a number of implementation problems such as ineffective tutorial strategies, but spurred further research into the application of AI techniques to education.

The prototypical ITS has four modules: an expert module, a tutorial module, a student model module, and a user interface. Although the degree of learner control could vary, the stereotypic ITS has traditionally been seen as being strictly system controlled (eg. Anderson's LISP Tutor) as opposed to earner controlled.

An ITS must have the ability to store and rapidly access both domain and learner information. The system can alter the tutorial strategies it employs according to what it is programmed to consider as most effective in a given situation. The basic instructional philosophy thus rests on the model the system has of the learner or student. The great majority of research on student modelling has occurred within the context of ITS research.

Recently however, a number of alternative approaches to the standard system controlled ITS have been proposed. These approaches can generally be differentiated on two dimensions: degree of learner versus tutor control and the role of the student model.

The "constructionist" approach to education (eg. [42]) maintains that students learn by exploring alternatives and constructing solutions rather than by being explicitly instructed or being led to a solution. Lesh [64] in a "Wizard of Oz" study found that tutors were most successful when the learner was in control and the tutor responded only to the learner's initiatives and queries. Holt and Wood [51] noted that many ITS researchers [32, 75, 82] have advocated architectures and approaches that favour a greater measure of learner control.

One might assume that the degree of learner control is negatively correlated with the complexity of the proposed student model. However, this is not necessarily the case. We next describe various systems ranging from complete learner control to very restricted system control and we argue that a student model may be very compatible with any degree of learner control. Conversely, Newman [69] argues for no student model in a system having very little learner control.

The LOGO learning environment approach [72] is a "microworld" approach consistent with an extreme constructivist approach. The environment provides toolkits with which the learners construct their own experiments and have complete control over all their actions. Proponents of such an approach assume all the necessary meaning or structure can be built directly into the environment without recourse to tutoring. An implicit model;of the learner is used to derive and implement all anticipated needs of the environment. It is not clear that an environment with an implicit student model will be as flexible as one that adapts to an evolving explicit student model but even if it were, the implicit model still has to be derived at some point [66].

There are several related approaches to learning environments based on the concept of a "mental model" [70]. Mental models have isomorphic relationships to external devices or domain knowledge, and play an important role in understanding a device, learning a concept, or performing a task [73]. Representing a "view" of a domain in a learning environment [82] appears to be the equivalent of representing "mental models" of a domain in the machine. (To avoid confusion we use the term "mental model" when referring to a learner's model, and "view" when referring to the ITS's presentation of that knowledge.)

Bhuiyan, Greer, and McCalla [8] have outlined how learners have different mental models of recursion at different stages of learning and have constructed a learning environment for supporting programming based on the relevant view to the learner. The presentation of predetermined views provides more structure than the Papert approach but Bhuiyan et al [8] still allow complete learner control in selecting the view. The views themselves are based on an implicit student model.

Cummings and Self [32] propose an approach they call collaborative learning which is somewhat like the stereotypic ITS approach in terms of learner versus system control of the environment and actions. In collaborative learning there are multiple views of the material with collaborative learning proceeding in the most suitable environment based on the student model. The tutor uses machine learning to parallel the learner's progress assisting at times and asking for assistance at other times. The system would require information about the learner's knowledge of the domain, as well as about the learner's goals and strategies. While machine learning techniques may be useful to update the model, there would also need to be facilities for the learner to inspect and make direct modifications to the student model.

White and Frederiksen [92] have developed a system with more system control of the learning than in Self's collaborative learning. They outline a series of qualitative mental models that a learner progresses through in learning basic electronic circuits. These models are used as the basis for computational qualitative views for teaching learners at various levels of expertise. Their system controls the learner's view based on the learner's prior history. Presumably, the selection of the appropriate views could be based on a diagnostic system using a more elaborate student model. Flexibility could be added by perhaps developing and changing these views based upon such a student model.

The apprenticeship approach to learning (e.g [69]) is based on the philosophy that self-regulation is acquired by a process which involves first experiencing outside regulation via interaction with mentors. Skills such as self-monitoring, error-checking and problem-solving strategies are acquired through the sharing of problem-solving experiences between learner and mentor. The approach is similar in some ways to collaborative learning but the mentor provides much more control than the collaborative tutor. This is the approach employed within INCROFT (Intelligent Conduct of Fire Trainer) [69]. Newman claims that the apprenticeship model provides an alternative to student modelling. It appears that the apprenticeship approach to instruction allows one to relax the role and subject-specificity of the student model. McCalla [66] argues that the student model is not eliminated but is implicit in off-line design and instructional decisions. Furthermore, we argue that an on-line student model would allow the system to tailor itself more to the learner's individual needs.

Recently there has been a focus on case-based tutoring [80] where the learner is presented with a series of case examples and is expected to learn from these vicarious experiences. Presumably case-based tutoring could have strong learner or strong system control of the presentation of cases. Advocates of case-based tutoring have questioned the necessity of developing detailed student models [39]; instead they concentrate on the tutoring strategy and presentation of the subject matter to the learner. However, case-based tutoring is based on a theory of how expertise is represented and how new knowledge is assimilated. Thus, despite questions about the relevance of student-model based diagnosis, research on how learners represent knowledge at different levels remains a central issue for this approach. Furthermore, with strong learner control a student model could support the generation of advice to the learner on case selection. With strong system control, a student model could be used to select the most appropriate cases.

Elsom-Cook [37] points out that systems control may be more desirable for tutoring in some domains than others. He suggests an approach where the degree of system versus learner control is discretionary. Guided Discovery Tutoring provides an environment in which both the "tutor" and the learners interact. The control of the learning could range from very learner-centred to tight tutor control depending upon a number of factors [37]. The role of the student model in such an environment would be to constrain and guide the collaborative work of the tutor.

We have outlined a number of approaches advocating various levels of learner versus system control. Proponents of several of these approaches have denied the need for any type of student modelling. We believe that there is a role for student modelling in all these approaches.

# 6 Current Issues

## 6.1 Developments in Artificial Intelligence

A number of areas of artificial intelligence should remain central to the development of the student modelling field. Many of these fields address real-world problems. Forbus and Gentner [41] maintain that the lack of research on such questions reflects a general strategy in AI research to focus on small precise models as opposed to large ones. Their work on similarity learning which attempts to build from and integrate with the CYC knowledge-base [63] demonstrates the tight links between general AI and student modelling issues.

This section looks at some ongoing research issues and the areas of qualitative reasoning, machine learning, neural networks, user modelling, and input bandwidth in relation to the future of student modelling.

Pragmatic concerns such as whether the student model needs fuzzy representation [58] or multi-layered inferencing (Woolf, this volume) will have to be addressed on an ongoing basis. Research in non-monotonic:representation will continue to be relevant to student modelling.

Typically the models within an ITS are qualitative in nature, which seems to make the field of qualitative reasoning very relevant to ITS. In a "qualitative" model [10], objects, processes, and their interrelationships are described analogically in terms of qualitative relationships such as "greater than" or "less than" without exact quantification. For example, a qualitative model would state that if the water in a steam boiler is hotter than the water in the cooling pipe, then heat will flow from the boiler to the cooling pipe. Exact quantities will not be stated. Researchers arguing from the qualitative reasoning viewpoint point out that experts frequently reason in qualitative terms rather than in quantitative terms. The relevance to intelligent tutoring system design lies in the problems posed by representing qualitative reasoning, which some ITS designs require. Recently the relevance of the qualitative reasoning for modelling physical processes has been questioned in special issue of Computational Intelligence [31] but the relevance to ITS is clear. Work by Baril et al. [5] also raises questions about the suitability of standard qualitative reasoning techniques for representing a student model.

Machine learning has played a minor role in student modelling [44] yet would seem to be central to the future of student modelling. A student model that learns relatively autonomously would be much more flexible than one that must be manually shaped and finely tuned. Ideally the student model would not just learn variations of existing expert knowledge but new, unpredictable structures generated by creative learners. Thus machine learning techniques should remain of central concern in student modelling research, although there may be a necessity for psychological validity not found in much of the rest of AI. Woolf (this volume) outlines how machine learning may be relevant to student modelling.

Neural network contributions to the current generation of ITSs have likewise been limited. Knowledge in neural net models is not represented in an easily articulated fashion and articulation of knowledge is the underpinning of current ITS technology. ITSs based solely on neural network models of expertise would be radically different from today's ITSs. In regard to student modelling, neural network technology could be used to provide the capability for recognizing a particular learner (perhaps by visual input or input device response patterns, much as old-time Morse telegraphists knew each other's "fist" or key-operating pattern). Even more immediately, neural nets might be used to provide a classification of a learner by patterns of response [7].

User modelling deals with modelling users of computer systems for support of on-line coaching and consulting. It addresses many of the same issues as student modelling: knowledge representation (eg., default or stereotype:representation[79], plan recognition [22], non-monotonic reasoning [13], and diagnosis [60]). However, user modelling largely ignores learning theory and the type of interaction with the user can be quite different from pedagogical interactions. Nevertheless, there is potential for a great deal of cross-fertilization.

Human teachers have a much wider variety of cues to work with than have computerized learning systems. An "eureka" look, a puzzled expression, or a hesitant tone of voice may all shape remedial action. Some such cues may be idiosyncratic or at least interpreted within an idiosyncratic standard. A computerized learning system does not have this wide band of input to deal with at this time but future student modelling may have to deal with such issues. Even available input measures such as response latency have apparently not been explored. Image processing techniques and neural networks may be relevant to endeavours to increase the input bandwidth. Knowledge representation techniques will have to expand to integrate spatial/visual knowledge and auditory/sequential knowledge, or new ways of representing knowledge will be developed.

## 6.2   Developments in Education, Cognitive Science, and Psychology

Student modelling is a multi-disciplinary endeavour. This section outlines issues from a few of the more relevant research fields from various disciplines: educational research into instructional design, context of learning, and metacognition; a new cognitive science concept of cognitive infrastructure; the psychological concept of "psychological validity"; and psychological research into mental models and other areas.

Instructional design is a field of education intrinsically related to student modelling. The representation of the learner's knowledge as simply knowing or not knowing something is not sufficient. The approach adopted by Brecht [13, 15] is to incorporate different levels of knowing into the student model representation. Based on Bloom's 6-level cognitive taxonomy [9], Brecht has chosen to incorporate three levels of cognition - facts, analysis, and synthesis - in the domain of LISP programming. Applying these cognitive abilities to each concept in the domain knowledge provides another dimension to the curriculum and hence to the corresponding student model. While Bloom's work has been largely superseded by concepts like situational learning, Brecht's attention to instructional design concepts is commendable. While there is work on instructional design and ITSs [76, 93], to a large extent they have remained different fields. For descriptions and discussions regarding the synthesis of instructional science with ITS design, see Jones and Winne [56].

Laurillard [61] argues that learning is context dependent. Simply teaching based on faults in the expert procedure leads to unhelpful instruction. She has more recently put forward an approach to the development of student models based on ascertaining the complete outcome space for a given concept in terms of the possible ways it can be understood and misunderstood. Like Anderson [2], she argues that it is necessary to examine how learners use a particular piece of knowledge. Laurillard suggests that one should not decouple what is being learned from the context. The approach she proposes is that of phenomenographic analysis: the description (graphs) of learners' experiences of learning a concept. The goal is to develop relevant categories or outcome spaces related to the knowledge of a particular concept that can then form the basis of the student model and diagnosis. For complex concepts, the approach undoubtedly provides valuable insight necessary for the construction of a student model. The concern is the effort required to accomplish the process. The key steps in order to describe the outcome spaces for a particular concept are as follows:
- generate questions to probe learners' understanding
- pilot questions
- refine questions
- interview at least 20 learners
- sort protocols into categories
- test reliability of categories with independent judges
- refine categories

The process is complex and requires substantial time, effort and subject expertise. It appears, however, to be a worthwhile endeavour for complex concepts. Laurillard [62] provides an illustration of the use of this technique to ascertain learners' understanding of Newton's Third Law.

The majority of work to date regarding student modelling concerns the representation of the learner's cognitive knowledge and processes. More recently, there has been the recognition within the ITS community that instruction should take into account learners' metacognitive processes; what learners know about their own knowledge and cognitive processing. In addition to the instruction of cognitive skills, it is often desirable to teach metacognitive skills. Derry [34] presents some convincing tales to illustrate the importance of metacognitive instruction. However, integrating metacognitive skills into the student model does have implications. In addition to capturing a student's model of the domain, the learner's metacognitive skills should also be represented, and instruction tailored accordingly. However, the underlying philosophy of metacognitive learning will influence all pedagogical aspects of the ITS. For example, if the philosophy of metacognitive learning emphasizes reflection, the pedagogical approach typically relies on experimentation, reflection and discussion. Such a system would then provide the learner with graphics-based cognitive toolkits, to allow the learner to construct models of the given problems and situations. The learner then receives feedback regarding the adequacy of his mental conceptualizations. There are several consequences of this approach, including that if the learner is in control (rather than the system), the role of the student model can be less dominant. For a discussion of concerns regarding this approach to instructional systems, see [34]. Derry and colleagues are developing an instructional system, TAPS, for arithmetic word problems which emphasizes the acquisition of metacognitive skills. Derry's approach to student modelling and diagnosis is global/holistic. The idea is to avoid overly breaking up the student model and to ensure that no one performance is unduly weighted in the course of diagnosis. To accomplish this within TAPS, the student model is represented as scores on fuzzy linguistic intervals.

Finally we argue learners are not blank slates, but possess a considerable amount of previously-acquired knowledge, a "cognitive infrastructure". What parts of this are relevant to a given situation is decided by the individual, and thus cognition and learning may be based on a learner's entire ontology for what they consider to be the specific domain [46]. Learners often appear to learn by drawing analogies between different areas. Clement and Gentner [30] have shown that for learning by analogybetween entities in different domains, the similarity of the contexts within their respective domains is as important as similarities between the specific entities. Keller and Lehman [59] have demonstrated that concepts within a domain may be defined only within the overall conceptual structure of the domain. Research by McCoy [68] has begun to address the issue of how such context dependent concepts might be represented or relative aspects of them highlighted. However, much basic research is required, not only on how learners represent concepts, but also on how the concepts' context and interrelationships are represented. An even more general question raised by Lesh [64] is how new learning is shaped by and integrated into the existing cognitive structures.

In the process of building the original Algebra Tutor, Anderson [2] learned a valuable lesson about psychological validity. He views the original Algebra Tutor as a failure because it did not result in instruction superior to classroom instruction, where as both the LISP Tutor and the

Geometry Tutor, which were built on the same underlying theory (ACT*), did so [2]. In the process of developing the Algebra Tutor, the developers came up with production rules, but had not extensively examined learner problem solving. In other words they produced a logical set of production rules which unfortunately did not accurately reflect how learners necessarily solve algebra problems. The result was a less effective instructional system. This has implications for the development and representation of the student model. It is critical that the learner's cognitive processes be understood.

The concept of a mental model has been referred to earlier in the chapter. Originally "mental models" [70] seemed to be limited to describing how a person represented in their mind the structure and function of a real-world device and their image of the inter-relationship of these elements. However, more recently the definition of mental model seems to have broadened to include isomorphic relationships of mental concepts to external devices or domain knowledge, and which play an important role in understanding a device, learning a concept, or performing a task [73], and programming [8]. More and more "views" of the domain are being built from explicit or implicit mental models of experts and novices [8, 92].

Psychological variables that have not been addressed by existing systems are intelligence/learning ability, learning styles, multiple and variable learning strategies, and gender differences. These last keep cropping up in such topic areas as Mathematics and Science; perhaps any such differences are the result of an interaction of teaching methods and gender-related learning styles. Research is needed on how female students learn vis-a-vis male students in the same subject area, and on the differences in the (somewhat indefinite) concept called "learning style" between the two genders. Some psychological variables such as learner motivation have only recently begun to be addressed [33].

## 6.3   Domain Issues

We know from research on learning theory that learners acquire knowledge and integrate it into their personal knowledge-bases in different ways and at different rates [49]. In addition, no two learners are identical in their achievement profiles, though a majority tend to have problems with the same subjects, eg. mathematics. It seems reasonable to assume that student models will always tend to be domain-specific; this implies that even if the methods of eliciting and updating each student model will be similar for a specific domain, they will vary across domains.

To date there has been no attempt to develop comprehensive student models for complex domains that may involve a number of different types of knowledge representation, different levels of knowledge (eg. domain, strategic, and metacognitive), different potential tutorial strategies [71], and different views of the domain. An example of such a domain is applied data communications as viewed by managers and technicians.

## 6.4 Meta-analysis of the Field

A great deal of work on the problems of student modelling has consisted of excellent research into specific systems. There needs to be ongoing review and meta-analysis of the field as a whole. Self and Dillenbourg (this volume) provide an interesting framework for analyzing various systems and examine a large number of systems within their framework. There may be a need to analyze systems at a finer level of granularity than their framework provides. Also they assume that the student model must be decomposable and be comparable on a piece by piece representation of knowledge at a micro-level. This assumption may be unfounded. Finally, their framework may eventually fall short in that it looks at student modelling within a traditional symbol manipulation and search perspective. Nevertheless, they make an excellent start at meta-analysis of the field.

# 7  Conclusions

Student modelling is constrained by both the state of the art in learning theory and in artificial intelligence technology. Much of the original work in student modelling was driven by work with "bug libraries" in restricted arithmetic domains and by a pragmatic decision to adapt expert systems technology to the field of computer-based learning. At the time there was no strong theoretical or empirical basis to assume that learner knowledge was a subset of expert knowledge or that tutoring systems based on an overlay model would be successful.

There is currently little ongoing research regarding overlay models. However, overlays continue to be used in the development of ITSs, often with extensions to the overlay knowledge base. It is only more recently that it has been recognized that a theory of learning is central to endeavors in artificial intelligence and education [71]. Although the student model is an essential component of an ITS, its nature and essence are still incompletely understood. To be effective, student models must provide descriptions of the learner's understanding and misunderstanding at a level of granularity that facilitates effective instruction. There is no "standard version" of the student model. Instead, student models are context-determined and content-specific. Ideally, they should consider both the role of context and metacognition in student learning. Current student models are typically shallow representations of the domain knowledge that is known or not known by the learner. Student modelling remains a difficult problem.

There is a need for more than analyzing the learner's performance in terms of procedural knowledge and mistakes. Moving beyond this to the identification of underlying conceptions and misconceptions of a domain and its interrelationship to other knowledge structures will be a difficult task. Research to date regarding diagnosis has had success only in limited domains. In a desire to develop instructional systems in more comprehensive domains, researchers are moving away from omniscient tutors capable of detecting all possible errors and misconceptions. One trend is towards co-operative instructional agents that choose from among several forms of interaction based on the content of the communication and the needs of the learner. This neither solves nor eliminates the need for student modelling, but rather shifts the focus.

Ohlsson [71] states that student modelling has been reduced to model tracing and bug libraries and is no longer a research problem. McCalla in [66], takes the opposite view that student modelling is the central research issue in the field. We maintain that model tracing and bug libraries were preliminary attempts in limited domains to come to grips with the problem of student modelling. As illustrated in this review the trend in student modelling representation has been towards increased sophistication, increased variability, increased generality, and increased flexibility.

This introductory review has uncovered a number of outstanding issues in regard to student modelling, including metacognition, the role of context, and cognitive infrastructure. Clearly, the subject is in its infancy as a research discipline. It is a major component of what has been described as a "theory of learning under instruction" [71] and much work is required in regard to both it and to artificial intelligence as a whole. At the same time that basic research in cognitive science is integral to the advance of intelligent learning systems, there are pragmatic needs for building working systems. The investigation and resolution of the issues outlined in this review will demand new developments in learning theory and artificial intelligence techniques as well as pragmatic approaches to building systems.

The papers in this book show excellent progress in several directions. The chapter by Ohlsson outlines a new technique for modelling learners. Katz, Lesgold, Eggan, and Gordin show an application of fuzzy set theory and Bayesian statistics to student modelling. Huang reports on an attention-focusing technique for increasing the efficiency of student model revision. The chapter by Frasson and Kaltenbach outlines work integrating various theoretical approaches to learning. The chapter by Moebus, Schroeder, and Thole shows the implementation of a theory of learning into an extension of a perturbation type model. Woolf and Murray outline the potential of machine learning to student modelling and Self provides a very good framework for further meta-analysis of the student modelling field.

## Acknowledgements

We would like to thank the various publishers who gave us permission to reproduce some of the figures in this paper. We would also like to acknowledge the financial support of the Natural Science and Engineering Research Council of Canada.

# References

1. Anderson, J. R.: *The Architecture of Cognition*. Cambridge, MA: Harvard University Press 1983
2. Anderson, J. R.: Talk on psychology and intelligent tutoring. Paper presented at the 4th International Conference on Artificial Intelligence and Education, Amsterdam, ND 1989
3. Anderson, J. R., Boyle, A. T., Corbett, A. & Lewis, M.: Cognitive modelling and intelligent tutoring. *Artificial Intelligence*, 42, pp. 7-51 (1990)
4. Anderson, J. R. & Pelletier, R.: A development system for model-tracing tutors. In: *The International Conference on the Learning Sciences: Proceedings of the 1991 Conference*, Evanston IL (L. Birnbaum, ed), pp. 1-9, Charlottesville, VA: AACE 1991
5. Baril, D., Greer, J. E. & McCalla, G. I.: Student modelling with confluences. Proceedings of the AAAI Conference, Anaheim, CA pp. 43-48, 1991
6. Barr, A., Beard, M. & Atkinson, R. C.: The computer as a tutorial laboratory: the Stanford BIP project. *International Journal of Man-Machine Studies*, 8, pp. 567-596 (1976)
7. Beale, R. & Finlay, J.: User Modelling with a Neural System. University of York, Department of Computer Science, Technical Report, Heslington, UK 1989
8. Bhuiyan, S. H., Greer, J. E. & McCalla, G. I.: Characterizing, rationalizing, and reifying mental models of recursion. Proceedings of the 13th Annual Meeting of the Cognitive Science Society, Chicago, IL, pp. 120-131, Hillsdale, NJ: Lawrence Erlbaum Associates 1991
9. Bloom, B. S. (ed.): *Taxonomy of Educational Objectives*. New York, NY: Mackay Publishing 1956
10. Bobrow, D. G.: *Qualitative Reasoning about Physical Systems*. Cambridge, MA: MIT Press 1984
11. Boder, A. & Cavallo, D.: An epistemological approach to intelligent tutoring systems. *Intelligent Tutoring Media*, 1(1), pp. 23-29 (1990)
12. Bonar, J. G. & Soloway, E. M.: Pre-programming knowledge: a major major source of misconceptions in novice programmers. *Human-Computer Interaction*, 1, pp. 133-161 (1985)
13. Brajnik, G. & Tasso, C.: A flexible tool for developing user modelling applications with non-monotonous reasoning capabilities. In: *UM92 Proceedings of the 3rd International Workshop on User Modelling*, Wadern, Germany (E. Andre, R. Cohen, W. Graf, B. Kass, C. Paris & W. Wahlster, eds.), pp. 44-64, Kaiserslautern: DFKI 1992
14. Brecht, B. J.: Determining the Focus of Instruction: Content Planning for Intelligent Tutoring Systems. Ph.D. Thesis, Department of Computational Science, University of Saskatchewan 1990
15. Brecht, B. J. & Jones, M.: Student models: the genetic graph approach. *International Journal of Man-Machine Studies*, 28, pp. 483-504, 1988
16. Brecht, B. J., McCalla, G. I., Greer, J. E. & Jones, M.: Planning the content of instruction. In: *Proceedings of the 4th International Conference on Artificial Intelligence and Education*, Amsterdam, ND (D. Bierman, J. Breuker & J. Sandberg, eds.)., pp. 32-41. Amsterdam: IOS 1989
17. Breuker, J. A. & Wielinga, B. J.: Model-driven knowledge acquisition. In: *Topics in the Design of Expert Systems* (P. Guida & G. Tasso, eds.), pp. 265-296, Amsterdam: North-Holland 1989
18. Brown, J. S. & Burton, R. R.: Diagnostic models for procedural bugs in basic mathematical skills. *Cognitive Science*, 2, pp. 155-192 (1978)
19. Brown, J. S. & VanLehn, K.: Repair theory: a generative theory of bugs in procedural skills. *Cognitive Science*, 4, pp. 379-42 (1980)
20. Burton, R. R.: Diagnosing bugs in a simple procedural skill. In: *Intelligent Tutoring Systems* (D. H. Sleeman & J. S. Brown, eds.), pp.157-184, London, UK: Academic Press 1982
21. Burton, R. R. & Brown, J. S.: A tutoring and student modeling paradigm for gaming environments. *ACM SIGCSE Bulletin*, 8(1), pp. 236-246 (1978)
22. Carberry, S., Karri, Z. & Lambert, L.: Modelling discourse, problem solving, and domain-goals incrementally in task-oriented dialogue. In: *UM92 Proceedings of the 3rd International Workshop on User Modelling*, Wadern, Germany, (E. Andre, R. Cohen, W. Graf, B. Kass, C. Paris & W. Wahlster, eds.), pp. 192-202, Kaiserslautern: DFKI 1992
23. Carbonell, J. R.: Mixed-Initiative Man-Computer Instructional Dialogues. Doctoral dissertation, Massachusetts Institute of Technology, Cambridge, MA 1970
24. Carr, B. & Goldstein, I.: Overlays: a theory of modelling for computer-aided instruction. *International Journal of Man-Machine Studies*, 5, pp. 215-236 (1977)
25. Cerri, S. A., Cheli, E. & McIntyre, A.: Nobile: user model acquisition in a natural laboratory. In: *Adaptive Learning Environments: Foundations and Frontiers* (M. Jones & P. Winne, eds.), pp. 325-348, NATO ASI Series F, Vol. 85, Berlin: Springer-Verlag 1992
26. Chi, M., Glaser, R. & Farr, M. J.: *The Nature of Expertise*, Hillsdale, NJ: Lawrence Erlbaum Associates 1988
27. Clancey, W. J.: GUIDON, *Journal of Computer-Based Instruction*, 10(1), pp. 8-14 (1983)

33

28. Clancey, W. J.: Qualitative student models. *Annual Review of Computer Science*, 1, pp. 381-450 (1986)
29. Clancey, W. J.: *Knowledge-Based Tutoring: The GUIDON Program*, Cambridge, MA: MIT Press 1987
30. Clement, C. A. & Gentner, D.: Systematicity as a selection constraint in analogical mapping, *Cognitive Science*, 15, pp. 89-132 (1991)
31. *Computational Intelligence*. Special Forum on Qualitative Physics, 8, 1992
32. Cummings, G. & Self, J.: Collaborative intelligent educational systems. In: *Proceedings of the 4th International Conference on Artificial Intelligence and Education*, Amsterdam, ND (D. Bierman, J. Breuker & J. Sandberg, eds.)., pp. 73-80. Amsterdam: IOS 1989
33. Del Soldato, T.: Detecting and reacting to the learner's motivational state. In: *Proceedings of the 2nd International Conference on Intelligent Tutoring Systems*, Montreal, Quebec, (C. Frasson, G. Gauthier & G. McCalla, eds.), pp. 567-574, Lecture Notes in Computer Science, Vol. 608, Berlin: Springer-Verlag 1992
34. Derry, S. J.: Metacognitive models of learning and instructional systems design. In: *Adaptive Learning Environments: Foundations and Frontiers* (M. Jones & P. Winne, eds.), pp. 257-286, NATO ASI Series F, Vol. 85, Berlin: Springer-Verlag 1992
35. Eggert, A., Middlecamp, C. & Jacobi, A.: CHEMPROF: the chemistry literacy problem. In: *Proceedings of the 2nd International Conference on Intelligent Tutoring Systems* (C. Frasson, G. Gauthier & G. McCalla, eds.), pp. 669-676, Lecture Notes in Computer Science, Vol. 608, Berlin: Springer-Verlag 1992
36. Elsom-Cook, M.: Guided discovery tutors and bounded user modelling. In: *Artificial Intelligence and Human Learning: Intelligent Computer-Aided Instruction* (J. Self, ed.), pp. 165-178, New York, NY: Chapman and Hall 1988
37. Elsom-Cook, M.: *Guided Discovery Tutoring : a Framework for ICAI Research*. London, UK: Paul Chapman 1990
38. Farrell, R. G., Anderson, J. R. & Reiser, B. J.: An interactive computer-based tutor for LISP tutoring. Proceedings of the 6th Cognitive Science Society Conference, Boulder, CO pp. 152-155, 1984
39. Feiffer, R. & Soclof, M. S.: Knowledge based tutoring systems: changing the focus from learner modelling to teaching. In: *The International Conference on the Learning Sciences: Proceedings of the 1991 Conference*, Evanston IL (L. Birnbaum, ed), pp. 151-157, Charlottesville, VA: AACE 1991
40. Finin, T. W.: GUMS - A general user modelling shell. In: *User Models in Dialog Systems* (A. Kobsa & W. Wahlster, eds.), pp. 411-430, Berlin: Springer-Verlag 1989
41. Forbus, K. & Gentner, D.: Similarity-based cognitive architecture, *SIGART Bulletin*, 2, pp. 66-69 (1991)
42. Frederiksen, N.: Implications of cognitive theory for instruction in problem solving, *Review of Educational Research*, 54(3), pp. 363-407 (Fall 1984)
43. Genesereth, M. R.: An automated consultant for MACSYMA. Proceedings of the 5th International Joint Conference on Artificial Intelligence, pp. 789, Cambridge, MA 1977
44. Gilmore, D. & Self, J.: The application of machine learning to intelligent tutoring systems. In: *Artificial Intelligence and Human Learning: Intelligent Computer-Aided Instruction* (J. Self, ed.), pp. 179-196, London, UK: Chapman & Hall 1988
45. Goldstein, I. P.: The genetic graph: a representation for the evolution of procedural knowledge. In: *Intelligent Tutoring Systems* (D. Sleeman & J. S. Brown, eds.), pp. 51-78, New York, NY: Academic Press 1982
46. Greeno, J.: Conceptual entities. In: *Mental Models* (D. Gentner & A. Stevens, eds.), pp. 227-251, Hillsdale, NJ: Lawrence Erlbaum Associates 1983
47. Greer, J. E. & McCalla, G. I.: A computational framework for granularity and its application to educational diagnosis. Proceedings of the 11th International Joint Conference on Artificial Intelligence, Detroit, MI, pp. 477-482, 1989
48. Greer, J. E., Mark, M. A. & McCalla, G. I.: Incorporating granularity-based recognition into SCENT. In: *Proceedings of the 4th International Conference on Artificial Intelligence and Education*, Amsterdam, ND (D. Bierman, J. Breuker & J. Sandberg, eds.). pp. 107-115, Amsterdam: IOS 1989
49. Hergenhahn, B. R.: *An Introduction to Theories of Learning (3rd ed.)*, Englewood Cliffs, NJ: Prentice Hall 1988
50. Hobbs, J. R.: Granularity. Proceedings of the 9th International Joint Conference on Artificial Intelligence, Los Angeles, CA pp. 432-435 1985
51. Holt, P. & Wood, P.: Intelligent tutoring systems: a review for beginners. *Canadian Journal of Educational Communications*, 19(2), pp. 107-123 (1990)
52. Huang X. & McCalla, G. I.: Instructional planning using focus of attention. In: *Proceedings of the 2nd International Conference on Intelligent Tutoring Systems*, Montreal, Quebec (C. Frasson, G. Gauthier & G. McCalla, eds.), pp. 433-450, Lecture Notes in Computer Science, Vol. 608, Berlin: Springer-Verlag 1992
53. Huang, X., McCalla, G. I., Greer, J. E. & Neufeld, E.: Revising deductive knowledge and sterotypical knowledge in a student model, *User Modelling and User Adapted Interaction*, 1, pp. 87-115 (1991)
54. Jones, M. & Poole, D.: An expert system for educational diagnosis based on default logic. Proceedings of the 5th International Workshop on Expert Systems and Their Applications. Vol. 2 1985

55. Jones, M. & Dubs, S.: Techniques for the Elicitation and Analysis of Mental Models, Alberta Research Council Technical Report IGI92-0025, 1992
56. Jones, M. & Winne, P. (eds): *Adaptive Learning Environments: Foundations and Frontiers*. NATO ASI Series F, Vol. 85, Berlin: Springer-Verlag 1992
57. Kass, R.: Student modelling in intelligent tutoring systems - implications for user modelling. In: *User Models in Dialog Systems* (A. Kobsa & W. Wahlster, eds.), pp. 386-410, Berlin: Springer-Verlag 1989
58. Katz, S. & Lesgold, A.: Approaches to student modelling in SHERLOCK tutors. In: *Proceedings of the 3rd International Workshop on User Modelling*, Wadern, Germany (E. Andre, R. Cohen, W. Graf, B. Kass, C. Paris & W. Wahlster, eds.), pp. 205-230, Kaiserslautern: DFKI 1992
59. Keller, J. D. & Lehman, F. K.: Complex concepts. *Cognitive Science*, 15, pp. 271-292 (1991)
60. Kobsa, A. & Wahlster, W. (eds.): *User Models in Dialog Systems*. Berlin: Springer-Verlag 1989
61. Laurillard, D. M.: The pedagogical limitations of generative student models. *Instructional Science*, 17, pp. 235-250 (1988)
62. Laurillard, D. M.: Phenomenographic research and the design of diagnostic strategies for adaptive tutoring systems. In: *Adaptive Learning Environments: Foundations and Frontiers* (M. Jones & P. Winne, eds.), pp. 233-248, NATO ASI Series F, Vol. 85, Berlin: Springer-Verlag 1992
63. Lenat, D. & Guha, R.: *Building Large Knowledge-Based Systems*. Reading, MA: Addison-Wesley 1990
64. Lesh, R.: *Foundations for AI-Based Tutoring: Obedient Butler versus All-Knowing Gurus*. Educational Testing Service (USA) 1990
65. Matz, M.: Towards a process model for high school algebra. In: *Intelligent Tutoring Systems* (D. Sleeman & J. S. Brown, eds.) pp. 25 - 49, London: Academic Press 1982
66. McCalla, G. I.: The centrality of student modelling to intelligent tutoring. In: *New Directions for Intelligent Tutoring Systems* (E. Costa, ed.), pp. 107-131, NATO ASI Series F, Vol. 91, Berlin: Springer-Verlag 1992
67. McCalla, G. I. & Greer, J. E.: Tracking student knowledge. Proceedings of the 2nd International Workshop on User Modelling, Honolulu, HI, 1990
68. McCoy, K. F.: Highlighting a user model to respond to misconceptions. In: *User Models in Dialog Systems*, (A. Kobsa & W. Wahlster, eds.), pp. 233-254, Berlin: Springer-Verlag 1989
69. Newman, D.: Is a student model necessary? Apprenticeship as a model for ITS. In: *Proceedings of the 4th International Conference on Artificial Intelligence and Education*, Amsterdam (D. Bierman, J. Breuker & J. Sandberg, eds.)., pp. 177-184. Amsterdam: IOS 1989
70. Norman, D.: Some observations on mental models. In: *Mental Models* (D. Gentner & A. Stevens, eds.), pp. 7-14, Hillsdale, NJ: Lawrence Erlbaum Associates 1983
71. Ohlsson, S.: Systems hacking meets learning theory: reflections on the goals and standards of research in artificial intelligence and education. *Journal of Artificial Intelligence in Education*, 3(1), pp. 5-14 (1991)
72. Papert, S.: *Mindstorms: Children, Computers and Powerful Ideas*. New York, NY: Basic Books 1980
73. Payne, S. J.: Methods and mental models in theories of cognitive skill. In: *Artificial Intelligence and Human Learning: Intelligent Computer-Aided Instruction* (J. Self, ed.), pp. 69-87, London, UK: Chapman & Hall 1988
74. Payne, S. J. & Squibb, H. R.: Algebra mal-rules and cognitive accounts of error. *Cognitive Science*, 14, pp. 445-481 (1991)
75. Pea, R. & Soloway, E.: The state of the art in education technology research and design: policy issues and opportunities. In: *Proceedings of the 2nd International Conference on Intelligent Tutoring Systems*, Montreal, Quebec (C. Frasson, G. Gauthier & G. McCalla, eds.), pp. 16-17, Lecture Notes in Computer Science, Vol. 608, Berlin: Springer-Verlag 1992
76. Pirolli, P. & Russell, D.: Towards theory and technology for the design of intelligent tutoring systems. In: *Proceedings of the 2nd International Conference on Intelligent Tutoring Systems*, Montreal, Quebec (C. Frasson, G. Gauthier & G. McCalla, eds.), pp. 350-356, Lecture Notes in Computer Science, Vol. 608, Berlin: Springer-Verlag 1992
77. Quinlan, R.: Learning efficient classification procedures and their application to chess endgames. In: *Machine Learning* (R. S. Michalski, T. M. Mitchell & J. Carbonell, eds.), pp. 463-482, Palo Alto, CA: Tioga Press 1983
78. Reiser, B. J., Anderson, J. R. & Farrell, R. G.: Dynamic student modelling in an intelligent tutor for LISP programming. Proceedings of the 9th International Joint Conference on Artificial Intelligence, Los Angeles, CA, pp. 8-14 1985
79. Rich, E.: Stereotypes and user modelling. In: *User Models in Dialog Systems* (A. Kobsa & W. Wahlster, eds.), pp. 34-51, Berlin: Springer-Verlag 1989
80. Schank, R. & Edelson, D.: A role for AI in education: using technology to reshape education. *Journal of Artificial Intelligence in Education*, 1(2), pp. 3-20 (1990)

35

81. Self, J. A.: Bypassing the intractable problem of student modelling. In: *Proceedings of the 2nd International Conference on Intelligent Tutoring Systems*, Montreal, Quebec (C. Frasson, G. Gauthier & G. McCalla, eds.), pp. 18-24, Lecture Notes in Computer Science, Vol. 608, Berlin: Springer-Verlag 1992
82. Self, J. A.: The case for formalizing student models (and intelligent tutoring systems generally). Paper presented at the 4th International Conference on Artificial Intelligence and Education, Amsterdam 1989
83. Self, J. A.: Bypassing the intractable problem of student modelling. In: *Intelligent Tutoring Systems: At The Crossroads of Artificial Intelligence and Education* (C. Frasson & G. Gauthier, eds.), pp 107-123, Norwood, NJ: Ablex Publishing Corporation 1990
84. Self, J. A.: Are theories of diagnosis applicable to cognitive diagnosis? In: *Proceedings of the 3rd International Workshop on User Modelling*, Wadern, Germany (E. Andre, R. Cohen, W. Graf, B. Kass, C. Paris & W. Wahlster, eds.), pp. 231-239, Kaiserslautern:DFKI 1992
85. Shortliffe, E. H.: *Computer-Based Medical Consultations: MYCIN*. New York, NY: American Elsevier Publishers 1976
86. Sleeman, D. H., Kelly, A., Martinak, W. & Moore, J. L.: Studies of diagnosis and remediation with high school algebra students. *Cognitive Science*, 13, pp. 467-506 (1989)
87. Sleeman, D. H. & Smith, M. J.: Modelling students' problem solving. *Artificial Intelligence*, 16, pp. 171-187 (1981)
88. Soloway, E. M. & Johnson, W. L.: Remembrance of blunders past: a retrospective on the development of PROUST. Proceedings of the 6th Cognitive Science Society Conference, Boulder, CO, p. 57, 1984
89. VanLehn, K.: Bugs are not enough: Empirical studies of bugs, impasses, and repairs in procedural skills. *Journal of Mathematical Behaviour*, 3, pp. 3-72 (1982)
90. VanLehn, K.: Learning one subprocedure per lesson. *Artificial Intelligence*, 31(1), pp. 1-40 (1987)
91. Wenger, E.: *Artificial Intelligence and Tutoring Systems*. Los Altos, CA: Morgan Kaufmann Publishers 1987
92. White, B. & Frederiksen, J.: Causal model progressions as a foundation for intelligent learning environments. *Artificial Intelligence*, 42, pp. 52-121 (1990)
93. Wipond, K. & Jones, M.: Curriculum and knowledge representation in a knowledge based system for curriculum development. *Proceedings of the 2nd International Conference on Intelligent Tutoring Systems*, Montreal, Quebec (C. Frasson, G. Gauthier & G. McCalla, eds.), pp. 97-102, Lecture Notes in Computer Science, Vol. 608, Berlin: Springer-Verlag 1992
94. Woolf, B.: Towards a computational model of tutoring. In: *Adaptive Learning Environments: Foundations and Frontiers* (M. Jones & P. Winne, eds.), pp.209-232, NATO ASI Series F, Vol. 85, Berlin: Springer-Verlag 1992
95. Young, R. & O'Shea, T.: Errors in children's subtraction. *Cognitive Science*, 5, pp. 153-177 (1981)

Part 2

Artificial Intelligence Techniques
for Student Modelling

# Granularity-Based Reasoning and Belief Revision in Student Models

Gordon I. McCalla and Jim E. Greer

ARIES Laboratory, University of Saskatchewan, Saskatoon, Canada

**Abstract:** In this chapter we discuss two important research topics surrounding student modelling: 1) how to represent knowledge about a student at various grain sizes and reason with this knowledge to enhance the capabilities of an intelligent tutoring system, and 2) how to maintain a consistent view of a student's knowledge as the system-student interaction evolves. The ability to represent and reason about knowledge at various levels of detail is important for robust tutoring. A tutor can benefit from incorporating an explicit notion of granularity into its representation and can take advantage of granularity-based representations in reasoning about student behaviour. As the student's understanding of concepts evolves and changes, the student model must track these changes. This leads to a difficult student model maintenance problem. Both of these topics are full of interesting subtleties and deep issues requiring years of research to be resolved (if they ever are), but a start has been made. In this chapter we characterize the main requirements for each topic, discuss some of our work that tackles these topics, and, finally, indicate important areas for future research.

**Keywords:** student modelling, granularity, belief revision

## 1 Introduction

Intelligent tutoring systems (ITS) research distinguishes itself from other educational software development in a number of ways. First, an ITS is concerned with **modelling** the knowledge of the learner in some computationally useful and inspectable way. Next, based on the cognitive model of the learner, the ITS **intervenes** in the interaction between system and learner with the goal of facilitating learning. Finally, the ITS **evaluates** the success of its intervention and adjusts its model of the learner; and the loop repeats.

The modelling phase involves understanding learner behaviour in the context of the

The modelling phase involves understanding learner behaviour in the context of the environment in which learning occurs. Understanding can be thought of as attributing meaning to behaviour. Although this is an uncertain business, it is the mainstay of ITS. This attempt to understand the learner's behaviour can be partitioned into four sub-tasks: 1) understanding pre-existing knowledge, 2) understanding gaps in knowledge, 3) understanding inappropriate or mis-conceived knowledge, and 4) understanding how the knowledge is changing and evolving over time. Each of these sub-tasks can be accomplished to some degree using artificial intelligence techniques such as pattern recognition and model-based diagnosis.

The intervention phase can be partitioned into two sub-tasks: 1) assisting to fill gaps in the learner's knowledge, and 2) facilitating the correction of learner misconceptions. Achieving these two sub-tasks requires planning the content of the intervention based on domain knowledge and the student model and then planning the delivery of the intervention according to some instructional theory. The learner may be told a fact, presented with an analogy or parable, engaged in a Socratic dialogue, given a problem to solve, or presented with a scenario that either engages or confronts the learner. In general, the environment in which the learner interacts is either directly or indirectly modified to highlight the misconception or knowledge gap. At the same time the necessary knowledge to fill the gap or correct the misconception must be made available.

The evaluation phase is, in effect, a more focused modelling activity, concerned only with aspects of the learner's knowledge in the neighbourhood where the intervention was targeted. This phase serves to validate the original model of the learner's knowledge and to test confidence in the future predictiveness of the model. Throughout all three phases the centrality of the modelling process is highlighted. A knowledge intensive student modelling system is, in our view, a critical aspect of any ITS.

It should be emphasized that in this paper we are speculating on long term research goals for intelligent tutoring systems and hard problems confronting the achievement of these long term goals. However, we do on occasion suggest possibilities for short term applicability of various techniques and comment on possible end runs around hard problems which together might lead more quickly to the construction of practical and reasonably sophisticated systems.

## 2  Student Modelling

### 2.1  The Role and Nature of Cognitive Models

A model can be defined as an abstraction of reality, faithful to the reality in ways deemed important. Models are used liberally in many design, prototyping, simulation, and evaluation activities. Models can serve as the basis for decisions and as testbeds for experiments. If a model is faithful, then experiments conducted with the model are generalizable to the real thing. From wind tunnel experiments on model cars, to simulation experiments on model nuclei, to teaching experiments on model learners, models are essential laboratory apparatus.

Some models, including student models in ITS, are constructive. Constructive modelling attempts to build up a model of the *real thing* based on clues acquired from interactions with the environment. Constructive models are often built up or refined over time; and eventually they may provide a useful description of the real thing. The reality that such models seek to represent may only be indirectly inspectable and is often highly uncertain. For example, a model of sub-atomic particles describes a real thing that can only be inspected indirectly and the true nature of the sub-atomic particle is not known with certainty. This is also the case in ITS, where a model of the cognitive state of the learner is sought. The cognitive real thing defies direct inspection. The best one can do is to create a constructive model of the cognitive activity or processes and hope that it behaves in ways comparable to the cognitive real thing. Even then, it is easy to question the faithfulness of such models.

Cognitive modelling, as done by psychologists, involves a great deal of detailed protocol collection and analysis. Given the narrow communication bandwidth in human-computer interaction, the complexity of protocol collection, and the *artistic* nature of protocol analysis, automatic cognitive modelling on this scale seems impossible. Nevertheless, there is a strong appeal to do cognitive modelling, because models, once they are constructed, serve as inspectable entities which can be both the subject and object of (pedagogical) experimentation. The models admittedly are difficult to verify, since they approximately represent a relatively uninspectable reality, ie. the learner's cognitive (and/or affective) state. The immensity of this task, combined with the ultimate uncertainty of the results, leads some to question the utility of the cognitive modelling approach to mediating learning. It is tempting to abandon the cognitive modelling approach and to focus on *engagement* of the learner in a richly situated learning environment. Rather than re-open the situated learning debate here, we state our view that in many learning situations, engagement of the learner ought to be punctuated with pedagogically relevant advice, and that adequate advice can arise only from some sort of student modelling. Moreover, engagement in learning situations that are individualized to the learner also requires knowledge of the learner's cognitive state in order to choose or restrict the learning environment appropriately.

The ultimate objective of cognitive student models in ITS is to represent genetic evolution in knowledge of the individual learner and to capture the context, focus, perspective, and viewpoint of the learner in the learning activity. This objective can only be accomplished to the extent that the cognitive model is a faithful abstraction of the learner's cognitive state. Having painted a seemingly impossible goal, that of creating a fully-automated cognitive student modelling system, it may seem pointless to proceed. However, we claim that only a modest amount of cognitive modelling is necessary for instruction. A teacher or tutor typically constructs an extremely simple and very approximate cognitive model of any individual learner. This frequently amounts to *classifying* the learner into one of a few categories or stereotypes with respect to learning the domain. This *classification* of the learner, however approximate, still serves to guide pedagogical decisions and to mediate advice.

One way to construct these more modest cognitive student models is to engage in two phases of modelling activity. The first phase, external student modelling, relies on deep analysis of tutoring and learning protocols from collections of learners to arrive at a generic model of novicehood and expertise and the stages in between. This phase is domain sensitive and is carried out by human experts during the design of an ITS. External student modelling identifies categories or stereotypes with respect to typical learners in the domain. The next phase, internal student modelling, can be carried out automatically by an ITS as it instantiates the external student model with evidence from the individual learner's behaviour. This individualizes the model to reflect (some modest approximation of) the cognitive state of the learner.

Even this more modest type of cognitive student modelling is very difficult. Challenges occur in representing the externally developed stereotypical models and in recognizing evidence of stereotypical models in individual behaviour. Problems exist in dealing with unexpected behaviour and in filtering out noise. In some domains, sufficient coverage of stereotypical models is a major concern. Also important is the context in which the instructional activity occurs. When a teacher and learner interact, a mutually agreeable context must be established in order to communicate advice "on the same wavelength".

## 2.2 The Structure of a Student Model

Before discussing further how to do student modelling, we describe the kind of architecture we have in mind for a student model. As shown in Figure 1, the tutor's knowledge is divided into a number of conceptual spaces. The four most important spaces are the tutor's goal space, the tutor's belief space, the student's goal space, and the student's belief space. Other spaces could be present but are unimportant relative to the current discussion. The tutor's goal space includes the pedagogical goals of the tutor and pedagogical planning algorithms to turn these goals into instructional plans. The tutor's belief space includes the knowledge the tutor has about the domain of concepts which the student is exploring. It can include knowledge about tasks which illustrate these concepts as well as knowledge about common misconceptions. These two spaces allow the tutor to be able to explicitly reason about its own knowledge and its own pedagogical goals.

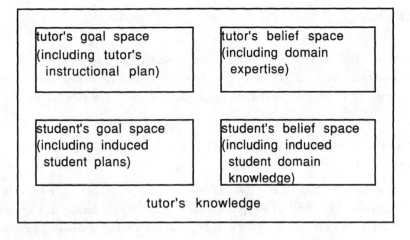

Figure 1: Goal and belief spaces

The student's goal space and the student's belief space represent the tutor's beliefs about the student and together constitute the student model. The student's goal space contains the tutor's perceptions of the cognitive goals of the student as well as plan recognition algorithms which the tutor can use to induce a student's plans for learning the concepts in the tutoring domain. The student's belief space contains the tutor's perceptions of what concepts from the domain the student has understood. The student's belief space has two interesting subspaces: the student's beliefs about the tutor's beliefs and the student's beliefs about the tutor's goals. These subspaces are essential if the tutor is to predict the student's reaction to the tutor. This general architecture is very similar to user models employed for dialogue planning in some natural language understanding systems (eg. [7]). The architecture makes important distinctions that will prove useful in the discussion to follow.

We next discuss two main student modelling issues: granularity-based reasoning and student model maintenance. In section 3 we indicate why we feel that it is essential that a student model be able to reason at many grain sizes and we then show a representation scheme that enables granularity-based reasoning to be flexibly carried out. In section 4 we discuss the challenge of trying to maintain a student model as the student-tutor interaction changes both the student's knowledge and the tutor's perceptions of the student's knowledge. We conclude section 4 with an approach to student model maintenance that combines stereotypical reasoning with truth maintenance using a focus attention mechanism to achieve tractability.

# 3 Granularity

Granularity is an oft-used term in ITS research, but is seldom considered as an issue in its own right. In this section we contend that it is essential for an intelligent tutoring system to be able to explicitly make use of granularity in both its organization of knowledge and in its reasoning.

## 3.1 Why Granularity is Important

Granularity is important, first because students seem to reason at many grain sizes, that is they can have both deep and shallow knowledge at the same time. This is especially true for problem solving abilities. For example, Bhuiyan et al [2] have shown that, in devising solutions to simple recursive programming problems, students have one or more mental models that underpin their strategy to solve the problem, which in turn is the basis for the code they actually produce. The range of understanding the student has, from deep mental model through more shallow strategy to surface code, encapsulates three simultaneously held perspectives on the problem solution at three different grain sizes. The student model must represent these multi-levelled perspectives (in the student's belief space) if it is to reflect the student's understanding.

Students also have only incomplete understanding of the environment they are exploring. This incomplete understanding ranges from total ignorance through partial knowledge to fully formed misconceptions. Of particular interest is partial knowledge. Partial knowledge may take the form of only knowing about some of the components that make up a concept or procedure (eg. knowing about reduction steps and base cases in recursion, but not about composition steps), or can take the form of ignorance about the complete details of a concept or procedure (eg. knowing that a recursion consists of reduction steps, base cases and composition steps, but not knowing that there are specific types of recursion). The relationship of partial knowledge to more complete knowledge is also a granularity relationship; that is, as a student refines his or her understanding, the student is, in Hobbs' terms [15], articulating his or her knowledge to finer grain sizes. Such articulation seems to happen along at least three dimensions: aggregation (where the student learns the components of some concept), abstraction (where the student learns specializations of some concept), and goals (where the student elaborates his/her goals into subgoals). Of course, the student could move in the opposite direction, simplifying his/her knowledge, from fine grained knowledge of particular situations to an understanding of inclusive, generic, coarse-grained knowledge.

Work in the ARIES Laboratory is aimed at trying to explicitly represent this kind of student knowledge in terms of granularity and making explicit use of it in the SCENT-3 program advising system [24][1]. Applying our approach to the student modelling architecture in Figure 1, we visualize domain knowledge as being represented in the tutor's belief space in granularity hierarchies, organized along two orthogonal dimensions: aggregation and abstraction. The goals in the tutor's goal space would also be organized in subgoal hierarchies, another granularity relationship. The student model would be structured similarly, with the tutor's perceptions of the student's knowledge of the domain arrayed in granularity hierarchies of concepts (and misconceptions), and the tutor's perceptions of the student's learning goals and subgoals being organized in a granularity hierarchy in the student's goal space. The knowledge in the student model would be much more sparse than in the tutor's own belief and goal spaces. For example, only very coarse-grained learning goals of the student may be induced by the tutor, and the student's knowledge of certain concepts may in some instances be general and coarse-grained and in others very specific and fine-grained.

Once granularity has been explicitly incorporated into a tutoring system it can be used to diagnose student behaviour, one of the key prerequisites for intelligent student modelling. A diagnostic system has a difficult time recognizing what a student is up to, especially when the student is allowed to roam freely through a large space of possible behaviours. Faced with such free-ranging behaviour, most diagnostic systems display a notorious lack of robustness. One way of controlling this problem is to restrict the student's freedom so that he or she stays within the scope of the student's knowledge (this is the approach taken in the LISP Tutor [1]). We believe, however, that if the range of student behaviour and student knowledge can be arrayed in granularity hierarchies, then we can still allow the student to have free rein. While it might be impossible to recognize what a student is doing at a fine grain size, it will surely be possible to recognize what he or she is doing at some grain size, even if it is quite coarse. For example, a student's solution to a programming problem might be so perturbed as to be unrecognizable as a tail-end recursion (due to extra parts, wrong parts, and/or missing parts), but it may at least be recognizable as a recursion, which is an island of certainty for use by the pedagogical component and other components of the tutoring system. Thus, granularity is not only useful to encode the range of student knowledge (fine-grained to coarse-grained), but is also useful to the tutoring system itself in its recognition of student behaviour. Such granularity-based recognition is very robust---student behaviour can be recognized at some level of detail, albeit not always precisely. Such robustness is rare in artificial intelligence systems.

---

[1] The ultimate goal of the SCENT-3 system is to guide a student towards understanding the programming language LISP, a goal which closely emulates that of guided discovery. In fact, it seems that far from being a dead research direction, the attempts to develop smart programming advisors are among the most common examples of research into guided discovery. They form a critical mass of research into how to interact with students as they learn complex procedural ideas in an exploratory fashion with guidance from an intelligent tutor. The growing body of interesting research being amassed around the CMU Lisp Tutor ([1, 28, 8] etc.), for example, shows a relatively rare occurrence within ITS of research cumulating into some coherent pyramid (heap?) of knowledge.

Of course, a clear distinction must be made between coarse grained recognition of a student's knowledge and recognition of a student's coarse grained knowledge. The former reflects the system's incomplete understanding of the student. The latter reflects the student's incomplete understanding of the domain. Using granularity to represent the system's incomplete knowledge is especially useful in the student's goal space since a student's goals are so hard to induce from behaviour. It seems possible that a student's goals can at least be understood at a coarse grain size, by looking at the kinds of tasks the student is working on and considering other behaviour patterns of the student. Using granularity to represent the incompleteness of student knowledge is especially useful in the student's belief space, since a student is constantly refining his/her understanding of the domain. At any given stage the student may only have coarse grained understanding of a concept.

## 3.2  A Representation for Granularity

In this section we discuss our notion of granularity in more detail. Granularity refers to the level-of-detail or perspective from which a concept or entity is viewed.  An entity may be considered at a refined, detailed level or at a more general, approximate level. It may be viewed as a set of parts or as a whole that is greater than the parts. We can think of a concept or entity described at various levels of detail as a collection of *models*. Models can be abstract (coarse-grained) or refined (fine-grained). They can refer to finer-grained sub-component models or coarser-grained aggregate models. Two key attributes of granularity emerge, namely *abstraction granularity* and *aggregation granularity*. When viewing an entity, granularity emerges as shifts in level of abstraction or shifts in level of aggregation occur.

When an entity is viewed at a particular grain-size, its refinements or components are *indistinguishable*. Irrelevant details and attention are focussed within the context of attributes of the object relevant at that grain-size. Shifting focus from one grain-size to another is mediated by two functions, namely *articulation* from coarser to finer-grained objects and *simplification* from finer to coarser-grained objects. These functions provide a mechanism for focus shifts, and implicitly, a definition for focusing attention on relevant objects. We follow Hobbs' [15] general description of granularity and use the terms *relevant attributes*, *indistinguishability*, *articulation*, and *simplification* in the same way he does.

We have taken the basic granularity definitions provided by Hobbs and implemented a hierarchical semantic-network-style knowledge representation scheme which we call a *granularity hierarchy*. The hierarchy contains three basic types of objects: *S-objects, clusters*, and *observers*. These objects are linked together with two orthogonal pairs of relations, namely*abstraction-refinement* relations;, and aggregation-component relations. These relations define two granularity dimensions, the *abstraction dimension* where movement from finer to coarser-grained objects crosses abstraction relations, and the *aggregation dimension* where movement from finer to coarser-grained objects crosses aggregation relations.

S-objects and the relations between them are the key components of the hierarchy. S-objects represent the domain models known by the system. For example, in Figure 2, abstract models of a car are illustrated. A car's abstraction refinements (convertible; family car, sports car; domestic, imported) illustrate specific types of cars (which may be clustered in various ways). The car's aggregation parts are also clustered, for example into structural components (wheels, motor, and seats) or functional components (means of transport and moves on roads, carries a few passengers). Refinements of cars, such as sports cars might have specialized parts such as magnesium wheels (depicted in Figure 3). There is little to distinguish granularity relationships in this example from a traditional ISA/Part-Of hierarchy or from a class-attribute object system. The distinction will be clarified later.

Observers are the interface between the environment and the S-objects in the hierarchy. Observers are depicted as ovals in Figure 3. They make direct observations on the environment through the evaluation of an associated function, called an *ofunction*. The observers enable granularity hierarchies to be used for recognition. S-objects are recognized when their component parts are recognized in an appropriate context. The finest-grained (in the aggregation dimension) S-objects are linked directly to observers, which are able to recognize these S-objects directly from environmental stimuli.

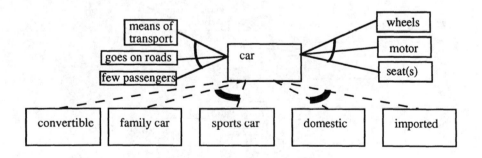

Figure 2: Granularity hierarchy fragment

Consider a formalization of the notation and concepts underlying the idea of granularity. S-objects are connected by granularity relations. Abstraction granularity connects specific, specialized S-objects to more general (coarser-grained) objects or to more approximate (coarser-grained views of) objects. Abstraction/refinement links are depicted as dashed lines in Figures 2 and 3. Aggregation granularity links component-parts or sub-objects to an aggregate S-object.

Aggregation/component links are depicted as solid lines in Figures 2 and 3. Clusters and observer objects are intermediate structures used for examining and retaining information relevant to the S-objects in the hierarchy. K- and L-clusters describe groupings of S-objects and observers. These groupings are important to the representation because an S-object can sometimes be recognizable in a variety of ways. Each "way" of aggregating parts into a recognizable S-object corresponds to a distinct K-cluster. These K-clusters are intermediate groupings of sub-objects in the aggregation dimension which gather a set of relevant component parts sufficient for describing the aggregate S-object. K-clusters are depicted as arcs on aggregation/component links. Similarly refinements of an S-object may be clustered into L-clusters (in the abstraction dimension), which group together refinements sharing a common basis for refinement (sport cars versus family cars). L-clusters behave like "one-of" selectors and are depicted as arcs on abstraction/refinement links.

We view a granularity hierarchy as a structured representation of separate domain models, arrayed in terms of abstractions and aggregations. Each S-object is itself a model (a theory) of some part of the domain. Each model is related to all other models in the hierarchy via the granularity relations. Each model occurs in some context relative to its abstraction and aggregation parents. Recognition of each model is constrained by local information in its clusters of parts or refinements. Articulation and simplification provide a mechanism for shifting focus from one model to another.

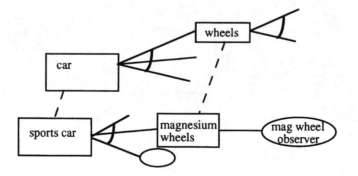

Figure 3: Components linked by refinement

Now consider the distinction between granularity and type-attribute (isa-partof) hierarchies. There are several differences. The abstraction-refinement relations do not make use of inheritance (as do normal isa relations). Articulation and simplification across these relations are mediated by local functions and local constraints. Isa links deal specifically with generalization/specialization relations. On the other hand, abstraction-refinement relations capture notions of approximation and induction as well as generalization and notions of instantiation and refinement as well as specialization. In addition, the existence of K- and L-clusters is a novel extension over the usual isa-partof semantics. Granularity hierarchies require a much greater concentration of local knowledge including local constraints and controls. Moreover, we employ granularity hierarchies for recognition, which, as will be seen in the next section, has quite different implications from the knowledge compaction role of traditional semantic networks.

## 3.3 Using Granularity Hierarchies for Recognition

Assume that a *generic granularity hierarchy* has been created corresponding to a particular content domain and particular anticipated strategies (S-objects) for solving problems in the domain. In the SCENT Advisor [24, 25], these objects represent typical LISP programming strategies and the real world environment is a solution to some programming task. This generic hierarchy can then be used to recognize behaviour in the domain, in SCENT to recognize student programming strategies implicit in students' code. For example, consider the fragment of a granularity hierarchy shown in Figure 4. In this figure, the **cdr recursion** object would recognize a LISP cdr recursion if the program contained a **cdr reduction** as well as a **null base test**. This means that objects are described in terms of their components, each of which is itself an object, ultimately bottoming out at observers responsible for actually accessing the environment. In the SCENT domain, observers look at the LISP program (or traces of the program's execution) for particular features (eg. a null test, the existence of a recursive call to the function, etc.). For example, the observer that is a direct part of the **cdr recursion** object in Figure 4 could make sure that the null base test and cdr reduction are in an appropriate order inside a LISP conditional. The *aggregation* dimension is complemented by the *abstraction* dimension that represents objects in terms of views ranging from abstract to refined. For example an abstraction of **cdr recursion** is **recursion**; a refinement is **tail-end cdr recursion**.

This generic hierarchy is *instantiated* for particular patterns of user behaviour using a *recognition scheme* that can incorporate either *top-down* or *bottom-up* control. In bottom-up control, observers look at the environment in order to recognize primitive objects, and recognized objects *simplify* (aggregate or abstract) into coarser-grained objects. In top-down control, higher-level objects *articulate* (refine or decompose) into finer grain sized objects until observers confirm that certain patterns exist in the environment. Multiple instances of objects are represented naturally, so the resulting instantiation pattern of objects is a true hierarchy. This *instantiated hierarchy*, complete with its recognized and partially recognized objects at various grain sizes, represents a particular pattern of strategies based on evidence from the environment, a "fingerprint" for a particular behaviour pattern in the world. In the LISP domain the generic hierarchy represents typical recursive programming strategies, and an instantiated hierarchy is created for a particular solution (correct or misconceived) to a programming task. Thus, the generic hierarchy is task- and solution-independent, while each instantiated hierarchy is task- and solution-specific. The recognition process is described in much more detail by McCalla et al [26].

An instantiated hierarchy constitutes a flexible and robust representation of the many levels at which particular behaviour can be recognized. There are various grain sizes at which the analysis of behaviour can be examined. Even if the behaviour cannot be completely recognized at the finest grain size, it can still be recognized at some level of detail. Following up on the example in Figure 4, say it is impossible to fully recognize a particular programming strategy (eg. **cdr recursion**) for some reason (perhaps the program contains an atom test rather than a null test in the base case). In this circumstance, it may still be possible to recognize at least a more abstract strategy (eg. **recursion**) because there are fewer constraints at this abstract level. Moreover, the representation can keep track of partially recognized objects (ie. objects where some of the components are not recognized). In the above example the instantiated hierarchy could record that the **cdr recursion** object is partially recognized, rather than throwing this information away. Thus, missing and/or highly uncertain information can be reasoned about.

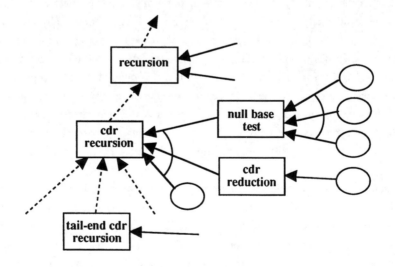

Figure 4: A fragment of a generic granularity hierarchy for LISP recursion

### 3.4 Constructing Student Models with Granularity Hierarchies

Constructing a granularity-based student model begins with external modelling. By examining behaviour in the world, it is possible in many domains to construct a *generic* granularity hierarchy corresponding to a particular content domain and particular anticipated strategies for solving problems in the domain. In the domain of LISP recursion, we have about 300 strategy objects in the generic hierarchy. Each object corresponds to some strategic model for solving a problem or sub-problem. For example, there are objects which recognize a tail-end recursion strategy, a strategy that tests for the end of a list, a strategy that composes lists, a strategy that performs a search in a list, etc.

When such strategy objects are organized into a granularity hierarchy, each object can be thought of as a model for an intended (or apparently intended) learner strategy. That is, if a cdr recursion is recognized in a learner's program, then the learner has correctly formulated that strategic concept. Further, each strategy object represents a perspective on the domain. For example, from the perspective of **cdr recursion** it would be relevant to consider its component parts (ie. **null base test** and **cdr reduction**), its abstractions (ie. **recursion**), or its refinements (**tail-end cdr recursion**, or **embedded cdr recursion**). Thus the hierarchy itself mediates shifts in perspective, and thus can be used to shift context within the domain models.

### 3.5 Case-Based Reasoning

As discussed earlier, the way we use granularity hierarchies in internal student modelling is by instantiating a granularity hierarchy specific to an individual learner's apparent use of strategic objects in a single problem-solving episode. The S-objects instantiated in the hierarchy correspond to strategies evident in the problem-solving episode. The hierarchy is an individualized snapshot of the system's best understanding of the learner's current cognitive state. For example, there might be strong evidence of an attempted **cdr recursion** with a slightly malformed **null base test**. There might be certain evidence of a **recursion** strategy. As can be imagined, with some three hundred potential strategies for simple LISP recursion, each of which may be instantiated zero or more times, the resulting instantiated hierarchy is very complex. After early attempts to make sense of these instantiated hierarchies by summarizing the information, we decided that another approach was necessary. Recently, we have adopted a case-based approach to reasoning about instantiated granularity hierarchies.

In this case-based approach, a particular instantiated granularity hierarchy, corresponding to some snapshot of learner problem-solving behaviour, is compared with a database of previously constructed hierarchies for the same task. Cases for the library are prepared by submitting various ideal and typical solutions to the recognition system, which automatically generates the library hierarchies. Before a new case is included in the library, it may need to be tailored to attach task specific advice to various S-objects, especially to those S-objects corresponding to mal-strategies.

Various matching algorithms retrieve the library case that matches most closely with the learner's solution hierarchy. This gives a reference point for the learner's solution. It also gives a basis for providing advice to the learner. If the learner's program closely resembles a correct solution with only minor strategic variations, the differences between the corresponding hierarchies precisely highlight those differences. Granularity thus guarantees recognition and matching, while the case-based approach ensures a degree of task-independence and generality. Weber's ELM system [31] gains a similar flexibility by adding a notion of cases to a model-based approach.

The advice attached to the strategies in a library case becomes the basis for advice given to the learner. The advice has been arrayed at the different levels of granularity in the corresponding recognized strategy. The system may make use of this granularity-based advice in a variety of ways. In our current implementations, learners are permitted to freely browse the advice hierarchy; but we have plans to extend explanation facilities by utilizing the contextual information afforded by the advice hierarchy.

## 3.6 Advantages of Granularity

There are many advantages of granularity-based reasoning. Granularity captures the notion of context within a content domain. Every S-object in a granularity hierarchy corresponds to a particular viewpoint on the entire content domain as well as a focal point for advice. The correspondence between the learner's behaviour that led to the hierarchy's instantiation and the particular hierarchy S-object in focus also affects the context. For example, when focusing on a particular **null test** that is part of some particular **cdr recursion**, advice can be given about the stopping case for a cdr recursion; and the actual LISP code fragment that corresponds to this **null test** strategy can be used as a context for discussion of the particular **null test**. Thus, the level of granularity can lead to an appropriate context for communication within the domain. In our future work we intend to capitalize on this granularity in advice and link instructional planning systems [3] into the SCENT advisor.

An important consideration in discussing a particular strategic element with a learner is the learner's knowledge of the technical terminology used to name and/or describe the S-object in focus. Again, the structure offered by granularity helps describe such a strategy object, since it will be a refinement or a part of some other strategy, and since it is contextually linked to the learner's problem-solving behaviour. Terminology can be introduced and explanations can be tailored with respect to the granularity-based organization of the content domain. Although our current implementations have not yet explicitly used granularity hierarchies to reason about advice and explanations, this is a priority in our upcoming research.

Granularity-based reasoning also allows a detailed model of the strategies apparently used by the learner to be obtained. This detailed model is really a hierarchy of simpler models, which is fully inspectable and useful for advising. The granularity hierarchy that records the strategic fingerprint corresponding to learner behaviour is the starting point from which advice at various grain sizes is generated. Any strategic element deemed important can be focused upon, enabling the organization of domain strategies to become the basis for focusing advice.

Granularity hierarchies deal with uncertainty in three ways. First, uncertainty in recognizing strategies from behaviour corresponds to partially recognized strategies in a granularity hierarchy. These partially recognized strategies point directly to the causes for their own partial recognition, that is, to the strategic entities which were expected but not found in the learner's behaviour. Thus, the system is knowledgeable about its own uncertainty. Second, the organization of granularity hierarchies guarantees that recognition of some strategies will occur at some grain size, no matter how bizarre the learner's behaviour might be. This guarantee of at least coarse grained recognition of strategies is important to maintaining some sort of dialogue with the learner, preventing system brittleness even in difficult situations. Third, the case-based matching deals with uncertainty in yet another way. If a learner's behaviour had many different plausible interpretations, the closest matching case can be used to focus on a single best interpretation. Remaining uncertainty in recognition of learners' strategies can thus be dealt with in a relatively reliable way, by using the information in the closest matching case hierarchy.

Another advantage to this granularity approach is its mechanism for monitoring the evolution in learners' strategies over time. While a learner makes numerous attempts at solving a single problem, the granularity hierarchies of these successive attempts can be analyzed to monitor how strategies evolve over time. If the learner continues to focus on unimportant details, the system is readily aware of this. If the learner has apparently mastered certain strategies, or has had difficulty with certain strategies, the selection of subsequent tasks can take this into consideration.

A final advantage to granularity is its natural adaptation to context within a domain. In an ITS interaction with a learner, the context for the interaction revolves entirely around the domain elements. Context can be thought of as a shared viewpoint on the domain. Establishing this viewpoint is facilitated by focus within the multi-grained models of a granularity hierarchy.

Granularity hierarchies provide a useful tool for reasoning, a tool that is practical right now. Further investigations into the nature of granularity should enhance the usefulness of granularity-based recognition. We especially wish to compare our notions of granularity to those found in other areas such as cartography, to define new kinds of granularity, and to more fully understand the implications of reasoning with granularity.

We also believe that granularity is a central notion in much of AI, not just in ITS, and thus we feel that lessons learned in an ITS research project can generalize beyond the field. ITS provides a great testbed for investigations into granularity since it is so important in the area. Of course, many of the granularity notions we have been working with have been originally sparked by research in other areas of AI such as computational vision and formal knowledge representation. This two-way street connecting AI to ITS is thus crucial for enriching both fields.

# 4  Maintaining the Student Model

The second main student modelling issue we wish to discuss in this chapter is the problem of maintaining a student model as the student's knowledge changes over time and the tutor's knowledge of the student is refined. At first this might appear to require a standard truth maintenance system such as explored by Doyle [10], de Kleer [9] and others. Such truth maintenance systems are able to spot how new information conflicts with existing information in some model of the world (encoded in propositional logic). The model contains facts which have been externally observed, implications which can be used to derive new facts from observed facts using modus ponens, and dependency relations showing how derived facts relate to the propositions that generated them. Conflicts are found only between new information and information that has already been derived; the truth maintenance system does not try to derive all of the internal implications of the information in its model of the world. Thus, unnoticed internal contradictions can exist in the world model. This is ideal for student modelling since students may well not derive all the implications of their knowledge, and may have numerous unrecognized internal contradictions.

## 4.1  Difficulties in Student Model Maintenance

Of course, being able to discern which inferences students have made and which they haven't made is a very difficult problem. This becomes an especially difficult problem when it is realized that students often have knowledge (and goals) they don't know they have, although their actions are clearly affected by this implicit knowledge. How can such implicit knowledge be handled by a standard truth maintenance system? If an implicit fact were added to the set of observed or deduced knowledge, then the student model would be able to accurately reflect student behaviour, although it would not accurately reflect what a student would claim to know. If, on the other hand, an implicit fact were left out of the set of observed or deduced knowledge, then the student model would accurately reflect what the student would claim to know, but would not be able to accurately reflect student behaviour.

Actual changes to the model are not carried out by a standard truth maintenance system (it simply points out the conflicts). Model updating is left to a separate domain-specific reasoning system which must choose how to resolve these conflicts according to rules relevant to the domain. Normally, this means removing old information that conflicts with new information, since a natural assumption is that new knowledge is more accurate than old. Such an assumption may not be valid in student modelling, given how difficult it is to accurately assess the student. An apparent change in the student's behaviour could well be a mistake in diagnosis, rather than a change in the student. To handle such uncertainty in diagnosis we advocate granularity hierarchies.

It is quite unclear how to extend truth maintenance systems to work with non-propositional knowledge structures such as granularity hierarchies. Even the definition of conflict changes, since no longer is logical contradiction the hallmark; odd kinds of pseudo-conflicts arise, where, for example, no conflict occurs between certain concepts at coarse grain sizes, but conflicts do occur among their finer grained descendants. Moreover, since much of the information that must be kept in an ITS is procedural, the very concept of conflict often seems a bit puzzling. How can conflicts between two procedures be defined? How can two student goals be said to be in conflict? Like speech acts in linguistics, knowledge of goals and procedures seems inherently non-propositional. This makes it doubtful that standard truth maintenance approaches will have much to say about maintaining the goal space of the student model, even if with some modifications such approaches can be adapted for use in the student's belief space. There are likely fundamentally different truth maintenance processes needed for belief spaces and goal spaces.

The problem of determining a conflict becomes even more difficult when it is realized that the whole point of instruction is to help the student's knowledge change. Often students are purposefully given information at a coarse grain size or are told incorrect information in order to get to the nub of an issue. Although any misconceptions that are thus generated must be corrected later, the tutoring system has in such situations decided to let the student live with some conflicts, at least temporarily. Similarly, a student may be encouraged to compare two analogous situations in order to spot a conflict, but until he/she actually carries out the analogy there will be no conflict.

What this means is that genetic relationships such as those proposed by Goldstein [12] underly any student's evolving knowledge, and such relationships are critical to determining when a conflict has occurred. A principled computational theory of instruction based on a deep understanding of the genetic paths through student knowledge would suggest what kinds of instructional actions would be appropriate at a given stage of a student's knowledge evolution. It would also suggest expected effects on the student model (both student beliefs and student goals) of these actions, and would define what kinds of actual student behaviour would be in conflict with these expected effects. Devising such a principled theory isn't going to be easy, and will require much in the way of empirical testing of actual student behaviour. It isn't even clear that such a theory would generalize beyond a particular domain, or whether instead a new theory must be devised for each domain outlining the genetic paths possible for that domain. It also isn't clear whether there would need to be many such theories for each different type of student or whether a single, all-encompassing theory could be projected onto each student. What this means for student model maintenance is that there may be many different kinds of maintenance procedures, depending on peculiarities of students and idiosyncrasies of domains.

An even tougher maintenance problem arises, however, if the student's knowledge isn't accumulated in an evolutionary way (predictably through expected genetic transformations in his/her knowledge), but instead undergoes revolutionary change. Students often seem to be immune to understanding a tough concept over an extended period of instruction; but then, suddenly, they make some sort of revolutionary change in their perception which radically improves their understanding of the concept. Presumably, the student has been accumulating exceptions to his/her standard perspectives over the extended period, but has not been willing and/or able to fundamentally alter those perspectives. When the accreted exceptions become too cumbersome and some key new insight comes along, a radical shift in perspectives occurs. This kind of change would seem to be quite difficult to deal with in that the exceptions must be tracked, but cannot be considered to be conflicts until the insight occurs. Once the insight occurs, a major reshuffling of the student model must take place, which promises to be much harder than the kinds of incremental change usually associated with truth maintenance.

One further problem that arises in student model maintenance is how to handle the fact that a student often forgets concepts he or she has learned. A student changes his or her goals as the situation changes, often withdrawing old goals. Knowledge does not simply accumulate, but can be forgotten as well. Forgetting is essential if an organism is to avoid being paralyzed by trying to sort through too much information. Presumably, it must be possible to predict certain kinds of forgetting. In fact, in some ways, truth maintenance systems are precisely designed to predict such forgetting since they identify sets of student beliefs which must change after new conflicting information arises. However, not all forgetting results from conflict resolution, so other principles must apply, perhaps based on theories of how students learn (eg. after general rules have been induced from specific instances of the rules, then the specific instances are often discarded). It must also be possible to directly discern certain kinds of forgetting as reflected in student behaviour (eg. a student who earlier could write tail-end recursive functions no longer can). Whether predicted or observed, however, in general it is very difficult to determine that a student no longer knows something. This is yet another manifestation of the core problem of not being able to fully understand a student's reasoning through observing his/her behaviour. In fact this is an even more difficult manifestation since at least when the student is learning new things it may relate to the current instructional goals of the student and tutor, whereas when he/she forgets something it may happen as background activity unconnected to the current situation. Even if such forgetting can be recognized, how does forgetting impact conflict detection and resolution? After a student has forgotten some key concept, certain things may now be in conflict which weren't before, and vice versa. Current truth maintenance systems only deal in accretion, not deletion, so this promises to be a tricky problem as well.

By any lights, student model maintenance is a very hard thing to do. The difficulty of clearly understanding a student's behaviour, combined with the extreme complexity of the knowledge structures in a student's mind, show up the simplicity of current truth maintenance approaches. Thus, research into extending truth maintenance into student model maintenance is another major area where ITS research can suggest deep and interesting problems for AI, while at the same time AI can provide some insights worthy of building upon. This has been the underlying motivation for a series of experiments carried out by Xueming Huang in the ARIES Laboratory. These experiments are described briefly in the next section.

## 4.2 Minimal Change, Focus of Attention, and Stereotypes

For some time, especially through Huang's Ph.D. thesis work [17], we in the ARIES Laboratory have been investigating student model maintenance. Given the extreme difficulty of solving the full-fledged student model maintenance problem, we have made a number of initial simplifying assumptions. Since we wanted this work to build on existing work in truth maintenance and user modelling, we decided to represent all knowledge and beliefs about the student and the domain as logical propositions. Thus, granularity has not played an explicit role at this stage of our research into student model maintenance. Moreover, the focus has not been on propositions inside the student belief and goal spaces (shown in Figure 1), since this would require a full fledged cognitive model of how students' beliefs and goals change. Rather, we have been focussed on the relatively more tractable problem of maintaining the consistency of the tutor's beliefs about the student, ie. those beliefs outside of the student's belief and goal spaces. Thus, we would not be upset if SB(x) and SB(¬x) co-existed in the student model, but would want to prevent the co-existence of SB(x) and ¬SB(x) since the latter would be a contradiction in the tutor's own beliefs. Preventing this kind of inconsistency suggests that there is indeed a role for truth maintenance systems. Finally, among all the possible student model maintenance issues, we have concentrated on three: minimal change, focus of attention, and stereotypes.

Research into the first issue has led to the creation of relatively efficient algorithms for identifying sets of beliefs which result in minimal changes being made to the tutor's beliefs about the student in order to keep them conflict free. This can make the job of adjusting the student model much easier than if all possible sets of conflicts are produced, rather than just minimal sets. Huang et al [16] have implemented a set of algorithms called the Evolutionary Belief Revision System (EBRS) that produces all minimal sets of conflicts by combining Reiter's diagnosis [29] approach with de Kleer's ATMS [9].

More recently, Huang et al [19] have begun to explore how to model belief spaces with limited consistency. Motivating this research is the recognition that the student model maintenance task is extremely hard and that maintaining total consistency, or even consistency to the level of the EBRS, throughout the entire student model is not achievable in the real world, nor (as we have pointed out) is it always necessary. Huang et al [18] have also worked out how to combine stereotypical knowledge of students with knowledge diagnosed during interaction with the student. Figure 5 shows the architecture of this limited consistency/sterotype-based student modelling system.

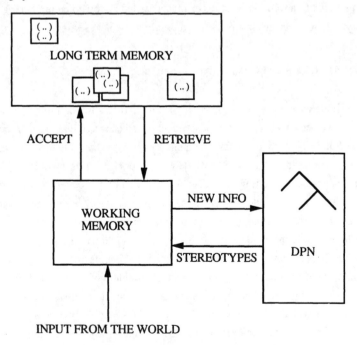

Figure 5: Huang's student model maintenance system

Briefly, the architecture suggests that there are two kinds of knowledge in a student model: 1) observed student beliefs and justifications for these beliefs, and 2) stereotypical beliefs held by typical students at various stages of their learning. Huang represents the observed beliefs by propositions stored in packages called *frames of mind* (a theoretical analysis of the frames of mind notion can be found in Huang's paper in this volume [21]). Only some of these frames are relevant to any problem the student might be working on, so these are *focussed* in *working memory*. The working memory is maintained by the EBRS, so must be internally consistent to at least the level of a truth maintenance system. When the student changes focus of attention, some of the frames from the working memory (perhaps modified by the addition or deletion of beliefs during their time under active consideration) are no longer needed so are *accepted* into the *long term memory* (LTM). Similarly, newly relevant LTM frames must be be *retrieved* into the working memory. Huang et al [19] provide algorithms (called, collectively, the Attention Shifting Belief Revision System, ABRS) for carrying out the accept and retrieve operations, as well as efficient algorithms for updating the LTM at least somewhat when frames are accepted into it. It must be emphasized, however, that the LTM updating, while efficient, does not even remotely guarantee total consistency in the LTM, so the tutor's beliefs about the student may be inconsistent. Huang and McCalla [20] show that such a limited consistency approach works efficiently and effectively in instructional planning, where the tutor has control of the agenda, but it isn't as clear how well it will work for the dual problem of tracking student beliefs.

Huang et al's [18] stereotype mechanism is specifically tailored to take into account how stereotypes change as a student's learning proceeds. The stereotypical beliefs are structured in hierarchies called "default package networks" (which is why the stereotype mechanism is called the "DPN"). Each node in the DPN represents some concept from the domain, and the beliefs arrayed at that node are typical student beliefs about the concept. Since student understanding of a concept can change over time, the beliefs are also categorized according to pre-specified learning stages at which they become appropriate. Novices may understand a concept incompletely or erroneously whereas an expert would know the finest nuances of the concept. The arcs connecting nodes in the DPN represent relationships among the concepts (eg. prerequisite relationships) and are used to keep track of data dependencies among the concepts as the student's learning progresses. Stereotypical beliefs appropriate to the perceived stage of learning are fed from the DPN into the working memory as required and these beliefs can then be used by the tutoring system as it reasons about student knowledge. As a student's understanding of the domain changes, the DPN is able to update the stereotypical knowledge that is appropriate by updating the learning category attached to relevant nodes in the DPN, and then doing constraint satisfaction and default propagation along arcs of the DPN to change related stereotypical knowledge. The old package of stereotypical beliefs can be removed from working memory and replaced with knowledge more appropriate to the current stage of learning.

Taken together, Huang's various belief revision algorithms provide some useful tools for student model maintenance. As mentioned earlier, however, Huang's system only reasons with beliefs that are propositional. An interesting research direction is to look at how to use Huang's approach while structuring beliefs in terms of granularity. Even more interesting is removing a layer of indirection and trying to reason directly with the beliefs "inside the brackets", that is to try to maintain the beliefs inside the student's belief and goal spaces. Reasoning inside the student's goal and belief spaces is a very hard problem, requiring serious cognitive modelling to see how students actually change and learn. Much evidence is out there, from cognitive science and instructional psychology, but as Section 3.1 has pointed out, the problems are subtle and deep.

# 5  Conclusions

There are many other issues inherent in student modelling, some of them touched upon in the discussion so far, and some brand new. How can the knowledge in a student model be generated as needed rather than prestored and just overlayed? Can a principled theory of misconceptions be devised? Are such theories inherently domain specific (like BUGGY [5]) or are there domain independent theories of misconceptions which take into account possible general principles of reasoning and mal-reasoning (eg. Repair Theory [6])? What is the relationship between domain knowledge and more general problem solving skills? Are there theories of cognition that can be used to explain the interconnections between a student's mental models, strategies, and surface behaviour? How can an episodic record of student history best be acquired and organized? How can the fact that a student's knowledge is necessarily incomplete and inconsistent, not to mention that a tutor's knowledge of the student is normally also incomplete and inconsistent, be dealt with, especially if the goal is to come up with a principled (ie. formal) approach to student modelling?

Research into any of these issues may well suggest whole new approaches to knowledge representation and innovative solutions to old problems, and conversely may necessitate the marshalling of many AI techniques to resolve them. This illustrates once again the synergy between ITS and AI.

We would like to draw several general conclusions from the preceding discussion:

1. Granularity is an important consideration in student modelling and in pedagogy. Explicit representations of granularity are central to being able to handle the uncertainties inherent both in diagnosis and in pedagogical decision making. Reasoning using granularity enhances the robustness of a tutoring system.

2. Standard artificial intelligence methodologies such as hierarchical knowledge representation techniques and truth maintenance approaches can be applied to student modelling, but they need to be substantially enhanced if they are to make a dent in the hard problems.

3. The enhancements to standard artificial intelligence techniques that are necessary if they are to apply to intelligent tutoring are deep and interesting, and should feed back much to artificial intelligence research outside of ITS. In this sense research into intelligent tutoring is a highly worthwhile AI activity.

4. The issues that must be resolved before an intelligent tutor can act with full subtlety are long term research issues, as tough as any that arise anywhere in AI. However, current research is suggesting certain student modelling techniques that might be directly applicable in the short term.

Overall, then, we argue for continued explorations of student modelling, the "key to individualized learning". The problems are hard, but even partial solutions may be useful and the research itself promises a plethora of interesting issues to explore that will enhance both artificial intelligence and intelligent tutoring systems.

## Acknowledgements

Particular thanks also go to all of our graduate students and research assistants, most especially to Xueming Huang, Randy Coulman, Dinesh Gadwal, Eric Neufeld, Barbara Wasson, Mary Mark, Bryce Barrie, and Paul Pospisil who have worked on research directly pertaining to the issues discussed in this chapter. We would also like to acknowledge the financial support of Canada's Natural Sciences and Engineering Research Council, the IRIS Network of Centres of Excellence, and the University of Saskatchewan.

## References

1. Anderson, J. & Reiser, B.: The LISP tutor, *Byte*, 10(4), pp. 159-175 (1985)
2. Bhuiyan, S. H., Greer, J. E. & McCalla, G. I.: Characterizing, rationalizing, and reifying mental models of recursion. Proceedings of the 13th Annual Meeting of the Cognitive Science Society, Chicago, IL, pp. 120-125, Hillsdale, NJ: Lawrence Erlbaum Associates 1991
3. Brecht (Wasson), B.: Determining the Focus of Instruction: Content Planning for Intelligent Tutoring Systems, Ph.D. Thesis, Department of Computational Science, University of Saskatchewan 1990
4. Brecht (Wasson), B., McCalla, G. I., Greer, J. E. & Jones, M.: Planning the content of instruction. In: *Proceedings of the 4th International Conference on Artificial Intelligence and Education*, Amsterdam (D. Bierman, J. Breuker & J. Sandberg, eds.)., pp. 32-41. Amsterdam: IOS 1989
5. Brown, J. & Burton, R.: Diagnostic models for procedural bugs in basic mathematical skills, *Cognitive Science Journal*, 2, pp. 155-191 (1978)
6. Brown, J. & Van Lehn, K.: Repair theory: a generative theory of bugs in procedural skills, *Cognitive Science Journal*, 4, pp. 379-426 (1980)
7. Cohen, P. R. & Perrault, C. R.: Elements of a plan-based theory of speech acts, *Cognitive Science*, 3, pp. 177-212 (1989)

8. Corbett, A. & Anderson, J.: Feedback timing and student control in the LISP Intelligent Tutoring System. In: *Proceedings of the 4th International Conference on Artificial Intelligence and Education*, Amsterdam (D. Bierman, J. Breuker & J. Sandberg, eds.)., pp. 64-72. Amsterdam: IOS 1989

9. de Kleer, J.: An assumption-based truth maintenance system, *Artificial Intelligence Journal*, 28, pp. 127-162 (1986)

10. Doyle, J.: A truth maintenance system, *Artificial Intelligence Journal*, 12, pp. 231-272 (1979)

11. Elsom-Cook, M.: *Guided Discovery Tutoring: a Framework for ICAI Research*. London: Paul Chapman 1989

12. Goldstein, I.: The genetic graph: a representation for the evolution of procedural knowledge. In: *Intelligent Tutoring Systems* (D. Sleeman & J. S. Brown, eds.).pp. 51-78, London: Academic Press 1982

13. Greer, J. E. & McCalla, G. I.: A computational framework for granularity and its application to educational diagnosis. Proceedings of the 11th International Joint Conference on Artificial Intelligence, Detroit, MI pp. 477-482 1989

14. Greer, J. E., Mark, M. & McCalla, G. I.: Incorporating granularity-based recognition into SCENT. In: *Proceedings of the 4th International Conference on Artificial Intelligence and Education*, Amsterdam (D. Bierman, J. Breuker & J. Sandberg, eds.)., pp. 107-115. Amsterdam: IOS 1989

15. Hobbs, J.: Granularity. Proceedings of the 9th International Conference on Artificial Intelligence, Los Angeles, CA, pp. 432-435 1985

16. Huang, X., McCalla, G. I. & Greer, J. E.: Student model revision: evolution and revolution. Proceedings of the 8th Canadian Conference on Artificial Intelligence, Ottawa, pp. 98-105 1990

17. Huang, X.: Updating Belief Systems: Minimal Change, Focus of Attention and Stereotypes. Ph.D. Thesis, Department of Computational Science, University of Saskatchewan 1991

18. Huang, X., McCalla, G. I., Greer, J. E. & Neufeld, E.: Revising deductive knowledge and sterotypical knowledge in a student model, *User Modelling and User Adapted Interaction*, 1(1), pp. 87-115 (1991)

19. Huang, X., McCalla, G. I.. & Neufeld, E.: Using attention in belief revision. Proceedings of the American Association for Artificial Intelligence Conference, Anaheim, CA, pp. 275-280 1991

20. Huang, X. & McCalla, G. I.: Instructional planning using focus of attention. In: *Proceedings of the 2nd International Conference on Intelligent Tutoring Systems*, Montreal, Quebec (C. Frasson, G. Gauthier & G. McCalla, eds.), pp. 433-450, Lecture Notes in Computer Science, Vol. 608, Berlin: Springer-Verlag 1992

21. Huang (1993). Modelling a student's inconsistent beliefs and attention. In: *Student Modelling: The Key to Individualized Knowledge-Based Instruction* (G. I. McCalla & J.E. Greer, eds.), pp. 277-290, Berlin, FDR: Springer-Verlag 1993

22. Macmillan, S. & Sleeman, D.: An architecture for a self-improving instructional planner for intelligent tutoring systems, *Computational Intelligence Journal*, 3, pp.17-27 (1987)

23. McCalla, G. I.: Knowledge Representation Issues in Automated Tutoring, Research Report 87-1, ARIES Laboratory, Department of Computational Science, University of Saskatchewan 1987

24. McCalla, G. I., Greer, J. E. & the SCENT Research Team: SCENT-3: an architecture for intelligent advising in problem solving domains. In: *Intelligent Tutoring Systems: At The Crossroads of Artificial Intelligence and Education* (C. Frasson & G. Gauthier, eds.), pp 140-161, Norwood, NJ: Ablex 1989

25. McCalla, G. I. & Greer, J. E.: Helping novices learn recursion: giving granularity-based advice on strategies and providing support at the mental model level. Proceedings of the NATO Advanced Research Workshop on Cognitive Models and Intelligent Environments for Learning Programming, Genoa, Italy, pp. 57-71 1992

26. McCalla, G. I., Greer, J. E., Barrie, B. & Pospisil, P.: Granularity hierarchies, *International Journal of Computers and Mathematics with Applications (Special Issue on Semantic Networks)*, 23, pp. 363-375 (1992)

27. Peachey, D. & McCalla, G. I.: Using planning techniques in intelligent tutoring systems, *International Journal of Man-Machine Studies*, 24, pp. 77-88 (1986)

28. Reiser, B., Anderson, J. & Farrell, R.: Dynamic student modelling in an intelligent tutor for LISP programming. Proceedings of the 9th International Conference on Artificial Intelligence, Los Angeles, CA, pp. 8-14, 1985

29. Reiter, R.: Diagnosis from First Principles, *Artificial Intelligence*, 32, pp. 57-95 (1987)

30. Spensley, F. & Elsom-Cook, M.: Dominie: Teaching and Assessment Strategies, CITE Report 37, Centre for Information Technology in Education, Institute of Educational Technology, The Open University, Milton Keynes, UK 1988

31. Weber, G.: Analogies in an intelligent programming environment for learning LISP. In: *Cognitive Models and Intelligent Environments for Learning Programming* (E. Lemut, B. du Boulay, G. Deltori, eds.), pp. 210-219, NATO ASI Series F, Vol. 111, Berlin: Springer-Verlag 1993

# Student Modelling Through Qualitative Reasoning

Bert Bredeweg[1] and Radboud Winkels[2]

[1]Department of Social Science Informatics (S.W.I.), University of Amsterdam, Amsterdam, The Netherlands
[2]Department of Computer Science & Law, University of Amsterdam, Amsterdam, The Netherlands

**Abstract:** A growing number of learning environments on the computer are simulation based. Research shows that such simulations are only effective when the student is guided by a tutor, for instance embedded in an intelligent tutoring system. However, most of the simulations are based on complex mathematical procedures. This makes it hard, if not impossible, for the intelligent tutoring system to use the simulator for explanations or student modelling, because it has no means to relate the calculations within the simulation to the conceptual framework that represents the knowledge the student possesses, or has to acquire. An alternative is to use causal, qualitative models as the basis for simulation. We present an integrated qualitative reasoning approach, implemented as a shell named GARP, that can be used to build both domain models and student models. The modelling language (at the conceptual level) appears to map directly on that of human reasoning about the domain. Furthermore, the resulting models in GARP are very suitable for different kinds of explanations, for diagnosis, and for generating critical tests to induce learning or awareness of misconceptions on the part of the student.

**Keywords:** qualitative reasoning, learning environments, diagnosis

## 1 Introduction

A growing number of learning environments on the computer are simulation based [18]. Usually these environments are based on the *discovery learning* educational philosophy (eg. [13]) and are aptly called discovery worlds. But research shows that such simulations are only effective when the actions of the students are monitored by a teacher (human or computer based) and guidance is provided [20, 27]. One solution is to embed the simulation in an intelligent tutoring system. However, most of the simulations are based on complex mathematical procedures that calculate how the specific aspects within the simulation are to be manipulated (eg. SOPHIE I/II [11], STEAMER [23], RBT [37]). These mathematical procedures, although quite efficient in simulating the physical world, provide no conceptual access to the objects and their behaviour in the simulation. This flaw makes it hard, if not impossible, for the intelligent tutoring system to use the simulator for explanations or student modelling, because it has no means to relate the mathematical calculations within the simulation to the conceptual framework that represents the knowledge the student possesses, or has to acquire. It is impossible to derive causal explanations of the behaviour of the particular device or system from the mathematical model, so these would have to be added *by hand*. Therefore we are looking for different models to use for simulations, models that explicitly represent the objects and their behaviours that play a role in the system. These models should enable causal reasoning, and preferably comply with the way humans reason about the system. In this paper we present an integrated approach for qualitative reasoning that can be used for this purpose.

The contents of this paper are as follows. In section 2 the important features of the three major approaches to qualitative reasoning are discussed. Section 3 then moves on by describing a unified framework for qualitative prediction of behaviour based on these approaches. Section 4 presents an example of how student models and domain models can be represented in this framework. This section consists of three parts. The first subsection 4.1 presents the example and discusses the cognitive plausibility of models represented in the unified framework. The second subsection 4.2 discusses how the integrated framework, implemented in GARP, can be used for generating critical tests to induce learning or awareness of misconceptions on the part of the student. The third subsection 4.3 shows how the framework facilitates different kinds of explanations. Finally, section 5 summarizes and discusses the important results of the research reported in this paper.

# 2  Qualitative Reasoning

During the last decade qualitative reasoning has evolved as an interesting research area of artificial intelligence that is concerned with automated reasoning about the physical world using qualitative representations [30]. Based on different ontologies about how to represent the physical world, three basic approaches have successfully been developed [4]. The major characteristics of these approaches are discussed in the first section below. The second section then moves on by discussing examples of qualitative reasoning techniques being used for teaching purposes. In the last subsection a number of problems are pointed out that must be solved in order to facilitate a more substantial use of qualitative reasoning techniques for teaching purposes.

## 2.1 The Three Major Approaches

The component centered approach of deKleer and Brown [19] models the physical world as consisting of components that manipulate materials and share information by means of conduits. Components behave independently from their surroundings, and they obey the *no-function-in-structure* principle. How components manipulate materials is described as a set *qualitative states*, each specifying a particular state of behaviour and associating it with a particular group of confluences, the latter being relations between parameters that describe the characteristics of the materials. After a configuration of components and conduits is specified (system topology) the behaviour prediction starts by generating a *cross-product* of qualitative states, ie. each qualitative state of one component is combined with each qualitative state of the other components. Every combination refers to a possible state of behaviour in which the system can be. Given these overall states of behaviour, the internal consistency of each state of behaviour is determined by applying *constraint satisfaction* and *generate and test*. The consistent states of behaviour are then analysed for state transitions by determining whether certain transformation rules are true between two states of behaviour. The final result is a *total envisionment,* ie. a set of state descriptions with for each description specified: its internal behaviour in terms of parameter values, its preceding states and its successor states. Together they describe all possible behaviours of the system specified in the initial description.

Important ontological primitives in Forbus' process centered approach [22] are *views* and *processes*. Views associate objects, or groups of objects, with parameter relations. These relations describe how the characteristics of materials and of objects are related to each other. Processes are similar to views, except that they can *influence* the characteristics of materials and objects. The behaviour prediction starts with a *scenario*, a collection of physical objects, and possibly some inequality relations between the quantities that describe the properties of these objects. The goal of the problem solving task is to find the views and processes that apply to that description. Given the set of applicable views and processes, the influences of the processes are determined first. The effects of these influences are then propagated by the available parameter relations, resulting in a complete description of the current situation. This description of the situation is then analysed in order to find out whether in the future the behaviour of the system becomes incompatible with this description. The process centered approach has a number of rules that specify how a particular situation description terminates, as well as how a transition to another (new) situation description can take place. The qualitative reasoning process continues until all states of behaviour have been determined as well as the possible transitions between them.

The Kuipers' constraint centered approach [25] takes a qualitative version of the differential equation, that is used in traditional physics for describing a particular situation, as a starting-point. This (mathematical) model is input for a *generate and test* cycle that determines all the possible behaviours of the modelled system. The total cycle stops when, similar to the process centered approach, for each situation an interpretation has been generated and all possible transitions between situations have been determined.

## 2.2 Using Qualitative Reasoning for Teaching Purposes

The only well known existing intelligent tutoring system that uses a qualitative model for its simulation is SOPHIE III [11], a reactive learning environment for teaching troubleshooting in electronic circuits, in which the coaching module was never realized. Notice however that although SOPHIE III is based on a qualitative approach, it does not have true causal models of the circuits, but uses circuit specific rules and links. More recently White and Frederiksen [31, 32] describe their work on QUEST, an instructional system for teaching the behaviour of electronic circuits. QUEST is based on a progression of mental models from a qualitative zero order model, via a qualitative first order model, to a full quantitative model. Both SOPHIE III and QUEST are essentially based upon a specific subset of the component oriented approach to qualitative reasoning. PRESTO [2] explicity uses qualitative differential equations as the basis for student modelling in order to help learners understand physical devices.

## 2.3 Improving the Use of Qualitative Models

To improve the use of qualitative reasoning techniques for teaching purposes the current state of the art needs to be extended in a number of ways. None of the approaches completely captures all the distinctions that are relevant for qualitative prediction of behaviour. Instead, each approach seems to be particularly suited for modelling a certain part of this problem solving task. On the other hand, the different approaches show a certain amount of similarity, but the precise relation between the conceptualizations used in each of the approaches is unclear. It is therefore fair to conclude that there is a need for an integrated approach to qualitative prediction of behaviour, not only for pointing out the similarities and differences between the individual approaches, but also for establishing a problem solving potential that currently cannot be realized by either of the original approaches. In particular, we want to facilitate the representation and use of different types of models of the physical world in a single intelligent tutoring system.

A second requirement for improving the use of qualitative models is that the conceptual framework underlying the qualitative reasoning technique must be represented explicitly [5] in order to facilitate *conceptual access* to the entities from the simulation at a level of detail that closely matches the human interpretation of the simulation.

In the next sections we present an integrated approach to qualitative reasoning, implemented as a shell called GARP that can be used for both modelling of the domain (the simulation) and the student, not only to reflect the learning (eg. QUEST where the different models are meant to specifically do that), but also as the basis for a systematic diagnostic process of lacks of knowledge or alternative conceptions.

## 3 Expertise in Qualitative Reasoning

Breuker and Wielinga [19] propose a framework (KADS) for modelling problem solving expertise which is based on the premise that knowledge used by people during reasoning processes can be distinguished according to several types, corresponding to the different roles the knowledge plays in the reasoning process (see Figure 1).

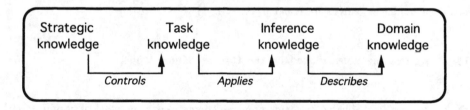

Figure 1: The KADS four layers

The *domain knowledge* describes the domain specific knowledge in terms of domain concepts, relations and complex structures such as models of processes or devices. This knowledge is static in nature, that is, it is not specified what control regime is needed in order to use the knowledge effectively.

The *inference knowledge* is concerned with the canonical problem solving actions (*knowledge sources*) that are the basis of reasoning. Knowledge sources are elementary in the sense that other parts of the problem solver can not influence their internal control. They represent the way in which a domain relation can be used to make inferences. For example: a *specification* and an *abstraction* inference might both use a *subsume* relation at the domain layer to make their inference. The different *roles* the domain knowledge plays in this reasoning process are described by *meta-classes*. For example, a domain concept like *faulty-transistor* may play the role of a *finding*, but may also play the role of a *hypothesis*. In this case finding and hypothesis represent domain independent use of domain concepts for diagnostic reasoning.

The third type of knowledge, the *task knowledge*, describes what goals are involved in a particular problem solving task and how the available knowledge sources can be ordered and applied to satisfy those goals.

The fourth type of knowledge concerns *strategic knowledge* that controls the overall reasoning process. It should, for instance, plan a particular task structure, monitor its execution, and, if needed, diagnose, repair or even substitute the current task structure with another task structure, until the desired problem solving goal is reached. There is a tradeoff between the task and the strategic layer. In the case of non-standard problems the problem solving process will use more strategic reasoning. This contrasts with more routine problems in which the problem solver is more likely to execute an already known task structure.

To model a students' knowledge about a specific system from the real-world domain knowledge, together with how this knowledge can be used in the reasoning process, is of crucial importance. In this paper we will therefore mainly concentrate on this topic and only partly discuss issues concerning task and strategic knowledge (discussions of the latter for intelligent tutoring systems can be found in [10, 34]).

## 3.1 Meta-classes: Roles Played by the Domain Knowledge

The approaches to qualitative reasoning provide different sets of ontological primitives for modelling domain specific knowledge. Typical examples are: components, qualitative states, views, processes, influences, and qualitative differential equations. Each modelling primitive is used by the qualitative inference engine in a certain way. This use represents the *role* that the modelling primitive plays in the reasoning process. In this section we will investigate which knowledge roles are relevant to qualitative prediction of behaviour (for an overview see Table 1). In particular, we will focus on (1) how the physical world is represented (system elements), (2) what is considered as behaviour (parameters, values and relations), and (3) how knowledge about behaviour is represented (partial behaviour models, system model descriptions and transformation rules).

| Meta-class name | Description of the role |
|---|---|
| *System model description* | A model that describes the real-world system during a period of time in which the behaviour of that system does not change |
| *System elements* | Abstractions from the real-world to which partial behaviour models apply |
| *Parameters* | Properties of system elements |
| *Parameter values* | Values of parameters |
| *Quantity spaces* | An ordered set of values that a specific parameter can have. |
| *Parameter relations* | Dependencies between parameters |
| *Qualitative calculi* | Semantics of a parameter relation |
| *Mathematical models* | A set of parameter relations that holds during a particular system model description |
| *Partial models* | Small units representing partial behaviours which are assembled into larger models that represent the behaviour of some real-world system |
| *Transformation rules* | Knowledge about how to find successive system model descriptions. Three types of rules have been identified: *termination*, *precedence*, and *continuity*. |
| *Behaviour descriptions* | A set of system model descriptions ordered in time, representing the potential behaviour of a system |

Table 1: Meta-classes in qualitative prediction of behaviour

## 3.1.1   System Elements

An essential step in qualitative reasoning is to determine (1) how objects from the real-world are represented in the prediction model, and (2) how these representations are applied to guide the behaviour analysis. The domain knowledge that is used for this purpose performs the role of system elements. Three aspects of system elements can be pointed out. The *hierarchy of generic concepts* provides the qualitative inference engine with a description of the entities that are believed to be present in the real-world. *Instances* refer to the specific entities that constitute the system that is the object of behaviour prediction (see also section 3.1.5). Instances always refer to a subset of the elements in the generic hierarchy. *Relations* are used for modelling structural dependencies between system elements, for example a container *containing* liquid or two heat-exchangeable objects having a *heat-path connection*[1]. We do not distinguish between generic relations and instances thereof. Relations are always 'instances' and specific for certain instantiated system elements.

### 3.1.2 Parameters, Parameter Values and Quantity Spaces

Qualitative prediction of behaviour is particularly concerned with reasoning about the properties of the physical world that gradually change over time. The domain knowledge that represents this class of properties plays the role of parameters. Important aspects of parameters are: (1) a *reference* to the system element whose property is described by the parameter, (2) the *physical quantity* that is described by the parameter (typical examples are: temperature, volume, current, resistance, etc.), (3) a reference to the type of values the parameter can have, and (4) the *quantity space* the parameter refers to (the set of specific values that the parameter can have).

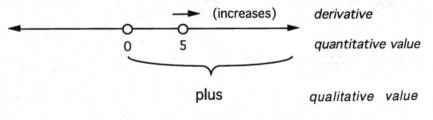

Figure 2: Parameter values

In the case of qualitative reasoning the parameter type is *qualitative*. This means that the quantitative values of a parameter are abstracted into a set of ordered intervals. This abstraction corresponds to an abstraction of real time into adjacent intervals. At each time interval the parameter has a value from this ordered set of intervals. In addition, the derivative of the parameter represents how the quantitative value of the parameter changes in real time (*decreasing*, *steady* and *increasing*). For example the value of parameter *volume* is *plus* and *increases* (see Figure 2).

The quantity space of a parameter refers to an ordered set of parameter values that a specific parameter can have. These values are usually represented as a sequence of alternating points and intervals. The intuitive understanding behind this approach is illustrated in Figure 3 for the parameter temperature as it is used to describe the characteristics of a substance. All the quantitative values a substance temperature can have are divided into six qualitative values,

---

[1] Relations should not be confused with parameters which describe properties of system elements that *continuously* change over time. These are discussed in section 3.1.2.

consisting of three intervals and three points. Each value resembles a characteristic period of constant qualitative behaviour for the substance. If, for example, the temperature has a quantitative value somewhere between the freezing point and the boiling point and this value increases, then the substance shows constant qualitative behaviour, until it reaches its boiling point, namely 'being a liquid'. As soon as it reaches this boiling point, the substance arrives at a new time interval in which it again shows constant qualitative behaviour, namely boiling.

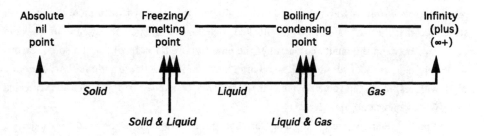

Figure 3: The quantity space for the temperature of a substance

### 3.1.3   Parameter Relations, Qualitative Calculi and Mathematical Models

Parameter relations represent the dependencies between the properties of system elements. They specify the constraints that hold between parameters of system elements. The qualitative calculus defines the semantics of a relation, ie. expresses how the relation must be used. The parameter relations that are true in a certain state of behaviour represent the mathematical model of the behaviour of some system in the real-world.

Parameter relations also depend on the type of parameter. If the parameter type is quantitative, then equations from traditional mathematics can be used to represent the constraints that exist between the 'behaviour' parameters. If the parameter type is qualitative then more specific relations and calculi are required. Typically used relations in qualitative reasoning are: (1) inequalities, (2) correspondences, (3) proportionalities, and (4) influences.

Inequalities can be used to define dependencies among parameter values and among derivatives of parameters. Inequality relations between parameter values means that the quantitative value of the parameters are equal[2]. Reasoning with inequality relations is complex and sometimes confusing. If, for example, two parameters have the 'same' interval as value (=qualitative value) this does not necessarily imply that they are equal. They may have different

---

[2]Notice that inequality relations can be specified without knowing the exact quantitative value.

quantitative values but be in the same qualitative interval. The values that a derivative can have are usually defined by the *min_zero_plus* quantity space. The derivative of a parameter can be negative (the parameter value decreases), zero (the parameter value does not change), or positive (the parameter value increases). This can respectively be modelled by the following inequality relations: *less-than zero, equal-to zero*, and *greater-than zero*.

Parameter relations can be divided into *directed* and *undirected* relations, modelling causal relationships and non-causal relationships respectively. It is, for example, valid to derive that there will be no flow of substance through a pipe (*flow_rate = zero*) when the flow area of the pipe is blocked (*flow_area = zero*), but it is not allowed to derive that when there is no flow of substance that the flow area must be blocked. Other aspects, such as absence of pressure difference between the input and output of the pipe (*press_diff = zero*) could also be reasons why there is no flow of substance. The relation between the *flow_rate* and the *flow_area* of a pipe, with respect to the value *zero*, can therefore only be applied in one direction (=directed value correspondence) [6].

Inequality relations are undirected. Correspondence relations can be used for modelling either directed or undirected dependencies between the qualitative values of a parameter. Correspondence relations are based on the notion of *value correspondence* as introduced by Forbus [22]. We have extended this notion resulting in four relations. *Value correspondence* specifies that the relation between two parameters is not known except for some values that always correspond between the parameters. Forbus gives the example of the *length* of a spring and the *force* exerted on the spring. Their values are unrelated except for the *rest-length* of the spring which corresponds to the force being *zero*. The *quantity space correspondence* relation extends the value correspondence by specifying that for all values in the quantity space of one parameter there is a corresponding value in the quantity space of the other parameter. Both the value and the quantity space correspondence can be used in an undirected or a directed manner. The causality introduced by the latter implies that the relation can only be used in one direction. Only if the value of a specific parameter is known (the causing parameter), can the value of the other parameter (the effected parameter) be derived (see [6] for more details).

For undirected relations between derivatives the inequality relation as discussed above can be used. Directed relations can be modelled by proportionalities [22]: a change in the causing parameter results in a change in the effected parameter in the *same* direction (positive proportionality), or in the *opposite* direction (negative proportionality). If a certain parameter is effected by two or more parameters in opposite directions then the resulting change in the effected parameter is ambiguous, that is the parameter may increase, stay constant, or decrease.

Influences [22] are parameter relations that model causal dependencies between the *value* of one parameter and the *derivative* of another parameter. They can be used for representing how the existence of a certain parameter (eg. *flow_rate*) changes the (quantitative) value of another parameter (eg. *amount_of* liquid): (1) if the qualitative value of the influencing parameter is greater than *zero*, then the effected parameter tends to increase (=positive influence) or decrease (=negative influence) as a result of this parameter, (2) if the qualitative value of the influencing parameter is less than *zero*, then the effected parameter tends to decrease (=positive influence) or to increase (=negative influence), and (3) if the value of the influencing parameter is *zero* then it has no effect on the derivative of the influenced parameter.

### 3.1.4  Partial Behaviour Models

The role of partial models is to represent knowledge about the behaviour of entities from the real-world in small units (partial behaviour models), which can be assembled into larger models that represent the behaviour of some real-world system as a whole. The partial models represent knowledge about physics and the physical world that is relevant to certain abstractions of that physical world (=system elements). They specify what features are important for such an abstraction as well as how these features are related to each other. More specifically, they are used to establish a mathematical model that specifies the behaviour of some system in the real-world.

| | |
|---|---|
| **IF** | a contained-liquid L1 exists |
| | and L1 has pressure P1 |
| | and a contained-liquid L2 exists |
| | and L2 has pressure P2 |
| | and a fluid-path between L1 and L2 exists |
| | and P1 is greater-than P2 |
| **THEN** | a liquid-flow F exists |
| | and F = P1 - P2 |
| | and the amount A1 of L1 is negatively influenced by F |
| | and the amount A2 of L2 is positively influenced by F |

Table 2: Partial model of the liquid flow process

In order to use partial models the qualitative inference engine must be able to derive when a particular partial model applies. Partial models are therefore conditional. The *conditions* specify what knowledge must be known in order for the partial model to be applicable. The *consequences* of a partial model specify the new knowledge that can be derived and added to the behaviour description of the real-world system when the partial model is applied. In Table 2 an .example of a partial model is shown that represents a *liquid-flow* process. The knowledge captured in this partial model specifies that a liquid flow is possible between two contained liquids when they are connected by a fluid path and the pressure of one contained liquid is greater than the pressure of the other contained liquid. The influences of this process are a decrease in the amount of liquid with the highest pressure and an increase in the amount of liquid with the lowest pressure

Based on the modelling primitives presented in the original approaches, the following integrated set of primitives for representing partial behaviour models can be defined:

**Static models** describe static dependencies between properties of system elements. Both component models [19] and views [22] fall within this class of partial behaviour models. Three types can be identified, depending on whether the models are context dependent or not:

**Single description models** are context independent, ie. they obey the no-function-in-structure principle. They describe (static) properties of *one* system element, for example the properties of a container or the behaviour of a component.

**Composition models** are context dependent. They model properties of a configuration (or number) of system elements, for instance a contained liquid, that has three system elements: a container, a liquid and a contain relation between the two. Usually a composition model requires other single description models to be active first. Given these behaviour descriptions of single system elements, a composition model adds additional behaviours to the assembly as a whole.

**Decomposition models** are modelling primitives that can be used for focusing on a specific system element, ie. for studying the behaviour of some part of the system at another level of detail, for example, decomposing a component into its subparts and reasoning about the behaviour of those subparts.

**Process models** represent changes in behaviour that happen because a number of system elements interact as a result of an inequality between them (with respect to some quantity). The descriptions are necessarily context dependent and are similar to the notions of processes in the process centered approach [22].

**Agent models** are used to model actors that enforce changes upon a system. These models are context independent, because they apply to a single system element (usually a component). An important difference between static models and agent models is that the latter *change* values of parameters, for example, a compressor, if it is modelled as a component that causes an increase in the pressure (which is different from describing the input-output dependencies).

In order to model specific behaviour into these partial models the knowledge roles (meta-classes) discussed in the previous sections are essential, especially the notions of system elements, parameters, parameter values and parameter relations, as well as the distinction between conditions and consequences. In addition, the different relations between partial models, such as applies-to and is-supertype-of, have to be taken into account. As a result, each of the modelling primitives for partial behaviour models must be represented in terms of the following knowledge representation:

**Super type relation.** The partial model can be a subtype of other partial models (multiple inheritance). This means that the super behaviour models must be applicable in order for the subtype to be applicable.

**Conditions.** Each partial model has its own specific conditions that must be true before the knowledge that is specified in the consequences of the model can be used. The following five knowledge types can be conditions:

1. System elements

   The abstraction from the physical world to which the partial model applies.

2. Parameters

   Properties of system elements used by parameter values and/or relations.

3. Parameter values

   Parameter values that must be true.

4. Parameter relations

   Relations (constraints) between parameters that must be true.

5. Partial behaviour models

   Other partial models that specify certain knowledge about the behaviour of the real-world system that must be known before the partial model may be used (=applies-to hierarchy).

**Consequences.** When a partial model is applicable, the consequences specify the additional knowledge about the behaviour of the real-world system that is derivable. The same five knowledge types can be derived:

1. System elements

   For processes it may be the case that new entities in the real-world are created because of the behaviour of the system (for example: gas when boiling liquid).

2. Parameters

   (New) properties that are introduced by the partial model.

3. Parameter values

   New values for parameters that hold.

4. Parameter relations

   Additional constraints that hold between parameters.

5. Partial behaviour models

   (Other) partial models that can be derived[3].

---

[3]When searching for partial models the qualitative inference engine needs to know which partial models are applicable. Therefore the partial model *itself* should be included here as a partial model that is from now on

The isa hierarchy allows the representation of detailed partial models as subtypes of more general ones. The general type represents the features that hold for the whole class whereas the more detailed ones represent features that are specific for the subclass. The function of the applies-to hierarchy is to define which other partial models have to be active in order to allow a particular partial model to be active. For example, a liquid-flow process (Table 2) requires two open-contained-liquids to be active before the flow process itself can be active. Composition models and process models often require other partial behaviour models to be active.

### 3.1.5 System Model Description and Input System

Central to qualitative reasoning is the way in which a system is described during *a period of time in which the behaviour of the system does not change*. The notion of change is subtle, because the actual (real-world) system may change whereas from a qualitative point of view its behaviour remains constant. During the evaporation of a contained liquid, for example, the liquid is transformed into a gas and as such the system changes, but from a qualitative point of view this process is seen as being in a constant state of behaviour, because none of the *qualitative* values that describe the system change. The modelling primitive that is used for representing a model of the real-world system during a period of constant behaviour plays the role of system model description.

Although a system model description should contain all the knowledge relevant to a certain state of behaviour, there are five aspects of special interest. These are used for referring to domain knowledge that models changeable aspects of the real-world system: system elements, parameters, parameter values, parameter relations, and partial models[4]. If the knowledge referred to by one of these aspects changes, then the system model description has to change as well, because the current system model description has become an incompatible model with respect to the changing aspect.

The input system (or case-model [29]) can be regarded as a specific type of system model description. It is used to represent a partial model of some real-world system. This model is used by the qualitative inference engine for behaviour prediction.

### 3.1.6 Transformation Rules

Knowledge used for deriving how a certain state of behaviour changes into another state of behaviour is represented by the original approaches in the form of rules. We will therefore refer to this knowledge as performing the role of transformation rules. Three types can be

---

applicable.
[4]Calculi, for example, do not change when the behaviour of the real-world system changes.

distinguished: (1) termination rules, (2) precedence rules, and (3) transition rules.

Termination rules specify the conditions under which a particular state of behaviour will terminate because the behaviour represented in the system model description is no longer compatible with the actual behaviour of the real-world system. An example of a termination rule is shown in Table 3. The knowledge in this rule represents a part of the *limit rule* [19]. It specifies that when a parameter has an interval value in the current state of behaviour and decreases, that it will have the point value below this interval in the next state of behaviour. Although changes in parameter values and parameter relations are the basis for terminations, other aspects can change as well. For example, the system element 'liquid' will disappear when its *amount_of* becomes *zero*.

The precedence rules specify the order in which changes take place. Take for example, two different kinds of liquids in one container. If the temperature increases then both liquids will reach their boiling temperature, introducing ambiguity because of two possible terminations. However, if it is known that the boiling point of one liquid is lower than the boiling point of the other liquid, the ambiguity can be solved. Only the liquid with the lower boiling point will reach its boiling point in the next state of behaviour.

| | |
|---|---|
| **IF** | a parameter Par has qualitative value V |
| | and Par is decreasing |
| | and Par has quantity space QS |
| | and V is an interval value from QS |
| | and P is the next value in QS below V |
| **THEN** | in the next state of behaviour SMD |
| | Par has value P |

Table 3: Termination rule for changing to a point 'below'

It is also possible that two, or more, terminations reflect aspects of the same change in behaviour. If, for example, the *amount_of* liquid goes to *zero* then also its *volume* and its *pressure* will go to *zero*. Parameters with corresponding values which are subject to termination should therefore be merged into one termination.

Finally, continuity rules specify additional conditions that must be satisfied by the new state of behaviour in order to be a valid successor state of behaviour. In particular, they deal with those aspects present in the current state of behaviour that are not part of a termination. All these aspects should stay constant between the old and the new state of behaviour.

A relevant feature of applying the rules as described above is that the transformation between two states of behaviour is not found by satisfying constraints, but by a *directed* search which provides a *causal account* of why a state terminated, how this termination was ordered with respect to other terminations and how this is used, together with transition rules, for deriving the next state of behaviour.

### 3.1.7   Behaviour Descriptions

The behaviour description is a graph of possible system model descriptions (states of behaviour). For each description the following must be specified: (1) its internal behaviour (in terms of system elements, parameters, parameter values, parameter relations, and partial models), (2) its preceding system model descriptions (from-list), and (3) its successor system model descriptions (to-list). Each system model description has a *to-list* and a *from-list*. The to-list specifies which terminations (and possibly how they were merged) caused each transformation to the next system model description. The from-list specifies which system model description preceded the current system model description.

### 3.2   Knowledge Sources: Canonical Inferences

Given this list of meta-classes (see Table 1) the canonical inferences used in qualitative prediction of behaviour can be described (see Figure 4). The purpose of the specification

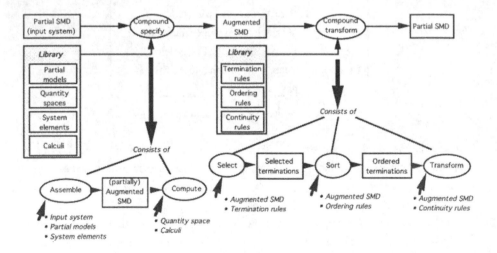

Figure 4: Inferences in qualitative prediction of behaviour

inference (*compound specify*) is to develop a complete[5] description of a particular state of behaviour of a system (=augmented SMD), which means satisfying the appropriate parameter relations and assigning qualitative values to parameters that are used to describe the system. More specifically, it has to find the partial behaviour models whose conditions satisfy the knowledge represented in the input system. If the conditions can be satisfied, the knowledge represented in the partial model becomes part of the system model description. This additional knowledge may lead to the satisfaction of conditions of other partial models (which could not be satisfied before). Finally, there may be partial models that have conditions which cannot be derived from the knowledge present in the system model description, but which are *consistent* with that knowledge. In such cases the compound specification inference should assume that these conditions are derivable, and add the knowledge of those partial models to the system model description. In the case of conflicting assumptions, alternative specifications must be made for each of these. The compound specification inference can be decomposed into two other inferences that must be carried out in order to arrive at a solution, namely *assembling* a mathematical model and *computing* the corresponding qualitative values.

**Assemble.** The mathematical model (=partially augmented SMD) is assembled by finding all the partial models that apply to the input system (=partial SMD). Each applicable partial model introduces parameter relations and parameter values (these make up the mathematical model). The partial models also specify which parameters are going to be used for describing the properties of the system elements.

**Compute.** Once the system model description is augmented with a mathematical model, the computation of qualitative values and the consistency checking of parameter relations can be done. The following outputs are possible: (1) *contradiction:* there is no set of parameter values consistent with the current set of parameter relations and/or there are inconsistent parameter relations, (2) *solution:* one or more sets of parameter values are consistent with the current set of parameter relations and there are no inconsistent parameter relations, and (3) *unknown:* there are parameter relations and/or parameter values which cannot be derived from the current parameter relations and parameter values specified in the system model description.

If there occurs an inconsistency, or any other kind of problem, when a partial model is being added to a system model description, then the system model description as a whole must be removed. An inconsistency in the consequences of a partial model means that the knowledge has not been modelled adequately. In other words, there is an inconsistency in the available domain knowledge.

The transformation inference (*compound transform*) is concerned with identifying successive states of behaviour. The inference can be decomposed into *selecting* terminations,

---

[5]Complete with respect to the knowledge that is available to the qualitative inference engine.

*sorting* terminations, and *transformation* (subsume or specify) to a new state of behaviour.

**Select.** *Termination* rules specify the conditions under which a particular state of behaviour will terminate and are used to *select* the possible terminations from the current system model description.

**Sort.** *Precedence* rules specify the order in which changes take place and are used to sort the possible terminations. There are three steps that must be carried out:

- *merge* all the terminations that are related and therefore form a single termination,
- *remove* those terminations that do not take place because of other terminations happening first, and
- *assemble* the cross-product of all terminations that have not been removed. The resulting set resembles all terminations that can take place.

**Transform (Subsume or Specify).** The *continuity* rules specify how unchanging aspects in the old system model description should reappear in the new system model description. They are, together with the ordered terminations, the input for transforming the current system model description into its successor. With respect to the new system model description there are two possibilities: either it has been generated before or it is a new state of behaviour. In the case of the former the partial system model description is a *subset* of an already existing system model description. In the case of the latter a new state of behaviour has to be *specified*.

## 3.3 Task and Strategic Knowledge

The task layer is used to represent typical chains of inferences that experts make in solving a particular, well-known task. However, in the prevailing approaches to qualitative reasoning the task layer is only minimally filled. They distinguish between: (1) finding all states of behaviour (total envisionment) and (2) finding one specific trace of behaviour (attainable envisionment). In the case of the latter additional input parameter values are taken into account to limit the number of system model descriptions that can be found.

Strategic knowledge, in the sense of the four layer model, is not present in the original approaches to qualitative reasoning. The approaches always execute the same task structure, are not able to monitor their own inference process, and as such are not able to modify or change their own reasoning process[6].

---

[6]There is some work going on as an extension of the constraint centered approach [24] to filter (and thereby reduce) the number of generated states.

# 4 Qualitative Reasoning in Intelligent Tutoring Systems

As mentioned in the introduction of this paper, qualitative models have several advantages over quantitative models for simulation, especially if we want to use them for teaching purposes. Qualitative models provide conceptual access to the objects and their behaviour. This makes them better suited for (causal) explanations. Moreover, if the qualitative models are the ones we want to teach and expect students to acquire, then they can be used for student modelling as well. The student's predictions about the behaviour of the system that is simulated can be compared with those of the model. If there is a discrepancy between the two, the model can be used to reason about the possible causes of the student's behaviour, ie. any difference between the expected (model) and observed (student) behaviour must be interpreted as an error on the part of the student, not as a fault in the model. This is the essence of model based diagnosis [17]. However, in order to do all this, the models represented in GARP will have to be the kind of models humans (can) work with; otherwise the explanations will not be understood, and the diagnoses will be of the wrong kind, or at the wrong level. The use of qualitative reasoning techniques for teaching purposes is therefore discussed in three subsections. The first part discusses the cognitive plausibility of the framework presented in the previous section. The second part shows how the models represented in the framework can be used for diagnosing the behaviour of the student. Finally, the third part points out a number of interesting explanations that are facilitated by the framework.

## 4.1 Cognitive Plausibility

In [7] we investigated the cognitive plausibility of the conceptual framework for qualitative prediction of behaviour. Think-aloud protocols of human subjects predicting the behaviour of a complex configuration of balances were compared with a computer model of the same problem solving task, implemented in GARP. This section first presents the balance problems as an example of how student models can be represented in the framework. The second part of this section discusses the cognitive plausibility of the model by summarizing the major results of the protocol analysis.

### 4.1.1 Balance Problems

The qualitative reasoning task has been operationalized with six balance problems (see Figure 5). The problem is to predict the behaviour of balances with containers on each balance arm.

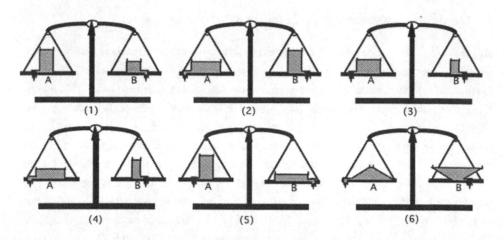

Figure 5: The balance problems

Both containers are assumed to be equal in weight. Depending on the difference in the mass of the water contained by the containers, one balance arm may be heavier than the other. Therefore, after releasing it from the starting position (*position = zero*), the balance may change its position. Through outlets near the bottom of the containers the water gradually flows out of the containers. Depending on the pressure at the bottom, the *flow_rates* of the two containers may be different. As a result the balance may move to a different position, because the difference

**System element relations:**

• Container contains water
• Balance arm supports container

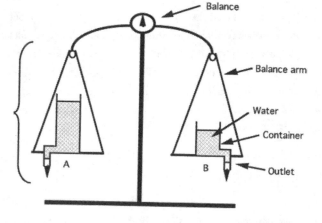

Figure 6: System elements of the balance problems

in weight between the two balance arms changes. Eventually, when both containers are empty, the balance will have reached an equilibrium. Predicting the different states of behaviour that the balance goes through after it is released, is the goal that must be solved in the balance problems.

**System Elements and Parameters.** The structural description of the balance problems is depicted in Figure 6. It consists of a balance with two balance arms. Each balance arm supports a container. Both containers contain a certain amount of water. There are equally shaped outlets near the bottom of each container. The parameters that describe the behaviour of the container and the water it contains, are shown in Figure 7. For the behaviour of the balance it is sufficient to give each of these parameters values from the quantity space *zero-plus* (the quantity is present or not). In addition to the parameters for the containers, a *position* parameter has to be introduced for the balance (see Figure 9). This parameter requires the quantity space *low-normal-high*, respectively referring to three possible positions of the balance. How the balance moves (the derivative of the position) is shown in Figure 10.

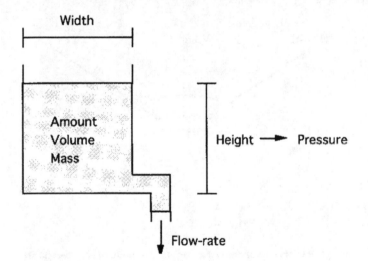

Figure 7: Parameters of a container

**Parameter Relations.** In each version of the balance problem, the two containers differ in shape and in the amount of water they contain (see Table 4). The different instances of the balance problem have been constructed in this way in order to allow as much variation as possible with respect to the factor(s) that determine(s) the *flow_rate* at the outlet. In particular, the parameters *height*, *amount*, and *width* will be important for capturing the different interpretations (including misconceptions) that the subjects may use. By varying these parameters for each of the balance problems, different behaviour predictions are to be expected

| Balance problem (Figure 5) | Width | Height | Amount |
|---|---|---|---|
| *Left (top)* | A = B | A > B | A > B |
| *Middle (top)* | A > B | A < B | A = B |
| *Right (top)* | A > B | A = B | A > B |
| *Left (below)* | A > B | A < B | A > B |
| *Middle (below)* | A < B | A > B | A > B |
| *Right (below)* | *unknown* | A = B | A = B |

Table 4: Inequality relations between parameters in the balance problems

depending on how the *flow_rate* is derived. Figure 8 depicts the possible interpretations. Notice that although none of the balance problems varies the outlet, it is possible that subjects use this as a factor for determining the *flow_rate*.

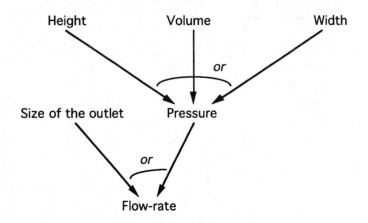

Figure 8: Possible ways of determining the *flow_rate* (including misconceptions)

**Partial Behaviour Models.** The partial behaviour models specify the different viewpoints that subjects may use in solving the balance problems. The different ways of determining the *flow_rate*, as discussed above, will be represented as alternative models for establishing the behaviour properties of a *contained_liquid* (composition model). In addition, partial behaviour models are needed for: (1) water flow from container to world (process), (2) balance arm supporting container (composition model), (3) position of balance configuration (composition model), and (4) movement of balance configuration (process).

The flow of water from the container into the world applies to a 'contained liquid' with an outlet near the bottom of the container. If this configuration exists and the outlet is open, then a liquid flow process introduces a *flow_rate* that influences the amount of water negatively. The

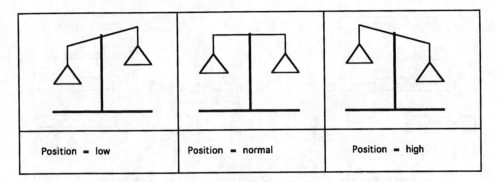

Figure 9: Partial behaviour models for the position of the balance

balance arm supporting a container is used to establish the total weight for each of the balance arms. The behaviours introduced by these composition models is used by the balance configuration to determine the position of the balance. Three possible positions are depicted in Figure 9. The movement of the balance depends on the difference in *mass_loss* between the two contained liquids. The three possible movements of the balance are: (1) left side down and right side up (*movement = plus*), (2) balanced (*movement = zero*) and (3) left side up and right side down (*movement = min*) (see also Figure 10). The movement represents the derivative of the position.

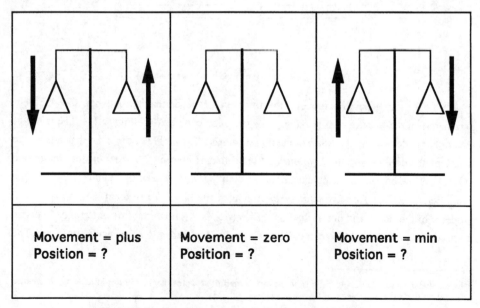

Figure 10: Partial behaviour models for the movement of the balance

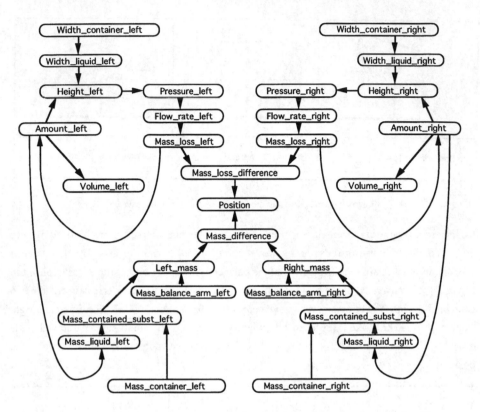

Figure 11: Detailed model of the parameter relations

Using all the behaviour models, the total set of dependencies between the different parameters of the balance configuration turns out to be complex (see Figure 11). The *width* of the container determines the *width* of the liquid column. The *height* of the latter depends on the *width* of the column and the *amount_of* liquid that is present. The *height* determines the *pressure* at the bottom of the container and as such the *flow_rate* of the liquid flow out of the container. The *flow_rate* is qualitatively similar to the *mass_loss* except that the latter is a property of the liquid and not of the liquid flow process[7]. The *mass_loss_difference* between the two arms of the balance depends on the individual *mass_loss* of each container. The

---

[7]Notice, that the *mass_loss* could differ from the *flow_rate* if there were other *flow_rates* influencing the *amount* of liquid. In the balance problems this is not the case.

*amount_of* liquid determines the *volume* and *mass*.[8]. The *mass* of the liquid and the *mass* of the container (and the *mass* of the balance arm itself), determine the *total_mass* for a balance arm. The difference between the *total_mass* of the two balance arms determines the position of the balance (and the initial movement of the balance after it is released from its starting position.)

**Task Knowledge and Strategic Knowledge.** It is to be expected that human subjects will concentrate only on attainable envisionments, ie. a prediction of the actual behaviour of the balance (and not a description of all possible behaviours). It is however, likely that subjects will encounter difficulties in the reasoning process, because the problem solving goal cannot be reached. We expect two types of difficulties to emerge: (1) problems with the available domain knowledge (=knowledge conflicts), in particular problems with missing, ambiguous, or contradictory facts in the domain knowledge, and (2) problems with insufficient processing capacity. For the knowledge conflicts we expect repairs as listed in Table 5 (for more details on this matter see, for example [3, 6,4]).

| Knowledge conflict | Type of repair |
|---|---|
| *Missing knowledge* | *Practical repairs:* <br> read the question again <br> ask for additional information <br> *Repairs by reasoning:* <br> continue reasoning after making an assumption <br> try extreme values <br> use analogy <br> use different/other domain knowledge |
| *Ambiguous knowledge* | try one (randomly or according to an estimate of success) <br> try all <br> reason backwards from a known final state |
| *Contradictory knowledge* | try again <br> check computations <br> use other domain knowledge |

Table 5: Repairs for knowledge conflicts

Once a repair is selected its plan is tuned to fit the specific instance of the impasse. This means that reasoning at the strategic level may involve a revision at the task level.

## 4.1.2 Protocol Analyses

To test the cognitive plausibility of the conceptual framework we compared problem solving activities as manifested by human subjects in think-aloud protocols with those predicted by the framework. The problem solving model that was built and implemented in GARP was therefore

---

[8]Depending on the specific conceptualization used by the subject *amount_of* and *volume* may represent the same entity or be different. In the case of the latter *amount_of* is used for referring to the number liquid molecules present.

translated into a coding template with which the think-aloud protocols could be analysed. The subjects were ten psychology sophomores who had taken high school courses in physics. Three protocols were coded entirely, resulting in 673 coded expressions, with the following distribution:

- Domain and inference layer: 62 percent
  - Specification: 37 percent
    *(assemble:compute $\Rightarrow$ 2:3)*
  - Transformation: 25 percent
    *(mostly selecting terminations)*
- Task and strategic layer: 40 percent
  - Detecting impasses: 7 percent
  - Repair impasses: 33 percent
    * Specification: 12 percent
    * Transformation: 11 percent
    * Others: 10 percent
- Not coded: 21 percent[9].
  *(all referred to relating different versions of the balance problems)*

All ten protocols were screened according to the following criteria: (1) the model is incomplete (there are expressions that cannot be encoded), (2) the model is too detailed (there are coding categories that are not used), and (3) the model is wrong (there are deviations in the expected order of expressions).

From the analysis it turned out that the framework as implemented in GARP provides an appropriate tool for describing and interpreting the reasoning processes involved in this problem solving task. Both the different viewpoints subjects had on the domain knowledge as well as their reasoning process could be modelled by the framework. The canonical inferences and the meta classes defined in the model provided strong means for interpreting the steps of the reasoning process in the protocols. The notion of strategic reasoning explained disruptions and changes in the order in which new states are determined.

However, from the experiment presented here it also becomes clear that the model can be refined in some places. In particular, the framework does not account for learning over a number of problem solving sessions. As the subjects moved from one problem to another they abstracted from irrelevant details in the description and the analysis of the problem. For example, *height* (or *amount* etc.) was seen as determining the *pressure*, which in turn determines *flow_rate* which equals *mass_loss* (see Figure 11). In the abstracted form the *height* determined the *mass_loss* directly (see Figure 12). The detailed model can be regarded as a *task independent* model, because it represents all the information for reasoning about the behaviour of the system.

---

[9] $21 = 100 - (62 + 40 - (12 + 11))$

The abstracted model, on the other hand, can be seen as a *task dependent* model. It abstracts from irrelevant details and focuses on those aspects of the system that are important for the problem solving task at hand [7]. The transformation of a task independent into a task dependent model as a consequence of practice (learning) can be represented by a compilation [1] or *chunking* [28] of invariant causal chains in the model of expertise. The different models can be represented in GARP, but incorporating the learning process would require additional mechanisms (see for example [8]).

The notion of task structures was less useful in analysing the protocols. Experts performing a particular problem solving task may develop, through the repeated execution of the same sequence of inferences, a trace of this sequence and as such learn a task structure. That is an instance of a strategic reasoning process. Non-experts, like the subjects in the experiment reported on here, just use general strategic reasoning.

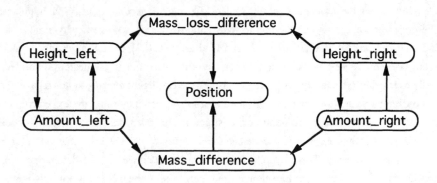

Figure 12: Abstracted model of the parameter relations

In conclusion, it is fair to assume that the conceptual model presented in the previous section does describe this problem solving task at the right level of abstraction, ie. it constitutes a knowledge level model of this problem solving expertise. In addition, the presented research provides a basis for further research on the way humans perform qualitative prediction of behaviour [26, 33]. Such research should in particular focus on the learning aspects and the knowledge structuring principles that people use for developing their domain knowledge.

## 4.2 Diagnosing Student Errors

As described in section 3.1.7 the output of GARP for predicting the behaviour of a system consists of so called *behaviour descriptions*, a graph of possible system descriptions ordered in time. If we want to compare the predictions of a student with those of the model in GARP, those predictions will have to be translated into the same form.

Suppose a student solving balance problem 1 (see Figure 5), predicts the following behaviour: First the balance will move in the *plus* (see Figure 10) direction towards position *low* (see Figure 9). It will remain in this position until container *B* is empty, after which the balance will gradually regain its *normal* position as container *A* continues to lose its contents. This is partly different from the predictions of the expert model. It also states that the balance will first move down on the left side (*plus*), and then up again to the *normal* position, but it gives two options. Since the flow-rate of container *A* is initially greater than that of *B*, the 'height' of the liquid in *A* will decrease faster than that of *B*. Two things can happen: either the heights become the same and the balance will already be in its *normal* position while the two containers are still losing liquid, or *B* is already empty before *A* has 'caught up', and the balance will reach the *normal* position when *A* is empty as well.

What is the cause of this discrepancy, and if there are several possibilities, how do we decide which one is the correct one for this student? Or in more general terms: What hypotheses can be generated, and how can they be tested? This distinction, generating hypotheses and testing them, is common in literature on diagnosis of artifacts [17], or natural physical systems [10], but when the 'system' to be diagnosed is a cognitive structure 'in the head of a human', it is hardly ever made. This last type of diagnosis is the one intelligent tutoring systems have to do when confronted with a discrepancy between the student's behaviour and the expected, norm behaviour. Most systems use decision tree like structures for this task, where tests are directly associated with hypotheses. In our case we can use the expert model as implemented in GARP for generating hypotheses. These hypotheses can then be tested against the data of the actual behaviour of the student, previously acquired data about the student's knowledge and competence at the task (as reflected by a user model, see below), or by presenting a new problem to the student that will discriminate between competing hypotheses. The outcome of this diagnostic process is either a lack of knowledge or a misconception of the student [35]. This lack of knowledge or misconception may concern one of the levels of expertise (see section 3), or the state of the reasoning process itself, eg. the student forgot an assumption that was made earlier.

### 4.2.1 Hypothesis Generation

In diagnosis there are basically two ways to generate hypotheses, depending on (our understanding of) the domain [36]: by 'decomposition' (of a part-of structure) and by 'specialization' (ie. descending a taxonomy). The first method assumes a hierarchical structure of parts or components at the domain level. A part stands for a physical part, some function or process. In artifacts the relation between a function and a physical component is a very explicit one, but many well understood natural systems can be decomposed in such a way too, eg. human anatomy. In principle the diagnostic process is very simple: partition the system according to its decomposition and eliminate the correctly functioning parts by testing. Essential in a test is that observed values are compared with norm (expected) values. Tests may consist of complex manipulations by varying inputs, or even by changing the structure of a system model. Also, the derivation of related norms may require complex inferences, and a possible solution is to use qualitative reasoning techniques (eg. the domain of SOPHIE III, [11]).

The second approach, generating hypotheses by 'specification', requires less structure in the domain, and works by descending taxonomies (eg. as in heuristic classification, [16]). Taxonomies are abstraction: hierarchies with intermediary concepts. Distinguishing 'viral' from 'bacterial' infections, or 'acute' from 'chronic' leukemia are simple examples.

We can use the model of expertise to generate hypotheses concerning the cause of deviant student behaviour, since this is the model we want the students to acquire, and it is at the right conceptual level for humans to be able to acquire and use it. The model of expertise can be decomposed in several ways to generate hypotheses. First of all the different levels of types of knowledge provide a basis for decomposition. One could first look for misconceptions or lack of knowledge at the strategic level and gradually work down until a conclusion is reached [34], or any other order for that matter. For our present purposes we are only concerned with the inference and domain layers. The inference structure of GARP was given in Figure 4. The domain layer will have to be filled in for a particular domain, so that leaves the inference structure of GARP as a general basis for generating hypotheses. This structure can be decomposed again, as can be seen from Figure 4. Every element of that structure is a possible cause for the deviant student predictions, though not all of them are as likely from a cognitive, psychological point of view. As we have seen from the experiments with students solving the balance problems, most of their misconceptions were about the factor that influences the flow rate out of the containers, ie. they used wrong partial (process) models to *assemble* an augmented system model description.

What can be wrong with each of these elements? In analogy with troubleshooting of artifacts it can be said that either the particular component does not work at all (the student does not possess or cannot retrieve the particular knowledge), or it functions incorrectly (the student has a misconception). The first case is relatively easy to check[10]. If the reasoning of GARP leads to the same predictions as those of the student after a deletion of the particular knowledge element, a lack of knowledge concerning that element is a possible hypothesis (eg., [12, 38]). The second case is more difficult. If the correct version of the knowledge is replaced by something else, what is it replaced with? We do not suggest a principled solution here, but provide GARP also with misconceptions, eg. a set of faulty partial models for the balance problems. GARP can

---

[10]We are not concerned with computational tractability for the moment.

reason with these faulty models, and if the outcomes are the same as the student's predictions, these misconceptions are again possible hypotheses.

### 4.2.2 Hypothesis Testing

After this hypothesis generation step a number of hypotheses remain (lack of knowledge and/or misconceptions of the student) that explain the student's predictions. Some of these may be rejected, or marked as less likely, because of what we know about the particular student. If, for instance, the student has shown in the past that she has the right conception concerning what determines the pressure at the outlet of the containers in the balance problems, we can reject any misconceptions to that effect. This information can be obtained from the user model, a knowledge base that reflects the knowledge of the student (correct and incorrect) about the domain in the eyes of the tutoring system. For our example of balance problems, an overlay of the expert model [15] and additional misconceptions will suffice.

After pruning the set of possible hypotheses on the basis of user model data, competing hypotheses may still exist. Analogous to diagnosis of physical systems, more tests are needed for discriminating between them. This means presenting the student with a new problem, preferably one that rules out all but one hypothesis: the conclusion. In principle, there are two solutions for picking the next problem: either selecting the best (most discriminating) problem from a stored set (eg. as in MOLE [21]), or constructing a critical test on the basis of the current hypothesis set (eg. like in IDEBUGGY [144]).

Starting with the former, the simpler solution, consider the example domain of the balance problems again. Suppose two hypotheses remain that explain an observed discrepancy between the predictions of the student and those of the expert model. Both state that the student has a misconception concerning the parameter that influences the pressure at the outlet of the containers, but one states that the student thinks the *width* of the liquid column determines the pressure instead of the *height,* the other that the student considers the *amount* to be the causing factor. If the program only has the six problems as specified in Figure 5, which of these will discriminate between the two competing hypotheses? One way to find out is to run both models on the examples and see which problem generates conflicting predictions. Given a pre-enumerated set of misconceptions and likely knowledge deficiencies, this could even be done off-line.

Since in the example there are only two competing hypotheses, a slightly smarter way would be to look at the differences between the problems (see Table 4) and find one that keeps the parameter of one hypothesis constant while varying the second one, for example, problems one (*width* is the same, *amount* varies) and two (*amounts* equal, *widths* not). In the case of more competing hypotheses, this would entail the presentation of more problems to subsequently differentiate between diads of hypotheses.[11]

For a relatively simple domain, as in the balance problems, it would be possible (although perhaps not very interesting) to generate critical tests on the basis of the hypothesis set, in a way similar to the one described above. For every two hypotheses, construct a test that keeps the parameter of one constant while varying the other. Given the two misconceptions concerning what influences the *pressure* and *flow_rate* at the outlet of the containers (*width*, or *amount*), this would result in the first two problems of Figure 5 (or mirrored versions), since the three parameters involved are not independent (*amount* depends on *width*, and *height*).

Once the problem is generated, the system can check whether it really differentiates between (some of) the hypotheses, by running all variants of the model on it and comparing the outcomes.

For more complex domains, with a larger amount and more complex misconceptions, the danger arises that the generated problems make no sense 'in the real world'. For example, if the domain is prediction of behaviour of the human body, a generated problem about a patient without a spine, would certainly raise some eyebrows.

### 4.3 Explanation of Domain Knowledge

The knowledge typing in the framework that is implemented in GARP facilitates an interesting set of possible explanations. In principle the whole model of expertise, as described in section 3, can be used as a basis for providing explanations. However, in this section we focus on how the meta classes, referring to the different roles of the domain knowledge in the reasoning process, can be used for explaining the different aspects of the domain knowledge. Below the most important knowledge roles are briefly discussed.

**Physical Structure and System elements.** The hierarchy of generic models can be used to point out what abstractions have been made of the physical world. The instances of these system elements specified in the case model (or input system), together with the relations between these elements, represent the specific physical structure for which the behaviour is predicted. Each of these entities is explicitly represented in the model that GARP reasons about and can therefore be accessed easily for explanation purposes. It can, for example, be used to drive a visual representation of the structure that is the object of the behaviour analysis.

**Using Different Types of Behaviour Models.** Each behaviour model that is used for behaviour prediction is a subtype of a specific class of behaviour models. Each of these classes

---

[11]This implies that problems 4 and 6 of the set shown in Figure 5 are not suited for testing misconceptions concerning the *width*, *height* and *amount* of the liquid in the containers. The first problem varies all three parameters at the same time, the second keeps two of them constant while the third is unknown.

provides further information about certain aspects of the physical world. Single description models and composition models specify features, or for that matter behaviour, of system elements. In contrast to these models, processes and agent models represent the changes that may occur. Processes are caused by inequalities that exist between two quantities, whereas agent models refer to changes that are enforced upon the physical structure by an actor. Finally, decomposition models specify how a certain physical structure can be decomposed into its subelements.

Each of these behaviour models represents a different aspect of behaviour as it manifests itself in the real-world and can be used to explain the specific characteristics of that behaviour. In particular, when presented in the context of the *no-function-in-structure* [6, 19] notion these behaviour models provide strong means for explanations.

**Causality in Parameter Relations.** Providing explanation about the causality in the behaviour of a physical system is of crucial importance. In our framework causality is represented at two places in the reasoning process, once as relations between parameters specified by the partial behaviour models (specify) and once as forward chaining rules that specify how one state of behaviour transforms into the next state of behaviour (see below). Causality between parameters in one state of behaviour is in particular represented by means of *proportionalities* and *influences*. Proportionalities specify how the change in one parameter effects the behaviour of another parameter whereas influences specify how flow rates introduced by processes cause a certain parameter to change. Both type of parameter relations are essential for reasoning about causality.

**Causality in State Transitions.** Different from previous approaches (see section 2) to qualitative reasoning which use constraint based techniques for determining state transitions, our framework uses a forward chaining mechanism of rules for determining behaviour transitions. Constraint based approaches can only derive that certain states of behaviour may follow each other, but they can not uniquely determine the cause of these transformations. This hampers the possibilities for providing explanations. In the framework presented in this paper the transformation inference deliberately searches for possible terminations, orders these if possible, and determines how a new state of behaviour follows from the resulting termination(s). This technique provides an explicit account of *why* a state of behaviour transformed into its successor. This knowledge can be used for explanation.

**Quantity Spaces as Indicators of Behaviour States.** Each partial behaviour model has a number of conditions that must be true for the model to be applicable. In particular, the values of different parameters (quantity spaces) are important in this respect. They specify the different states of behaviour that a single system element or a configuration of system elements can manifest. Consider, for example, the parameter *temperature* as shown in Figure 3. Each value of this parameter corresponds to a specific state of behaviour of a substance. The quantity space provides a rationale of why certain states of behaviour have been represented in partial behaviour models.


# 5 Concluding Remarks

Research shows that simulation based learning environments are only effective when the student is guided by a tutor. However, most of the simulations are based on complex mathematical procedures, which hampers the possibilities for the intelligent tutoring system to use the simulator for explanations or student modelling because it has no means to relate the calculations within the simulation to the conceptual framework that represents the knowledge the student possesses or has to acquire. In this paper we have investigated the use of qualitative models as the basis for simulation in order to cope with these problems.

Although qualitative reasoning has evolved over the last decade as an interesting research area of artificial intelligence, only a few well known existing tutoring systems use qualitative models. We concluded that for improving the use of qualitative reasoning techniques for teaching purposes the current state of the art needs to be extended in at least two ways. Firstly, the different approaches to qualitative reasoning must be integrated into a unified approach in order to (1) point out similarities and differences between the approaches and, (2) possibly even more importantly, to facilitate a problem solving potential that currently cannot be realized by any of the original approaches. Secondly, it is essential that the conceptual framework underlying the qualitative reasoning technique is represented explicitly in order to facilitate *conceptual access* to the entities from the simulation at a level of detail that closely matches the human interpretation of the simulation.

Based on these conclusions, we have presented an integrated approach to qualitative prediction of behaviour, based on the three basic approaches in this area of research, that we believe to be of crucial importance for student modelling. We have also discussed a qualitative reasoning shell, GARP, that implements the integrated framework and that therefore can be used within an intelligent tutoring system, both for modelling the domain and for representing alternative conceptions of the student. Of particular importance in this respect is whether the models represented in GARP are the kind of models humans (can) work with; otherwise the tutoring system that uses these models will not be of much help. A significant part of this paper is therefore concerned with investigating the 'cognitive plausibility' of the presented framework. From the protocol analysis it turned out that the framework does facilitate representing conceptual models that describe qualitative prediction of behaviour at the right level of abstraction, ie. it constitutes a knowledge level model of this problem solving expertise.

The last two subsections of our paper discuss how the framework can be used for systematic diagnosis of students' problem solving behaviour and for explanation of the domain knowledge that has to be learned. First of all, the models of expertise represented in GARP provide a sound basis for generating the 'norm' against which to test student predictions. Next, these models can be used for systematic generation and testing of hypotheses concerning the cause of deviations from the norm, ie. for model based diagnosis. Some tentative ideas were given concerning the selection and construction of critical problems to differentiate between competing hypotheses in the diagnostic process. Finally, the use of qualitative models for explanation was discussed by presenting examples of different uses of knowledge structures in GARP. These sections are tentative in the sense that no tutoring system has been built yet that uses GARP in this respect. However, we think that the model based approach to teaching environments is an essential one. Realizing these functionalities in an implemented system will be an important aspect of our coming research.

# References

1. Anderson, J. R.:  Knowledge compilation: the general learning mechanism. In: *Machine Learning: An Artificial Intelligence Approach*, volume 2, (R. S. Michalski, J. G. Carbonell, & T. M. Mitchell, eds.). pp. 289-310. Los Altos, CA: Morgan Kaufmann 1986
2. Baril, D., Greer, J. E. & McCalla, G.I.:  Student modelling with confluences. Proceedings of the AAAI Conference, Anaheim, CA pp. 43-48, 1991
3. Bartsch-Sporl, B., Reinders, M., Akkermans, H., Bredeweg, B., Christaller, T., Drouven, U., van Harmelen, F., Karbach, W., Schreiber, G., Vob, A., & Wielinga, B.:  A Tentative Framework for Knowledge-Level Reflection. ESPRIT Basic Research Action P3178 REFLECT, Deliverable IR.2 RFL/BSR-ECN/I.3/1, BSR Consulting and Netherlands Energy Research Foundation ECN, August 1990
4. Bobrow, D. G. (ed.):  *Qualitative Reasoning about Physical Systems*. Amsterdam: Elsevier Science Publishers 1984
5. Bredeweg, B.:  Introduction of meta-levels to qualitative reasoning. *Applied Artificial Intelligence*, 3(2), pp. 85-100 (1989)
6. Bredeweg, B.:  Expertise in Qualitative Prediction of Behaviour. PhD thesis, University of Amsterdam 1992
7. Bredeweg, B. & Schut, C.:  Cognitive plausibility of a conceptual framework (for modelling problem solving expertise). Proceedings of the 13th Conference of Cognitive Science Society, Chicago, IL, pp. 478-479, Hillsdale, NJ: Lawrence Erlbaum Associates 1991
8. Bredeweg, B., Schut, C., van den Heerik, K., & van Someren, M.:  Reducing ambiguity by learning assembly behavior. Proceedings of the Sixth International Workshop on Qualitative Reasoning about physical systems.
9. Breuker, J. A. & Wielinga, B. J.:  Model driven knowledge acquisition. In: *Topics in the Design of Expert Systems* (P. Guida & G. Tasso, eds.). pp. 265-296. Amsterdam: North-Holland 1989
10. Breuker, J. A. & Winkels, R. G. F.:  The use of the KADS methodology in designing an Intelligent Teaching System for diagnosis in physiotherapy. In: *Knowledge Based Systems in Medicine: Methods, Applications and Evaluation* (J. L. Talmon & J. L. Fox, eds.). pp. 3-26, Berlin: Springer-Verlag 1991
11. Brown, J. S., Burton, R R., & deKleer, J.:  Pedagogical, natural language and knowledge engineering techniques in SOPHIE I, II and III. In: *Intelligent Tutoring Systems* (D. Sleeman & J. S. Brown, eds.), pp. 227-279, London: Academic Press 1982
12. Brown, J. S. & VanLehn, K.:  Repair theory: a generative theory of bugs in procedural skills. *Cognitive Science*, 4(2), pp. 379-426 (1980)
13. Bruner, J. S.:  The act of discovery. *Harvard Educational Review*, 31, pp. 21-31 (1961)
14. Burton, R. R.:  Diagnosing bugs in simple procedural skills. In: *Intelligent Tutoring Systems* (D. Sleeman & J. S. Brown, eds.). pp 157-184. London: Academic Press 1982

15. Carr, B. & Goldstein, I. P.: Overlays: A Theory of Modelling for Computer-aided Instruction. Technical Report AI Memeo 406, AI Lab. MIT, 1977
16. Clancey, W. J.: Heuristic classification. *Artificial Intelligence*, 27, pp. 289-350 (1985)
17. Davis, R., & Hamscher, H.: Model-based reasoning: troubleshooting. In: *Exploring Artificial Intelligence* (H. E. Shrobe, ed.). pp 297-346 San Mateo, CA: Morgan Kaufmann Publishers 1988
18. DeJong, T. (ed.): Computer simulations in an instructional context. *Education and Computing (Special issue)*, 6, 1991
19. deKleer, J. & Brown, J. S.: A qualitative physics based on confluences. *Artificial Intelligence*, 24, pp. 27-83 (1984)
20. Elsom-Cook, M. (ed.): *Guided Discovery Tutoring*. London: Paul Chapman Publishing 1990
21. Eshelman, L.: MOLE: A knowledge-acquisition tool for cover-and-differentiate systems. In: *Automating Knowledge Acquisition for Expert Systems* (S. Marcus, ed.), pp 37-80. The Netherlands: Kluwer Academic Publishers 1988
22. Forbus, K. D.: Qualitative process theory. *Artificial Intelligence*, 24, pp. 85-168 (1984)
23. Hollan, J. D., Hutchins, E. L., & Weizenbaum, L.: Steamer: an interactive inspectable simulation-based training system. *AI Magazine*, 5, pp. 15-27 (1984)
24. Jansweijer, W., Elshout, J., & Wielinga, B.: The expertise of novice problem solvers. Proceedings ECAI-86, Brigthon, 1986
25. Kuipers, B.: Qualitative simulation. *Artificial Intelligence*, 29, pp. 289-388 (1986)
26. Larkin, J. H.: The role of problem representation in physics. In: *Mental Models* (D. Gentner & A. L. Stevens, eds.). pp 27-39. Hillsdale, NJ: Lawrence Erlbaum Associates 1983
27. Lavioe, D. R., & Good, R.: The nature and use of prediction skills in a biological computer simulation. *Journal of Research in Science Teaching*, 25, pp. 335-360 (1988)
28. Rosenbloom, P. S., & Newell, A.: The chunking of goal hierarchies: a generalized model of practise. In: *Machine Learning: An Artificial Intelligence Approach*, volume 2, (R. S. Michalski, J. G. Carbonnel, & T. M. Mitchell, eds.). pp 247-288. Los Altos, CA: Morgan Kaufmann 1986
29. Steels, L.: Components of expertise. *AI Magazine*, Summer 1990. Also as: AI Memo 88-16, AI Lab, Free University of Brussels
30. Weld, D. S., & DeKleer, J.: *Readings in Qualitative Reasoning about Physical Systems*. Los Altos, CA: Morgan Kaufmann 1990
31. White, B. Y. & Frederiksen, J. R.: Qualitative models and intelligent learning environments. In: *Artificial Intelligence and Education, Volume 1*, pp. 281-305. Norwood, NJ: Ablex Publishing 1987
32. White, B. Y. & Frederiksen, J. R.: Causal model progressions as a foundation for learning environments. *Artificial Intelligence*, 42, pp. 99-157 (1990)
33. Williams, D. M., Hollan, J. D., & Stevens, A. L.: Human reasoning about a simple physical system. In: *Mental Models* (D. Gentner & A. L. Stevens, eds.). pp 40 51, Hillsdale, NJ: Lawrence Erlbaum Associates 1983
34. Winkels, R. & Achthoven, W.: Methodology and modularity in ITS design. In: *Proceedings of the 4th International Conference on Artificial Intelligence and Education*, Amsterdam (D. Bierman, J. Breuker & J. Sandberg, eds.), pp 314-322, Amsterdam: IOS 1989
35. Winkels, R. G. F: A new framework for describing and designing intelligent tutoring systems. In: *Artificial Intelligence in Higher Education* (V. Marik, O. Stepankova, & Z. Zdrahal, eds.). pp. 230-243, Lecture Notes in Computer Science, Vol. 451, Berlin: Springer-Verlag 1990
36. Winkels, R. G. F., & Breuker, J. A.: Modelling expertise for educational purposes. *Proceedings of the 2nd International Conference on Intelligent Tutoring Systems*, Montreal, Quebec (C. Frasson, G. Gauthier & G. McCalla, eds.), pp. 633-642, Lecture Notes in Computer Science, Vol. 608, Berlin: Springer-Verlag 1992
37. Woolf, B. & Cunningham, P. A.: Multiple knowledge sources in intelligent tutoring systems. In: *IEEE Expert*, pp 41-54, 1987
38. Young, R. M. & O'Shea, T.: Errors in children's subtraction. *Cognitive Science*, 5, pp. 153-177 (1981)

# Modeling the Student in Sherlock II[1]

Sandra Katz, Alan Lesgold, Gary Eggan, and Maria Gordin

Learning Research and Development Center, University of Pittsburgh, Pittsburgh, PA USA

**Abstract:** Student modeling—the task of building dynamic models of student ability—is fraught with uncertainty, caused by such factors as multiple sources of student errors, careless errors and lucky guesses, learning and forgetting. Various approaches have been developed in recent years to make student modeling more tractable. One approach, which is based on fuzzy set theory, aims at building *imprecise*, or "fuzzy" diagnostic student models; (eg. [18]). We have built upon this approach by developing techniques for representing and updating discrete student knowledge variables in our avionics troubleshooting tutor, **Sherlock II**. We describe these techniques and, more broadly, the student modeling component in this tutor. Future work will focus on calibrating the student modeling knowledge base and updating rules, evaluating the approach, and comparing it with other approaches to imprecise student modeling that we have implemented and are currently developing.

**Keywords:** student modeling, fuzzy set theory, fuzzy reasoning, Bayesian belief networks, Sherlock, error diagnosis, assessment, intelligent tutoring systems

## 1 Introduction

It has often been said that the chief potential advantage of computer-based learning systems over other forms of instruction is that these systems will be able to tailor instruction to the individual student's needs. As Ohlsson [37] has stated it:

... the main promise of computer tutors ... lies in their potential for moment-by-moment adaptation of instructional content and form to the changing cognitive

---

[1]This chapter also appeared in the *Journal of Artificial Intelligence in Education*, 3(4), pp. 495, (1993). Reprinted with permission of the Association for the Advancement of Computing in Education (AACE, P.O. Box 2966, Charlottesville, VA 22902 USA).

needs of the individual learner, and our task ... is to find principles which can guide the construction of tutors which fulfill that promise (p. 204).

Some functions of adaptive instruction that developers of tutoring systems have attended to include selecting the appropriate level of advice and explanations; determining readiness for advancement and dynamic planning of the student's curriculum; and giving the student feedback on his or her current performance and progress through the curriculum.

Each of these functions requires the tutoring system to be able to dynamically model the student's knowledge state. This capability is one of the main factors which distinguishes "intelligent" tutoring systems (ITS's) from other computer-based learning programs. Although significant progress in developing a technology for student modeling has been made over the last decade (eg. [1, 15, 18],) the task is a big one, so fraught with difficulties that Self [44] has pronounced it, "the intractable problem of student modeling." The intense difficulty of constructing and dynamically updating models of student understanding is one reason why, more than two decades after computers have been introduced to learning in schools, the promise of computers to provide individualized instruction has not yet been fulfilled [3, 17].

There are several sources of uncertainty in modeling student knowledge. Ambiguity is one; there is often more than one possible explanation for students' errors and inappropriate actions. Multiplicity is another; an error or inappropriate problem-solving action can often be traced to several misconceptions and skill deficiencies. Factor in idiosyncratic errors such as computational or mechanical slip-ups (eg., typos), lucky guesses, the fact that students often forget prior knowledge, etc. and the modeling problem compounds.

Several approaches to making student modeling more tractable have been developed in recent years. These approaches vary across a spectrum of precision in the models produced.[2] At one extreme lie model-tracing methods (eg., [1]) and buggy diagnostic approaches (eg., [48]), which are often combined. With model-tracing technology, the knowledge that the student is expected to acquire is represented within the tutor as a set of executable production rules. Common buggy productions also may be included in the model. Student performance is matched to expected performance based on the expert model. By restricting the student to a particular problem space, it is technically possible for the system to understand exactly what the student is doing using these model-tracing techniques. However, model-tracing methods tend to eliminate trial-and-error search and exploration, thereby reducing opportunities for metacognitive skill development and for system modeling of metacognitive skill [11].

Examples of less precision-oriented modeling approaches include *bounded student models* [14] and *granularity-based recognition* of students' problem-solving plans and strategies (eg., [16, 29]). These approaches are grounded in the belief that student models do not need to be precise and accurate to be useful. Similarly, the approach we have taken is grounded in fuzzy set

---

[2]See the Introduction to [23] for a more in-depth discussion of this issue.

theory [51], which attempts to capture the notion that items can have varying *degrees* of membership within a set, as opposed to the standard view that an item either belongs or does not belong in a set. For example, a student might have partial membership within the set of people who are expert in a particular skill, as reflected in teacher comments such as, "Joe is *fairly good* at two-column subtraction."

This "fuzzy" student modeling approach was originally proposed by Hawkes, Derry and their colleagues (eg.[11, 18]). Hawkes et al. [18] present the following rationale for applying fuzzy set theory to student modeling:

> [Partial membership within a set] is an important concept to the field of ITSs [intelligent tutor systems] because there are different aspects of vagueness inherent in real world data. There is the inherent vagueness of classification terms referring to a continuous scale, the uncertainty of linguistic terms such as "I almost agree," or the vagueness of terms or concepts due to statistical variability in communication [55]. Fuzzy set theory is an attempt to provide a systematic and sound basis for the modeling of [those] types of imprecision which are mainly due to a lack of well-defined boundaries for elements belonging to the set of objects. The use of fuzzy terms [eg., "rather high," "possibly," "not likely," etc.] allows for imprecision and vagueness in the values stored in the database. This provides a flexible and realistic representation that easily captures the way in which the human tutor might evaluate a student ... Also, many tutoring decisions are not clearcut ones and the capability to deal with such imprecision is a definite enhancement to ITS's. (pp. 416-17)

We have built upon Hawkes' and Derry's work by developing techniques for representing and updating discrete "fuzzy" student knowledge variables in our avionics troubleshooting tutor, **Sherlock II** [25]. In our system, each knowledge variable is associated with a *fuzzy probability distribution* that is upgraded or downgraded at different rates depending upon the type and strength of the evidence that appears in a student problem-solving trace. For example, the variable *ability to interpret test results* receives a strong upgrade each time a student tests the input signals to a circuit card when a previous test shows that the card's output signals are faulty, but receives a weaker upgrade if the student performs the input verification after receiving system advice to do so. Knowledge variables are linked together in a lattice where higher order variables, which we call "global variables" (eg., *ability to use test equipment)* represent aggregations of more primitive knowledge components, which we call "local variables" (eg., skill in using each type of test equipment - ie., *ability to use the hand held meter; ability to use the digital multimeter; ability to use the oscilloscope*). The updating techniques we have developed propagate changes in local variables "upwards" through layers of associated global variables.

Several researchers who have been experimenting with imprecise modeling approaches are finding that the incomplete and inaccurate models produced are nonetheless useful for carrying out the system's knowledge assessment and didactic functions (eg., [8, 11, 15, 30]). In our own work on the forerunner of **Sherlock II (Sherlock I)**, we found that a very crude categorization of student ability into discrete knowledge levels (ie., *unlearned, perhaps, probably, and strong*) worked quite well in guiding system decisions about the level of detail to provide in hints [25]. This is not surprising, since there is an increasing body of evidence that human tutoring decisions seldom involve precise diagnosis (eg., [31, 42]) - that is, a detailed model of the misconceptions or "bugs" that motivate student errors - although research has not yet directly addressed the issue of exactly what kinds of student models expert human tutors in action do construct. We share with Derry and Hawkes [11] the belief that in low-risk decision-making situations such as tutoring, where new information is constantly being made available for modifying diagnostic hypotheses, imprecise student modeling is adequate. Future evaluations of our system and others incorporating imprecise modeling approaches will help to determine how effective these approaches actually are.

A major technical aim of our work was to simplify the knowledge and software engineering requirements involved in building a student modeling component that can produce fuzzy (imprecise) probabilistic student records which are adequate to guide system functions such as coaching, feedback, and problem selection. There is a tradition of formal probabilistic approaches to reasoning under uncertainty in the field of AI, most notably *Bayesian inferencing networks*[3] and an outgrowth of fuzzy set theory known as *possibility theory* (eg., [12, 13, 51-54). However, some approaches to possibility theory have been criticized for overwhelming computational complexity, while simpler ones compromise expressibility [43]. And Bayesian reasoning, although computationally manageable (eg., [39]), has often been criticized for high knowledge engineering demands (eg., [49])[4]. That is, knowledge engineers (often domain experts) face the difficult and unnatural task of specifying prior :probabilities for variables and conditional probabilities for link matrices. In contrast, our modeling scheme allows system developers to state in broad, categorical terms how indicative a particular action is of a particular knowledge attribute (eg., *strong, medium, weak*). In addition, as the following pages will demonstrate, the techniques we use to update primitive knowledge variables and draw inferences from these primitives about higher-order knowledge variables are far simpler computationally than those used in either Bayesian or fuzzy reasoning systems.

---

[3]For a thorough technical discussion of Bayesian belief networks see [40]. A more accessible introduction can be found in [6] or [35].

[4]There is also a long-standing debate about the relative adequacy of fuzzy and Bayesian approaches for representing and reasoning about vague concepts. It is beyond the scope of this paper to discuss this issue, but we refer the interested reader to [7, 9, 43, 54].

A long-term goal of our research is to determine just how much simplicity and imprecision a student modeling engine can get away with and still be useful. It may well be, for example, that the mathematical rigor afforded by Bayesian inferencing networks are worth the added costs in knowledge engineering and programming complexity—at least for certain system functions. In the near future, we plan to explore this issue by building a Bayesian network from a calibrated version of the student modeling network described in this paper, and then compare the effectiveness of using Bayesian reasoning techniques for student modeling with those we have developed.

The remainder of this paper consists of four main sections. First, we introduce **Sherlock II** We then describe in more detail the imprecise student modeling component we have developed for this tutoring system. Next we discuss our plans for future work, focusing on the issues that will guide comparisons of the imprecise modeling approach described in this article with others we have implemented and are currently developing. Finally, we conclude with a summary of our work and its potential contributions to student modeling.

# 2 Overview of Sherlock II

**Sherlock II** is an intelligent coached practice environment developed to train avionics technicians to diagnose faults in a complex electronic testing system—in particular, a test station which checks out F-15 aircraft modules[5]. Ordinarily, when a module is brought into the repair shop because of suspected malfunction, the technician attaches the module (referred to as the "unit under test" or UUT) to a *test station* and, by carrying out a series of checkout procedures, is able to locate the fault. However, sometimes the airman discovers that he[6] continues to get an unexpected reading even when he replaces the UUT with a shop standard. When this occurs, the airman should know that the problem is not with the UUT; rather, the test station itself is malfunctioning and needs to be repaired. Locating a faulty component within the test station requires the technician to troubleshoot a much larger problem space than does diagnosing a faulty module. The test station contains approximately $70ft^3$ of circuitry! However, not all of this circuitry is needed to carry out each checkout procedure. So, the essential task confronting the airman is to construct a mental representation of the *active* circuitry - what we refer to as the *active circuit path* - and to troubleshoot this path until he locates the fault. Sherlock's job is to

---

[5]The system is written in Smalltalk/V286, an object-oriented programming language, and runs on 386 workstations equipped with Sony videodisc hardware. Discussions of Sherlock I, the predecessor of Sherlock II, can be found in [24, 25, 27].

[6]We use the masculine pronoun, since most Sherlock students are male.

scaffold the process of learning to construct these abstract representations and of developing efficient troubleshooting strategies.

**Sherlock II** is a realistic computer simulation of the actual job environment. Trainees acquire and practice skills in a context similar to the real setting in which they will be used. The tutor, Sherlock, presents trainees with a series of exercises of increasing difficulty. There are two main episodes in each exercise: *problem-solving* and *review*. During problem-solving, the student runs the checkout procedures on a simulation of a test station with a particular UUT attached. Using interactive video with a mouse pointer interface, the student can set switches and adjust knobs and dials on test station drawers, take measurements, and view readings. If he gets an unexpected reading on one of the measurement devices (hand held meter, digital multimeter, or oscilloscope), he should see if the aircraft module is the "culprit" by replacing it with a shop standard. If after doing this the student still gets an unexpected reading, he should troubleshoot the test station. He can test components by "attaching" probes to measurement points in a video display, replace a suspect component with a shop standard and rerun the failed checkout test, etc. These and other options are available through a menu-driven interface, as shown in Figure 1.

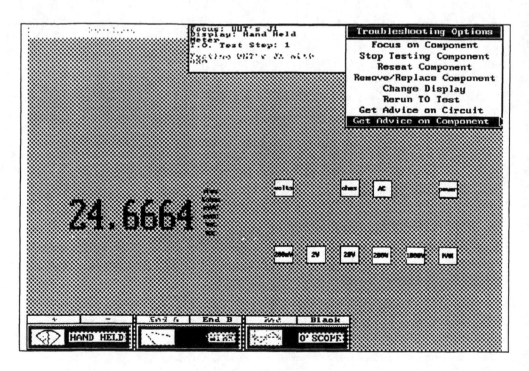

Figure 1: Sherlock's troubleshooting menu

Perhaps most importantly, the student can ask for advice at any point while troubleshooting. Sherlock provides advice at both the circuit path and individual component levels of investigation. (See Figure 1.) At each level, Sherlock offers functional, strategic, and procedural advice: via the **how it works, how to test,** and **how to trace** options, respectively. The student is then asked to specify the type and amount of help he wants, via a sub-menu of advice options. For example, if the student asks for **how to test** help at the component level, he will be prompted to choose between receiving a simple summary of the troubleshooting goals he has already achieved; a suggested goal to achieve next (eg., *You should verify the component's data flow signals.*); a goal to achieve **plus** specific advice about how to achieve it (ie., the exact type of measurement to take and pins to test), etc. The basic idea behind this coaching scheme is to give students control over their own learning, and to help them develop metacognitive skills by requiring them to figure out for themselves what type of information they need. At times, though, Sherlock will advise a student to select a particular help option. For example, Sherlock may suggest that the student ask for help with tracing through the schematics if he continues to be way off target.

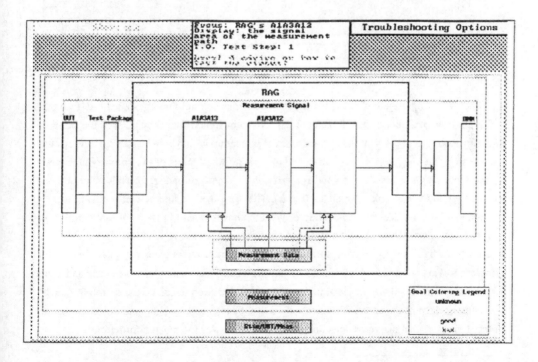

Figure 2: Abstract representation of the active circuit path

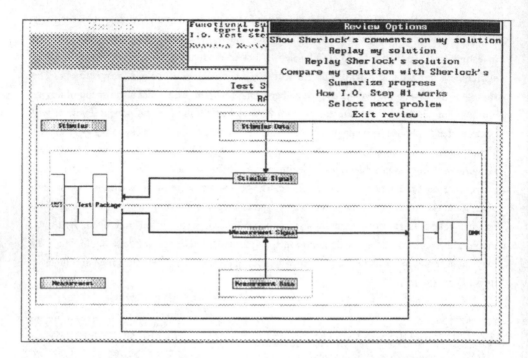

Figure 3: Reflective follow-up options

The major cognitive tool provided by **Sherlock II** is an intelligent graphics interface that helps students construct a mental model of the active circuit path and keep track of the status of troubleshooting goals. A sample abstract schematic diagram is shown in Figure 2. Although not visible here, these diagrams are color-coded to indicate which parts of the circuitry have been found from previous tests to be good (green); which areas are bad (red); and which are not suspect (yellow) or of unknown status (black). The drawings are interactive: mousing on any component box produces an explanation of what is known about the status of that component given the actions (such as measurements and swaps) carried out so far. An intelligent schematic producer configures these drawings to match the coach's current explanatory goal, the current problem solving context, and information about the trainee. For example, more space and more expanded circuit detail are provided in the part of the circuit on which an expert might now be focusing or the part the coach wishes to emphasize. Component labeling and color coding are filtered to assure that diagrams don't unintentionally give away too much information[7].

---

[7]A component is only labeled if the student has already tested it, if it has been referred to in a help message, or if the student has identified the component when prompted. This restriction ensures that students have to use schematics to trace through the active path.

In designing **Sherlock II**, we embraced Vygotsky's [50] notion of cognitive tools: "objects provided by the learning environment that permit students to incorporate new auxiliary methods or symbols into their problem-solving activity that otherwise would be unavailable" [11, 23].

Each problem-solving session is followed by a review phase, which we call *reflective follow-up* (RFU). Psychological experimentation [38, 45, 46] and theoretical models of case-based learning (eg., [33]) indicate why a review phase is important for acquiring cognitive skills. Students often suffer from "cognitive overload" during problem-solving sessions. Consequently, it is best to parcel out some of the instruction to a post-problem reflective phase.

The following options are available during reflective follow-up : (a) *Show Sherlock's comments on my solution*, (b) *Replay my solution*, (c) *Replay Sherlock's solution*, (d) *Compare my solution to Sherlock's*, (e) *Summarize my progress through the Sherlock program*, (f) *Explain what the test station was supposed to be doing at the point of failure in the problem just finished*, and (g) *Let me help determine the next problem Sherlock assigns*. Menu labels are actually more terse than described here, as shown in Figure 3.

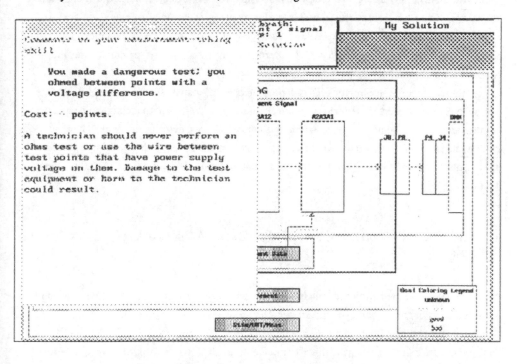

Figure 4: Sherlock's comments on a troubleshooting action

It is beyond the scope of this paper to describe each menu option, but we will give the reader a sense of what the main review activity we want students to engage in is like: namely, a coached replay of the student's problem-solving session. While stepping through his solution within the *Replay my solution* option, the student receives a summary of each action and feedback pointing out its good and bad aspects. A **Sherlock II** comment is illustrated in Figure 4[8]. The student can ask to see what Sherlock would have done instead, and receive other kinds of coaching, including the chance to re-examine the dynamically labeled and color-coded schematic diagrams visible during problem-solving. (See Figure 4.)

# 3  Building Imprecise Student Models

While the student is working on a problem, the system records a trace of his actions, including the components he tested; the actual measurements made; replacements ("swaps") of components with shop standards; requests for help, etc. This *student trace* is the crucial input to the student modeling component, which interprets the trace in order to update the tutor's assessment of the student's knowledge state.

A student record[9] in **Sherlock II** is represented as an instantiated lattice of knowledge variables. In this section, we describe in more detail the generic student modeling lattice and the representation of individual variables within this lattice. We then describe the rules that are used to draw inferences about student ability from observable student actions; the updating algorithms that respond to rule "firings"; and the procedure that orchestrates the modification of a student record.

# 4  The Student Modeling Knowledge Base: A Network of "Fuzzy Variables"

To review what we said earlier, the main structure used in **Sherlock II** to store the knowledge required for student modeling is the *student variable lattice*. Each node in the lattice is an indicator about some characteristic of student capability. The lowest level variables, which we call *local variables*, represent distinct components of expertise - in particular, conceptual knowledge (eg., *understanding of how a relay card works*), skills (eg., *ability to use an*

---

[8]Johanna Moore is currently developing tools to generate more intelligent explanations during reflective follow-up, drawing from ideas in her dissertation [34].

[9]The terms student model and student record are used interchangeably in this chapter.

*oscilloscope*), behavioral dispositions (eg. *tendency to replace components rather than test them*), and affective factors (eg. *self-confidence vs. coaching dependency*). Local variables are thus close to an overlay of competence estimates on the system's expert model. The higher-level variables in the lattice, which we call *global variables*, represent abstractions over groups of these "local" competencies (eg. *ability to use test equipment*, which includes *ability to use the digital multimeter*, *ability to use the hand held meter*, and *ability to use the oscilloscope*). Figure 5 contains a list of the main types of variables tracked by **Sherlock II's** student modeling component[10].

```
o   Global testing ability variables
o   Circuit variables
o   Circuit strategy variables by path type
o   Circuit tactical variables by path type
o   Component variables: strategic
o   Component variables: tactical
o   Overall score on testing component (strategic plus tactical ability)
o   Test equipment usage skills
o   Other test-taking skills
    □   overall ability to interpret test results
        ▶   circuit-level ability to interpret test results
        ▶   component-level ability to interpret test results
    □   ability to read schematics
o   Domain knowledge
    □   system understanding
    □   TO understanding
o   Dispositions
    □   swapping vs testing
    □   testing for the appropriate signal type
    □   thrashing
    □   history-taking
    □   overall systematicity and completeness
    □   attention to safety preconditions
    □   redundant testing
    □   attention to probability of failure
    □   independence and self-confidence
    □   accepting help
```

Figure 5: Types of modeling variables in Sherlock II

Where do these modeling variables come from? We relied upon two main sources of information about which aspects of students' understanding and performance should be modeled by the system: cognitive task analysis and expert judgments. Local variables, and the rules for updating them, were derived mainly from observable properties of troubleshooting performance, as revealed during cognitive analysis of the job of troubleshooting the F-15 manual test station

---

[10]The most indented items under each category are local variables; the rest are global.

[26, 27]. To a lesser degree, local variables also reflect domain experts' judgments about what properties of local performance are important to measure. Global variables, on the other hand, are anchored primarily in expert evaluations of trainee performance. Policy-capturing techniques helped us to identify the evaluation criteria experts use to rate student performance traces [36][11]. Indirectly, global variables are also anchored in observations of human performance, since they represent cumulations of local variables. These relationships between modeling variables and their sources are summarized in Figure 6[12].

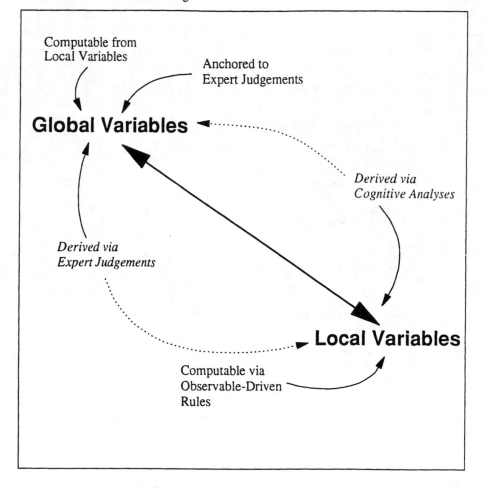

Figure 6: Multi-level assessment scheme

---

[11]The set of evaluation criteria identified by using policy-capturing techniques keeps the amount of sensible cumulations of local variables (i.e., global variables) to a tractable size.

[12]Solid lines represent primary sources of information about variables; dotted lines represent secondary sources.

Currently, all student modeling variables are represented as *fuzzy variables*. A fuzzy variable can be thought of as a distribution over the set of possible levels of competence (ie., knowledge states) a trainee might have in a particular skill, or understanding of a particular domain concept. **Sherlock II** tracks five such knowledge states for each modeling variable: *no knowledge, limited knowledge, unautomated knowledge, partially automated knowledge,* and *fully developed knowledge*. The distribution of a fuzzy variable can be denoted by the vector $F$, with the $i$th probability interval being denoted by $F_i$.

For most knowledge variables, we assume that each of the five states has equal probability (20%), and we initialize the distributions accordingly, as illustrated in Figure 7[13]. However, since we have some prior knowledge about student ability on certain variables, we can bias these distributions. For example, since we know that most of our students have had little experience using an oscilloscope, we can initialize the associated distribution as (20 60 20 0 0). This would indicate that we are 60% certain that the skill indexed by this particular variable is limited in any given student, but it might be non-existent, and it might even have reached the level of being established but not automated. The updating procedures described below control revisions of these initial hypotheses about student ability.

## 4.1 Variable Updating

Updating rules for local variables. Everything that a teacher - human or machine - can infer about a student's knowledge and misconceptions is conveyed through the student's actions, be they speech acts or non-linguistic actions. Indeed, no user modeling system can peer directly into an agent's mind; language and action are the sole media through which modeling information passes, and there will invariably be gaps and distortions in the image conveyed. This is, in essence, why the user modeling task is so hard. In a system like **Sherlock II**, which does not have natural-language processing capabilities[14] student actions serve as the sole "window" or "keyhole" [10] through which diagnostic information about the student is conveyed. **Sherlock II**'s modeling window is the student trace.

Of course, only a subset of student actions observable by a computerized tutor are significant, from a diagnostic standpoint. And they are significant only when certain constraints are met. For example, in *Sherlock II*, the student can select a menu option that will allow him to

---

[13]More rigorous analysis of student data is needed to more accurately initialize our modeling variables.

[14]As noted in footnote 7, Johanna Moore is currently extending the dialogue capabilities within Sherlock II's reflective follow-up phase. One goal of her work is to enable trainees to ask follow-up questions about the comments that the system generates while replaying the student's (or an expert's) solution. Eventually, similar dialogue capabilities will be incorporated within Sherlock II's problem-solving phase. Kass [19] has commented upon the importance of flexible interaction between the system and the user for building a user model.

test a component. (See Figure 1.) But the student's selection of this **Test Component** option is only interesting in light of the current test situation. Is the component on the active circuit path? If not, then the student might have a weak model of the diagnostic procedure that the test station is currently performing, or of the test station itself. (These knowledge components are associated with the fuzzy variables *understanding of the checkout procedures* and *system understanding*, respectively. See Figure 7.) Did other tests made on other components already verify that the currently tested component is functioning alright? If so, then the student is carrying out a redundant test, and his troubleshooting approach might be inefficient and unsystematic, or he might have difficulty interpreting the results of prior tests. (These tendencies are tracked as *redundant testing*, *systematicity*, and *ability to interpret test results*, respectively.)

---

ABILITY TO USE THE HANDHELD METER

**description:** measure of knowledge about when to use the handheld meter; tactical ability is assumed

**initial distribution:** (20 20 20 20 20)

**upgrading rules:**
1) uses handheld meter appropriately to measure resistance, i.e., when there is no power, without help from Sherlock (+++)
2) uses handheld meter appropriately to measure DC voltage, i.e., DC power is on, without help from Sherlock (+++)
3) uses handheld meter appropriately to measure AC voltage, i.e., AC power is on (+++)

**downgrading rules:**
1) uses handheld meter to measure resistance when power is on (e.g., shorting in the data area) (---)
2) uses handheld meter to measure voltage when there is none (---)
3) uses handheld meter to measure DC voltage when it's AC (--)
4) uses handheld meter to measure AC voltage when it's DC (--)

---

Figure 7: A sample fuzzy variable

In our tutoring system, we refer to these 'diagnostically significant' aspects of student behavior as *performance conditions*. Performance conditions comprise the "left hand side" of rules for updating local variables, in conventional terms: the events that trigger the system to update the current distribution for a local fuzzy variable. In fact, we view local variables as abstractions over performance conditions, just as global variables are meaningful abstractions over local variables.

The performance conditions that update the fuzzy variable representing a student's ability to use a hand held meter are shown in Figure 7. Adjacent to each condition is a symbol indicating how rapidly the variable should be updated when the rule fires. We use an arbitrary convention in this example, where +++ means to upgrade the variable relatively quickly, ++ means a moderate upgrade, + means a slower upgrade, --- means a rapid downgrade, etc. Below, we formalize the procedure that carries out modifications of fuzzy distributions at these varying rates.

There are two main observations to be made about performance conditions. First, although the updating rules shown in this example are derived from simple observations (eg., what test type the student set the meter to, voltage or ohms), not all local variables need to be fixed by simple events. Rather, some may have their values inferred by relatively complex qualitative patterns over multiple observable events. For instance, the local variable for the student's strategy in testing a particular functional area of the test station (eg., the signal path between the UUT and the digital multimeter) may operate on implications of actions, such as an index of the extent to which a *series* of measurements on components within this functional area helped to identify the location of the fault[15].

Perhaps a more important observation to be made about performance conditions is that they are redundant across variables. This is not surprising, since in reality there could be more than one valid explanation for a student action. An action can be part of different plans and/or motivated by different aspects of conceptual understanding, as illustrated above in our example of a student's selection of an inappropriate component to test.

To take another example with reference to the hand held meter (Figure 7), an incorrect setting on this measurement device - eg., ohms instead of voltage - could mean that the student does not realize that setting the meter before testing is necessary, or does not know how to do this, from a purely mechanical standpoint. This aspect of domain knowledge is tracked by the variable *tactical test equipment skill*. What is more likely, though, is that the student does not know that the correct setting for the test he is conducting is VDC (direct current voltage), because he does not realize that current was in the active circuit path for the diagnostic procedure that the test station was carrying out when failure occurred. In other words, the student probably has an inadequate mental model of the failed checkout test[16].

---

[15]See [25] for additional examples of performance conditions used to update local variables.

[16]This situation provides a good example of how violations of expected behavior can serve as indicators of gaps in students' knowledge. Kass [19] stipulated a general rule for acquiring information about an agent called the Sufficiency Rule. The rule is based upon Grice's principles of cooperative interaction. It essentially states that a cooperative agent does everything necessary (and nothing more) to enable the system to achieve its goal. In a

In our system, we handle the ambiguity in interpreting student actions by allowing the same performance condition to update *several* variables. Regarding our example, the act of performing the wrong type of test will update *tactical test equipment skill, ability to use the hand held meter, testing for the appropriate signal type*, etc. However, we vary the rate-at which updating occurs for a given condition across variables. Two factors govern the update rate that our knowledge engineers assign to a performance condition for a particular variable: (1) the condition's strength as an indicator of competency in that variable, and (2) the frequency with which the action associated with the condition might occur during any given problem-solving session. If the same upgrading speed was used for all events, some variables would reach expert level way ahead of others. For example, there are many more opportunities to set the hand held meter, to place probes on pins, and to carry out other test-taking actions on a component than there are to respond to an indicator light which fails to come on.

Identifying updating rates that take both factors (indicative strength of a behavior, and its frequency of occurrence) into account is indeed a tricky matter at times. There are two clear-cut cases: weak indicators that occur frequently should update a variable slowly; strong indicators that occur infrequently should update a variable quickly. We generally handle the other cases, in which the indicative strength of a condition and its frequency of occurrence are at odds, by assigning a moderate updating rate. As with all parameters in our modeling system, these rates need to be adjusted empirically.

The updating rate is expressed in the "right hand" side of an updating rule—the "action" part, in conventional terms. More formally, we specify the updating rate for a fuzzy variable, $F$, by two pieces of information: a *range vector*, $V$, and a *change percentage*, $c$. The change percentage controls the rate of updating. The downgrading procedure for a fuzzy variable, $F$, can be expressed as follows, where $V$ represents the range vector[17] and $c$ the change percentage:

$$F = (f_1\, f_2\, f_3\, f_4\, f_5),$$
$$V = (v_1\, v_2\, v_3\, v_4\, v_5),$$
$$c = \text{constant},$$
$$f_i = f_i - f_i v_i c + f_{i+1} v_{i+1} c, \qquad \text{where } v_1 = 0, \qquad i = 1,\dots 4,$$
$$f_5 = f_5 - f_5 v_5 c$$

---

tutorial situation, it is usually the agent, not the system, who has the goal of solving the problem, but the Sufficiency Rule still applies to a large extent. That is, we can expect that the student will do what is required to solve the problem (e.g., find the fault in a test station's active circuitry), barring some satisficing. If he does not, it is probably because of a lack of understanding, or lack of capacity due to insufficiently automated knowledge.

[17]In our system, we vary the range according to the student's current level of expertise—novice, journeyman, or near-expert. The percentage for each interval in the range decreases as skill increases. For example, the range for a journeyman might be (0, 20, 30, 30, 30), for a near-expert (0, 15, 25, 25, 25). This scheme enables us to control updating so that the system does not deem the student an "expert" too readily.

## Initial settings:

$F = (20\ 20\ 20\ 20\ 20)$,
$V = (0\ 30\ 100\ 100\ 100)$,
$c = 10$

## After one downgrade:

$f_i = f_i - f_i v_i c + f_{i+1} v_{i+1} c$, where $v_1 = 0$, $i = 1,...4$
$f_5 = f_5 - f_5 v_5 c$

$f_1 = f_1 - f_1 v_1 c + f_2 v_2 c$
$\quad = 20 - 20 \times 0 \times .1 + 20 \times .3 \times .1 = 20 - 0 + .6 = 20.6$

$f_2 = f_2 - f_2 v_2 c + f_3 v_3 c$
$\quad = 20 - 20 \times .3 \times .1 + 20 \times 1 \times .1 = 20 - .6 = 2 = 21.4$

$f_3 = f_3 - f_3 v_3 c + f_4 v_4 c$
$\quad = 20 - 20 \times 1 \times .1 + 20 \times 1 \times .1 = 20 - 20 + 20 = 20$

$f_4 = f_4 - f_4 v_4 c + f_5 v_5 c$
$\quad = 20 - 20 \times 1 \times .1 + 20 \times 1 \times .1 = 20 - 20 + 20 = 20$

$f_5 = f_5 - f_5 v_5 c$
$\quad = 20 - 20 \times 1 \times .1 = 20 - 2 = 18$

$F = (20.6\ 21.4\ 20\ 20\ 18)$

## After 10 downgrades:

$F = (28.7\ 32.9\ 18.2\ 13.9\ 6.3)$

Figure 8: Example of variable downgrading

An example is shown in Figure 8. The basic idea behind downgrading is to "shift" the current distribution to the left, by successively adding some amount of probability interval $F_{i+1}$ to $F_i$. The leftmost interval in the change vector is set to 0, to prevent "spillover." As the example shows, downgrading proceeds conservatively, since a single instance of an error is insufficient for drawing conclusions about student ability. However, as Figure 8 shows, multiple behavioral events *are* significant, and effect dramatic changes in the distribution.

Upgrading occurs in a similar manner except that the shift is to the right, by successively adding some amount of $F_i$ to $F_{i+1}$. The rightmost interval in the change vector is set to 0, again to prevent spillover:

$$f_1 = f_1 - f_1 v_1 c,$$
$$f_i = f_i - f_i v_i c + f_{i-1} v_{i-1} c, \text{ where } v_5 = 0, \ i = 2,...,5$$

Given the same initial values for $F$, $V$, and $c$ shown in Figure 8, a single upgrade would change $F$ to (18 20 20 21.4 20.6). After ten rule firings, the distribution would be (6.3 13.9 18.2 32.9 28.7).

Updating rules for global variables. Reasoning under uncertainty can be viewed as a two-sided operation. One involves *pooling* evidence to arrive at hypotheses; the other involves *propagating* the uncertainty in one or more hypothesis through an inferencing process aimed at arriving at some conclusion [9]. In the preceding section, we described how our system pools behavioral evidence (performance conditions) to formulate hypotheses about student competence on "primitive" (local) skills. In this section, we describe how Sherlock combines these hypotheses to reason about more complex, "global" skills.

In **Sherlock II**, updating rules for global variables are expressed as weighted linear equations. Just as the change rates in updating rules for local variables reflect a performance condition's strength as an indicator for that variable, so do the weights in aggregation equations reflect the relative strength of each local knowledge variable in determining the student's ability on the associated global knowledge variable. Below are some sample weighted equations for updating global variables.

**Circuit testing ability** = .85 *circuit testing strategy* + .15 *circuit testing tactical ability*

**Test equipment usage** = .60 *ability to use the oscilloscope* + .20 *ability to use the digital multimeter* + .20 *ability to use the hand held meter*

**Domain understanding** = .75 *system understanding* + .25 *understanding of the checkout procedures*

The result of applying these equations is a composite distribution, expressing the system's degree of belief that the student is competent in the skill represented by the global variable. The procedure for updating a global variable $G$, using local variables $Fl$ *and* their associated weights, $w_l$, can be expressed as shown below.

$$G = w_1 F_1 + w_2 F_2 + ... + w_k F_k,$$

$$F_1 = (f_{11} f_{12} f_{13} f_{14} f_{15})$$
$$F_2 = (f_{22} f_{23} f_{24} f_{25} f_{26})$$
...
$$F_k = (f_{k1} f_{k2} f_{k3} f_{k4} f_{k5})$$

We use the following formula to calculate $G = (g_1 \ g_2 \ g_3 \ g_4 \ g_5)$:

$$g_1 = w_1 f_{11} + w_2 f_{21} + ... + w_k f_{k1},$$
...
$$g_5 = w_5 f_{15} + w_2 f_{25} + ... + w_k f_{k5}$$

An example for test equipment usage, where the number of associated local variables, $k$, equals 3 is shown in Figure 9.

*G - test equipment usage*

*$F_1$ - ability to use the oscilloscope*        $F_1 = (0\ 40\ 30\ 30\ 0)$
*$F_2$ - ability to use the digital multimeter*   $F_2 = (0\ 20\ 60\ 20\ 0)$
*$F_3$ - ability to use the handheld meter*       $F_3 = (0\ \ 0\ 30\ 50\ 20)$

$G = .6F_1 + .2F_2 + .2F_3$

$G = (g_1\ g_2\ g_3\ g_4\ g_5)$
$g_1 = .6 \times 0 + .2 \times 0 + .2 \times 0 = 0$
$g_2 = .6 \times 40 + .2 \times 20 + .2 \times 0 = 28$
$g_3 = .6 \times 30 + .2 \times 60 + .2 \times 30 = 26$
$g_4 = .6 \times 30 + .2 \times 20 + .2 \times 50 = 32$
$g_5 = .6 \times 0 + .2 \times 0 + .2 \times 20 = 4$

$G = (0\ 28\ 36\ 32\ 4)$

Figure 9:  Example of global variable updating

# 5  Putting it All Together: Updating an Individual Student Model

Building the Student Trace.  The "intelligence" in object oriented systems like **Sherlock II** is encapsulated in computational "objects."  An object is an independent piece of computer program that stores its own local data and can thus respond to various requests that other parts of the system might make of it. In **Sherlock II**, the information needed to model the student gets recorded by objects at two levels: the active circuit path, and individual component objects within this path. The circuit path object records global information such as the order of components tested, and the order in which circuit testing goals (eg., verification that the signal path between the UUT and the digital multimeter is functioning okay) were achieved. Component objects record more local information about what happened while the student was testing a particular component - in particular, the order in which tests were made and component testing goals (eg., verification that the inputs to the component are okay) were achieved; which particular pins were measured and how the probes were placed; what test equipment was used, and how it was set up; what types and levels of coaching were requested, etc. The modeling information gathered by these circuit and component objects is stored in the object that we call the 'student trace.'[18]

Interpreting the trace to update the student model. A few variables are updated dynamically while the student is solving a problem. However, most variables are updated between problem completion and reflective follow-up, since updating takes time and would slow down the system considerably if it were all done dynamically. Dynamically updated variables primarily correspond to safety hazards, such as attempting to conduct an ohms test when current is on. Dynamic updating is triggered by rule "firings," as soon as these dangerous events occur. The appropriate variables are updated the rate specified by their updating rules - in particular, the "right hand" side which encodes the updating rate.

Post-solution updating proceeds as follows. First, **Sherlock II** imports the student's record, thereby gaining access to the student's score on all local variables up to the current exercise. If the student is new to the system, initializes variables to a pre-specified level, as indicated by the "initial distribution" slot in Figure 7. Using its updating routines, **Sherlock II** examines the student's solution trace, searching for performance conditions that trigger rule firings. Each performance condition is recorded in a structure called the *conditions table*. **Sherlock II** simply notes how many times each performance condition has been identified in the student trace. Each local variable associated with that indicator will then be updated the recorded number of times. After each local variable has been updated, **Sherlock II** uses its weighed linear equations to propagate these values "upwards" through the student modeling lattice, thereby updating global variables.

# 6 Current Status and Future Directions

A prototype version of **Sherlock II** underwent initial field trials in August of 1991. The system contained an uncalibrated student modeling component, implemented using the approach described in this article. These initial system trials underscored the need to fine-tune the student modeling knowledge base in light of student data. We found, for example, that student records were being updated too slowly to be useful for problem selection. In general, students were much better than the modeler made them out to be. This was one of a cluster of reasons why

---

[18]Actuallly, the student trace consists of a cluster of objects, each one holding a different type of information - e.g., one records the student's measurements, one holds the sequence of achieved goals and the tests used to achieve these goals, another stores information about test device settings, etc. This division of labor makes updating the model more efficient, since individual updating routines need only access those objects that contain the information that they need. However, for conceptual simplicity and ease of exposition, it is best to think in terms of one student trace object.

some students were given too many easy problems and became frustrated with the tutor.[19]

Calibrating the student modeling component will involve validating the structure and content of the student variable lattice, as well as the parameters used in updating rules. We need to ensure that we have the right set of modeling variables - ie., those that human experts actually use to diagnose and assess student ability - and that the aggregations of local and global modeling variables are correct. The parameters that need to be adjusted include the rates that control local variable updating, and their two-part expression as a range vector and change percentage; the initial fuzzy distribution for local variables; and the weights in aggregation equations.[20]

In the near future, we plan to revise the variable lattice and its updating rules using the results of an empirically validated study of expert scoring criteria [41]. This study revealed the competency indicators (behaviors) that experts watch for, the high-level ("global") skills they associate with these behaviors - in particular, *understanding of the testing system (test station)*, *test-taking ability*, and *strategy* - and the relative import experts attach to a particular behavior as evidence of a particular skill. Although it will be an important first step to ensure that our network is consistent with this information, the study yields only coarse-grained associations between student behaviors and a small set of global variables. In order to develop a finer-grained variable lattice such as that described above, which would in turn afford finer-grained student modeling and assessment, we will also have to use other knowledge engineering techniques.

We could also use various psychometric and scaling methods to calibrate the modeling network and updating rules. Regression analysis techniques are certainly a possibility. For example, decisions concerning which local variables are related to one another and which are the most sensitive indicators of competence can be made empirically on the basis of initial student data, especially if the fuzzy distributions' central tendencies are converted to scalars. One can then perform regression analyses in which the global variables, as estimated by experts, are predicted by medians or means of local variable distributions, which are in turn generated through the updating process described above.

It is also possible to search for indicators of competence using scaling techniques. For example, we have looked at a variety of specific indicators of progress and how they change as trainees get more experience using the tutor. By applying scaling techniques such as factor analyses and cluster analyses to means or medians of local variables, we could examine the covariation of these indicators. That in turn would suggest possible global student modeling variables, one for each cluster. The indicators that cluster together tend to give clues about which

---

[19]Other factors contributing to sluggish curriculum planning included a problem set that was too large, and a non-robust file backup procedure which caused some student trace files to be deleted. The latter led the tutor to consider students who had already worked on the tutor beginners!

[20]These values were mainly initialized by our in-house domain expert, Gary Eggan.

local variables might be aggregated to produce the corresponding global variable.[21]

Once we have calibrated the modeling lattice and updating rules, we will be able to compare our updating techniques with other student modeling approaches we have implemented and are currently developing. We expect such fine-tuning to take considerable effort, and more student data than was made available during the preliminary field trials. Since we were in need of a more empirically valid student modeling/assessment component in order to demonstrate and field test the tutor in the summer of 1992, we implemented an interim scheme based on the results of the Pokorny and Gott [41] study discussed above. The approach is based on a more traditional, point-scoring scheme, in which students are "charged" a certain number of points for inappropriate as well as some appropriate troubleshooting actions (eg., extending a circuit card for testing; replacing a malfunctioning component). Their total charge is then compared with that incurred by the expert model run on the same problem. The ratio of expert-to-student "costs" constitutes the student's score for a particular problem, and then this score is used to update a recency-weighted average of the student's performance on particular problem types (eg., problems in which a switch is malfunctioning; problems that require use of the oscilloscope). This information is then used to guide selection of the next problem[22]. In addition, a shallow clustering of inappropriate actions under global variable labels (ie., *system understanding*, *test-taking ability*, and *strategy*) is presented to the student for feedback purposes.

Field testing will enable us to assess the effectiveness of this rather standard assessment approach. The approach itself will also serve as a useful basis for future comparisons of a calibrated version of the more experimental approach to student modeling and assessment described in this paper with another we are currently developing. As forecasted in the Introduction, the latter involves applying Bayesian inferencing techniques (eg., [6, 35, 39]) to student modeling and assessment. Our plan is to apply these techniques to the revised student modeling network and to the same network we will apply our calibrated fuzzy modeling techniques.

There are several motivations for experimenting with a Bayesian student modeling approach. The variable lattice we have developed is already quite close to a Bayesian belief net. Its nodes represent discrete knowledge variables, encoded as distributions over meaningful knowledge states (*unautomated*, *partially automated*, etc.). However, the current network structure will have to be checked to ensure that it adheres to the constraint of *conditional independence*, which prevents updating inertia by ensuring that all of the nodes that a given node depends upon are linked directly to it [40]. We might find that Bayesian inferencing techniques do a better job than ours at updating the student's knowledge state on variables within the revised network.

---

[21]See [20] for a more in-depth discussion of approaches to evaluating and fine-tuning the student modeling network and its updating rules.

[22]See [21] for a more detailed discussion of this approach to problem selection.

One possible reason for this is that unlike our updating scheme, where reasoning takes place in only one direction, Bayesian belief nets are quite capable of *bi-directional reasoning*. This has been demonstrated extensively in other domains, especially medicine. That is, in addition to formulating diagnostic hypotheses, a Bayesian reasoning system such as MUNIN [2] can make *predictions* about the occurrence of symptoms as these hypotheses are strengthened or weakened, which can then be used to guide the selection of further tests. Similarly, a bi-directional, Bayesian student modeling scheme might enable the system to reason about student ability on knowledge variables for which little or no evidence has been gathered, as well as predict student performance on particular types of problems.

Another motivation for experimenting with Bayesian student modeling is that belief networks are already a standard AI technique. As such, they are understood and taught, which increases the likelihood that Bayesian student modeling components will be implemented in other tutors. This would in turn lead to the development of a well-codified, standard technology for Bayesian student modeling. Several researchers have already begun to experiment with this approach (eg., [49]).

Our future comparisons of the three modeling approaches described above - imprecise (fuzzy) modeling, the point-scoring scheme, and Bayesian modeling - will focus on several issues, mainly:

(1)  the types of tutoring system functions each approach is best-suited for,
(2)  the amount of knowledge engineering effort required to implement an initial version of a given approach,
(3)  the amount of knowledge engineering effort required to calibrate the modeling component, and
(4)  the difficulty of programming the updating procedures.

It may well be, for example, that Bayesian student modeling is superior to our current fuzzy modeling scheme for problem selection, because of the greater mathematical rigor of Bayesian belief nets, and their bi-directional reasoning capability. However, this increased functionality might have to be bought at greater costs in terms of knowledge engineering and programming effort.

The difference in engineering effort might not be as great as we originally expected, however. In the first place, our fuzzy modeling component turned out to require more effort to prototype than we anticipated, and we expect the work required to calibrate the many parameter settings (eg., updating rates, and the weights in aggregation equations) to be substantial. If calibration remains difficult, then the marginal cost of implementing a Bayesian scheme could be low. Recent work in test theory provides some rigorous computational methods for deriving probability estimates (eg., [4, 28, 32, 47]) for Bayesian belief nets. However, *calibrating* these estimates might prove to be unwieldy, due to feedback loops. That is, it could be nearly impossible to assign blame correctly when estimated student knowledge states in the network fail to match human expert ratings. For example, if variable $B$, which depends upon variable $A$, appears to be inaccurate, is it because $A$'s prior probabilities are wrong, or is it because $B$ at some point made an incorrect prediction about $A$, which then "backfired" (propagated upwards) to $B$? Our future experiments with both modeling approaches will enable us to address these knowledge engineering complexity issues.

# 7 Summary and Conclusions

Our aim has been to further the development of an approach to imprecise modeling of student ability based upon fuzzy set theory (eg., [11, 18]). Technical concerns included minimizing the knowledge engineering effort required to initially develop and fine-tune the student modeling knowledge base, while also lessening computational (programming) complexity. Our main contribution so far has been in specifying and implementing relatively simple procedures that can dynamically update fuzzy (imprecise) probability distributions which represent student competence on discrete knowledge components. The adequacy of these procedures will be determined when the student modeling knowledge base and updating routines in **Sherlock II** have been calibrated, and the tutoring system is evaluated.

The adequacy of fuzzy set theory-based modeling approaches in general awaits our system's evaluation, and that of other systems which take this approach (eg., [8, 11, 18]). An evaluation of the approach should include comparisons with other student modeling approaches. Such comparisons should focus on the knowledge engineering effort needed to develop an initial version of the student modeling component within a given approach, and then to fine-tune it; the difficulty of implementing the approach; and, perhaps most importantly, how useful the approach is for different system functions (ie., coaching, versus curriculum planning, versus assessment, etc.). Other researchers (eg., [5, 22]) have stressed the importance of designing user modeling components by taking into account situational factors such as what the model will be used for, what the available human resources are, and what the developmental stage of the system (ie., prototype, or near-release) is. We believe that empirically validated comparisons of various approaches to student modeling - addressing functionality and engineering complexity issues such as those listed above - will better equip tutoring system designers to take these situational factors into account, and thereby make more informed decisions about which modeling approach (or combination of approaches) to take in their tutor.

The work on **Sherlock II** described in this chapter is funded by the United States Air Force. The funding agency and the collaborators acknowledged below do not necessarily endorse the views expressed.

# Acknowledgements

Sherlock II has been a collaborative effort by a team that has included (either currently or in the recent past) Marilyn Bunzo, Richard Eastman, Gary Eggan, Maria Gordin, Linda Greenberg, Edward Hughes, Sandra Katz, Susanne Lajoie, Alan Lesgold, Thomas McGinnis, Rudianto Prabowo, Govinda Rao, and Rose Rosenfeld. As with its predecessor, *Sherlock I,* Dr. Sherrie Gott and her colleagues at Air Force Human Resources, Armstrong Laboratories, are active contributors to the effort. We would especially like to thank Linda Greenberg for help with preparing the manuscript; Sharon Derry for many informative discussions about the work on fuzzy diagnosis and assessment that she has been doing with Lois Hawkes and her colleagues at Florida State University; the editors, and the reviewers for many insightful comments and helpful suggestions on an earlier version of the manuscript.

# References

1. Anderson, J. S., Boyle, C. F. & Reiser, B. J.: Intelligent tutoring systems. *Science,* 228, pp. 456-468 (1985)
2. Andreassen, S., Woldbye, M., Falck, B. & Andersen, S. K.: MUNIN: a causal probabilistic network for interpretation of electromyographic findings. Proceedings of the 10th International Joint Conference on Artificial Intelligence, Milan, Italy, pp. 366-372 1987
3. Becker, H. J.: Using computers for instruction. *Byte,* 12(2), pp. 149-291 (1987)
4. Bock, R. D. & Aitkin, M.: Marginal maximum likelihood estimation of item parameters: an application of an EM-algorithm. *Psychometrika,* 46, pp. 443-459 (1981)
5. Cahour, B. & Paris, C.: Role and use of user models. In: *Proceedings of the 12th International Joint Conference on Artificial Intelligence Workshop, W4: Agent Modelling for Intelligent Interaction,* Sydney, Australia, (J. Kay & A. Quilici, eds.). 1991
6. Charniak, E.: Bayesian networks without tears. *AI Magazine,* 12(4), pp. 50-63 (1991)
7. Cheeseman, P.: Probabilistic versus fuzzy reasoning. In: *Uncertainty in Artificial Intelligence* (L. N. Kanal & J. F. Lemmer, eds.). pp. 85-102, Esevier Science Publishers, North-Holland 1986
8. Chin, D. N.: KNOME: modeling what the user knows in UC. In: *User Models in Dialog Systems* (A. Kobsa & W. Wahlster, eds.). pp. 74-107. New York, NY: Springer-Verlag 1989
9. Cohen, P. R.: *Heuristic Reasoning About Uncertainty.* Boston: Pitman Advanced Pub. Program 1985
10. Cohen, P. R., Perrault, C. R. & Allen, J. F.: Beyond question answering. In: *Strategies for Natural Language Processing* (W. G. Lehnert & M. Ringle, eds.), pp. 245-274 Hillsdale, NJ: Lawrence Erlbaum Associates 1982
11. Derry, S. J. & Hawkes, L. W.: Toward fuzzy diagnostic assessment of metacognitive knowledge and growth. Paper presented at the annual meeting of the American Educational Research Association, San Francisco, CA 1992
12. DuBois, D. & Prade, H.: *Fuzzy Sets and Systems: Theory and Applications.* New York, NY: Academic Press 1979
13. DuBois, D. & Prade, H.: Necessity measures and the resolution principle, *IEEE Transactions on Systems, Man and Cybernetics,* 17, pp. 474-78 (1987)
14. Elsom-Cook, M.: Guided discovery tutoring. Preprint for Nato Workshop on Guided Discovery Tutoring, Italy 1989
15. Greer, J. E. & McCalla, G. I.: A computational framework for granularity and its application to educational diagnosis. Proceedings of the 11th International Joint Conference on Artificial Intelligence, Detroit, MI Vol. 1, pp. 477-82 1989

124

16. Greer, J. E., McCalla, G. I. & Mark, M. A.: Incorporating granularity-based recognition into SCENT. In: *Proceedings of the 4th International Conference on Artificial Intelligence and Education*, Amsterdam (D. Bierman, J. Breuker & J. Sandberg, eds.)., pp. 107-115. Amsterdam: IOS 1989
17. Hativa, N. & Lesgold, A.: The computer as a tutor--can it adapt to the individual learner? *Instructional Science*, 20, pp. 49-78 (1991)
18. Hawkes, L. W., Derry, S. J. & Rundensteiner, E. A.: Individualized tutoring using an intelligent fuzzy temporal relational database. *International Journal of Man-Machine Studies*, 33, pp. 409-429 (1990)
19. Kass, R.: Building a user model implicitly from a cooperative advisory dialog. Paper presented at the 2nd International Workshop on User Modeling, Honolulu, HI 1990
20. Katz, S. & Lesgold, A.: Modeling the student in Sherlock II. In: *Proceedings of the 12th International Joint Conference on Artificial Intelligence Workshop, W.4: Agent Modelling for Intelligent Interaction*, Sydney, Australia (J. Kay & A. Quilici, eds.). pp. 73-80, 1991
21. Katz, S. & Lesgold, A.: Self-adjusting curriculum planning in Sherlock II. Paper presented at the 4th International Conference on Computers and Learning, Wolfville, Nova Scotia 1992
22. Kay, J.: Generalised user modelling shells—a taxonomy. In: *Proceedings of the 12th International Joint Conference on Artificial Intelligence. Workshop W.4: Agent Modelling for Intelligent Interaction*, Sydney, Australia (J. Kay & A. Quilici, eds.). pp. 169-85, 1991
23. Lajoie, S. P. & Derry, S. J.: Introduction. *In: Computers as Cognitive Tools* (S. P. Lajoie & S. Derry, eds.). Hillsdale, NJ: Lawrence Erlbaum Associates (in press)
24. Lajoie, S. P. & Lesgold, A.: Apprenticeship training in the workplace: computer-coached practice environments as a new form of apprenticeship, *Machine-Mediated Learning*, 3, pp. 7-28 (1989)
25. Lesgold, A. M., Eggan, G., Katz, S. & Rao, G.: Possibilities for assessment using computer-based apprenticeship environments. To appear in: *Cognitive approaches to automated instruction* (W. Regian & V. Shute, eds.). Hillsdale, NJ: Lawrence Erlbaum Associates (in press)
26. Lesgold, A. M., Lajoie, S. P., Logan, D. & Eggan, G.: Applying cognitive task analysis and research methods to assessment. In: *Diagnostic Monitoring of Skill and Knowledge Acquisition* (N. Frederiksen, R. Glaser, A.M. Lesgold & M. Shafto, eds.). Hillsdale, NJ: Lawrence Erlbaum Associates 1990
27. Lesgold, A. M. & Lajoie, S. P.: Complex problem solving in electronics. In: *Complex Problem Solving: Principles and Mechanisms* (R. Sternberg & P. A. Frensch, eds.). Hillsdale, NJ: Lawrence Erlbaum Associates 1990
28. Lewis, C.: Estimating individual abilities with imperfectly known item response function. Paper presented at the Annual Meeting of the Psychometric Society, Nashville, TN, 1985
29. McCalla, G. I., Greer, J. E., Barrie, B. & Pospisil, P.: Granularity hierarchies.*International Journal of Computers and Mathematics with Applications (Special Issue on Semantic Networks)*, pp. 363-375 (1992)
30. McCalla, G. & Greer, J. E.: Enhancing the robustness of model-based recognition. Paper presented at the 3rd International Workshop on User Modeling, Wadern, Germany 1992
31. McArthur, D., Stasz, C. & Zmuidzinas, M.: Tutoring techniques in algebra. *Cognition and Instruction*, 7(3), pp. 197-244 (1990)
32. Mislevy, R. J.: *Randomization-Based Inference About Latent Variables from Complex Samples*. Psychometrika (in press)
33. Mitchell, T. M., Keller, R. M. & Kedar-Cabelli, S. T.: Explanation-based generalization: a unifying view. *Machine Learning*, 1, pp. 47-80 (1986)
34. Moore, J. D.: A Reactive Approach to Explanation in Expert and Advice-Giving Systems. PhD thesis, University of California, Los Angeles, CA, 1989
35. Morawski, P.: Understanding bayesian belief networks. *AI Expert*, May, pp. 44-48 (1989)
36. Nichols, P., Pokorny, R., Jones, G., Gott, S. P. & Alley, W. E.: Evaluation of an Avionics Troubleshooting Tutoring System. Special Report. Brooks Air Force Base, TX: Air Force Human Resources Laboratory (in press)
37. Ohlsson, S.: Some principles of intelligent tutoring. In: *Artificial Intelligence and Education* (R. W. Lawler & M. Yazdani, eds.), pp. 203-238 Norwood, NJ: Ablex Publishing 1987
38. Owen, E. & Sweller, J.: What do students learn while solving mathematics problems? *Journal of Educational Psychology*, 77(3), pp. 272-284 (1985)
39. Pearl, J.: Evidential reasoning under uncertainty. In: *Exploring Artificial Intelligence: Survey Talks from the National Conferences on Artificial Intelligence* (H. E. Shrobe & the American Association for Artificial Intelligence, eds.), pp. 381-418. San Mateo, CA: Morgan Kaufmann 1988
40. Pearl, J. : *Probabilistic Reasoning in Aartificial Intelligence: Networks of Plausible Inference*. San Mateo, CA: Morgan Kaufmann 1988
41. Pokorny, B. & Gott, S. P.: The Evaluation of a Real-World Instructional System: Using Technical Experts as Raters. Technical Report. Brooks Air Force Base: Air Force Human Resources (in press)
42. Putnam, R. T.: Structuring and adjusting content for students: a study of live and simulated tutoring of addition. *American Educational Research Journal*, 24(1), pp. 13-48 (1987)

43. Schwartz, D.: Outline of a naive semantics for reasoning with qualitative linguistic information. Proceedings of the 11th International Joint Conference on Artificial Intelligence, Detroit, MI, Vol. 1, pp. 20-25, 1989
44. Self, J. A.: Bypassing the intractable problem of student modeling. In: *Intelligent Tutoring Systems: At The Crossroads of Artificial Intelligence and Education* (C. Frasson & G. Gauthier, eds.) pp. 107-123. Norwood, NJ: Ablex 1990
45. Sweller, J.: Cognitive load during problem solving: effects on learning. *Cognitive Science*, 12, pp. 257-285 (1988)
46. Sweller, J. & Cooper, G. A.: The use of worked examples as a substitute for problem solving in learning algebra. *Cognition and Instruction*, 2(1), pp. 59-89 (1985)
47. Tsutakawa, R. K. & Johnson, J.: The effect of uncertainty of item parameter estimation on ability estimates. *Psychometrika*, 55, pp. 371-90 (1990)
48. VanLehn, K.: Toward a theory of impasse-driven learning. In: *Learning Issues for Intelligent Tutoring Systems* (H. Mandl & A. Lesgold, eds.) pp. 19-42. New York, NY: Springer-Verlag 1988
49. Villano, M.: Probabalistic student models: bayesian belief networks and knowledge space theory. Paper presented at the 2nd International Conference on Intelligent Tutoring Systems, Montreal, Quebec 1988
50. Vygotsky, L. S.: *Mind in Society*. Cambridge, MA: Harvard University Press 1978
51. Zadeh, L. A.: Fuzzy sets. *Information and Control*, 8, pp. 338-353 (1965)
52. Zadeh, L. A.: The concept of a linguistic variable and its application to approximate reasoning, Part I: *Information Science*, 8, pp. 199-249; Part II: *Information Science*, 8, pp. 301-357; Part III: *Information Science*, 9, pp. 43-80 (1975)
53. Zadeh, L. A.: Fuzzy sets as a basis for a theory of possibility. *Fuzzy Sets and Systems*, 1, pp. 3-28 (1978)
54. Zadeh, L. A.: Outline of a theory of usuality based on fuzzy logic. In: *Fuzzy Sets: Theory and Applications* (A. Jones, A. Kaufmann & H. J. Zimmerman, eds.) Dordrecht: Reidel 1986
55. Zemankova-Leech, M. & Kandel, A.: *Fuzzy Relational Data Bases—a Key to Expert Systems*, Köln TÜV Rheinland/Springer-Verlag 1984

# Using Machine Learning to Advise a Student Model[1]

Beverly Park Woolf and Tom Murray

Department of Computer Science, University of Massachusetts, Amherst, MA USA

**Abstract:** Human learning is complex, dynamic, and non-monotonic. Currently it cannot be accurately modeled or measured, and present-day student models are too simplistic and too static to reason effectively about it. This paper explores several machine learning mechanisms which might enhance the functionality of a student model. Human learning experiments are described demonstrating the spontaneous nature of learning, for which action-oriented student model components are needed. An existing student model, built as part of a physics tutoring system, is described which begins to handle non-monotonic reasoning, makes little commitment to a static model of student knowledge, and uses a Multi-layered representation of inferences about student knowledge. The paper asks how a learning mechanism might inform such a student model and represent the dynamicism and spontaneity of human learning.

**Keywords:** machine learning, non-monotonic reasoning, physics tutoring

## 1 Overview

Human learning is dynamic, spontaneous, and unpredictable; it can be contradictory and uncertain in some situations while robust and predictable in others. A mechanism such as a 'student model,' which proposes to assess human learning, will need information at a great enough "bandwidth" to make reliable inferences about the complex activities involved in human learning. In addition, inferences made about human learninglearning:humanmight have to be retracted at a later time and the system will have to reason about what was actually learned and what was incorrectly presumed to have been learned.

Few AI systems exhibit recursive learning (hierarchical use of past learning). "Invention" in the Piagetian sense is almost non-existent. Many AI systems are brittle (input which deviates

---

[1]This chapter also appeared in the *Journal of Artificial Intelligence in Education*, 3(4), pp. 429 (1993). Reprinted with permission of the Association for the Advancement of Computing in Education (AACE, P.O. Box 2966, Charlottesville, VA 22920 USA).

from the rules will be rejected). We suggest that behavior of a student model not be based on inferences from axioms, but rather result from learning and case-based reasoning based on a vast array of examples (cases) encoded in the system. These cases (due to limited experience) cannot constitute a completely consistent axiom-based logical system. We suggest that learning is case-based, explanation-based chunking, or that cases can be used to acquire new operations, new representations, and indeed whole new problem specifications.

In this paper we argue that machine learning be incorporated into a student model and inductive processes be added to deductive reasoning to account for human inconsistency, spontaneity, and forgetting. The mechanism will have to make assumptions and diagnostic decisions about a student's knowledge, update information about the modelling process, and improve its own diagnostic power. Just as a new teacher must *learn* to evaluate and diagnose student behavior and decide which are the best analogies or examples to present at specific times, so a student model must *learn* how to evaluate a specific student and make decisions about the presentation of instructional material. A new teacher requires time to observe master teachers before he or she becomes an effective teacher. Similarly, a student model requires a learning mechanism and a large amount of knowledge about conventional and nontraditional student behavior, alternative teaching strategies, and how to assess teaching decisions, before it becomes effective as a component of a tutoring system.

This paper describes some human learning experiments which demonstrate the dynamic and spontaneous nature of learning. A student model within a current tutoring system is discussed, showing rudimentary non-monotonicity and allowing for uncertainty in knowledge about the student. This student model does not now have a learning model, and we describe several machine learning mechanisms which might be used to improve its functionality.

## 2 Observations About Human Learning

Human learning is dynamic and appears to proceed in a specific order, involving several unique thresholds. Piaget hypothesized that learning is a function of a schema or internal representation built by an organism for each concept [10]. Bruner suggested that humans hold multiple such schemas at distinct periods of their life [1]. Improved performance (learning) is suggested to result from spontaneous upgrading of a particular schema. In Piaget's experiments, researchers presented children with models of situations in which children naturally experiment, eg., liquid in a bottle or a series of rods. Figures 1 and 2 show a variety of drawings produced by children of different ages when asked to draw a situation (top of each figure) both during the experiment and then again six months later *without* seeing the experimental set-up during the lapsed time. The age at which children comprehended each phenomenon varied based on the phenomenon.

For instance, understanding of horizontality of liquids is achieved at around 9 years. Figure 1 shows decanters filled with water filled and covered. Drawings made from long term memory are shown in order of increasing accuracy and age. Children improved in their drawings based on the age at which they first saw the situation, thus children between 5 and 7 improved 30% in their drawings. The greatest improvement was found in children who were first tested several years younger than the stage at which understanding of the concept is suggested to occur. Through such experiments, a hypothesis of spontaneous readjustment, growth and contradiction was first supported in areas of human learning from geometry to ethics. Such research suggests that a student model should be able to represent spontaneous change and constant growth in addition to the concept of gradual and reasoned learning.

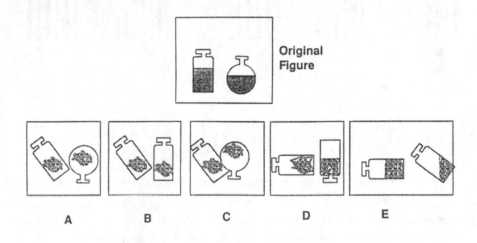

Figure 1:  Knowledge about horizontality of liquids

Human learning is also "deeply and unavoidably" non-monotonic [11]. Information about what a person understands is always subject to revision. Suppose that a student exhibits some knowledge about physics, specifically Newton's third law. Does he or she then also understand which forces are involved in this law? You may assume, since Newton's law involves resulting equal and opposite forces, that the student probably understands simple cases involving force and movement. A little reflection shows this isn't necessarily true, since the student might have memorized a formula for Newton's laws and in fact not understood about forces themselves. On the other hand, it seems to be a "plausible inference" of a not-too-daring sort that we make all the time to avoid complete skepticism [2]. A computerized teacher will need to make robust assumptions and plausible inferences about a student's knowledge which can also be overturned if necessary.

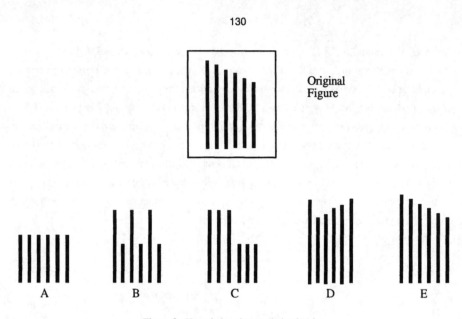

Figure 2: Knowledge about ordering by size

## 3 Constraints on a Student Model

Observations about human learning constrain the design of a student model. We have shown that the model should reflect a student's changing knowledge, spontaneous reorganization of that knowledge and changes in its own beliefs about that knowledge. It should also generate non-persistent inferences which can later be overturned. It should continually reassess student knowledge and expect dynamic movement through stages.

Traditional inferencing mechanisms in computer science allow plausible inferences which cannot be easily removed. Thus if we had rules in a student model that said knowledge of Newton's Third Law implies knowledge of force, such a student model might infer that a student knows about force even after exhibiting a lack of knowledge about forces. Even if we added a new axiom that said if a person cannot express (through vectors) the forces in a static situation then that person does not understand force, this new axiom would not erase the initial inference made by the system.

A logic in which a conclusion stands no matter what new facts are added is called *monotonic* [2]. Classical formal systems are all monotonic. This means they cannot possibly capture inferences about student knowledge since human learning is replete with cases where new inferences contradict earlier inferences. Similarly the following reasoning is impossible for a traditional system:

> Freda is a professor of Psychology. Therefore, Freda has a graduate degree in
> Psychology. Of course, maybe she hasn't. If we are told by a trustworthy source
> that she hasn't, we just withdraw the conclusion.

In this case, new information causes an old conclusion to be withdrawn. Such a reasoning system is non-monotonic[2].

Figure 3 represents knowledge units in both a domain network and in a student model. Changes in a student's learning should be represented in the student model. Alternative tutorial interactions are listed on the left, including communication, analogical reasoning, and reflection. A learner might not be knowledgeable about a particular concept (top of Figure 3) and ask for explanations, definitions or hints. In this case, the student model should deduce that the student does not understand the topic based on the questions asked or the unknown concepts discussed. Alternatively, a student might have overgeneralized a concept (middle of Figure 3) and the tutor might suggest the use of an analogy to persuade the student, or patch or differentiate critical factors. Finally the student might just need time to reflect, reorganize or resolve impasse;s (bottom of Figure 3). In this case, the tutor should get out of the way and through an interactive environment allow the student to experiment, providing a simple question to analyze changes in the student's knowledge. A student frequently learns through impasse and his or her response to that impasse. In such a case, the student should be placed in a situation to acquire expertise for him or herself.

Current student models attempt a kind of "dead reckoning" reasoning:  calculate a diagnosis of current student knowledge and act on it. Such results are often formulated in a static and deterministic manner. Protocols of human learning are frequently compared to an assumed or predicted mechanism, when in fact, empirically-based student data does not compare well with model-based actions. Efforts to validate student models are ill-advised.

We propose a more action-oriented student model. Rather than rendering a diagnosis and a prescription for further action, a student model might integrate its reasoning and action with that of traditional reasoning mechanisms. For instance, a paradigm of 'lazy planning' [7] in which reasoning and action are interleaved is a possibility. The student model might reason a little, act a little, assess a little. It might sketch a plan of action (diagnosis and prescribed strategy), execute a small portion of this plan, assess the effectiveness of the plan, and then reformulate its goal. Such a formulation would be more efficient and by being action-oriented, the system would teach only when appropriate.

---

[2]Even in cases in which the inference is technically monotonic, like playing chess, in practice a program must choose a move after a bounded length of time; increasing the length of time allowed for making a decision could change the system's conclusion. In such a case the program may be thought of as using a non-monotonic approximation of the "real" theory.

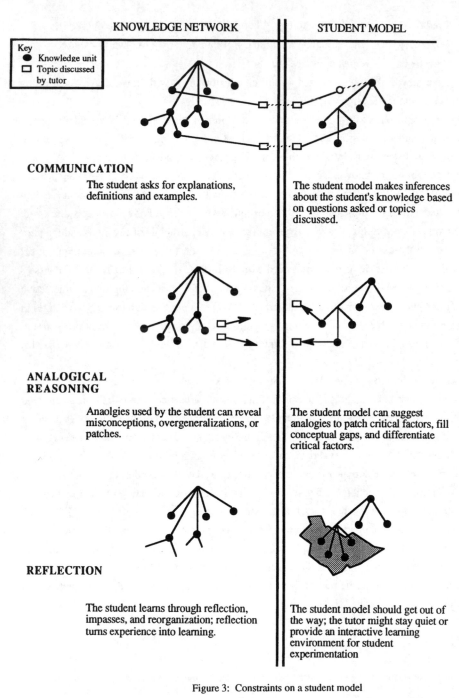

KNOWLEDGE NETWORK                    STUDENT MODEL

Key
● Knowledge unit
☐ Topic discussed
   by tutor

**COMMUNICATION**

The student asks for explanations, definitions and examples.

The student model makes inferences about the student's knowledge based on questions asked or topics discussed.

**ANALOGICAL REASONING**

Anaolgies used by the student can reveal misconceptions, overgeneralizations, or patches.

The student model can suggest analogies to patch critical factors, fill conceptual gaps, and differentiate critical factors.

**REFLECTION**

The student learns through reflection, impasses, and reorganization; reflection turns experience into learning.

The student model should get out of the way; the tutor might stay quiet or provide an interactive learning environment for student experimentation

Figure 3: Constraints on a student model

# 4 A Student Model with Rudimentary Non-monotonic Reasoning

In this section we describe a student model which begins to handle non-monotonic reasoning, makes little commitment to a static model of student knowledge, and uses a Multi-layered representation of inferences about student knowledge. This student model does not yet have a learning component, although it is relatively unconstrained and could incorporate a learning mechanism such as that described in the next section. It was developed within a large physics tutoring system described elsewhere (eg., see [8, 9]) which focused on developing a knowledge acquisition interface for tutoring knowledge. In this section we describe design considerations and architecture of the student model.

## 4.1 Building a Student Model: Design Considerations

We propose a minimalist approach to building a student model. Since the problem of student modeling is so complex, and since only piecemeal solutions have been demonstrated thus far, designers should carefully consider both the intended uses of a student model and the limitations and tradeoffs inherent in the technology at their disposal. Designers often attempt to model too much or too deeply, or to build complex mechanisms which infer information about the student's state that a) will not actually be used by the end system, or b) will be too uncertain or abstract to be effectively used. Two closely related design issues are knowledge representation and diagnostic inference; ie., a system cannot diagnose what it can't represent, and should not represent what it cannot make inferences about. In designing the student model's knowledge representation a decision must be made about *what* will be represented (eg., student mastery, types of knowledge, behavior history, certainty levels, student goals, preferences, etc.), and *how* these entities will be represented (eg., by frames, networks, rules, etc.). In designing the diagnostic mechanism, a decision must be made about what can be *measured* (eg., the nature of the raw data) and what *diagnostic technique* to use (eg., model tracing, plan recognition, etc.--- see [14]).

Unless the goal is to do research on student modeling[3], the student model should be only complex enough to meet the foreseen needs. In the system discussed here, the focus was on knowledge acquisition of instructional contentand strategies;, and the potential of a student model was evaluated in this context. Useful lists of student model functions or purposes have been given by others [12, 14, 15]. Our system does not attempt to build a cognitively accurate

---

[3]For the purpose of this discussion, people designing student models fall into two groups: a) those doing research in student (or user) modeling, and b) those doing research in other aspects of tutoring, e.g., domain knowledge or tutoring strategy.

model of the student's mental states of thoughts, so the following **student model purposes**, listed from most essential to least essential to our project, are based on pragmatic, rather than theoretical, considerations.

1. **Prevent unwanted repetition.** Minimally, the student model keeps a record of what the tutor has done, what the student has seen, or what the student is assumed to know, in order to prevent instructional material from being given repeatedly (unless the repetition is intentional). This record keeping answers the question "Has the student *been given* X?"

2. **Present information at an appropriate level.** The most important purpose of most student models is to infer answers to the question "Does the student *know* X?" We use this information to present instructional material that is neither too boring (easy) nor too complex (difficult).

3. **Facilitate remediation.** Student models can represent common bugs or misconceptions. This helps the tutor remediate bugs or misconceptions or postpone teaching a topic until a misconception has been cleared up.

4. **Parameterizing tutorial behavior.** The information in a student model can support decisions to alter the style of presentations, determine the number of hints given, the need to interrupt a student's task with advice, or whether to give summaries after each topic.

5. **Adapt the content of information presented.** Information in the student model can support decisions about the content of real-time generated communications, as in the generation of problems and explanations that have features matched to the student's strengths and weaknesses.

6. **Compare student behavior with expert or novice behavior.** The student model can be represented in executable form, so that it can be 'run' to compare student behavior with what an expert would have done, or to view how a student would behave in particular situation, such as when a particular skill bug is present. Though this feature was not important to us for this project, it is the key element of many student models.

The tutoring system described in this section required a student model that supported the first four facilities above. A "discourse model" which recorded the actions of the student and tutor was used to prevent unwanted repetition (#1 above). An overlay student model performed inferencing for presenting information at the appropriate level (#2 above). A library of objects called "Mis-knowledge-units" represented incorrect facts, misconceptions, and buggy skills (#3 above).[4] Finally, parameterized action networks and tutoring strategies (#4 above) adapted student information at several levels of granularity.

---

[4]Traditionally, overlay student models assign a simple symbolic or numeric value for each topic or skill, indicating whether the student is assumed to know that topic or skill.

Our student model had several features not found in traditional models. First, a layered representation and inferencing architecture allowed more precision, expressiveness, and flexibility in diagnostic reasoning. Second, the model had rudimentary, yet effective, mechanisms for dealing with uncertainty and non-monotonicity. These features are discussed after a brief description of the teaching purpose of the system.

## 4.2 Involving Teachers in the Design of Tutors

The tutor described here was designed primarily to assist teachers in on-line transfer of their physics knowledge to an intelligent tutor. A framework based on graphic user interfaces was developed to support considerable teacher involvement in the design and construction of the computer tutor. The framework was used by three educators (non-programmers) who logged more than 300 hours of curriculum design and debugging and found the framework easy to use. The physics tutor design focused on issues of knowledge representation and acquisition. Involvement of educators in these processes is important because insights, principles, and rules used in machine tutors should originate from a rich synthesis of learning and instructional theories, insights from practicing teachers and on-line experimentation.

Using the interface, teachers were able to debug, update, and expand system knowledge "pieces" for topics, examples, hints, prerequisites, etc.; they also created or modified the strategies that determined how the tutor will behave. Development of this system illustrated the need for consideration about epistemological, pedagogical, and cognitive issues before and during the design of an intelligent tutor.

The physics tutor gave students a qualitative, intuitive understanding of the relationships between forces in static (non-motion) situations. The topic network of about 40 topics focused on Newton's Third Law, linear equilibrium, the properties of different types of forces (tension, gravity, and contact forces), and how to evaluate free body diagrams. Part of the curriculum centered around a learning environment called the "crane boom" in which the student manipulated a simulated physical system and observed the resulting forces and force components.

## 4.3 Multiple Layers in the Student Model

In order to deal with uncertainty, change, contradictions, inconsistencies, and assumptions in student knowledge, the student model for the physics tutor consisted of multiple layers and a bug library. Non-monotonic reasoning was supported in a rudimentary way by generation of non-persistent inferences which could be overturned based on later inference driven by subsequent student behavior. Recorded data ("raw data") included only information with no uncertainty, such as the actual student response or number of examples provided. In this way, inferences made about the level of a student's knowledge of a single topic could change over time irrespective of the student's actual performance while explicitly learning that topic. For example, a presentation might be used to teach topic #1 and then the same presentation used to teach topic #2. The student's presumed knowledge of topic #1 might increase as a result of revisiting a presentation even though topic #1 was not itself the reason for re-introducing the presentation.

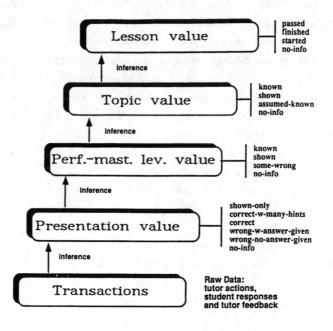

Figure 4: Layered student model

**Multi-layered inferencing**. The student model employed five layers of data and/or inferencing: lesson, topic, performance-mastery (corresponding to performance and mastery levels within topics), presentation (the activity presented by the tutor and associated with a student task or question), and transaction (individual student and tutor actions), as shown in Figure 4. The value of objects at each layer was constrained to a set of symbolic values. For example, *presentations* had a value of no-info, shown-only, correct-with-many-hints, correct, wrong-with-answer-given, or wrong-no-answer-given. The value at any layer was calculated using a symbolic function with arguments (input) from the next lower layer. For example, the value of a performance-mastery level was determined by a function which takes as input value any of the presentation values listed above, eg., no-info and shown-only and produces as output values such as known, shown, some-wrong, or no-info. The set of allowed values for each level was defined to cover the needs of the "rules" invented by the domain expert and knowledge engineer. For example, the domain expert wanted a topic marked as "known" if most of its performance-mastery level values were "known," but a few skills could be "wrong." Thus the performance-mastery level has values of some-wrong as well as known and shown.

**Reasoning with uncertainty**. The language used to express knowledge in this student model explicitly represented and reasoned with uncertainty [3]. For example, we incorporated the terms "no-info," "shown," and "assumed" into the representational language. "Shown" was used to indicate that a topic or presentation (or a part of one) was presented to the student and that not enough evidence had accumulated to determine whether the student did or did not know the topic or presentation. The domain expert or teacher might initialize the student model with some topics assumed to be known and the system might then accumulate evidence to the contrary. The "familiarity" value represents the fact that the system has uncertainty about student knowledge about a topic (it indicates that the topic has been introduced but the student has not yet answered questions relative to the topic). The "suspected" Mis-knowledge-unit value also represents system uncertainty, as compared with the "confirmed" Mis-knowledge-units value.

**Non-monotonic reasoning**. Non-monotonic reasoning involves making inferences which may have to be abandoned in light of new information. Non-monotonic reasoning is needed because 1) running the tutor may contradict assumptions made by the teacher about initial student knowledge and 2) student knowledge changes during the session. When the tutor tried to teach a topic (giving the student the presentations associated with it) it inferred the level of the student's understanding of the topic based on how well he or she did on the topic's component presentations. But these same presentations may be given again for other reasons, such as for teaching a second topic, or from a student initiative (the student asks to be given the presentation). Therefore evidence of the student's understanding of a topic might change even though the topic itself is not explicitly taught. By not storing or caching inferences, each deduction made by the system always refers to the most recent student behavior. Raw data stored in the transaction layer (see Figure 4) includes only information with no uncertainty, such as the student responses to answers, the number of hints given, etc. By allowing inferences to flow from the raw data up the data layers every time a student behavior is recorded, inferences about a student's knowledge of a topic may change over time even though that topic may not have been visited[5].

---

[5]Recalculating values every time they are accessed has not affected the response time of the tutor perceptibly.

# 5  Machine Learning

The student model described above does not 'learn,' although a machine learning mechanism might be added to enhance its tutoring behavior. In this section we describe two machine learning systems, one an early example-based system and the other an explanation-based learning system. We ask how these computer learning mechanisms might inform us about encoding the dynamicism and spontaneity of human learning. In the next section we describe how such learning mechanisms might be included in an intelligent tutor.

## 5.1  Learning from Examples

Winston's system learned about concepts, such as an arch, from a series of examples and near-misses [16]. Figure 5 shows input required for the program to decide that an arch is made from a brick or wedge supported by two bricks which do not touch. This system had two powerful features which are important for machine learning: 1) some prerequisite or pre-knowledge is required; and 2) no learning took place until primitive knowledge, such as the concepts "straight line" or "next-to" were encoded.

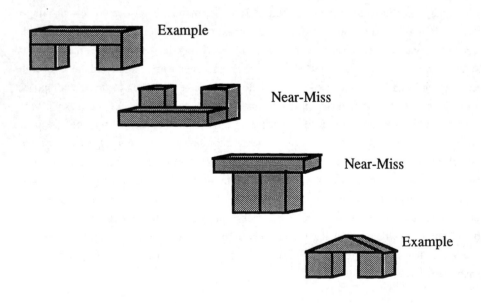

Figure 5:  A Mechanism to learn about arches [16]

This system had an axiomatic knowledge base in which a clear distinction was made between primitive concepts and defined concepts. Assimilation, or a transient modification of each schema, took place with each new example. An internal representation of an arch was updated when the system learned more about the definition of an arch (Figure 6). Interestingly, more information was garnered when a "near-miss" was presented (Figures 6 and 7) than when a prototypical example was presented. Then new information was generalized and the schema updated accordingly.

INITIAL SAMPLE

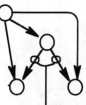

IS-SUPPORTED-BY

NEAR MISS

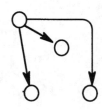

NEAR MISS

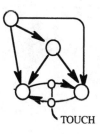

TOUCH

Figure 6: Internal representation of an arch and a near miss [16]

Note that only strong features were learned by this system. Irrelevant features were lost, while noisy data and subtle features could not be learned. Knowledge in this system was declarative; ie., an arch could be described but the rules for constructing an arch, including the steps needed to build one, were not immediately available.

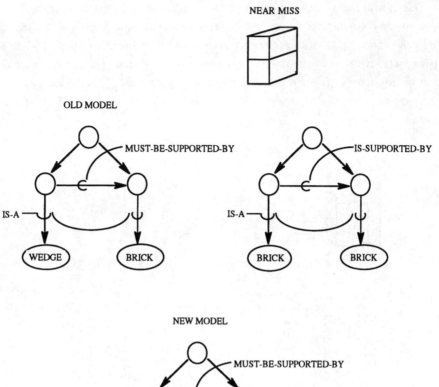

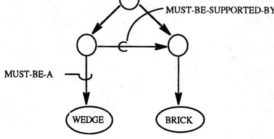

Figure 7: Adding knowledge based on a near miss [16]

This learning mechanism is a simple first approximation for machine learning which can be used in a student model. For instance, such a mechanism might observe several cases of student learning and non-learning and make deductions about plausible student knowledge and effective pedagogical principles. Implementing such machine learning inside a student model is proposed in a later section.

## 5.2 Explanation-Based Learning

A second mechanism to use for implementing machine learning in a student model is explanation-based learning (EBL), a kind of learning from observation [5]. It allows a system to acquire general knowledge through analysis of a few specific examples. Here background knowledge plays a crucial role in the analysis process.

EBL provides a way to incorporate pre-existing knowledge, and begins with a high-level target concept, eg. does a student understand a specific topic, and a set of training examples. Let's assume the student answered questions #40 and #43 correctly and these questions concern topic X. Then, using a domain theory (a set of axioms describing the domain), EBL would generate an explanation of why the particular training sequence of correct answers is an instance of the target -- ie. understanding topic X. The explanation provided by the system is proof that the training example satisfies the target example [6].

**THE FAR SIDE**
By GARY LARSON

"Hey! Look what Zog do!"

Figure 8: Early use of explanation based learning

Figure 8 (from [4]. The Far Side cartoon by Gary Larson is reprinted by permission of Chronicle Features, San Francisco, CA. All rights reserved.) provides an early instance of explanation-based learning. Zog is an advanced thinker and has discovered something entirely new: a cooking skewer. The smartest of the three gentlemen in the foreground has noticed Zog's invention, learned from it, and will no doubt adopt it to prevent further burned fingers.

Many AI learning systems try to learn as did Zog using original creative problem solving for difficult world problems. This is beyond current AI technology. EBL, on the other hand, is a process which attempts to acquire new concepts by observing, as did the gentlemen in the foreground, instances or examples in which someone else more intelligent has already made some discovery. There are three steps to learning via this method:

1) observe instances of the concept or procedure;
2) explain how or why the procedure or concept works; and
3) generalize the explanation of the single observed instance into a useful, broadly-applicable problem-solving concept.

Thus the person in the foreground noticed the invention. He appreciated the generality of Zog's cleverness and recognized, for instance, that the skewer will work for a variety of meats and reptiles. And he probably understood the limitation of the invention and would for instance not try to use a skewer for supporting a giant turtle egg.

The determining feature of an EBL system is not the presence of an explanation; rather it is how the explanation is used that qualifies a system as taking an EBL approach [4]. Each EBL system uses the explanation of a very few examples to define the boundaries of a concept or process, such as "student understands the concept". The concept's definition is determined by an inspection of why it worked, not by similarities and differences between this example and previous instances.

Why is EBL appropriate for a student model? Because an EBL mechanism should begin with a rich knowledge base of student behavior and inferences made by master teachers. The explanations to be constructed by the learning system would arise from observation of the large number of examples of student behavior along with observations and assessments made by expert teachers of the *presumed* knowledge of each student. Ultimately, the student model would assess the student's behavior as might a very experienced teacher. EBL is a type of apprenticeship learning, eg. it requires knowledge about many students and many situations, and thus is an appropriate approach to becoming a good teacher. It provides a way to encode in the student model some examples of student activity, pedagogical materials supplied by a teacher and evaluations by master teachers on the effectiveness of the materials. Thus a human expert would inform the student model about presumed student knowledge. The student model would learn to make similar assessments at a later time. Apprenticeship learning is key to being a good teacher and an extended period of close observation of an established master is key to its successful application.

# 6   A Possible Scenario Using Machine Learning

Initially, a learning mechanism might identify pedagogical materials, such as examples or questions, that seem in retrospect to have "enabled" correct student responses to conceptual questions. During processing, such a mechanism might annotate effective sequences of materials within the knowledge base in order to improve a system's ability to select more appropriate materials during subsequent sessions with users.

Consider a learning mechanism based on EBL but with a slight example-based component as in Winston's Learning System. The initial background knowledge might consist of rules about how people interact with materials when forming new concepts. This background knowledge might contain descriptive features about user activities, such as questions asked, evaluations of answers, and student modification of variables. Human concept formation might be first described as patterns of correct and purposeful activity in the environment. This background knowledge, together with general knowledge about evidence of concept possession, form the mechanism's domain theory. A large number of examples would be provided to the mechanism to be embellished and interpreted using the background knowledge. The mechanism would then produce hypotheses about the characteristics that materials should possess to be effective for promoting concept formation. Materials and sequences of materials that seem to most clearly enable concept formation would be annotated in the knowledge base and further tested.

**Multi-Level Architecture**. The task under investigation is sufficiently complex that we would need a learning mechanism that uses a multi-level architecture such as that developed by Soloway [13]. Such an architecture would permit analysis of the problem at several levels as shown in Figure 9, perhaps 1) pattern matching, 2) attention focusing, 3) hypothesis generation, 4) hypothesis generalization, and 5) knowledge base modification, where each level would be tailored to match the requirements of the subproblem.

The learning mechanism might move from one level of description to another [13]. For instance, at a low level it might interpret isolated events, such as the user answers questions or modifies parameters. This is input data and is non-intentional. At a higher level, the mechanism might move to a new description of those same events which includes new features such as "concept formation." This is an intentional (purposive) level of interpretation which corresponds to making inferences about human concept formation. The non-intentional levels (at the lower levels) describe the inferred cognitive changes (eg. a correct answer is evidence of possible knowledge).

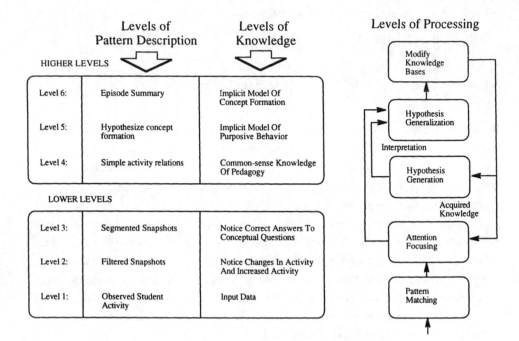

Figure 9: A possible learning mechanism, adapted from [13]

The higher levels of inferencing would make observations concerning whether or not a student can comprehend a concept after extensive and deliberate activity. By equipping the learning mechanism with some interpretation of student activities (expressed as background domain knowledge), it can infer a causal relationship between student modifications of parameters and concept formation based on the student's answers.

The following generalized behavior pattern, encoded as a rule, might be included as background knowledge: a student engages in increased, more purposeful, and more directed activity as he or she forms new concepts. Other general schemas about purposeful activity would permit the system to hypothesize about formation processes. For example, the following will help assess whether or not the student is involved in concept formation: the student is involved in exploration in the domain, he or she asks questions or responds to the tutor's questions, and persistent activity is observed. At this point the learning mechanism might make an assessment about whether or not the student has formed new concepts.

145

# 7 Discussion

Student modeling can be seen as a mapping from observed student behavior to hypotheses about that student's mental state. This is a complex process and beyond the ability of current technology. We have proposed that learning mechanisms might be used to provide a more powerful observational and inferential component to existing student models. We described a student model which was not very general, especially in its vocabulary and diagnostic mechanisms, but one which allows for non-monotonic reasoning. We suggested a possible Explanation-Based Learning mechanism extension to an existing student model.

As a community, we know little about modeling observable human behavior and identifying parameters of mental states in learning. In specific cases, such as the statics domain, we believe we can know more about cognitive processing by building and testing limited and focused systems. As we learn more about individual domains, we can begin to build useful student models. As we understand more about human cognition, we can begin to incorporate machine learning into a system's reasoning ability.

One step towards developing an AI theory about student models is to characterize representations and reasoning of such models in specific cases. Our goal in this research has been to generate a few data points useful in this characterization. We propose that in order to develop an AI theory, an empirical approach is needed. The process of developing such theories is still imperfectly understood. However, methods which appear to be effective must be examined to identify how those techniques, representations, and mechanisms work. Successfully applied techniques might evolve into a theory of student models. Based on this paradigm, we have begun to define a usable foundation for describing student models *en route* to the development of a usable theory of building student models.

# References

1. Bruner, J. S.:. The ontogenesis of speech acts. *Journal of Child Language*, 2, pp. 1-20 (1975)
2. Cherniac, E. & McDermott, D.: *Introduction to Artificial Intelligence*. Reading, MA: Addison-Wesley 1986
3. Cohen, P. & Gruber, T.: Reasoning About Uncertainty, A Knowledge Representation Perspective. COINS Technical Report 85-24. Amherst, MA: University of Massachusetts at Amherst 1985
4. DeJong, G.: An introduction to explanation-based learning. In: *Exploring Artificial Intelligence* (H. Schrobe & American Association for Artificial Intelligence, eds.). San Mateo, CA: Morgan Kaufmann 1988
5. DeJong, G. F. & Mooney, R. J.: Explanation-based learning: an alternative view. *Machine Learning*, 1(2), pp. 145-176 (1986)
6. Eskay, M. & Zweban, M.: Learning search control for constraint-based scheduling. Proceedings of the 8th National Conference on Artificial Intelligence, pp. 908-915. Menlo Park, CA: AAAI 1990
7. Fennema, C. L. Jr.: Interweaving Reason, Action and Perception. Ph.D. Dissertation, University of Massachusetts at Amherst. (Also available as COINS Technical Report 91-56, Amherst, MA: University of Massachusetts at Amherst) 1991
8. Murray, T. & Woolf, B.: A knowledge acquisition framework for intelligent learning environments. *SIGART Bulletin*, 2(2), pp. 1-13 (1991)

9.  Murray, T. & Woolf, B.:  Tools for teacher participation in ITS design. In: *Proceedings of the 2nd International Conference on Intelligent Tutoring Systems*, Montreal, Quebec (C. Frasson, G. Gauthier & G. McCalla, eds.), pp. 593-600, Lecture Notes in Computer Science, Vol. 608, Berlin: Springer-Verlag 1992
10. Piaget, J.: *Genetic Epistemology*. New York, NY: Norton 1971
11. Self, J.: Formal approaches to student modelling. Chapter in this volume.
12. Self, J.: User modeling in open learning systems. In: *Tutoring and Monitoring Facilities for European Open Learning* (J. Whiting & D. Bell, eds.). pp. 219-237, Amsterdam: Elsevier 1987
13. Soloway, E.: Learning = Interpretation + Generalization: A Case Study in Knowledge Directed Learning. Ph.D. thesis, Computer and Information Science Department, University of Massachusetts 1978
14. VanLehn, K.: Student modeling. In: *Foundations of Intelligent Tutoring Systems* (M. Polson & J. Richardson, eds.), pp. 55-78, Hillsdale, NJ: Lawrence Erlbaum Associates 1988
15. Winkels, R.: User modeling. In: *EUROHELP, Developing Intelligent Help Systems* (J. Breuker, ed.). Amsterdam: EC 1990
16. Winston, P. H.: Learning structural descriptions from examples. In: *The Psychology of Computer Vision*, (P. H. Winston, ed.), pp. 157-210 New York, NY: McGraw-Hill 1975

# Building a Student Model for an Intelligent Tutoring System

M. F. Verdejo

E.T.S. Ingenieros Industriales. U.N.E.D, Ciudad Universitaria, Madrid, Spain

**Abstract:** A *user* model can be roughly described as the information that a system keeps about an individual user. This paper address the problem of building a user model for an intelligent tutoring system. In this framework the main purpose of a learner model is to provide the instructional planning component with the information it needs to select a suitable instructional action. Our system, CAPRA, teaches novice students about program specification. The approach to building the student model relies on gathering a great deal of information about the student behavior in a non-intrusive way. CAPRA provides a problem solving environment with intermediate languages, a Spanish natural language interface for communication activities, and a knowledge-based debugger.

**Keywords:** student modelling, knowledge-based instruction, interfaces for educational systems

## 1   Introduction

Intelligent tutoring systems should actively support the student's learning process. This task has to be performed according to each learner and therefore the teaching process should also be carried out tailored to the individual user.

The term "user model" refers to the information that a system keeps about the individual user. Planning techniques provide a way to formalize instructional knowledge in order to automatically develop an interactive teaching session. A dynamic planner can generate the appropriate next instructional step taking into account both the goal and the current situation of the learner. Thus the main purpose of a learner model is to provide the planning component with the information it needs to select a suitable instructional action.

Self [16] proposes a functional characterization of the learner model including the following aspects: *elaborative,* to support the selection of the next topic, *diagnostic* for bug identification, *corrective* for selection of appropriate remediation, *strategic* to provide information for the selection of a tutorial strategy, *predictive* to anticipate how the learner will perform and *evaluative* for both the learner and the system. We will consider one more: *communicative*, to support a mixed-initiative style of interaction.

Two ways have been explored to acquire the information for the user model: *implicit* and *explicit*. The implicit approach relies on inference techniques based on knowledge about the domain and the observed behavior during the course of the interaction. Under the explicit approach information about the user is provided by the system designer when defining the content of a generic (classes of) user model.

A major problem with incorporating a learner model is the difficulty of building this model implicitly. However the explicit pre-coding of knowledge about the user is also time consuming for the designer and usually bothersome for the user.

One way to reduce the complexity of the implicit approach is to design appropriate task-oriented interfaces: on one hand they give support to structure and visualize the problem solving process, while on the other hand information about student behaviour is acquired in a non-intrusive way.

This paper presents the student modelling component of CAPRA, an ITS to teach elementary programming domain. Our approach relies on gathering a great deal of information about the student behavior. The system provides an environment with intermediate languages facilitating problem solving tasks, and a Spanish natural language interface for communication activities. Next we give an overview of the system. In section 3 some aspects of general user modelling are briefly discussed. Section 4 describes the student model in CAPRA, analysing its content, how it is built and its use following the functional criteria mentioned above. Finally a summary and important conclusions are reported.

## 2 Overview of the System

The system [10] was designed to teach program construction. The teaching methodology distinguishes four main steps: problem comprehension, problem classification, algorithm design and coding.

Currently the implemented domain knowledge is related to problem specification ie. the prototype teaches the first step, problem comprehension. The student learns to express problems stated in natural language in terms of the input and output required and to rewrite them using a formal specification language.

The CAPRA system offers a tutorial dialogue integrating a natural language interface and an interactive tool to perform problem solving activities. Instruction follows a Socratic style combining explanation and practice.

During a teaching session the Tutor presents exercises to assess the student's acquisition of the domain knowledge. The selection of the problems is based on the student model, the concept to be checked, and the current state of the session. The Tutor has an interactive debugger to supervise the pupil during the solving process.

The student is presented with a problem stated in natural language and is asked to write a formal specification. This activity must be performed with a particular approach: a top-down design. The system provides an interactive tool for this task. The student writes the solution incrementally, selecting options from a menu of design plans and writing fragments to complete the schema selected by previous design decisions.

The CAPRA system is able to:

- Plan and carry out an instructional session in a dynamic way, adapted to a particular learner.
- Develop a mixed-initiative dialogue. The system understands Spanish sentences.
- Design a problem specification, in parallel and adapted to, the student's solution.
- Detect errors, comparing the system and student solutions.
- Interrupt the student activity when there is an important conflict between the tutor's and student's goals.
- Correct the student's errors, taking into account the student 's characteristics.

## 2.1 Design of the System

The system is composed of five major parts: the Tutor, the Knowledge-based Debugger, the Interface, the Domain Knowledge Base and the Student Model.

The Tutor includes a planner and the instructional knowledge needed to carry out a teaching session. Teaching strategies are independent of the domain and are represented declaratively. The knowledge-based debugger works with the Tutor component; as the student solves a problem, it performs an intention-based diagnosis supported by knowledge about the domain, the problem to be solved and the inferred student model.

The interface includes two components: a translation system and a natural-language interface.

The translation system handles the problem solution window, where the student develops his solution using a syntactic editor. There is an edit menu to explicitly indicate the design decisions. The edit menu presents series of options to select either a goal/subgoal to focus on, or a plan to apply to a previously selected problem goal. The plan selected is then inserted automatically into the problem solution window by the syntactic editor. Thus, when solving a problem, the student interacts with the system through the edit menus and the solution window.

The natural language interface operates in close cooperation with the Tutor module. Communication between the natural languageinterface and the Tutor is performed by messages containing relevant information about the current state of the instructional task. A teaching dialogue is composed of interrelated sentences, reflecting the underlying pedagogical strategy. Each dialogue is structured on segments aggregating the linguistic expressions produced by the student and the tutor to communicate a particular instructional goal. A parser interprets the students' natural language sentences, and sends this information to the tutor. Natural language understanding is carried out using contextual, semantic and syntactic knowledge.

The Domain Knowledge Base includes both definitional knowledge about program specification, represented as a structured network of concepts, and procedural knowledge about how to specify problems in form of generic plans and rules. It also includes a problem library, an abstract description of required input and goals to be solved. The meta-description of the domain provides a pedagogical view of the domain topics, and gives support to the tutor to organize the sequence and the content of the instructional actions. For example one of the meta-descriptors indicates genetic links between domain elements. Knowledge about categorization from a learning point of view, difficulty, ways of explanation, mapping to problems in the library, typical bugs, etc. is part of the domain meta-description.

CAPRA was implemented with a blackboard architecture, on a Lisp machine using Knowledge Craft. The natural languageinterface is implemented too. The morphologic and syntactic components include a large dictionary and a Spanish grammar (which is used in other applications as well). The semantic component is based on a frame formalism. The sublanguage accepted has been defined to cover the experimental material collected during 140 hours of interactive teaching. Portability has been considered; for instance the taxonomy for verbs contains three groups: the first one is related to the communication process (to say, to tell, etc.), the second one to the instructional task (to explain, to make clear, etc.) and the third one to the domain (to specify, to program, etc.). A change of domain will require modifications only to this third class.

# 3  User Modelling

From the very beginning of ICAI student modelling was recognized as critical to tailoring the teaching/learning process to the individual learner. The difficulty of inferring a model from the student behaviour is one of the main reasons for questioning, in recent years, the feasibility of this approach. However, with the growing spread of systems requiring intelligent interaction, user modelling has become an important research topic of its own. In this section we briefly review two aspects discussed in the literature: the content of a user model, and the dimensions that have been suggested to characterize a user model.

## 3.1 The Content of the User Model

User modelling in a broad context should consider cognitive, perception and motor activities. We will focus on the first: cognitive user modelling. Usually five kinds of features are distinguished in modelling the cognitive aspects of a system user: his (meta) knowledge, intentions, capabilities, preferences, and motivations.

Knowledge and intentions have received a lot of attention both from AI and Cognitive Science. Capabilities, preferences and motivations, although studied in traditional Psychology and Education, are still at the very beginning of a computational treatment.

Knowledge can be further classified into the user beliefs about the domain, and world knowledge. Meta-Knowledge can be considered as reflexive knowledge and reciprocal knowledge (user's beliefs about other agents, including the system itself) .

Intentions are captured in form of user goals. To infer objectives from user behaviour, it is proposed that planning techniques using discourse and domain knowledge in the form of plans be used.

Capabilities are described more informally in terms of cognitive style and intellectual abilities. Each one in turn is characterized by a set of attributes. For example for cognitive style, attributes such as field dependence/independence, reflectivity, and risk-taking are considered.

Preferences are expressed through a set of features mainly to support a classification of interaction styles.

Motivation has been specified in terms of traits such as achievement motivation, anxiety, competence motivation, and locus of control.

Depending on the kind of situation, a variety of user model functions are required, and the model content, scope and granularity differ accordingly.

Natural language understanding systems have largely explored knowledge and intentions because both are key issues in communication [1, 5]. Motivation has been explored in the design of games and simulation software [13] . Expert systems have dealt extensively with domain and task modelling [3, 6, 19], in order not only to solve problems but also to provide effective explanations and to support knowledge acquisition. Intelligent Tutoring Systems have focused on representing the user's acquired knowledge [11], and particularly misconceptions, [2, 17] in order to understand the student's behaviour and give him adequate instruction.

## 3.2 Dimensions

A number of authors [15, 18, 4, 12, 16] have suggested criteria to characterize user modelling; they focus on the content, the use, and the ways of building a user model. Figure 1 adapts and summarizes dimensions relevant to Intelligent Tutoring Systems. These dimensions are discussed below.

Observability
Specialization
Number of models
Variability
Temporal scope
Content
Extent
Knowledge level
Representation
Implementation
Construction technique
Use

Figure 1: Dimensions to characterize a user model

## Observability

When a system has been designed with users in mind, and those design decisions are embedded in the code, then it is called externaluser modelling. On the contrary, internalmodels are separate components enabling the system to deal explicitly with the user representation.

## Specialization

A system can have a unique or canonical user model, a set of users classes/profiles, or an individual model for each user.

## Number of models

There can be an unique model, or multiple models, of each user.

## Variability

When the user model is defined all at once, it is called *static*; models that change during the interaction are called *dynamic*.

## Temporal scope

Short term models stand for the duration of an interaction. Long term ones keep information for future interactions.

## Content

This includes knowledge, intentions, capabilities, preferences, and motivation.

*Extent*

The acquired domain knowledge represented can consist of *overlays,* which capture only correct knowledge represented as as subset of the expert domain knowledge, or *differential* models, which encode misconceptions.

*Knowledge level*

The distinction between *deep knowledge* versus *surface* knowledge based systems characterizes whether a system contains a problem solver is able to construct and reason about domain models. A deep knowledge representation makes explicit the various models of the domain (causal, associational, structural, functional) needed for a particular task, while a surface knowledge representation supports inference techniques to solve a problem, without explicit use of domain models. Deep knowledge representation facilitates better explanations and more principled knowledge acquisition techniques.

*Representation*

The method for content representation can be *inferential* or *non-inferential.* The former supports executable models to simulate a user's behaviour, while the latter only records features in a descriptive way.

*Implementation formalism*

(Inferential) knowledge representations can be implemented under production systems, frame-based representations or logic languages.

*Construction technique*

There are two basic approaches to construction: *implicit* and *explicit.* The former involves automatically building a user model and can be done using deductive or inductive (machine learning) techniques. The latter is covered by diverse techniques relying on the system designer and/or the user.

*Use*

One common way to categorize "use" is as *descriptive* and *predictive.* Descriptive can be subcategorized as supporting *elaborative, diagnostic, corrective, strategic, evaluative* and *communicative* functions.

# 4 Student Modelling in CAPRA

CAPRA's instructional strategies make use of the learner's previous domain knowledge, information about the teaching/learning process itself (current learner goals, level of acquisition attained, explanations given, problems solved, and bugs detected), learner attributes such as preferred learning style and aptitude, and temporal data (time remaining, interval from previous session, etc.) All this information is encapsulated in three modules: learner component, session-context, and system objects.

The learner component is structured in two submodules. One of them is long-term, where learner attributes, learner's previous domain knowledge, and information about the end of the last session are represented. The other module is the learner's current task component containing detailed information about the on going process of teaching/learning.

The session-context component is in turn a structured object containing information about conflicts between tutor and student goals, current general and local strategies, and current student goals, concepts and the problem in focus.

Starting time and elapsed time for the current session are recorded in one of the system objects.

A detailed description of each component is presented below.

## 4.1 The Content of the Model

The student model primarily includes information about acquired knowledge and current task performance. Motivations are ignored, preferences and capability are roughly represented along a qualitative scale.

### 4.1.1 The Knowledge Acquired

The acquired domain knowledge is represented as a network of structured elements. This is nominally an overlay model but enriched with information from the learning process, such as related elements known, acquisition level, explanations given, examples/counterexamples used, problems solved, and bugs detected. Figure 2 shows the generic structure of an element.

```
ACQUIRED ELEMENT
Reference: an element of the domain knowledge
Related elements known: other acquired-elements of the network
Acquisition-level: one of {remember, know, use}
Acquired degree: one of {weak, medium, sure}
Explanations given: list of text references
Examples: list of example/counterexample references
Problems solved as main goal: list of problems solved involving this
        element as main goal
Problems solved as secondary goal: list of problems solved involving
        this element as secondary goal
Errors: list of errors
```

Figure 2: The generic structure of an acquired element of the domain

The reference descriptor is a pointer to an element of the domain description, where knowledge about program construction is codified. Explanations, examples and problems are references to the pedagogic meta-level of the domain description. The error descriptor contains the list of errors involving that element, that the student made while using CAPRA.

Semantic errors are detected by the debugger and are classified along two dimensions: superficial (as they appear in isolation) and global (combinations of superficial ones). Superficial errors are further classified as errors of omission, excess, change, or wrong approach. Global errors are obtained by the debugger by combining the student's superficial errors. Three subtypes are considered: malformed, malsituated and false. The description of a particular error follows the structure shown in Figure 3. The "type" descriptor characterizes the error class while the "composed by" and "is part of" descriptors express the relationships between student errors. The "importance" descriptor is qualitative, taking into account the type of the error, the level of acquisition of the concept involved, and the level of difficulty of the problem to be solved.

```
ERROR-DESCRIPTION
concept involved: reference to the acquired-element affected
where: problem solving activity where the error was detected
type of error: one of {omission,excess, ...}
related information:
importance:
teaching strategy:
composed by:
is part of:
```

Figure 3: The structure of an error description

## 4.1.2 The Communication Model

The student communicates with CAPRA through an interface organized into different task spaces. The student-tutor communication window allows the student to communicate with the system using natural language. The communication report window provides a record of the current session. This window is inspectable and scrollable. When solving a problem two additional spaces are visible: the problem statement window, and the problem solution window in which the student writes his solution to the proposed problem.

The student-tutor communication window is controlled by a natural language interface, and the problem solution window by a translation system with an embedded syntactic editor.

The student activity in the problem solving process concentrates on two steps. First the student chooses an option from the menu to indicate what s/he wants to solve or how s/he wants to solve it. Then the student fills the chosen plan by completing a sentence pattern written in the solution window by the syntactic editor.

The translation system creates the student's objectives from the information obtained through the windows. The student interacts through the edit menus and the solution window. The translation system derives two kinds of student's objectives called *edit* and *informative*. The edit objectives contain information about the design decision taken from the edit menus.

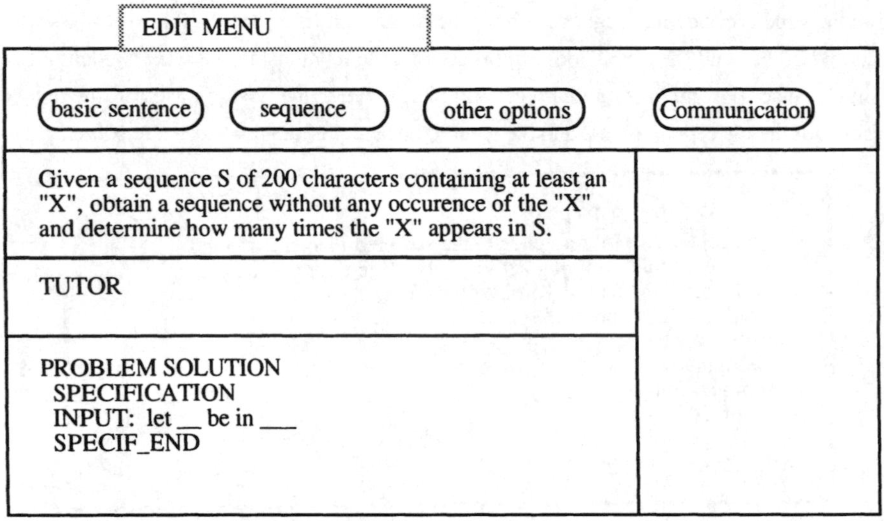

```
┌─────────────────────────────────────────────────────────────────────┐
│ ┌─ EDIT MENU ──────────────────┐                                      │
│ ╎                              ╎                                      │
│ ╎                              ╎                                      │
│ ┌──────────────┐  ┌──────────┐  ┌──────────────┐   ┌──────────────┐  │
│ ( basic sentence )  ( sequence )  ( other options )  (Communication) │
│ └──────────────┘  └──────────┘  └──────────────┘   └──────────────┘  │
│ ┌─────────────────────────────────────────────────┐                  │
│ │ Given a sequence S of 200 characters containing  │                  │
│ │ at least an "X", obtain a sequence without any    │                  │
│ │ occurence of the "X" and determine how many times │                  │
│ │ the "X" appears in S.                             │                  │
│ ├─────────────────────────────────────────────────┤                  │
│ │ TUTOR                                             │                  │
│ ├─────────────────────────────────────────────────┤                  │
│ │ PROBLEM SOLUTION                                  │                  │
│ │   SPECIFICATION                                   │                  │
│ │   INPUT:  let __ be in ___                        │                  │
│ │   SPECIF_END                                      │                  │
│ └─────────────────────────────────────────────────┘                  │
└─────────────────────────────────────────────────────────────────────┘
```

Figure 4: The interface for problem-solving tasks

In the example shown in Figure 4 we see that the student has chosen the *basic sentence* option to specify the data. The student's objective created to represent this activity is an *edit* objective describing *the basic sentence plan* selected. Whenever the student modifies the solution window, *informative* objectives are created containing a translation (into an internal representation language) of what the student has written.

The natural language interface interprets the student's interventions, generating a communication objective. We distinguish several major types of student communicative acts:

- Confirmation: the student indicates that he does or does not understand the explained concepts. For example "*I don't understand what you are talking about*".
- Request: The student proposes that the Tutor perform an action, to solve a problem, for instance, or give a more detailed explanation.
- Query: The student is in doubt about a concept and wants an explanation.

- Information: The student states precisely which concepts he knows and which he does not.
- Comment: messages included in this group are related to the student activity (learning state) not belonging to one of the previous types.

Request, query, information and confirmation are further divided into a hierarchy taking into account the focused objects of the student's intervention. For thematic objects we distinguish the following cases:

- Thematic objects related to the subject matter:
  - an item, either to validate a hypothesis or to know its conceptual definition, the value of a property, its relationship with other items.
  - a related subset of subject-matter items to perform some comparative operations.
- Thematic objects related to the Tutor's activity:
  - asking for the purpose of the teaching task itself.
  - requesting explicitly a teaching concept (a problem, an example, etc.).

Thematic objects are derived by the parser in two different ways, either implicitly (inferred from the dialogue attentional structure) or explicitly (the student gives information about the potential focus).

Illocutionary acts, together with thematic objects, define the set of possible objectives for a student's intervention. The next table (Figure 5) shows the relationships between illocutionary acts (columns) and thematic objects (rows).

| | How / What | Query concept explain | Query activity explain | Request example | Request problem | Request correct | Request confirm | Request continue | Request stop act. | Information not known | Information known | Neg. | Conf. | Evaluab. Answer |
|---|---|---|---|---|---|---|---|---|---|---|---|---|---|---|
| Validate hypothesis | Implicit | | | | | | | | | | | | | |
| | Explicit | Obj: 8 | | | | | Obj: 8 | | | Obj:8 | | | | |
| Concept definition | I | Obj: 4 | Obj: 4 | | | | | | | Obj: 4 | Obj: 6 | Obj: 7 | Obj: 6 | |
| | E | Obj: 4 | Obj: 4 | | | | | | | Obj: 4 | Obj: 1 | | | |
| Value of a property | I | Obj: 4 | Obj: 4 | | | | | | | Obj: 4 | Obj: 6 | | | |
| | E | Obj: 4 | Obj: 4 | | | | | | | Obj: 4 | Obj: 1 | | | |
| Related concepts | - | | | | | | | | | | | | | |
| | E | Obj: 4 | Obj: 4 | | | | | | | Obj:4 | Obj: 1 | | | |
| Tutor's aim justification | I | | | | | | | | | | | | | |
| | E | Obj: 5 | Obj: 5 | | | | | | | Obj: 5 | | | | |
| Items related to teaching process | I | | | | | | | | | | | Obj: 7 | Obj: 6 | Obj: 9 |
| | E | | | Obj: 2 | Obj: 3 | Obj: 9 | | Obj: 6 | Obj: 7 | | | | | |

Figure 5: Illocutionary acts vs. thematic objects

Nine different types of objectives have been identified: (1) "give information" (2) "get an example related to a concept", (3) "get a problem related to the concept explained in order to acquire practice", (4) "obtain an explanation about a concept", (5) "obtain an explanation about the teaching activity", (6) "continue the teaching activity", (7) "change the teaching activity", (8) "obtain a confirmation for a hypothesis", and (9) "verify the correction of a problem".

The natural language interface keeps the student's objectives on the context data, along with current goals and strategies stored there by the tutor component.

## 4.2  How the Model is Used

Instructional knowledge is represented as a set of generic goals, plans to achieve classes of goals, and rules for deciding which plan to instantiate for a given goal in a particular situation. The tutor dynamically plans, executes and supervises a sequence of instructional actions. The planning process is performed by instructional goal-refinement at different levels of abstraction, from the most general where the global approach is decided to the more concrete where a specific action is executed.

Goals, plans and rules are expressed in a declarative formalism and organized as knowledge sources. Each knowledge source is specialized in a particular class of instructional task. Currently the tutor includes four knowledge sources: pedagogic, thematic, teaching and supervisory. The pedagogic KS establishes and develops the global strategies, and the thematic KS refines the learning goals to be attained in terms of the subject matter. Delivery and control of the acquisition are the tasks carried out by the teaching component. Detection and resolution of conflicts between the tutor and the student's objectives are dealt with by the supervisor KS.

The knowledge-based debugger follows the same representational approach. Its knowledge sources are: designer, verifier and diagnosis. The designer KS generates a solution to the problem in parallel with and adapted to the student's solution; the verifier supervises the student's objectives to determine which design plan he has selected and detect the differences between the two solutions. Detection involves matching the student's partial version to the partial versions implicitly defined by the domain knowledge bases.

Whenever relevant differences between the solutions are found, an error is detected. Thus, the debugger does not need to have an extensive bug library of student misconceptions since errors are detected by incrementally matching the student and the designer solutions. When there is an error, a diagnosis process determines its classification (superficial or global) and whether is necessary to interrupt the student.

Figure 6 shows a partial view of the system configuration.

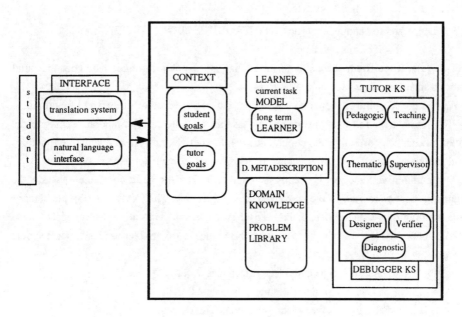

Figure 6: System configuration (partial view)

Different plans in a knowledge source represent different ways to attain a goal. Rules for selecting plans express conditions for selecting a generic plan and create an instance representing the current situation. Conditions in a rule can refer to information contained in the learner model; the pedagogic component, for instance, has two main classes of goals: *strategic* and *common*. The former are used to state global strategies while the latter refine a selected strategy. The rules for solving strategic goals are shaped by the following general schema:

    If conditions about

- Tutor's objectives
- student learning characteristics
- domain knowledge already acquired
- last session outcome
- temporal constraints

    then    Select X as a possible strategy

One of the rules to solve the strategic goal "decide an instructional strategy" says

    If       the current tutor objective is "Decide an instructional strategy", and

            the student does not know all concepts in the curriculum, and

            the interval from the last session is less than MAXINTERVAL, and

            the estimated time is less than PRESENTATIONTIME

then    add to pending strategies TO INTRODUCE NEW CONCEPT, and
          modify estimated time

This rule, when fired, selects the instructional strategy "to introduce new concepts" and performs an elementary action on a system object.

As mentioned in the introduction, the student model can be used for different functions. In CAPRA we have the following uses: strategic (as the example above), elaborative, diagnostic, student evaluative, corrective and communicative. Predictive and system evaluative functions could also be supported but the current instructional strategies have not focused on them.

The elaborative function is mainly invoked from the thematic component, while the diagnostic function is used by the knowledge-based debugger. The following example belongs to the teaching knowledge source. In this case the rule selects a plan stating two subgoals: one to explain a concept and the other one to evaluate the acquisition. Variables not instantiated should get values as the plan is elaborated.

If      current tutor objective is "the student has acquired X", and
          X has neither prerequisites nor subconcepts, and
          elapsed time in the session is less than TMAX, and
          the student has not acquired X, and
          the desired level associated with X is "use"
then    explain X with detail level Y, and
          the student knows how to use X with a degree of certainty Z

The student model records for each element of the acquired domain knowledge a *level* and a *degree* of acquisition. Level is one of remember, know, or use. The "use" value is given when the student has performed problem solving activities involving that element. *Degree* takes qualitative values in a scale between sure and weak evidence.

Each domain element has an associated level of difficulty and a way of evaluation. All of this information is used when selecting a plan for student assessment. An example of such a rule is given below:

If      the tutor objective is "the student knows how to use X with a degree of certainty Z", and
          the student acquisition level is less than "use"
then    apply the plan "verify comprehension with problem solving"

Corrective actions are classified as global or local. They are decided either by the pedagogic KS (to solve a severe mismatch between tutor expectations and student current state, detected by the supervisor) or the knowledge-base debugger. They are further refined and carried out by the thematic and teaching components. Thus the corrective function of the student model is invoked from different system components. Two examples of such cases are shown by the rules below:

    If       the current debugger goal is "decide whether to interrupt", and

              the type of the error is "Omission", and

              the importance of the error is "high"

    then   insert the goal "decide Z corrective strategy"

    If       the current tutor goal is "decide a corrective strategy", and

              the importance of the current error is "high", and

              the concept involved is "difficult", and

              the acquired student level is not the desired level, and

              the student type is "medium", and

              the number of problems solved is less than NMAXP

    then   communicate change of activity, and

              insert the local strategy "solve simpler problem"

When carrying on a dialogue, student sentences are translated in terms of objectives. These objectives are always compared with tutor expectations in order to detect conflicts. Responses to student's interventions are given in the form of either an instructional action, a communicative action, or both, as shown by the following rule:

    If       the current tutor goal is "brief review of the concept X", and

              the student objective is "solve problem related to X", and

              time of the session is "start"

    then   acknowledge, and

              insert the strategy "problem solving"

## 4.3  How the Model is Built

The student model includes a learner component and a communicative component. The former includes two subcomponents: *long term* and *current* task. The long-term model is created at the first teaching session when initially attributes get default values. This long term model is updated at the end of each teaching session to incorporate the newly acquired domain knowledge and eventually to modify the attributes. The current task model is created at the beginning of the session, and updated during the interaction whenever an action of the class "actualize student model" appears as one of the steps in an instantiated instructional plan.

The communicative model has a temporary life. It is included as a part of the context component due to its shareability with the interfaces. Thus, it is consulted and updated by the translation system, the natural languageinterface and the instructional planner.

A fuller description of these topics can be found in [7 - 9, 20].

# 5 Summary and Conclusion

Student modelling is a key feature to give either instruction or adequate help in teaching/learning environments. We have presented an ITS system able to build an internal model of each individual user, representing mainly his knowledge and intentions. The model contains long and short term components, evolving during the interaction. It gives elaborative, diagnostic, corrective, strategic, evaluative, and communicative functionality to the tutor and debugger modules.

The feasibility of our approach relies on two techniques: first, gathering information about the student behaviour through an appropriate task-oriented interface complemented with natural language dialogue; second, using knowledge about the problems to be solved, the domain and the learning process followed by the student.

The difficulty of inferring the model is reduced because student goals are stated step by step through the interface. Interactivity and the use of a top-down methodology to solve a problem facilitates the detection of buggy behaviour.

Tutorial dialogue in natural language for a particular domain is feasible, but still an expensive feature both in terms of resources needed to develop the interface and to run it. However, a menu-like dialogue explicitly supporting the expression of communication goals [14] is a realistic compromise to enhance tutor cooperation without increasing the complexity of the complete system.

# References

1. Bobrow, D.: *Representation and Understanding* (Collins, ed.). Academic Press 1975
2. Brown, J. S. & Burton, R. R.: Diagnostic models for procedural bugs in basic mathematic skills. *Cognitive Science*, 2, pp. 155-191 (1978)
3. Clancey, W. J.: The epistemology of rule-based expert systems: a framework for explanations. *Artificial Intelligence*, 20(3), pp. 215-251 (1982)
4. Clancey W. J.: Qualitative student models. *Computer Science Annual Review*, 1, pp. 381-450 (1986)
5. Cohen, R., Morgan J. & Pollack, M.: *Intentions in Communication.* System Development Foundation Benchmark Series. Cambridge, MA: MIT Press 1990
6. Chandrasekaran, B. & Mittal,S.: Deep versus compiled approaches to diagnostic problem solving. *International Journal of Man-Machine Studies*, 19, pp. 425-436 (1983)
7. Diaz, A., Fernandez, I. & Verdejo, F.: A nl interface for intelligent tutoring systems. In: *Education and Application of Computer Technology* (M. deBlasi, E. Scuri & E. Luque, eds.). pp 1-12, Editione Fratelli Laterza, Set 1990
8. Fernandez, I., Diaz, A. & Verdejo, F.: Building a programming tutor by dynamic planning: case studies and a proposal. *Proceedings of the 2nd International Conference on Intelligent Tutoring Systems*, Montreal, Quebec (C. Frasson, G. Gauthier & G. McCalla, eds.), pp. 230-237, Lecture Notes in Computer Science, Vol. 608, Berlin: Springer-Verlag 1992
9. Fernandez, I., Diaz, A. & Verdejo, F.: A cooperative architecture for tutoring tasks. Proceedings of the 8th International Workshop on Expert Systems and their Application (Vol 2), Avignon, pp 107 -126, 1988

10. Garijo, F., Verdejo, F., Diaz, A., Fernandez, I. & Sarasola, K.: CAPRA: an intelligent system to teach novice programmers. In: *Perspectives in Artificial Intelligence* (P. Campbell & Cuena, eds.). Vol 2, pp 179-196, Chichester, UK: Ellis Horwood 1987

11. Goldstein, I. P.: The genetic graph: a representation for the evolution of procedural knowledge. In: *Intelligent Tutoring Systems* (D. Sleeman & J. S. Brown, eds.). pp 51-77. London: Academic Press 1982

12. Kass, R. & Finin, T.: Modelling the user in natural language systems. In: *Computational Linguistics: Special Issue on User Modelling.* , 14, pp 5-22 (September 1988)

13. Malone, T.: Heuristics for designing enjoyable user interfaces: lessons from computer games. Proceedings of the Conference on Human Factors in Computer Systems (ACM), pp 63-68, 1982

14. Mayorga, I. & Verdejo, F.: Creacion de una biblioteca ejecutable de estrategias de ensenanza en GTE. Technical University of Cataluna, Technical Report LS1-91-29, 1991

15. Rich E.: User modelling via stereotypes. *Cognitive Science*, 3, pp. 329-354 (1979)

16. Self, J.A.: User modelling in open learning systems. In: *Tutoring and Monitoring Facilities for European Open Learning* (Whiting & Bell, eds.). pp 219-237, Amsterdam: North-Holland: 1987

17. Sleeman, D. & Smith, M.: Modeling student's problem solving. *Artificial Intelligence*, 16, pp. 171-188 (1981)

18. Sleman, D.: UMFE: a user modelling front-end subsystem. *International Journal of Man-Machine Studies*, 23, pp 71-88 (1985)

19. Steels, L.: Components of expertise. *A.I. Magazine*, 11, pp. 28-49 (1990)

20. Urretavizcaya, M. & Verdejo, M. F.: A cooperative system for an interactive debugging of novice programming errors. In: *Instructional Models in Computer-Based Learning Environments*. (S.Dijkstra, H.P.M. Krammer & J.J.G. van Merrienboer, eds.). pp 421-444, NATO ASI Series F, Vol. 104, Berlin: Springer-Verlag 1993.

Part 3

Human Cognition and
Student Modelling

# Constraint-Based Student Modeling[1]

Stellan Ohlsson

Learning Research and Development Center, University of Pittsburgh, Pittsburgh, PA USA

**Abstract:** A new approach to the student modeling problem is based on the idea of representing subject matter knowledge in sets of constraints. Constraint violations on the part of the student indicate incomplete or incorrect knowledge and can therefore be used to guide the response of an intelligent tutoring system. This approach promises to eliminate the need for runnable models of *either* the expert *or* the student and to reduce the computations required for student modeling to pattern matching. An application in the domain of subtraction illustrates the feasibility of the concept.

**Keywords:** bug library, constraint: satisfaction, intelligent tutoring systems, machine learning, model tracing, overlay model, path constraints, student modeling

## 1 Introduction

This chapter proposes a new technique for student modeling which is based on the idea of representing subject matter knowledge as a set of constraints on problem states. In this technique, the model of a particular student consists of those constraints that he or she violates during problem solving. This technique does not require a runnable expert model, nor does it necessitate extensive empirical research of student errors. Furthermore, it does not rely on computationally expensive inference algorithms; pattern matching will do. In spite of its computational simplicity, the technique is robust in the face of inconsistency on the part of students. The constraint-based student modeling technique is also neutral with respect to pedagogy. The technique can be used both on-line, to monitor ongoing practice, and off-line, to analyze test results.

[1]This chapter also appeared in the *Journal of Artificial Intelligence in Education*, 3(4), pp. 429, (1993). Reprinted with the permission of the Association for the Advancement of Computing in Education (AACE, P.O. Box 2966, Charlottesville, VA 22902 USA).

Although an implemented demonstration for off-line use will be reported here, the technique has not been employed in an intelligent tutoring system. The main purpose of this chapter is to communicate the idea to other researchers who might want to use it. In order to situate the new technique within current research on student modeling, I begin with a brief summary of some relevant aspects of existing techniques.

## 2  The Art of Describing 'What Ain't So'

The student modeling problem in its general form can be stated as follows [14]:

> *Given a behavioral record (of some sort), infer what the student knows **and does not know** about the relevant topic.*

Two pedagogical insights led to this problem, one commonplace and one deep. It is a trivial observation that one should not teach students what they already know; hence, individualized instruction requires a representation of which subject matter units the student has already learned. If this was *all* that was needed, a so-called overlay model [5] would be sufficient. In the overlay technique the relevant instructional topic is broken down into subject matter units (concepts, principles, subskills, etc.); the student is modeled as the subset of those units which he or she has mastered so far. Such a model can be constructed with a computationally cheap and easy to implement inference rule:

> *If subject matter unit X is a prerequisite for correct performance on a practice problem or question Y, and student S performs correctly on Y, then infer that S knows X (or upgrade the probability that he or she knows X).*

If an assessment of what the student knows was sufficient basis for instruction, the overlay technique would be a complete solution to the student modeling problem. (I have argued elsewhere that although overlay models are incomplete, they are better than no model; see [16].)

The difficulties begin with the second insight: Students who have not yet mastered a topic are not blank slates who merely lack certain subject matter units. Instead, students act on the basis of previously acquired misconceptions of the subject matter and/or misconstruals of the instruction they have received. In the apt phrase of Mark Twain, students know a lot of things that 'ain't so'. Because there are many different ways to misconstrue a topic, adaptive tutoring requires a description of what, exactly, the student knows that ain't so. The student modeling problem is thus the problem of how to describe and diagnose false knowledge. The three approaches to this problem developed so far--bug libraries, machine learning, and model tracing--set the stage for current developments.

## 2.1 The Bug Library Technique

The bug library technique exploits the obvious way to describe false knowledge: Study students' problem solutions and make a list of their (recurring) errors; construct explanations[2] for how each type of error comes about. The list of explanations (buggy procedures, misconceptions) is a list of the various ways in which students misunderstand or misconstrue that topic. The identification of recurring errors might require extensive empirical research and it is often difficult to find and empirically verify explanations for observed error patterns. Nevertheless, bug libraries for many instructionally relevant domains have been created.

Once the bug library is reasonably complete, some inference algorithm must be found which can identify which explanation, or combination of explanations, is true of a particular student at a particular moment in time. The inference from an erroneous answer or solution to what the student knows that ain't so is more complicated than the inference from a correct answer to what he or she knows correctly. This asymmetry is not paradoxical: The universe of mal-knowledge is incomprehensibly more vast than the universe of correct knowledge and the inference problem correspondingly more complicated.

In principle, the task for a bug library system is simple: To identify that bug which provides the best explanation for the student's performance. In practice, there are many complexities. In a sophisticated knowledge representation, the bugs are not explicitly listed, but represented generatively in terms of buggy components and a mechanism for combining them. Thus, the modeling system must generate combinations of correct and buggy components to explain the observed performance. There might be a huge number of such combinations, so the system has to have a method for choosing which is the best one. In spite of these difficulties, there are highly successful modeling systems that operate from a list of (explanations for) errors. Two of the most successful are Burton's [4] and Brown and Burton's [3] DEBUGGY system which maps incorrect answers to subtraction problems onto buggy subtraction procedures and Johnson's [8] PROUST system which maps incorrect Pascal code onto buggy programming plans. Bug library systems can often infer from the student's *answer* (arithmetic difference, algebraic derivation, Pascal code, etc.), rather than from his or her *solution path* (ie., the sequence of steps by which the answer was produced or arrived at). This feature provides the advantage that the systems can be used for off-line diagnosis of test results as well as for on-line monitoring of problem solving practice.

The successes and advantages of the bug library technique come at considerable cost: successful bug library systems typically build on extensive empirical research and use

---

[2]For the sake of uniformity of expression, I am deliberately stretching the term "explanation" to cover procedural domains. An 'explanation' for an incorrect answer is thus a faulty ("buggy") procedure which, when executed, generates that answer.

sophisticated and computationally expensive AI techniques to contain the combinatorial explosion that results from the large number of ways in which incorrect knowledge units (subskills, programming plans, rules) can be combined to yield an explanation for an observed error.

The amount of work involved in constructing a bug library is unimportant, if the library can be used in many tutoring systems. Sophisticated technological devices, eg., bridges and airplanes, often require years of construction. Why should the construction of an educational tool necessarily require less work than, for example, a nuclear power plant? This argument is based on the assumption that a bug library abstracted from one student population can be used to tutor other student populations. The recent results by Payne and Squibb [23] are somewhat disturbing for this point of view. They found that the bug library constructed by Derek Sleeman and co-workers for algebra [28-30] was minimally relevant for two new student populations, which in turn were not similar to each other. This finding, if replicated, implies that bug libraries cannot be transferred from one student population to the next, a conclusion which constitutes a major argument against extensive practical use of the bug library technique.

## 2.2  The Machine Learning Approach

In an attempt to improve on the bug library technique, Patrick Langley and I attempted to dispense with bug libraries and to invent a student model on-line by searching the space of possible models [9, 10, 19, 20]. This approach amounts to a computer implementation of the type of analysis proposed by Allen Newell and Herbert A. Simon in the context of protocol analysis (see [11], Chapter 6; see [15], for a second application). In this bottom-up technique, a model of a particular performance is constructed by first identifying a solution path that explains the performance, and second, constructing a procedure that generates that path.

This two-step inference technique requires two generator-evaluator pairs, one for paths and one for procedures. The generator for solution paths used in the Diagnostic Path Finder (DPF) system [19] is heuristic search through the relevant problem space; one can search a problem space for a path that ends with an incorrect answer just as one can search a space for a path that ends with the correct answer. The search can of course, be very costly. DPF used a domain-specific method for constraining the search in the domain of subtraction. There might be more than one path through the space which ends with a particular incorrect answer. Psychologically motivated principles for choosing between alternative paths have been described in Ohlsson and Langley [20].

Once the most plausible solution path has been identified, the next step is to infer the procedure that generated it. The generator in this step can be any machine learning method. A machine learning method is precisely a method for searching the space of possible procedures for a procedure that generates a particular path. Such methods are designed to infer correct procedures from correct paths, but the techniques are, in fact, insensitive to the correctness of either the paths they are given as input or the procedures they generate. Hence, they can be used as generators for incorrect procedures. This insight is entirely due to Patrick Langley and was the basis for the Automated Cognitive Modeler (ACM) system, which combined DPF with a version of the ID3 machine learning technique [9]. It is possible that there is more than one procedure that can generate the chosen path, so the problem of evaluation recurs in this step. A technique for utilizing information from more than one path in choosing between alternative procedures has been discussed in Langley, Wogulis, and Ohlsson [10].

The main advantage of the machine learning technique is that it dispenses with the need for empirical research to construct a bug library. Unfortunately, the computational complexity of the machine learning technique can be even greater than that of the bug library technique. Searching the problem space for a path to an incorrect answer can be very costly in large problem spaces with many possible errors and searching through the procedure space can be even more costly.

The computational complexity of the bug library and machine learning techniques might be a moot point, however, because there is now an empirical reason to doubt the validity of either technique. Both techniques implicitly assume that the student can meaningfully be characterized as having a *single* mental procedure or strategy for the relevant instructional task. The mental procedure might be more or less complete and more or less correct, but it is a single, integrated procedure which is consistently applied over some period of time. This *single strategy assumption* implies that the task for a student modeling system is to identify *the* procedure possessed by the student.

Recent research has shown that the single strategy assumption is false, at least for simple mathematical tasks. Instead of possessing a single strategy, each student has a family or space of different strategies for each task and he or she selects a strategy from that space on a trial-by-trial basis. Ohlsson and Bee [18] found that a group of students who worked for several weeks on a computer-based microworld for fractions solved posttest problems with a wide variety of different strategies, some correct and some incorrect. Rapid moves back and forth between different strategies for simple addition and subtraction problems have also been observed by Siegler [25, 26]. Within-student strategy variability has been observed by Nwana and Coxhead [12] in the domain of fractions, by VanLehn [32] in the domain of multi-digit subtraction ("bug tinkering"), and by Payne and Squibb [23] in algebra. Radical strategy variability is not confined to mathematical tasks. In previous work, I observed problem-by-problem strategy shifts in a verbal reasoning task [13] and Simon and Reed [27] reported intra-trial strategy shifts in a puzzle solving task.

The claim is not that there are interindividual differences or that bugs migrate over time. The claim is that *each* individual student has several strategies at *each* moment in time, that he or she switches between them on a problem-by-problem basis, *and this is the normal case*. I refer to this phenomenon as *radical strategy variability*, to distinguish it from interindividual differences and bug migration over time. Radical strategy variability, if verified for a wide variety of task domains, implies that student modeling techniques which describe the student as consisting of a single strategy, correct or incorrect, are invalid and that student modeling techniques cannot assume consistency from problem to problem on the part of the student. The next technique to be described can proceed without the assumption of consistency, either between or even within a single problem.

## 2.3 The Model Tracing Technique

The model tracing technique proposed by John Anderson and co-workers [1] avoids several of the problems afflicting other techniques. The basis of this technique is to replace the intractable problem of inferring from final *answers* to entire *procedures* (a la DEBUGGY, PIXIE, PROUST, and ACM) with the problem of inferring from single *problem solving steps* to single *rules*. The student is monitored step by problem-solving step and each step is interpreted (modeled) as it occurs by identifying a rule (out of a library of all relevant correct and incorrect rules) which could have generated that step. The student is modeled as the set of rules which matched his or her steps in the traced performance. The model can include both correct and incorrect rules. The model tracing technique achieves its success through increased modularity (single rules instead of entire procedures) and decreased grain size (single problem solving steps instead of entire paths).

The model tracing technique is computationally cheap. The basic computation involved is to interpret an observed situation-action pair by finding a rule that applies in the given situation and which would, if evoked, execute the given action. If both correct and incorrect procedures are encoded as production rules, then this computation can be accomplished through pattern matching: any production rule that matches the relevant situation and which evokes the relevant action is a possible hypothesis about how the student decided what to do in that situation. Thus, no inferential machinery beyond that used in standard production system architectures is needed for this type of student modeling.

The model tracing technique ought to be insensitive to the problem posed by radical strategy variability [18]. The student's steps are matched against a library of rules. That library can contain rules from many different strategies. The final model of the student is the set of rules needed to account for his or her steps; that set might include rules belonging to different strategies. The modularity of the production system format makes the model tracing technique robust against inconsistency on the part of the student (as long as there is no attempt to *execute* the possibly inconsistent student model).

However, the model tracing technique requires a rule library and is in this respect in the same boat as the bug library technique. "The set of ideal and buggy rules [in the Geometry Tutor] are based on considerable theoretical analysis of the characteristics of the problem domain and on a great deal of empirical observation of student behavior." ([2], p. 2) The extensive empirical work might result in a rule library which cannot be used with any other student population than the one in which it was found.

Another difficulty with the model tracing technique is that it might be impossible to interpret the student's problem solving steps outside a narrow neighborhood around the correct path. The local interpretation of each individual step draws upon the modeling system's knowledge of where in the problem solving effort the step occurs, ie., which goal or subgoal the student is currently pursuing. Once the student leaves the correct path, it becomes less clear what he or she is doing. Without knowledge of the problem solving context, the interpretation of individual steps might become impossible. One would expect the model tracing technique to have difficulties with widely incorrect behavior, but also with exploratory behavior, whether mindless or intelligent.

## 2.4  Summary

Three conceptually distinct approaches to student modeling have been defined to date: map the student's solution onto a pre-defined library of error types, search the procedure space for a fitting model on-line, or follow the student step by step. Almost all implemented systems are variants of one of these three. All three approaches represent considerable progress in our ability to infer what a student knows and does not know from a record of his or her behavior. No perfect solution has been forthcoming and none should be expected. The universe of false knowledge is truly vast and the problem of inferring what the student knows that ain't so is computationally intractable in its general form and perhaps even conceptually incoherent. (What counts as an incorrect way of doing X?) Instead of a single general solution, we have a slowly growing library of imperfect but useful techniques. Each technique has a unique combination of positive and negative features, of advantages and disadvantages. The more student modeling techniques we know, the more likely it is that we have a technique that will fit a given pedagogical purpose.

# 3 A Constraint-Based Modeling Technique

Two considerations guided the present approach to the student modeling problem. First, the main purpose of student modeling in the context of intelligent tutoring is to guide pedagogical decision making. There is little need for a description of the student's knowledge, unless there is some way for a tutoring system to make use of, or react to, that description. It is not useful for a tutoring system to know that student S has bug A rather than bug B, unless the system has in its repertoire some instructional action that is more relevant for A than for B. If all its instructional actions are equally appropriate (or inappropriate) for both bugs, then the distinction between the two bugs does not matter (for purposes of implementing that system). In general, a student modeling component should identify the classes $C_1, C_2, ..., C_n$ of situations (learner states) in which instructional actions $A_1, A_2, ..., A_n$ are appropriate.

Second, the vastness of false knowledge implies that we must deal with it in terms of abstractions. The combinatorial explosions that wreck student modeling efforts come about because most modeling techniques deal with the specifics of students' solution paths and because they try to infer the particular mental procedures (strategies) the students are executing. Psychologists ponder rich data sources such as reaction time measures, videotapes, and think-aloud protocols for hundreds of hours in the attempt to identify the particular cognitive strategy used by a particular subject on a particular occasion [11, 15, 24, 33]. It is unreasonable to expect an AI algorithm to solve this complicated diagnostic task during on-going interaction with a student. We need a type of description which abstracts from the details of the student's mental code while capturing the pedagogically important properties of his or her current knowledge.

These two considerations imply that we need to model students in terms of *equivalence classes* of solutions rather than specific solutions or strategies. The members of a particular equivalence class are those learner states that warrant the same instructional response. In short, I propose that the student modeling problem can be conceptualized as the problem of defining instructionally relevant equivalence classes in a computationally tractable way.

## 3.1 Instructionally Relevant Equivalence Classes

All problem solving steps are not equally significant for diagnostic purposes. Some steps spring directly from the student's conceptual understanding of the problem, while others are mere errands or practicalities which spring from pragmatic considerations and which carry little conceptual significance. As a consequence, some problem solving steps are more diagnostic than others. This implies that we can achieve abstraction by selectively focussing on the significant steps and ignoring the others.

For example, consider a child who is adding two simple fractions. The problem he or she is facing might be written as:

$$1/4 + 2/3 =$$

Suppose that this student proceeds to draw a fraction bar on the other side of the equal sign:

$$1/4 + 2/3 = \text{---}$$

This action is a problem solving step, but a minimally significant one. The drawing of a fraction bar to the right of the equal sign is consistent with any number of correct and incorrect procedures for adding fractions. It tells us nothing about how the student thinks or about what he or she knows. However, if the next step is to fill in the numerator on that fraction bar as follows:

$$1/4 + 2/3 = \frac{3}{}$$

then we immediately know what the student is doing: he or she is adding the two fractions by adding numerators and denominators separately and we can predict that the final answer will be 3/7. We now also know something about this student's knowledge. Briefly put, he or she does not understand that fractions must have the same denominator in order to be added. Hence, without further ado, we have a significant clue as to what instruction is needed. The action of adding the numerators of two fractions with unequal denominators is a highly diagnostic problem solving step which is closely related to the meaning of fractions. Once we have observed this step, we need to know little else about the student's behavior to decide upon the appropriate instructional action: instruct him or her in the meaning of the denominator.

As a second example, consider a student practicing the routine scientific skill of constructing the structural formula, the so-called Lewis structure, for a given organic molecule. This cognitive skill is typically discussed in the beginning of a college level text on organic chemistry (eg., [31]). The rationale for this skill is the elementary theory of the covalent bond, which asserts, among other things, that each bond between two atoms results in the sharing of two electrons.

Suppose that a student is trying to construct the Lewis structure for the $C_2H_4$ compound, and suppose that he or she begins by connecting the two carbon molecules and continues by attaching one hydrogen to each carbon atom:

H-C-C-H

At this point we have learned very little about what this student knows about the covalent bond, even though he or she is seven steps[3] into the solution to this problem. However, if the next step is to attach one of the remaining hydrogen atoms to a hydrogen atom, as in

---

[3]Counting *the selection of an atom* and *the drawing of a bond* as steps: Select C, select C, draw the C-C bond, select H, draw H-C bond, select H, and draw H-C bond.

H-H-C-C-H,

then we learn something significant: this student does not understand that each covalent bond uses up two electrons, one from each atom; alternatively, he or she does not know that a hydrogen atom has only a single valence electron. Whereas the initial seven steps on this path are largely uninformative and conceptually distant from the theoretical rationale of the skill of constructing Lewis structures, this fatal eighth step immediately shows us that the student is not applying the constraint that each covalent bond requires two shared electrons. The appropriate instructional action is obvious: ask how many electrons a hydrogen atom has, and if the student knows the right answer, then instruct him or her in the fact that each bond requires two electrons. Once again, we see that some problem solving steps are more diagnostic than others.

The two examples also illustrate a second, even more significant point: the diagnostic information does not reside in the *sequence of actions* the student executed, but in the situation -- the problem state -- he or she created. It does not matter which sequence of steps the student took to arrive at a fraction which has the sum of the numerators of two given fractions with unequal denominators as its numerator. *There exists no correct solution path which traverses a problem state in which there is a fraction which has the sum of the numerators of the unequal fractions as its numerator.* Any path that goes through a problem state which has this property is incorrect; it violates the constraint that if two fractions have unequal denominators, then the denominators must be equalized before the fractions can be added. Violating this constraint indicates that the student is not thinking about the denominator as the unit in terms of which the numerator is expressed.

The property "a numerator equal to the sum of the numerators of two unequal fractions" defines an equivalence class of problem states, namely the set of all states that contain such a numerator. This property divides the universe of possible solution paths into two disjoint classes: paths that pass through a state that is a member of the class and paths which do not. For every path in the former class, it makes sense to instruct the student about the meaning of the denominator. We need not have any further information about the student to decide what instruction is needed.

This observation is true for the second example as well. The problem space for Lewis structures is characterized by a large number of alternative paths for both correct and incorrect solutions. Once again, we can define instructionally relevant equivalence classes by describing crucial properties of the problem states, while ignoring the student's actions. It does not matter which sequence of steps led to a structural formula in which one hydrogen atom is bound to two other atoms. *There exists no correct path which traverses a problem state in which one hydrogen atom has two co-valent bonds.* The property of containing a hydrogen atom with two bonds divides the universe of all possible paths into two equivalence classes, those which contain such an atom and those which do not. All paths in the former class indicate a lack of understanding of either the facts about hydrogen atoms or the principles of the covalent bond, or both. The instructional implication is obvious: teach the student these facts. Once again, the diagnostic information is in the problem state, not in the steps that led to it.

In summary, some problem solving steps are more diagnostic than others; some problem solving steps are more closely related to the conceptual rationale for the correct solution than others. These two aspects are interdependent: the highly diagnostic steps are informative precisely *because* they are closely related to the conceptual rationale for the skill. Furthermore, the pedagogically useful information does not reside in the sequence of actions the student takes, but in the resulting problem state. A problem state is diagnostically informative when it violates one or more of the fundamental ideas or basic principles of the relevant domain. These observations suggest that a tutoring system can extract the information it needs from the student's behavior by expressing the knowledge of the domain as a set of constraints on correct solution paths and recording when the student violates those constraints. Each constraint defines two equivalence classes: solutions that violate the constraint and solutions which do not. If the constraints are chosen to represent fundamental ideas of the domain, then these two classes of situations require different tutorial responses. To implement this idea requires a formal representation for constraints.

## 3.2 A Representation for Constraints

Ohlsson and Rees [21] introduced a representational format which makes it easy to express domain knowledge as a collection of constraints. The unit of this format is appropriately enough called a *state constraint*. Each state constraint is an ordered pair

$$<C_r, C_s>,$$

where $C_r$, the *relevance condition*, identifies the class of problem states for which the constraint is relevant, and $C_s$, the *satisfaction condition*, identifies the class of (relevant) states in which the constraint is satisfied. Each member of the pair can be thought of as a conjunction of features or properties of a problem state.

For example, the idea that fractions have to have equal denominators before they can be added can be expressed in state constraint form as *if the problem is $n_1/d_1 + n_2/d_2$ and if $n = n_1 + n_2$ then it had better be the case that $d_1 = d_2$* (or else something is wrong). This constraint is only relevant when one is adding fractions; fractions do not have to have equal denominators to be multiplied, for instance; hence the condition that *the problem is $n_1/d_1 + n_2/d_2$*. Also, the denominators do not have to be equal until the step of adding the numerators is taken; hence the condition that $n = n_1 + n_2$. It is only when both of those conditions are true that it also has to be true that $d_1 = d_2$ for the solution to be correct. To reiterate, the relevance pattern is a conjunction of properties that define the class of situations in which the constraint is relevant, while the satisfaction pattern defines the additional property (or properties) that have to be present for the constraint to be satisfied.

In the chemistry example, the principle that an atom cannot exceed its maximum number of valence electrons can be written in state constraint form as *if substance X has a maximum of $N_1$ valence electrons and if atom Y in a particular Lewis structure is of substance X and if the current number of electrons for Y is $N_2$, then it had better be the case that $N_1$ is smaller than or equal to $N_2$* (or else something is wrong with that Lewis structure). Unlike the previous constraint, this constraint has a relevance condition that is always satisfied in every problem state. Every substance has some maximum number of valence electrons, every atom belongs to some substance, and so on. This means that the constraint is always relevant, ie., an atom can never exceed its maximum number of valence electrons so the relation between $N_1$ and $N_2$ has to be monitored continuously while constructing a Lewis structure.

A state constraint can be implemented in a variety of ways. The most convenient and obvious way is to code each constraint as a pair of *patterns*, where each pattern is a list (conjunction) of elementary propositions which may or may not contain variables. In this implementation, the two parts of a state constraint are analogous to the condition side of a production rule. Examples of state constraints expressed as pairs of patterns for several domains are available in Ohlsson and Rees [21] and in Ohlsson [17]. Alternatively, the state constraints can be represented as pairs of Lisp predicates or as Horn clauses with two antecedents. The important point is that each state constraint is a pair of (possibly complex) tests on problem states.

The state constraints have to be evaluated with respect to the current problem state. Hence, a student modeling system using this format has to have an internal representation of the current problem state. If the state constraints are implemented as patterns, then it is convenient to represent the problem state as a list (conjunction) of elementary propositions. (Such a list is analogous to the working memory of a production system architecture.) Furthermore, the system must update that representation in the appropriate way as the student acts on the problem. The actions need not necessarily be represented, but their effects on the problem state have to be.

Once the problem state and the set of constraints have been encoded, the computations required to test whether a given problem state is consistent with a particular set of constraints are trivial: compare that state against all constraints and notice any constraint violations. The comparison can be carried out with any standard pattern matching algorithm, eg., a RETE network [6]. In a first step, the pattern matcher matches all the relevance patterns against the problem state to identify those constraints that are relevant in that state. In a second step, the satisfaction patterns of the relevant constraints are matched against the problem state. If the satisfaction pattern of a relevant constraint matches the state, then that constraint is satisfied and the tutoring system need not take any action. If the satisfaction pattern of a relevant constraint is not satisfied, then the student has violated that constraint. The output of this computation is the list of constraints the student has generated in a given problem state or throughout an entire solution path.

In what sense is this a student modeling technique? What kind of student model does this procedure give rise to? *The model of the student is the set of constraints which he or she violates.* The student is described in terms of those constraints that apply in the relevant domain but which he or she is *not* conforming to. As we saw previously, to describe what the student knows correctly is not sufficient; to specify his or her incorrect knowledge in detail is too complicated. The goal of student modeling is to describe what the student knows that ain't so in a compact way. The set of violated constraints is such a description. It is an abstract specification of the student's knowledge which is precise enough to guide instruction and also computationally tractable.

### 3.3 An Implemented Example

There are two distinct ways of using a student modeling system: on-line and off-line. A system is used *on-line* when it is implemented as a component of a tutoring system and used to monitor ongoing student behavior during tutoring. A modeling system is used *off-line* when it is implemented as a stand-alone system and applied outside the context of tutoring, as in the analysis of test results. Although most student modeling techniques can, in principle, be used in both ways, there is a tendency for actual systems to fit one mode better than the other.

Student modeling operates either on final answers to practice problems, on solution paths, or on some combination of the two. Although most modeling techniques could, in principle, benefit from both types of information, there is in practice a tendency to rely more on one type of information than the other. For example, both model tracing and the technique used in the POSIT tutor [22] diagnose each step along a solution path and neither attaches any particular importance to the final step, while a system like ACM could not work at all without access to final answers. On the other hand, ACM *can* perform diagnosis using nothing but final answers, something model tracing cannot do.

In practice, there is a correlation between the two dichotomies just described. On-line systems tend to work with entire solution paths while off-line systems work with final answers. An off-line implementation of the constraint-based student modeling technique that works with final answers is described in this section. An informal discussion of how constraint-based modeling would operate in on-line mode is offered in the next section.

The task domain chosen for this demonstration was that old standby of procedural skills, subtraction; with regrouping. This domain was chosen because it is tractable and well understood, and because it enables us to compare the constraint-based technique with the bug library technique used in DEBUGGY as well as with the machine learning technique used in ACM. Stringent evaluation of constraint-based modeling in the context of tutoring is still a task for the future. The main purpose of the example below is to document that the constraint-based technique is feasible.

Constraint-based modeling begins with a task analysis that aims to identify constraints that capture central concepts of the domain. Two constraints from the domain of subtraction will be discussed here. A central concept in subtraction is *place value*, ie., the idea that the position (or *place*) of a digit in a numeral determines which quantity (or *value*) it refers to; in particular, that the value of a digit increases by a factor ten for each change in position from right to left. A second important idea is the concept of *regrouping*, ie. the idea that a numeral can be rearranged by decrementing one digit with some amount and then incrementing another digit in the same numeral by the same amount, and that this operation does not change the number indicated by that numeral. The two ideas of place value and regrouping are connected because the amount that must be paid back, as it were, after decrementing a particular digit is determined by the place value interpretation of the decremented and incremented digits.

These ideas take expression in behavior in a variety of ways. Correct understanding of regrouping implies that one cannot decouple the two operations of decrementing and incrementing from each other. To decrement one digit in a numeral without performing a corresponding increment on some other digit, or vice versa, is to switch to another number, rather than to rearrange the numeral. Therefore, we can formulate the following constraint:

Constraint 1: Increments should not occur in the absence of corresponding decrements (and vice versa).[4]

There exists no correct solution path in subtraction which contains an uncompensated increment, so this constraint implicitly specifies an equivalence class of incorrect paths. Also, this constraint is closely related to the meaning of the regrouping operation. Hence, it is a good candidate for a pedagogically relevant constraint.

Another aspect of regrouping is that the difference between each column and the next is a factor of ten, so decrementing with unity and moving one step to the right implies incrementing with ten; moving two steps to the right implies incrementing with a hundred. In short, there is an intrinsic relation between the place in which decrementing occurs, the place in which incrementing occurs, and the amounts involved. The standard procedure is to always decrement with unity, increment the digit immediately to the right, and increment with ten. Breaking this

---

[4]Formally but less idiomatically: *If there is an increment in column C, then there had better be a corresponding decrement in the column to the left of C* (or else the solution is incorrect).

relationship between place and amount indicates a lack of understanding of the relation between regrouping and place value. Thus, we can formulate:

Constraint 2: An increment by ten should not occur unless there is a decrement by unity in the column immediately to the left.

There exists no correct path in the subtraction space that increments one column without decrementing the column immediately to the right. Violation of this constraint indicates that instruction is needed, because the constraint is a direct expression of the relation between place value and regrouping.

In order to apply constraints to solution paths, we must first have some way of generating the paths. In off-line diagnosis on the basis of final answers, the solution paths of the students have to be reconstructed. As in previous work on the ACM system [10], heuristic search was used as a path generator. The modeling system was built on top of HS, a standard flavored production system architecture [17]. HS performs a best-first, forward search of whatever problem space it is given. The standard problem space for subtraction, as defined in Ohlsson and Langley [20], was implemented within HS. The search was not guided by the mechanism described in Ohlsson and Langley [20], but by a numerical evaluation function, the details of which are not important for present purposes[5]. For purposes of this chapter, I shall refer to the resulting system as $HS_d$ (for "HS, diagnostic version").

Given the standard problem space for subtraction, a subtraction problem and an answer (correct or incorrect), $HS_d$ first finds a path which explains that answer. In the runs discussed here, this task was accomplished in 50-100 production system cycles, depending on the number of columns in the problem and the exact evaluation function used. (In on-line use, the solution paths would be generated by the student so this step would be unnecessary.) Having found the path, the system compares each state on the path with all available state constraints. The output is a list of constraints violated by that path. This list is the diagnosis of the (hypothetical) student who generated the answer.

For example, given the problem (404-187 = ?) and the correct answer 217, the system proposes the following (correct) solution path:

Path 1:
1. Decrement 4 to 3.
2. Increment 0 to 10.
3. Decrement 10 to 9.
4. Increment 4 to 14.
5. Take difference between 14 and 7; write 7.

---

[5]We experimented with several different evaluation functions and found that they all picked out the same solution paths, but that the cost involved in finding a particular path varied. However, no single evaluation function gave better results for all problems.

6. Take difference between 9 and 8; write 1.

7. Take difference between 3 and 1; write 2.

Because this is a correct path, the system reports no constraint violations.

Given the same problem and the incorrect answer 327, the system suggests a solution which is known in the standard bug library for subtraction as Decrement-No-Borrow, ie., the answer is explained by postulating that each column is incremented without any corresponding decrement:

Path 2:

1. Increment 4 to 14.

2. Take the difference between 14 and 7; write 7.

3. Increment 0 to 10.

4. Take the difference between 10 and 8; write 2.

5. Take the difference between 4 and 1; write 3.

$HS_d$ reports that this path violates Constraint 1. Notice that the computational work performed by $HS_d$ is trivial (once the solution path has been found). The system makes no attempt to analyze the solution path, to instantiate plans, or to infer goals or strategies or the like. Its only action is to compare each constraint with each state along the path and make a list of the constraints that have been violated. The assertion that this path violates Constraint 1 contains, I claim, all the information that is needed in order to decide how to instruct this student.

To illustrate how constraints provide abstraction, consider the effect of giving the system the alternative incorrect answer 227. In this case, the system suggests a path in which the Borrow-No-Decrement is applied in the right-most column, as before, but in which a correct regrouping operation is executed in the other two columns:

Path 3:

1. Increment 4 to 14.

2. Take the difference between 14 and 7; write 7.

3. Decrement 4 to 3.

4. Increment 0 to 10.

5. Take the difference between 10 and 8; write 2.

6. Take the difference between 3 and 1; write 2.

In this case, the hypothetical student inconsistently applies the Borrow-No-Decrement bug to one part of the problem, but not to another part in which it could have applied. This type of inconsistency causes difficulties for student modeling systems which try to explain what the student is doing at the level of specific problem solving strategies. However, the $HS_d$ system has no more trouble with this example than with the previous one. It notices that Constraint 1 has been violated and reports this fact. No extra computational work is required to diagnose an inconsistent student. Notice that $HS_d$ provides the same diagnosis for Paths 2 and 3, although they are procedurally different. This amounts to a claim that there are no pedagogically interesting differences between the two paths and that an intelligent tutoring system should react in the same way to both of them.

Consider, finally, the effect of giving $HS_d$ the incorrect answer 127 to the same problem. In this case, the system suggested a path that exemplifies the Borrow-Across-Zero bug: the 4 in the left-most column is decremented and the right-most column is incremented, but the middle column is unchanged. Thus, the 100 subtracted from the hundreds column is paid back, as it were, as ten in the units column. This incorrect operation is followed by a correct regrouping in which the left-most column is decremented one more time:

Path 4:

Decrement 4 to 3.
Increment 4 to 14.
Take the difference between 14 and 7; write 7.
Decrement 3 to 2.
Increment 0 to 10.
Take the difference between 10 and 8; write 2.
Take the difference between 2 and 1; write 1.

In this path, Constraint 1 is not violated, because each increment is balanced by a corresponding decrement. There is no evidence in this path that the compensatory nature of the regrouping operation is not understood by the student. The problem with this path is that the place value of the decremented column is 100 and the place value of the incremented column is unity, so the amounts involved are incorrect. Consequently, the system reports a violation of Constraint 2, indicating that the student does not understand the relation between place value and regrouping.

By reporting a violation of Constraint 1 for both Path 2 and Path 3, the $HS_d$ system implicitly claims that the two incorrect answers 327 and 227 are of a kind, pedagogically speaking. They belong in an equivalence class of paths, all of which should trigger the same instruction. Although the answers come about through two different solution paths, they are both expressions of the same conceptual error: the student does not understand the compensatory nature of the regrouping operation. The simple statement that Constraint 1 has been violated is a compact expression of this diagnosis. By the same token, $HS_d$ implicitly claims that Path 4 is qualitatively different from the other two, and should trigger different instruction. These results are in accordance with pedagogical intuition.

## 3.4 Discussion

The simplicity of this type of student modeling is worth emphasizing. Admittedly, identifying a set of constraints which identify pedagogically relevant equivalence classes of paths requires extensive reflection on the task domain. However, the implementation of the constraints, once identified, is a trivial programming task. Furthermore, the constraints can be compared to problem states through pattern matching, a cheap computation. In the application described in this section, the modeling system also had to reconstruct the paths by searching the relevant problem space. However, this is an artifact of the off-line, final-answers-only mode; in on-line mode the path would be generated by the student.

A constraint-based student model differs from other types of student models in several ways. Unlike buggy models, constraint-based models are not runnable. Constraints are not procedures or strategies or inference rules. (Constraints state what ought to be true, not what is, in fact, true.) They cannot be executed to generate the solution to a problem. Also, constraint-based models do not describe what the student *does* know. Those constraints which the student had an opportunity to violate but did not, in fact, violate are candidates for concepts which he does know, but this indirect inference cannot be trusted; the student's behavior may accidentally have conformed to those constraints.

However, constraint-based modeling shares several features of the modeling approach proposed by Hawkes and Derry [7]. They use deviations of student solutions from correct paths to trigger tutorial interventions in their TAPS tutor for complex arithmetic word problems. Such deviations from the correct path are similar to constraint violations. Also, Hawkes and Derry achieve abstraction by ignoring the details of the student's cognitive strategy: "Deep modeling of procedural bugs is not necessary. In order to derive an effective tutorial intervention, it is not necessary to know the exact nature of the buggy routine that produces a particular error. Rather, it is sufficient to know that a particular error pattern indicates that a particular skill must be targeted for instruction." ([7], p. 55)

Like the modeling technique used in the TAPS tutor, constraint-based models ignore issues of control. Because the constraints express properties of problem states rather than action sequences, they are necessarily silent about goal hierarchies, plans, weak methods, and other entities that figure so prominently in information processing analyses of cognitive strategies. Constraint-based models ignore the question of how behavior, correct or incorrect, is generated. The student is described in terms of the kinds of *situations* he or she believes are consistent with the concepts he or she is trying to learn, rather than in terms of his or her cognitive skills. To the extent that instruction is concerned with how the student understands the subject matter; this is a pedagogically appropriate description.

Ignoring issues of control buys several advantages. First, the constraint-based technique should be robust in dealing with creative students who produce solution paths which the system implementer did not think of. If such a path satisfies all constraints (which it must, if it is truly correct and if the constraints have been formulated correctly), then a constraint-based system will (implicitly) recognize it as correct and thus refrain from interrupting. Second, for the same reason, a constraint-based system has the potential to monitor unrestricted exploration of a problem space. Because it deals with equivalence classes of paths, not particular paths, it can recognize any incorrect path as incorrect. No restrictions need to be imposed on the student for this to be possible. Third, a constraint-based system should be robust in the face of radical strategy variability [18]. Because issues of control are ignored, it does not matter that the student is using multiple strategies. The technique is not trying to model student strategies, so it is not affected by strategy inconsistency.

What research is required to construct a constraint-based system? No runnable expert or ideal student model is necessary, nor is there a need to construct a bug library. A careful task analysis is required to identify constraints which are closely related to the basic concepts of the domain. To repeat, each constraint should specify a property that is shared by all correct paths, so that a problem state that violates one or more constraints is known to be incorrect without further analysis. In addition, each constraint should express a property that derives from the basic concepts of the problem domain, so that a violation of the constraint is diagnostic with respect to the student's understanding of the domain. Close comparative analysis of correct and incorrect solution paths can be expected to facilitate the identification of most diagnostic constraints, so the need for empirical research is not entirely circumvented.

# 4  Design for a Constraint-Based Tutor

A tutoring system based on constraint-based student modeling would be significantly simpler than a system based on current tutoring technologies. Such a system would not need a separate expert model, nor would it contain a runnable student model. An important component of such a system is the interface, including the internal representation of what the student sees on the screen. It is imperative that the effects of each action are recorded in the internal state description. Furthermore, such a system would have a collection of constraints and a pattern matcher that can determine when the constraints are satisfied and not. Finally, there is the tutoring component which decides which instruction to deliver on the basis of the output from the student modeling component.

How could a constraint-based student model be used to guide instruction? The technique is in and of itself neutral with respect to pedagogy. A constraint violation is only an indicator that instruction is called for; it does not dictate which instructional action should be taken. In the simplest case, instructional messages are attached directly to the constraints (analogous to the way in which instructional messages are associated with buggy rules in model tracing tutors). Whenever the student violates constraint C, the instructional message associated with that constraint is typed out. The cycle of events in this scheme would be as follows: the student takes a step, the problem state is matched against the available constraints, and if it violates a constraint, then the instructional message associated with that constraint is typed out.

The basic scheme can be made more sophisticated in various ways. For example, the discussion up to this point has assumed that only a single constraint is violated in any one state. If more than one constraint is violated, then the tutoring system must have some procedure for choosing which constraint to react to or some method for how to deal with combinations of constraint violations. A simple solution is to impose a pre-defined priority ordering on the constraints. A more sophisticated solution requires various relations between the constraints and an algorithm which can reason intelligently about how to react to combinations of constraint violations. The basic scheme also presupposes that the last problem state is the only one considered, but this is not a necessary feature of the technique. The system can wait and collect repeated constraint violations before deciding what to do. In principle, the system could store all constraint violations generated by a particular student during an entire course, although it might not be easy to define tutoring strategies that can make use of such information.

In short, constraint-based student modeling does not force a particular pedagogy. It provides a description of the student in terms of the constraints which he or she has violated (in the current state, throughout the current problem, or consistently over a long period of time), but it leaves open the question of what instruction is implied by that description. In the basic scheme a remedial message is attached to each constraint and printed when that constraint is violated, but this scheme is just the simplest of many possibilities.

# 5   Conclusions and General Discussion

Constraint-based student modeling is based on the notion that the student can be described in terms of entities more abstract than particular solution paths or strategies. Abstraction can be achieved in two ways. First, some problem solving steps are highly diagnostic because they follow from the fundamental ideas of the subject matter, while other steps are a function of the pragmatics of the task and thus less informative. Second, the diagnostic information associated with a highly informative step does not reside in the step *per se*, but in the properties of the resulting problem state. Classes of problem states can therefore be defined by expressing the fundamental ideas of a domain in terms of constraints on correct problem states. The student is represented by the set of constraints that he or she violates. Instructional messages can be associated with individual constraints. Alternatively, the set of violated constraints can be input to a tutoring module which decides which instruction is called for.

The constraint-based technique warrants attention because of its potential to provide the following advantages:

1.  There is no need to create a *runnable* expert (or ideal student) model, and, consequently, no need for large scale empirical studies of domain experts (although interviews with experts might be helpful in identifying key ideas in a domain).
2.  There is no need to create a bug library, and, consequently, no need for large scale empirical studies of students to create and validate such bug libraries (although studies of incorrect solution paths might suggest useful constraints).
3.  There is no need for sophisticated and computationally expensive AI inference mechanisms. Constraints can be compared to problem states with off-the-shelf pattern matching algorithms.
4.  A constraint-based student model ignores the student's problem solving strategy. Consequently, a constraint-based system should be able to monitor free exploration, to recognize creative and novel solutions as correct, and to succeed in the face of various types of inconsistency on the part of the student, including radical strategy variability.
5.  The constraint-based technique is neutral with respect to pedagogy. A student can be tutored after each constraint violation or after a sequence of them, as seems most appropriate for the domain.

If these potential advantages can be realized in practice, then the effort required to implement an intelligent tutoring system would be significantly reduced.

The potential disadvantages of the constraint-based technique include the following: first, for some domains it might be impossible to identify properties of problem states which are highly informative with respect to the student's understanding. Second, the set of constraints might provide too loose a net, as it were, so that many incorrect solutions slip through without violating any constraints. As a result, the tutoring system might *underinstruct*, ie., not react to errors on the part of the student. This possibility must be taken seriously, because the student is likely to interpret system acceptance of a solution as active endorsement, rather than as mere failure to find faults with the solution. Third, it might be that the state constraints provide the wrong type of abstraction. They might not partition student behaviors into pedagogically relevant equivalence classes after all.

The constraint-based technique has not yet been subject to a realistic test. No tutoring system using this technique has as yet been implemented. The implementation for off-line diagnosis described above only proves that the technique is feasible. No evidence has been presented here that the technique yields psychologically realistic or pedagogically useful student models that can guide instruction. The main purpose of this chapter is to encourage researchers and system builders to experiment with the constraint-based technique so that we may learn something about its potential.

## Acknowledgement

Preparation of this manuscript was supported by Grant No. N00014-89-J-1681 from the Cognitive Science Program of the Office of Naval Research. The opinions expressed are not necessarily those of the sponsoring agency, and no endorsement should be inferred. Approved for public release; distribution unlimited.

## References

1. Anderson, J. R., Boyle, C. F., Corbett, A. T., & Lewis, M. W.: Cognitive modeling and intelligent tutoring. *Artificial Intelligence*, 42, pp. 7-49 (1990)
2. Anderson, J. R., Boyle, C. F., & Yost, G.: The geometry tutor. Proceedings of the Ninth International Joint Conference on Artificial Intelligence, pp. 1-7. Los Angeles, CA: University of California at Los Angeles 1985
3. Brown, J. S., & Burton, R. R. : Diagnostic models for procedural bugs in basic mathematical skills. *Cognitive Science*, 2, pp. 155-192 (1978)
4. Burton, R.: Diagnosing bugs in a simple procedural skill. In: *Intelligent Tutoring Systems* (D. Sleeman & J. S. Brown, eds.). pp. 17-183. New York, NY: Academic Press 1982
5. Carr, B. & Goldstein, I.: Overlays: A Theory of Modeling for Computer-Aided Instruction. Technical Report A. I. Memo 406. Cambridge, MA: MIT 1977
6. Forgy, C. L.: Rete: A fast algorithm for the many pattern/many object pattern match problem. *Artificial Intelligence*, 19, pp. 17-37 (1982)
7. Hawkes, L. W. & Derry, S. J.: Error diagnosis and fuzzy reasoning techniques for intelligent tutoring systems. *Journal of Artificial Intelligence in Education*, 1, pp. 43-56 (1989/90)
8. Johnson, W. L.: *Intention-Based Diagnosis of Novice Programming Rrrors*. Los Altos, CA: Morgan Kaufmann 1986
9. Langley, P., Ohlsson, S., & Sage, S.: A Machine Learning Approach to Student Modeling. Technical Report No. CMU-RI-TR-84-7. Pittsburgh, PA: Carnegie-Mellon University 1984
10. Langley, P., Wogulis, J., & Ohlsson, S.: Rules and principles in cognitive diagnosis. In: *Diagnostic Monitoring of Skill and Knowledge Acquisition* (N. Frederiksen, R. Glaser, A. Lesgold & M. G. Shafto, eds.).pp. 217-250. Hillsdale, NJ: Lawrence Erlbaum Associates 1990
11. Newell, A., & Simon, H. A.: *Human Problem Solving*. Englewood Cliffs, NJ: Prentice-Hall 1972
12. Nwana, H. S., & Coxhead, P.: Towards an intelligent tutoring system for fractions. *Proceedings of the 2nd International Conference on Intelligent Tutoring Systems*, Montreal, Quebec (C. Frasson, G. Gauthier & G. McCalla, eds.), pp. 403-408, Lecture Notes in Computer Science, Vol. 608, Berlin: Springer-Verlag 1992
13. Ohlsson, S.: Induced strategy shifts in spatial reasoning. *Acta Psychologica*, 57, pp. 47-67 (1984)
14. Ohlsson, S.: Some principles of intelligent tutoring. *Instructional Science*, 14, pp. 293-326 (1986)
15. Ohlsson, S.: Trace analysis and spatial reasoning: An example of intensive cognitive diagnosis and its implications for testing. In: *Diagnostic Monitoring of Skill and Knowledge Acquisition* (N. Frederiksen, R. Glaser, A. Lesgold, & M. G. Shafto, eds.). pp. 251-296. Hillsdale, NJ: Lawrence Erlbaum Associates 1990
16. Ohlsson, S.: The impact of cognitive theory on the practice of courseware authoring. In: *Authoring Environments for Computer-Based Courseware*. (R. Lewis, ed.). New York, NY: Springer-Verlag (in press)

17. Ohlsson, S.: The interaction between knowledge and practice in the acquisition of cognitive skills. In: *Cognitive Models of Complex Learning*. (A. L. Meyrowitz & S. Chipman, eds.). Norwell, MA: Kluwer (in press)
18. Ohlsson, S., & Bee, N.: Strategy variability: A challenge to models of procedural learning. In: Proceedings of the International Conference of the Learning Sciences (L. Birnbaum, ed.). pp. 351-356. Charlottesville, VA: Association for the Advancement of Computing in Education 1991
19. Ohlsson, S., & Langley, P.: Identifying Solution Paths in Cognitive Diagnosis. Technical Report No. CMU-RI-TR-85-2. Pittsburgh, PA: Carnegie-Mellon University 1985
20. Ohlsson, S., & Langley, P.: Psychological evaluation of path hypotheses in cognitive diagnosis. In: *Learning Issues for Intelligent Tutoring Systems* (H. Mandl & A. Lesgold, eds.). pp. 42-62. New York, NY: Springer-Verlag 1988
21. Ohlsson, S. & Rees, E.: The function of conceptual understanding in the learning of arithmetic procedures. *Cognition & Instruction*, 8, pp. 103-179 (1991)
22. Orey, M. A., & Burton, J. K.: POSIT: Process oriented subtraction-interface for tutoring. *Journal of Artificial Intelligence in Education*, 1, pp. 77-104 (1989/90)
23. Payne, S. J., & Squibb, H. R.: Algebra mal-rules and cognitive accounts of errors. *Cognitive Science*, 14, pp. 445-481 (1990)
24. Schoenfeld, A. H., Smith III, J. P., & Arcavi, A.: Learning: The microgenetic analysis of one student's evolving understanding of a complex subject matter domain. In: *Advances in Instructional Psychology*, Vol. 4 (R. Glaser, ed.). Hillsdale, NJ: Lawrence Erlbaum Associates (in press)
25. Siegler, R.: The perils of averaging data over strategies: an example from childrens' subtraction. *Journal of Experimental Psychology: General*, 116, pp. 250-264 (1987)
26. Siegler, R.: Hazards of mental chronometry: an example from childrens' subtraction. *Journal of Educational Psychology*, 81, pp. 497-506 (1989)
27. Simon, H., & Reed, S.: Modeling strategy shifts in a problem solving task. *Cognitive Psychology*, 8, pp. 86-97 (1976)
28. Sleeman, D.: Assessing aspects of competence in basic algebra. In: *Intelligent Tutoring Systems* (Sleeman, D., & Brown, J. S., eds.) pp. 185-199. New York, NY: Academic Press 1982
29. Sleeman, D., Hirsch, H., Ellery, I., & Kim, I.-Y.: Extending domain theories: two case studies in student modeling. *Machine Learning*, 5, pp. 11-37 (1990)
30. Sleeman, D., Kelly, A. E., Martinak, R., Ward, R. D., & Moore, J. L.: Studies of diagnosis and remediation with high school algebra students. *Cognitive Science*, 13, pp. 551-568 (1989)
31. Solomons, G.: *Organic Chemistry* (4th ed.). New York, NY: Wiley 1988
32. VanLehn, K.: Bugs are not enough: empirical studies of bugs, impasses and repairs in procedural skills. *Journal of Mathematical Behavior*, 3, pp. 3-71 (1982)
33. Williams, M. D., & Santos-Williams, S.: Method for exploring retrieval processes using verbal protocols. In: *Attention and Performance VIII*. (R. S. Nickerson, ed.). Hillsdale, NJ: Lawrence Erlbaum Associates 1980

# Strengthening the Novice-Expert Shift Using the Self-Explanation Effect[1]

C. Frasson[2] and M. Kaltenbach[3]

[2]Université de Montréal, Département IRO, CP 6128 Montréal, Canada
[3]Bishop's University, Department of Management and Information Science Lenoxville, Canada

**Abstract:** A critical assessment is given of a model of skill acquisition (Cascade) and of its account of the "self-explanation effect." This model reproduces result differences observed between students with apparently the same level of intelligence and pre-requisite knowledge. However it does not seem to account for the transformation of novices into experts. We are proposing an alternative interpretation of the psychological facts, based on learning contexts, that does not have this limitation. A brief account is given of a system that would make the benefits of self-explanations more widely distributed.

**Keywords:** constraint satisfaction, educational technology, feed-back messages, intelligent tutoring systems, one-on-one tutoring, student modeling, task analysis

## 1  Introduction

In an Intelligent tutoring system (ITS) the student model is one of the most important components. It can be used for various purposes such as evaluating the degree of student's mastery of a topic and determining the next topic to be taught, choosing the most suitable time to interact, generating adapted exercises and explanations or selecting the best teaching strategy. However the model is complex to build and more complex to maintain. The important challenge remains how to acquire knowledge about a student's knowledge.

Most of the approaches to student modelling compare a student's knowledge to an expert's knowledge, or to some referential model. Very few take into consideration the learning conditions in which the student was placed. Since the student model governs an important part

---

[1]This chapter also appeared in the *Journal of Artificial Intelligence in Education*, 3(4), pp. 477, (1993). Reprinted with permission of the Association for the Advancement of Computing in Education (AACE, P.O. Box 2966, Charlottesville, VA 22902 USA).

of the tutoring process, it must be very close to reality. According to VanLehn [26] it must reflect the sequence of mental states the student experiences when solving problems, and should help us understand how knowledge is acquired and reliably predict the results (in terms of knowledge acquisition) of tutoring sessions.

Particular learning strategies can strengthen knowledge acquisition. Recent investigations have revealed that students learn more when they explain examples to themselves [4, 28]. A set of findings, called the *self-explanation effect*, has been observed that seems to provide much needed insights on how students solve problems. The main finding is that different processes, used by different students, seem to account for different levels of performance, distinguishing Poor solvers from Good solvers [9]. Others studies have considered the impact of self-explanations on learners gradual shifts from novices to experts [7, 20] and the resultant implications on learning strategies for tutoring systems [10].

We have misgivings concerning an interpretation that to us seems excessively mechanistic. Many of the valuable observations of VanLehn et al. would benefit from reinterpretation in a wider context, inspired by Gagné's work [13] on the conditions of learning. We also think that the learning conditions in which students successively acquire knowledge should be considered. Frasson and de la Passardière [11] call these conditions "the learning context", and the corresponding student model the "contextual student model". An important aspect of this student model is that the level of learning is related to the conditions of knowledge acquisition experienced by the student. For instance if a student has only been motivated to acquire some specific knowledge items, he or she will be unable to integrate this knowledge without guidance and a variety of exercises. On the practical side we are developing a system (Dynaboard) for facilitating knowledge abstraction.

In the following we comment on VanLehn et al.'s current interpretation of the self-explanation effect. Then we broaden the context in which the self-explanation effect can be interpreted by conjecturing a structure for the conditions of learning. Finally we propose some integrating tools to elicit self-explanation at the appropriate time in a learning sequence. The aim is to strengthen knowledge acquisition in ITS and promote novice to expert shifts.

## 2 The Self-Explanation Effect

### 2.1 The Experimental Facts

Several experiments have shown that students learn more when they explain examples to themselves. A set of findings around this principle has been called the self-explanation effect [4] and reproduced in models or simulation programs [28, 22]. The study by Chi et al. was conducted on students involved in a physics course (learning particle dynamics) and distinguished between two classes of students: Good solvers (students with the highest scores) and Poor solvers (the others). After having studied a chapter on Newton's laws, students were presented example problems with solutions; afterward they were asked to solve similar problems. The main findings are the following:

*F1*:   Good solvers utter more self-explanations than Poor solvers when they study examples.

*F2*:   When reading the examples, Good solvers tend to say that they do not understand whereas Poor solvers say that they do understand.

*F3*:   During problem solving Poor solvers tend to refer back to the examples more often then the Good solvers.

*F4*:   Good solvers' references to examples are better targeted; the Good solvers read fewer lines than the Poor solvers who start at the beginning of the example.

These findings have been called the self-explanation effect, analyzed in several studies and used in several models. Pirolli and Bielaczyc [22] observed the same effect on students learning Lisp. Fergusson-Hessler and de Jong [9] studied works on the applications of principles of electricity and magnetism to the Aston mass spectrometer. These two studies confirmed the Chi et al. findings in different experimental settings. Moreover, Bielaczyc [22] and Recker [23] showed that a teaching strategy based on the self-explanation effect might be used efficiently in a tutoring system. Pirolli and Recker [23] developed a model that involves several levels of elaboration and abstraction, allowing details of the encoding, indexing and retrieval of mental information. This approach, which is based on Soar's data chunking principle [21], gives interesting insights on how information is organized when studying text and examples.

The interpretations and analysis made by VanLehn [28] are best given by quoting them, (the numbering is added for later references to the specific points):

"1.   We argued that students were inventing new knowledge during example studying and problem solving rather than recalling and operationalizing knowledge acquired by reading the text.

2.   We noted that when a derivation utilizes previously unpresented knowledge, only a few small pieces of knowledge are new.

3.   We noted that detecting a gap (in a proof) is difficult, because some impasses arc caused by poor search control decisions or slips. We claimed that subjects usually check their partial derivation for slips and to determine if an alternative solution path exists. Only when they are satisfied that the impasse is inevitable given their current knowledge do they proceed to search for knowledge to fill it.

4.   We conjectured that subjects use the derivations produced while explaining examples to constrain their generation of derivations while problem solving.

5.  Subjects have multiple methods for finding new knowledge. The most productive one for our subjects seems to be explanation-based learning of correctness (EBLC), wherein new domain knowledge is created by specialization of overly general knowledge.

6.  The effective learner learns more rules while studying the example than the poor learner. The Good solvers merely choose to explain more example lines than the Poor solvers."

We have no difficulty agreeing with the first point. Learning is an active process that involves students in a variety of creative ways. VanLehn et al. have confronted the difficult task of explaining why and how example studying enhances learning. Few would disagree with their argument that example studying provides much needed control knowledge for problem solving. Where we tend to disagree is on the "how" part. VanLehn et al. state "little is known about human knowledge acquisition methods"; only general processes have been identified involving the acquisition and the compilation of knowledge. We feel reluctant to follow them and other researchers in the position of making a very sharp distinction between these two processes. They consider that the slow changes in performance that accompany practice occur as a result of genetically coded operators. This denies any individual involvement or responsibility in semi-conscious or dimly perceived processes occurring in the recesses of the mind. This leads to a rather mechanistic and reductionist view of learning. In the following, at times, we shall take the liberty of adopting an introspective point of view in an attempt to produce a less one-sided account of the self-explanation effect.

Points 2 to 6 follow from the particular conception of knowledge adopted by VanLehn et al. Though some statements in their writings seem to indicate otherwise, the general impression is that knowledge is a bag of rules. These rules, for the kind of domain studied, are of an apparently simple type such as binary associations or equations. An attempt to order them has been made by distinguishing general rules from domain rules. The general rules may include variables which when instantiated produce domain rules. VanLehn et al. have proposed a model of knowledge acquisition that need not involve the way rules are indexed and structured in memory. A permanent organization of rules is not considered important for forming analogies between examples and problems: "Most models of analogical problem solving divide the process into three phases: retrieving an example, forming a mapping between the example and the problem, and applying information from the example to the problem." The overall conclusion is that students learn rules rather than cases. What is disturbing here is that at other points in their paper, VanLehn et al. state that "experts classify problems according to the solution method while novices classify problems according to their surface characteristics. However, we believe this finding can be explained...if one assumes that experts have a vast store of derivations that they use to quickly plan a solution to the given problem. This allows them to determine the main solution method." A derivation is not made up of a single rule; therefore the model of knowledge acquisition represented by the Cascade system does not account for the achievement of expertise, only for its external manifestations. Point 4 above would provide an arguable refutation of this conclusion, were it not for the fact that the derivations students produce while explaining examples are presented only as temporary constructs. Nothing has been made clear concerning the life span and ultimate fate of these derivations. If they persist, what is their role?

That the Cascade model accounts for the experimental facts is not surprising, since the model is constructed on the basis of protocols collected while students studied examples and solved problems. VanLehn et al. disagree with this conclusion, saying that the model could have given contrary results, claiming also for it "computational sufficiency" (as to externally observed facts) and "empirical sufficiency" (as a matter of opinion). In short, the validity of the Cascade model as a model of human learning hinges on the fact that the results it produced were unlikely, a kind of Turing test!

We now elaborate further on the more specific findings concerning the self-explanation effect.

*Fact F1:* (See also point 6: "The effective learner learns more rules while studying the example than the poor learner"). This is the most actively defended point in the argumentation by VanLehn et al. and in their view the root cause of all the others. It is a purely quantitative account. The quality of the rules produced is dismissed as secondary since no perceptible differences were found in the recorded protocols. As an account of what happens externally we are ready to concur, but with some alternative interpretations. It is likely that in a proof concerning a completely new domain, as was the case for the students tested by VanLehn et al., only simple propositions (rules) could be adequately indexed by old knowledge; by this we mean that the students do not have in memory knowledge structures with which the current example can be compared, so they concentrate on simple associations, inventing simple rules. Another possibility is that expressing complex structures is not as easy as reporting simple rules; the reported rules are the only practical things to report, a sort of language to express more complex things.

*Fact F2:* While the understanding process is going on students have no firm grip on the subject matter and may express statements of lack of understanding, only as tension releases and/or encouragements to study at a deeper level. Such negative statements can be expected to last until the new knowledge has been made commonplace, usable as a new chunk of knowledge or concept. Also, when the new knowledge has just been acquired and supported by a rational argument, the Good student may not be completely sure yet. "Fallacious arguments are always lurking around the corner and one is never too cautious." On the other hand, the Poor student has plenty of self-confidence and glances over the study material, acquiring only surface knowledge and by-passing any abstraction process; he or she is prone to jump to conclusions and to reduce the new material to some supposedly already familiar one. He or she fails to recognize the originality of the new knowledge. For very specific facts (eg., mathematical formulae), he or she learns by rote.

Also, Good students are often uncertain about a new chunk of knowledge (say, an abstract element of a problem solution) while it is being elaborated; so it is not surprising that their self-explanations remain mainly negative so long as this process lasts. By contrast, the Poor students having been only into surface knowledge and having avoided any deep abstraction process can mistake the appearance of the example for all that there is to know, and so express that they understand.

*Fact F3:* One tentative explanation for this fact could be that Poor students, in their unsuccessful attempts to solve a problem will return to the only potential source of a solution, that is the example. What is puzzling in the account given by VanLehn et al. is that if it is only the number of extracted rules while studying examples that differentiates Good students from Poor students, why then the Poor students do not become Good students as a result of their more frequent return to the examples? Clearly, the Poor student does not extract the same kind of rules as the Good student. We have here another reason to doubt an account of the difference between Good students and Poor students based only on the number of rules extracted during example studying.

*Fact F4:* As VanLehn et al. have mentioned, this is a corollary to fact F3. We add the observation that this better targeting of references to examples is an indication that, as a result of example studying, good students are grasping the structure of the example and not just a collection of rules. When using analogical problem solving, as defined by VanLehn et al., students would match their problem elements one by one with the elements of a knowledge structure they have in memory; this would contradict fact F4. In summary, example understanding is not limited to collecting rules. There is more to it, and what it is deserves a better account than just saying that the student immediately sees the relevant rule to extract from the example.

In summary, we cannot fully subscribe to VanLehn et al's account of the self-explanation effect just on the strength of their having obtained a computationally efficient model that reproduces experimental facts (student protocols). Within this self-imposed constraint they have built what may appear as an empirically sufficient model but which has in our view two major limitations:

1. It makes reference to some internal mental processes in humans that are not convincingly modeled by the machinery of a prolog interpreter.

2. More importantly, it does not account for the transfer of expertise from novice to expert.

Despite this criticism, the Cascade model sets a standard against which future models of skill acquisition will have to be measured.

In our opinion, a shift of emphasis is needed to further our understanding of the self-explanation effect. In the next section, we show how some aspects of the self explanation effect can be explained within the framework of the theory of Gagné [12].

# 3 The Learning Context

We consider that the conditions of learning in which the student has to acquire knowledge are fundamental for in-depth knowledge acquisition. These conditions form the *learning context* which, from our point of view, is composed of two elements : the *learning level* and the *learning capability*.

| Learning level | Conditions of acquisition |
|---|---|
| 0 Indetermination | unknown state |
| 1 Acceptance | prerequisites available |
| 2 Motivation | motivation activated and objectives given |
| 3 Attention | attention directed and recall stimulated |
| 4 Presentation | learning guidance provided |
| 5 Initiation | simple exercises provided and passed |
| 6 Integration | more complex exercises provided and passed |
| 7 Generalization | retention and transfer of knowledge |

Figure 1: The learning levels

According to Gagné [12], instruction is a set of events external to the learner which are designed to support the internal processes of learning. We are not interested here in all the instructional design aspects of the external events but consider that these events can place the student into different learning states (internal states). Using the conditions of learning established by Gagné [13], we have determined several *learning levels* corresponding to the main steps of the cognitive process (Figure 1). The conditions of acquisition characterize the type of external events to be activated in order to reach the corresponding learning level. A student reaches a certain level if the corresponding conditions of acquisition are satisfied. This set of levels constitutes the first part of the learning context

Level 0 may correspond to two possibilities : either the student does not have the prerequisites, or there is not enough information on the learning conditions.

Level 1 indicates that the prerequisites exist but no information related to the knowledge was given before.

Level 2 indicates that the learning process has started; the student is motivated and knows the target objectives.

Level 3 corresponds to the fact that the attention was drawn and that a recall of previously learned capabilities was done.

Level 4 corresponds to the introduction of learning tools and stimuli (text, video, demonstration,...); learning guidance adapted to the individual learner.

Level 5 specifies student mastery of knowledge in particular and simple situations.

Level 6 indicates that the student is in an intermediate state, aware of some solutions for more complex situations than the previous one.

Level 7 indicates that the student can transfer the knowledge in various situations.

Levels 1 to 4 represent the conditioning steps (the student is prepared to learn), while levels 5 to 7 correspond to the steps of effective knowledge acquisition. Notice that during the first steps (levels 1 to 4) the student is not really active in the learning process (he or she is guided). His active participation increases from levels 5 to 7 where he or she is finally capable of generalizing the solution. According to Gagné, the external events which can occur to transfer the knowledge from short term memory to long term memory, lead successively (for the levels indicated above) to phases of semantic encoding, recall of previously learned material and reinforcement of the acquired knowledge.

Another distinction considered in learning deals with human capabilities, which can be classified according to five types of learned capabilities: verbal information (V), intellectual skill (I), cognitive strategy (C), attitude (A) and motor skill (M), as indicated by Gagné [12]. Each type of learned capability is associated with a learning level in Figure 1.

Finally, we consider four types of knowledge [15]:

- acquisition of facts or "knows",
- executive knowledge or "can-dos", corresponding to the application of an intellectual or a physical process,
- capability knowledge or "can-uses" corresponding to the effective use of different "can-dos" according the situation, and
- explanatory knowledge or "can-explains", used to describe some properties.

Each type of knowledge will be mastered according to specific types of external events.

All these elements are important to determine the *learning context,* or more simply *the context.* The *context* is defined by the couple:

$$C = (L, A)$$

where, for a given knowledge, L is a learning level and A a capability (or ability).

In addition, we think that *learning strategies* used to present knowledge to the student should be specified and tested successively with the student in order to determine the conditions and the strategy which would give the best results. Depending on the situation, specific rules for simulating a student can be elaborated.

If we consider now the self-explanation effect, we see that it corresponds to the steps of knowledge acquisition in the model of Gagné. The conditions 5 to 7 are of particular concern: the student is in an active phase and tries to generalize the solutions. Only level 5 seemed to be passed by the good students in the Chi et al. experiment. However, why might Poor solvers not reach this level? Our interpretation is that :

* Poor solvers had only reached level 3 or 4 when examples were presented to them,
* even if, according to Chi [4], Good and Poor solvers had the same prerequisites in term of knowledge, we think that Good solvers had previously acquired operational knowledge (can-dos, can-uses or can-explains) and Poor solvers did not (knowing only facts and rules but not how to use them).

The analysis conducted by Chi and VanLehn [5] showed that 68.5% of the propositions deduced by both categories of student were inferred from previous knowledge (example, common sense or knowledge acquired from the previous example lines) and not from the text. If Good solvers uttered more self-explanations, this implies that they had reached a *different learning context* and particularly cognitive strategies and explanatory knowledge.

An analogy can be made to the differences in learning behaviors between the Poor and the Good students and between the novice and the expert. Self-explanations contribute to the generation of general skills, and conversely general skill (in learning conditions) enhances the effectiveness of self-explanations. We think that an additional and deeper interpretation of the self-explanation effect can be found in the experiments made in transforming expert systems into tutoring systems. Moreover, the self-explanation effect is a way to improve the shift of the novice to the expert.

## 4 The Novice-Expert Shift

Transfer of knowledge is still a complex problem. The experiments conducted by Shortliffe and Buchanan [25] in developing the tutoring system GUIDON from MYCIN, produced a spectacular demonstration that tutoring systems studies could contribute to fundamental aspects of knowledge management and organization in artificial intelligence. As an expert system, MYCIN proved efficient in several hundred cases, giving in the majority of them a better recommendation than human experts. However, an important weakness of MYCIN and

GUIDON is that they suppose that the student has the knowledge of all the technical vocabulary terms used by specialists and this aspect reflects the main problems of MYCIN :

- the system was designed by specialists in the field, and intended for specialists,
- the rules represent a compiled expertise but this compiled form is incomprehensible to students. The inconvenience is that only the reasoning of the expert is available and this reasoning is not explicit for the novice. The reasoning process implemented in MYCIN used a backward search, a knowledge deployment generally not used by humans, except by human experts, and that is efficient when the set of possible conclusions is small.

MYCIN was reconfigured into NEOMYCIN, separating strategic knowledge from domain facts and rules, and using a control structure based on a domain-independent set of rules about how to use the rules. The system can then move forward, proposing hypotheses. According to Clancey and Letsinger [6] "it is precisely NEOMYCIN's forward, non-exhaustive reasoning and management of a space of hypotheses that makes its strategy more human-like". Also, the set of metarules (organized in a hierarchy) represents the reasoning strategy expressed in terms of tasks on specific information.

The most important aspect to consider is that expert and novice reasonings are different. Novices function in a forward chaining mode also called data-driven (starting from the data and trying to reach the conclusion), while experts function in a backward goal-directed mode (starting from a goal and trying to verify a well founded hypothesis).

The self-explanation effect is a good illustration of how experts function: the Good students choose intermediate goals (or a final goal) to demonstrate, using some specific references to the examples. The Poor students proceed in a forward mode, referring back to the examples very often but, as novices, they are often lost and cannot reach the goal. Going from the goal to the data is also called an abstraction process and in fact the same process occurs when the Good students try to explain examples to themselves. They try to relate the problem to a list of well defined and recognized cases in order to reach the conclusion as to what was observed more easily [25]. The study by Farand et al. [8] showed that the development of ITS could benefit from a case-based methodology. The problem of novice-expert shift is deep and we recommended in [10] that the next generation of ITS include capabilities of modification of the inference mechanism in order to adapt the explanation of the problem to the reasoning form of the student. In fact, when Good solvers try to explain to themselves the solution of a problem they reduce the reasoning to their own reasoning approach. Also, when they do this explanation, students use a refreshing technique able to transfer knowledge from short-term to long-term memory (also called "encoding" in Gagné's theory). They can link new knowledge with previously acquired chunks, using their own knowledge base in which they are confident, thus making abstraction easier.

A major problem is how can one detect when a self-explanation method could be most effective? We propose the spiral model (described in the next section) to help in detecting the student's learning context. If the student has really acquired the highest level of context and operational knowledge, then he or she will benefit from the self-explanation effect.

To strengthen this novice-expert shift we think that an ITS should be supported by *specific tools* that promote the *self-explanation effect* in the context of a *student model* that distinguishes the different learning states or, at least, possible learning states of the student. In the next section we examine what kind of student model could be used for that purpose.

## 5 The Spiral Student Model

When a course is being taught, the conditions of learning (learning context) and the results obtained can be known for each activity. It is, however, difficult to determine the level of previously acquired knowledge in a context that is partly or totally unknown; it is even more difficult to predict the future results of a candidate activity. Since only hypotheses can be made in that case, our model must be capable of generating hypotheses drawn from various sources. The range of hypotheses can be reduced by specific questions directed to the student before delivering the course. We recall here the main components of this model [11] and show how it can be used to detect the conditions of activation of tools able to strengthen acquisition of knowledge using the self-explanation effect or other methods.

We consider an element $K$ of *knowledge* as a basic element of learning. Each element K is the most simple element of the curriculum corresponding to either a "know", "can-do" or "can-use", category of knowledge. For instance, K0 corresponds to how to make a selection (in a word processing curriculum, see Figure 2), K2 how to indent a paragraph, etc.

This knowledge K is acquired, presented or supposed to be mastered at a given time, in a *context C* composed of the couple: (*learning level, ability*), as indicated in section 3. For instance, we may suppose that K0 is acquired in context (4, V) and K2 in context (3, A). This means that learning guidance has been provided for K0 with verbal information and only attention has been directed for K2 giving a model of attitude.

A *strategy S* is the type of learning strategy used to present knowledge K (coaching, guided discovery, tutoring by example, tutoring by emulation,...). We may consider that K0 has been presented in a guided discovery strategy (S1) and K2 was just shown in an example (S2).

Our contextual student model is based upon real and hypothetical schemas.

A schema is a 4-tuple, *(K, C, S, E)* where $K$ is a knowledge, $C$ a context, $S$ a strategy, and $E$ an evaluation. The evaluation can range from 0 to 10 and indicates that the corresponding knowledge has been acquired in context C, using a given strategy and resulting in the indicated value.

A *real schema*, $S_R = (K, C, S, E_R)$ corresponds to a real evaluation $E_R$ of the student's activity for a given knowledge K, in a context C with a strategy S.

An *hypothetical schema* $S_H = (K, C, S, E_H)$ specifies that the knowledge K presented in the context C with a strategy S should give the evaluation $E_H$. This one is deduced by the system using meta-rules. Notice that an hypothesis can be made either on knowledge to be acquired or previously acquired. In fact, we have recently built a model and an algorithm able to predict the acquisition level of a knowledge unit, using an inheritance principle between the knowledge units [24] and some real evaluations.

The real schema gives an evaluation of knowledge K in the context C, while the hypothetical schema is a belief of the system of the student's capability to acquire knowledge K in context C (using the same strategy).

For example, let us consider the following schemas:

$$S_{R1} = (K0, (4, V), S1, 8) \quad S_{R2} = (K3, (3, A), S2, 7) \quad S_{H1} = (K2, (5, V), S1, 2)$$

The first two schemas result from real evaluations: the student has successfully reached the learning level of attention and presentation, respectively, for underlining and copying a paragraph. The third schema is an hypothesis that when presented with simple exercises to indent a paragraph should lead to a bad result.

Hypotheses and evaluations can be performed either on the context (for a given strategy) or on the strategy (fixing the learning level). The comparison of hypothetical schemas to the corresponding real schemas adjusts the accuracy of the student model, which may or may not serve for guiding the tutoring process. The question is how can we obtain the hypothetical evaluations?

Some of the rules used for the management of hypotheses are based on the principle of *coherence*. The coherence is the degree of linking existing between the different knowledge elements of a curriculum. Some similar ideas can be found in [2] with the genetic graph approach. Given a certain knowledge chunk, acquisition of another knowledge chunk can be achieved more or less quickly according to their relationship. If we consider a curriculum as a set of objects, *inheritance* between object classes provides an important concept which can be related to knowledge acquisition. The idea of inheritance links between elements of Ki and Kj knowledge-units relies on a replication of properties and attributes of Kj in Ki [18].

Ki -----------> Kj      inheritance link (Ki inherits from Kj)

This basic idea allows calculation of hypothetical schema from real schema knowing the coherence between knowledge-units. A formal algorithm to calculate the coherence values of a curriculum is defined in [24].

The following principle applies: if two knowledge elements, K1 and K2, are related, the conditions (context) of acquisition of K1 *will either facilitate the acquisition or the misunderstanding* of K2. For example, if the student is supposed to be aware of the backspace key but only at level 3 (motivation), the knowledge "can-do erase-backspace", which is strongly dependent on the backspace key, cannot be acquired in a higher context. In such a situation for instance, the application of a self-explanation method will prove inefficient.

Knowing (or supposing) that knowledge K0 was acquired at a given level, then different hypotheses can be generated by the system according to the *knowledge environment* of K0 and some meta-rules. The knowledge environment of K0 is the set of Ki elements linked to K0 by coherence degrees and on which reasonable hypotheses can be formulated. Beyond the last coherence, no hypothesis concerning the acquisition context can be formulated. These coherence degrees are determined by the subject matter expert.

To illustrate the process, let us consider an example of a knowledge environment in word processing. The meaning of knowledge elements (K0 to K6) is indicated below in Figure 2.

The subject matter expert determines the knowledge environment of K0 (Figure 2). For instance, he or she may consider that K0 and K1 are strongly coherent (so are K0 and K5). On the other hand, K2 and K6 are weakly related to K0, as they concern formatting functions. Finally, K3 and K4 can be situated in an intermediate position. We represent by different circles the degrees (from 1 to 5) of coherence, the smallest circle representing the strongest coherence level . The reason for this schematic representation is that it allows a repartitioning of the knowledge to be taught within different learning contexts, as indicated in Figure 3. However, in reality, there is no discontinuity among the coherence levels, as they are measured on a continuous scale [24].

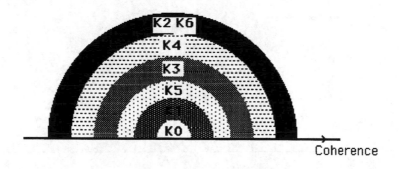

Figure 2: Knowledge environment

| | | |
|---|---|---|
| K0 : make selection | K1 : bold or any character style | K2 : indenting paragraphs |
| K3 : copy/paste | K4: save    K5 : underlining | K6 : formatting features |

In addition, the different possible acquisition contexts are distributed from right to left. Knowledge K0 stands in the center of the circle and the hypotheses on the related knowledge elements can evolve in different layers on a set of contexts. As soon as we know the acquisition context of K0, hypotheses can be made to determine possible evaluations of related knowledge presentation in different contexts. Figure 3 represents the possible contexts for knowledge K1 to K6.

For instance let us consider that knowledge K0 is acquired in context 7 (generalization, the highest context) and that strategy S1 is used to present the different knowledge. As one can understand, K1 being strongly coherent with K0 and so inheriting a large part of K0 attributes, it is reasonable to think that the effort to acquire K1 should be low and thus that K1 could be successfully presented in context 6. The corresponding subsequent evaluation would result in a high value (for instance 10, according to the evaluation scale).

For the same reason, K5 could be presented in context 6 or 5, but evaluation of K5 in context 5 would give a better (safer) result (9). Again, K3 could be presented in context 6, 5 or 4. The range of variations for each related knowledge is represented by a shadow area and the context in which the best result should be reached is determined by the position of the knowledge in Figure 3. The rest of hypothetical evaluation could be:

If we present     K4 in contexts 6 to 3, the results would be between 5 to 8,

                 K2 and K6, in contexts 6 to 2, the results would be between 3 to 7.

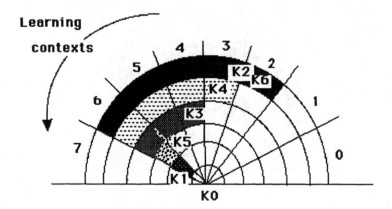

Figure 3: The hypotheses environment

As we can see, the spectrum of learning contexts evolves as a spiral. The different coherences are facts (provided by the curriculum expert) while the position of each knowledge in a context is an hypothesis made by the system using some rules (on the subset of contexts fixed by the expert, according to the objectives).

If K0 is now acquired in a lower context (for instance 6 or 5), then the projected contexts will be lower and the spiral area will be reduced. In particular, the spiral model would make it clear whether a knowledge chunk or a set of knowledge chunks would benefit from the self explanation effect. If the knowledge does not range between levels 5 to 7, only Poor students would result. At a given time the system builds a network of hypotheses which will be shrunk or expanded according to the comparisons of hypotheses with the real results of the student, (ER1 to ER6).

Reciprocally, if the results obtained are different from the hypotheses, then the initial level of learning of K0 was not correct and must be reconsidered. For instance we cannot efficiently apply the self-explanation method when we are faced with Poor students. The strategy to apply would be to gradually improve the degree of learning of K0 before choosing strategies that require mastering of "can-use" or "can-explain" knowledge.

This spiral student model would be a first way to detect not only the conditions for application of strategies like the self-explanation method, but also the conditions for use of some tools that aim at strengthening knowledge acquisition. In the next section we give a brief account of a system that would make the benefits of the self explanation effect more widely distributed.

# 6 Implications for an ITS System

The foregoing analysis has implications for the design of Intelligent Tutoring Systems (ITS). The various requirements we can identify at present for the further development of an ITS can be classified as needs for *incitation facilities* [30], and needs for *learning assistance facilities*. Tools must be provided to promote the kind of mental activities or actions that characterize Good students, independently of the subject matter. Assistance tools are needed to ease the performance of these mental activities or actions.

## 6.1 Incitation Tools

The work by VanLehn et al., among others, has demonstrated the fundamental role of example studying in "fleshing out" what would otherwise remain as abstract (obscure) concepts, disconnected from the previous learning and day to day common sense experience of students. The fundamental question that has not been addressed yet is how one would elicit from the students the kind of relating, abstracting, indexing, and archiving activities that characterize the Good student .

Our hypothesis is that many students have simply never been exposed to the kind of conversational freedom and distance which a mature person has relative to the material he or she is presented. High school training and the practical contingencies of mass education may in part be responsible for that. The Good students have acquired that sort of freedom, possibly as a result of having grown up in an enlightened family environment or having had particularly dedicated teachers. If this hypothesis can be sustained, then it follows that Poor students still need to experience that distancing from the study material.

This experience can be provided in a computer learning environment. For instance just adding an explanation module to the Cascade system would demonstrate to students the type of solution searching attitudes that correspond to EBLC (Explanation-based Learning of Correctness [27]). Other modes of reasoning could equally be presented in various example studying/problem solving contexts. Thus Poor students need more than sample solutions presented in terse style. They have to be made aware that such terse presentations constitute only an outline of the real proof, and of the pitfalls of cursorily scanning the material.

A good way to drive this point home is to propose proof presentation and exploration scenarios (different possible solutions) at various levels of detail. Development of such an enhanced presentation system has begun with the Dynaboard project [16] aiming at the creation of a sophisticated editor and exploration system for mathematical proofs. The main idea behind project Dynaboard is to create a computer platform to display complex reasonings (specifically mathematical proofs) as demonstration graphs that can be inspected at various levels of details. Demonstration graphs are not assembled in the same way as in the Geometry Tutor [1]. Instead the student can expand a statement associated with a node into a sub-graph of statements giving a more detailed proof derivation. The "intelligence" of the system resides in the management of constraints to insure that at all times only coherent (ie. compatible) information is displayed in the various nodes that are simultaneously visible. For instance if at some level of detail some nodes show a particular variable, the node that includes the definition of that variable must be visible. Most of the work done so far has focussed on finding ways to manage the graph transformations so that they appear natural to the student. In particular we use smooth animations [17].

With this system a student can read an example at a comfortable level of detail. By expanding some parts of the display students can test their understanding at a given level of generality. By compacting parts of the graph the reader derives structures that are more general (abstract). Finally the student can compose a view of the proof that is adequate for consignment to memory (human or computer) and can be efficiently exploited in an ulterior phase of information recall.

We are experimenting with ways of inciting the reader to adjust the level of a presentation. For instance, we let him or her know that a particular information item has associated comments, can be detailed, or that a collection of items can be regrouped. All he or she has to do is select a particular cursor shape; then when he or she places the cursor on a particular information item he or she gets visual cues on what would happen if he or she clicked the mouse.

In summary, when using Dynaboard, a student is placed in the position of a proof editor to the extent that he or she is able to specify a level of presentation that he or she feels is adequate for his current needs. He or she does not actually make the derivation, but on the other hand he or she is not forced to make the big step of reconstructing all by himself some missing steps, as often occurs with paper printed proofs. We conjecture that it is the magnitude of that gap that discourages many students from engaging in beneficial self-explanations. However this still has to be verified by experimental tests. It could be argued that providing students with a multitude of views of the same proof will make it more difficult to refer to examples while solving problems. But, as VanLehn et al. have observed, the student who has made an in-depth study of the example needs to make much less reference to it afterwards.

## 6.2   Assistance Tools

Apart from motivation, Poor students often need assistance in order to gain confidence in exercising the kind of freedom needed to distance themselves from the study material. Awareness of the gap between what they feel they can achieve and what they would like to achieve is often a discouraging factor that negatively affects performance.

Self-confidence can be raised by providing simultaneous assistance at the strategic and the tactical levels of understanding while students study solved problems and work at elaborating proofs. In conformity with the observations by VanLehn et al., the objective is to avoid students attempting many unmotivated exploratory steps in a blind search for a possible breakthrough when trying to solve a problem.

The method of instruction consisting of reading/studying worked out examples and then trying to solve problems, can be seen as an extreme case of the approach we suggest. For some (Poor) students this approach may separate the steps where strategic and tactical expertise are acquired and applied too much.

In studying worked out examples, the Good students discover rules and proof strategies. Experiments indicate that the Good students do not seek to extract all of the elementary associations (or rules) that could be needed in solving the problems; they concentrate on extracting strategy statements (ie. high level rules). Conversely the Poor students extract mostly shallow rules, based on surface features, such as variable names, that are often false or not applicable in the problem solving phase.

In order to assist students in better analyzing and understanding given proofs at the strategic level, it is necessary to involve them in activities at that level. The fact that the Poor students in the experiments of VanLehn et al. said that they understood the worked out examples well, in opposition to what the Good students reported, indicates that they read the successive lines without questioning, created rules on the basis of surface features, and were satisfied with only an appearance of logic in their reasonings.

VanLehn et al. have reported that the Good students created more rules during example studying than the Poor students; does this contradict our analysis? We do not think so. Ideas, rules, and plans, are better integrated and lend themselves better to discursive statements, whereas the surface feature rules, being of merely associative nature, can remain mainly tacit (or misunderstood by the study evaluators as simple rephrasing of lines in the solved example) and are also more quickly forgotten.

The question then is how to engage all students in extracting strategic information when studying the worked examples? In the current phase of the Dynaboard project we are testing a possible answer to this question. The student is given a terse proof, as in the examples used by VanLehn et al., and is asked to structure it as a demonstration graph (the different steps of the demonstration are linked in a graph). If he or she cannot do it, more details are added to the solved example. Once the demonstration graph is obtained, the student is engaged in the reverse process to summarize the proof while giving it a form best adapted to his/her current level of understanding. We are also planning to offer sequences of solved examples that provide a continuum between tasks corresponding to studying worked out examples and problem solving tasks.

# 7 Conclusion

We have elaborated upon the findings by VanLehn concerning the role of worked out examples in scientific training. We felt that the reported self-explanation effect was not distributed randomly among students but itself could be explained in terms of learning contexts. We have proposed a view of learning contexts as highly structured, non domain-specific, groups of abilities. These contexts actually condition the acquisition of specific knowledge.

This analysis results in practical recommendations on the design of teaching and knowledge discovery systems. The most important ones concern reducing the gap between example studying and problem solving. According to the context of the student, assistance tools can be useful to bridge the gap between data and intermediate goals. More emphasis is placed on the abstraction process and less on problem solving abilities that may be more apparent than real.

# Acknowledgments

We would like to thank the reviewers for their comments. In particular, one of the reviewers made extensive and detailed comments which were greatly appreciated and which helped to improve the article significantly. We also thank Pierre Mckenzie for proof reading a draft of this paper.

# References

1. Boyle, C. E. & Anderson, J. R.: Acquisition and automated instruction of geometry skills. Paper presented at the Annual Meeting of the American Educational Research Association, New Orleans 1984
2. Brecht, B. & Jones, M.: Student models: the genetic graph approach. *International Journal of Man-Machine Studies*, 28, pp. 483-504 (1988)
3. Buchanan, B. G. & Shortliffe, E. H.(eds.): *Rule-Based Expert Systems: The Mycin Experiments of the Stanford Heuristic Programming Project.* Reading, MA: Addison-Wesley 1984
4. Chi, M., Bassok, M., Lewis, M., Reimann, P. & Glaser, R.: Self-explanation: how students study and use examples in learning to solve problems. *Cognitive Science*, 13, pp. 145-182 (1989)
5. Chi, M. & VanLehn, K.: The content of physics self-explanation. *Journal of the Learning Science*, 1(1), pp. 69-106 (1991)
6. Clancey, W. J. & Letsinger, R.: NEOMYCIN: Reconfiguring a rule-based expert system for application to teaching. In: *Readings in Medical Artificial Intelligence: The First Decade.* (W. J. Clancey & E. H. Shortliffe, eds.). pp. 361-381, Reading, MA: Addison-Wesley 1981
7. Elio, R. & Scharf, P.: Modeling novice to expert shifts in problem solving strategy and knowledge organization. *Cognitive Science*, 14, pp. 579-639 (1990)
8. Farand, L., Patel, V., Leprohon, J. & Frasson, C.: A case-based approach to knowledge acquisition for ITS in medicine. Paper presented at the International Conference on Advanced Research on Computers in Education, IFIP, Tokyo 1990
9. Ferguson-Hessler, M. & de Jong, T.: Studying physics texts: differences in study processes between good and poor solvers. *Cognition and Instruction*, 7, pp. 41-54 (1990)
10. Frasson, C.: From expert systems to intelligent tutoring systems: advanced models of cognition for medical training and practice. Paper presented at the NATO Advanced Scientific Workshop, Italy 1991
11. Frasson, C. & de La Passardière, B.: A student model based on learning context. Paper presented at the International Conference on Advanced Research on Computers in Education, IFIP, Tokyo 1990
12. Gagné, R. M.: *Les Principes Fondamentaux de Lapprentissage.* Montréal: Les éditions HRW Ltée. 1976
13. Gagné, R. M.: *The Conditions of Learning,* 4th ed, Montréal: Les éditions HRW Ltée 1984
14. Gauvin, D. & Lefebvre, B.: Méthodes d'analyse de bases de connaissances dans un système tutoriel intelligent dédié à l'apprentissage de ART 4ème congrés de Reconnaissance des formes et intelligence artificielle, Paris 1984
15. Hopper, C. & Imbeau, G.: Organizing practical domain expertise in an ITS as knows, can-dos, can-uses. Proceedings of the 13th annual Western Educational Computing Conference, San Diego 1989
16. Kaltenbach, M. & Frasson, C.: Dynaboard: user animated display of deductive proofs in mathematics, *International Journal of Man Machine Studies*, 21, pp. 149-170 (1989)
17. Kaltenbach M., Robillard F. & Frasson C.: Screen management in hypertext: systems with rubber sheet layouts. Proceedings of the Hypertext '91 Conference, San Antonio, TX, pp. 15-18, December 1991
18. Kappel, G. & Schrefl, M.: Object/behavior diagrams. Proceedings of the IEEE 7th International Conference on Data Engineering, Tokyo, Japan, 1991
19. McCalla, G. I.: Some issues for guided discovery tutoring research: granularity-based reasoning, student model maintenance, and pedagogical planning. Paper presented at the NATO Advanced Workshop, Italy 1989
20. Möbus,C., Schröder, O. & Jürgen Thole, H.: Runtime modeling the novice-expert shift on a rule-schema-case continuum. Paper presented at the Nato Advanced Scientific Workshop, St.Adele, Quebec 1991
21. Newell, A.: *Unified theory of cognition.* Cambridge, MA: Harvard University Press 1990

22. Pirolli, P. & Bielaczyc, K.: Empirical analysis of self-explanation and transfer in learning to program. Proceedings of the 11th Annual Conference of the Cognitive Science Society, Ann Arbor, MI, pp. 450-457, Hillsdale, NJ: Lawrence Erlbaum Associates 1990

23. Pirolli, P. & Recker, M.: *A model of self-explanation strategies of instructional text in the acquisition of programming skills*. Technical Report CSM-1, Berkeley, CA: University of California, School of Education 1991

24. Ramazani, D. & Frasson, C.: Using an extended object oriented model for contextual student modelling. Proceedings of the 6th International Conference on Systems Research Informatics and Cybernetics, Baden-Baden 1992

25. Teach, R. L. & Shortliffe, E. H.: An analysis of physicians' attitudes. In: *Rule-Based Expert System: the Mycin Experiments of the Stanford Heuristic Programming Project.* (B. G. Buchanan & E. H. Shortliffe, eds.). pp. 635-652. Reading, MA: Addison-Wesley 1984

26. VanLehn, K.: Student modeling. In: *Foundations of Intelligent Tutoring Systems* (Polson & Richardson, eds.). Hillsdale, NJ: Lawrence Erlbaum Associates 1988

27. VanLehn, K., Ball, W. & Kowalski, B.: Non-LIFO execution of cognitive procedures, *Cognitive Science*, 13, pp. 415-465 (1990)

28. VanLehn, K., Jones, M. & Chi M.: Modeling the self-explanation effect with Cascade 3. Proceedings of the 13th Annual Conference of the Cognitive Science Society, Chicago, Il, pp 137-148, Hillsdale, NJ: Lawrence Erlbaum Associates 1991

29. VanLehn, K., Jones, M. & Chi, M.: A model of the self-explanation effect. *Journal of the Learning Science* (1991)

30. Winne, P. H.: Theories of instruction and of intelligence for designing artificially intelligent tutoring systems. *Educational Psychologist*, 24(3), pp. 229-259 (1989)

# Diagnosing and Evaluating the Acquisition Process of Problem Solving Schemata in the Domain of Functional Programming

Claus Möbus, Olaf Schröder, and Heinz-Jürgen Thole*

Department of Computational Science, University of Oldenburg, Oldenburg, Germany

**Abstract:** This paper describes an approach to model students' knowledge growth from novice to expert within the framework of a help system, ABSYNT, in the domain of functional programming. The help system has expert knowledge about a large solution space. On the other hand, in order to provide learner-centered help there is a model of the student's actual state of domain knowledge. The model is continuously updated based on the learner's actions. It distinguishes between newly acquired and improved knowledge. *Newly acquired knowledge* is represented by augmenting the model with rules from the expert knowledge base. Although they are expert rules, only rules able to explain the student's action sequences are incorporated in the model. *Knowledge improvement* is represented by rule composition. This allows the prediction of various knowledge acquisition phenomena, like performance speedup and a decrease of verbalizations.

In this way, the knowledge contained in the model is partially ordered from general rules to more specific schemas for solution fragments to specific cases (= example solutions). The model construction is implemented but not yet actually used for help generation within the help system. This paper focuses on knowledge diagnosis as accomplished by the model, and on an empirical analysis of some of its predictions.

**Keywords**: knowledge acquisition, knowledge optimization, schema identification, empirical validation of student models, analysis of time-based and correction-based data

---

* We thank Jörg Folckers for reimplementing ABSYNT in LPA-PROLOG for the Macintosh computer. Now we can switch off our LISP machine.

# 1 Introduction

The problem of student modelling has become an important research topic especially within the context of help and tutoring systems [5, 9, 18, 26, 53, 54, 64] because the design of such systems raises questions like: Which order is the best for a set of tasks to be worked on? Why is information useless to one person and helpful to another? How is help material to be designed? Advance in answering these questions seems to be possible only if the actual knowledge state of the learner can be diagnosed *online* in an efficient and valid way. This is difficult [50, 51] but necessary for a system in order to react adequately to the student's activities. Furthermore, it has been well recognized that progress in student modelling depends much on understanding what the student is doing (and why). Thus, detailed assumptions about problem solving, knowledge representation and acquisition processes are needed.

We face the student modelling problem within the context of a help system in the domain of functional programming: The ABSYNT Problem Solving Monitor. ABSYNT ("Abstract Syntax Trees") is a functional visual programming language designed to support the acquisition of basic functional programming knowledge. The ABSYNT Problem Solving Monitor provides help and proposals for the student while constructing ABSYNT programs to solve given tasks. In order to make the system's actions adaptive to the student, we model the growth of the student's knowledge state. Our basic approach rests on three principles:

- To try to "understand what the student is doing", and why. This amounts to constructing a *theoretical framework* which is powerful enough to describe the continuous stream of hypothetical problem solving, knowledge acquisition and utilization events, and to explain the stream of observable actions and verbalizations of the student.
- To use a subset of this theoretical framework in order to construct a student model containing the actual hypothetical state of domain knowledge of the student. This *state model* must be (and can be) simpler than the theoretical framework because its job is *efficient online diagnosis of domain knowledge* based on the computer-assessable data provided by the student's interactions with the system.
- To fill the gap between the theoretical framework and the state model by constructing an offline model of knowledge acquisition, knowledge modification, and problem solving processes. This *process model* provides hypothetical *reasons* for the changing knowledge states as represented in the state model.

In accordance with these principles, we pursue a three-level approach:

- A theoretical framework of problem solving and learning serves as a base for interpreting and understanding the student's actions and verbalizations. We call this framework *ISP-DL Theory* (Impasse - Success - Problem - Solving - Driven Learning Theory).

- An *internal model* (*IM*) diagnoses the actual domain knowledge of the learner at different states in the knowledge acquisition process (*state model*). It is designed to be an integrated part of the help system ("internal" to it) in order to provide user-centered feedback.

- An *external model* (*EM*) is designed to simulate the knowledge acquisition *processes* of learners at a level of detail not available to the IM (for example, including verbalizations). Thus the EM is not part of the help system ("external" to it) but supports the design of the IM.

Thus ISP-DL Theory, IM, and EM are designed to be mutually consistent but serve different purposes. This paper is concerned with the IM. It is organized as follows: First we will briefly describe the ISP-DL Theory, our help system, the ABSYNT problem solving monitor, and the domain of functional programming knowledge as incorporated in ABSYNT. Then the IM is described and illustrated in some detail. Empirical predictions and a first evaluation are presented. Finally we will discuss some possible extensions and the role of the IM for adaptive help generation.

## 2   The ISP-DL Knowledge Acquisition Theory

As indicated, the ISP-DL Theory is intended to describe the continuous flow of problem solving and learning of the student as it occurs in a sequence of, for example, programming sessions. In our view, existing approaches touch upon main aspects of this process but do not cover all of them. Consequently, the ISP-DL Theory is an attempt to integrate several approaches. Before describing it, we will briefly discuss three theoretical approaches relevant here:

- In VanLehn's [56, 58, 60] theory of Impasse Driven Learning, the concept of an impasse is of central importance to the acquisition of new knowledge. Roughly, an impasse is a situation where "the architecture cannot decide what to do next given the knowledge and the situation that are its current focus of attention" [60, p. 19]. Impasses trigger problem solving processes which may lead to new information. Thus, impasses are an important source for the acquisition of new knowledge, though probably not the only one [57, 60]. Impasses are also situations where the learner is likely to actively look for and to accept *help* [56]. There is also empirical evidence that uncertainty leads to active search for information [30]. But problem solving or trying to understand remedial information might as well lead to secondary impasses [10].

  The idea of impasse-driven learning is also found elsewhere. As an example from machine learning, Prodigy [11, 35] acquires new domain knowledge and new heuristics in response to noticing differences between expected and obtained outcomes. As an example from memory research, scripts may be augmented with information about exceptions in response to mispredicted events [31, 47]. Refining hypotheses in the context of concept learning [15] may be considered another instance.

Impasse Driven Learning Theory is concerned about *conditions* for problem solving, using help, and thereby acquiring new knowledge. It is not concerned about optimizing knowledge already acquired. "Knowledge compilation ... is not the kind of learning that the theory describes" [56, p. 32]. Thus Impasse Driven Learning Theory covers an important part of the processes we are interested in, but not all of them.

- In SOAR [28, 29, 45] the concept of impasse driven learning is elaborated by different types of impasses and weak heuristics performed in response to them. Impasses trigger the creation of subgoals and heuristic search in corresponding problem spaces. If a solution is found, a chunk is created acting as a new operator in the original problem space.

  In SOAR all learning is triggered by impasses. But these impasses can be more fine-grained than in VanLehn's theory. Since our intention is to describe and understand students' actions and verbalizations, we are interested in coarse-grained impasses corresponding to observable behavior. At this level of analysis, it seems questionable whether all knowledge acquisition events can reasonably be described as resulting from impasses [57, 60]. For example, existing knowledge may be deductively improved as a result of its successful application without changing the problem space.

- ACT* [1, 2, 4] focuses on the success-driven optimization of already existing knowledge by knowledge compilation but pays less attention to the problem of where new knowledge comes from. This is a main topic of PUPS [2-4] which provides mechanisms for the inductive acquisition of rules from the perception of causal relationships and from analogy. But conditions for knowledge acquisition events (like impasses) is less focused on.

We think that for our purposes it is necessary to cover problem solving, impasse-driven learning, and success-driven learning as well. Thus ISP-DL Theory incorporates the following aspects:

- The distinction of different problem solving phases [19, 20]: *deliberating* with the result of choosing a goal, *planning* a solution to it, *executing* the plan and *evaluating* the result.
- The *impasse-driven acquisition of new knowledge*. In response to impasses, the problem solver applies weak heuristics, like asking questions, looking for help, etc. [29, 56-58, 60]. Thus *new* knowledge may be *acquired*.
- The *success-driven improvement of acquired knowledge*. *Successfully used* knowledge is *improved* so it can be used more effectively. More specifically, by *rule composition*

[1, 2, 32, 43, 61], the number of control decisions and subgoals to be set is reduced. In our approach, composition is based on resolution and unfolding [24].

We describe the ISP-DL Theory by *hierarchical higher Petri nets* [25], though alternative modelling formalisms are possible, eg., *stream* communication [22]. Petri nets show temporal constraints on the order of processing steps more clearly than a purely verbal presentation. Thus they emphasize empirical predictions. The whole process is divided into 4 recursive subprocesses (*pages*): "Problem Processing", "Goal Processing", "Nonoperational Goal Processing" and "Operational Goal Processing" (Figures 1-4). *Places* (circles/ellipses) represent states (eg., the content of data memories); *transitions* (rectangles) represent events or process steps.

Places may contain tokens which represent mental objects (goals, memory traces, heuristics etc.) or real objects (eg. a solution or a behaviour protocol). Places can be marked with tags (*In* for entering, *Out* for exiting place, *FG* for global fusion set). An FG tagged place is common to several nets (eg. the Knowledge Base). Transitions can be tagged with HI (HI for hierarchical invocation transition). This means that the process is continued in the called subnet. The dotted boxes show which places are corresponding in the calling net and in the called net. Shaded transitions and places are taken into account by the IM (see below).

Problem Solving is started in the page *"Problem Processing"* (Figure 1). The problem solver (PS) strives for one goal to choose out of the set of goals: *"deliberate"*.

A goal may be viewed as a set of facts about the environment which the problem solver wants to become true [44]. A goal can be expressed as a *predicative description* which is to be achieved by a problem solution. For example, the goal to create a program which tests if a natural number is even, "even(n)", can be expressed by the description: "funct even = (nat n) bool: exists ((nat k) 2 * k = n)". The "even" problem can be implemented by a function with the same name, one parameter "n" which has the type *"natural number"*, the output type of the function is a *boolean* truth value, and the body of the function has to meet the declarative specification: "There exists a natural number k such that 2 * k = n". The goal is achieved when a program is created which satisfies this description.

The goal is processed in the page *"Goal Processing"* (Figure 2). If the PS comes up with a solution, the used knowledge is optimized: *deductive knowledge optimization*. When the PS encounters a similar problem, the solution time will be shorter. The net is left when there are no tokens in *"Goals"*, *"Goal"* and *"Solutions"*.

In the page "Goal Processing" (Figure 2) the PS checks whether his set of problem solving operators is sufficient for a solution: *"operational?"/"non-operational?"*.

An operational goal is processed according to the page *"Operational Goal Processing"* (Figure 3). A plan is *synthesized* by applying problem solving operators, or it is created by

216

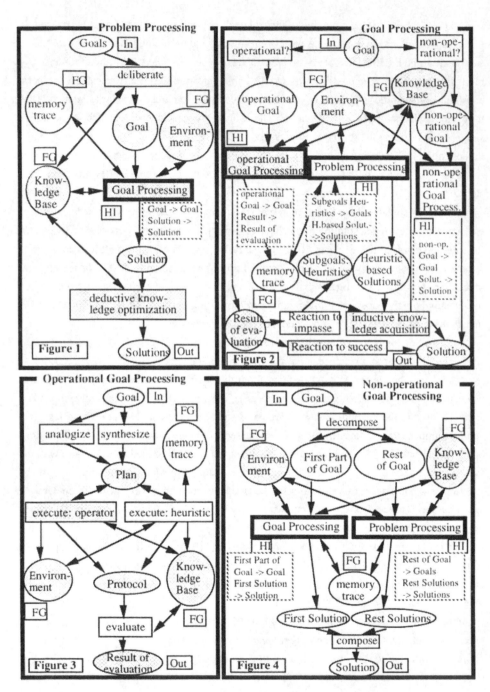

Figures 1 - 4: The ISP-DL theory of problem solving and learning

*analogical* reasoning. The plan is a partially ordered sequence or hierarchy of domain specific problem solving goals (or of domain-unspecific heuristic goals, this will be explained in a moment). In either case, the goals in the plan are pursued by *executing* domain specific or heuristic operators. Execution leads to a problem solving *protocol* which is used in combination with the knowledge base to *evaluate* the outcome. The *result of the evaluation* generates an impasse or a success. The result of the evaluation is transferred back to the page *"Goal Processing"*.

Within the page "Operational Goal Processing", the cause of an impasse may be located at different points. For example, the "synthesize" process might create an insufficient plan because of missing planning knowledge or insufficient control knowledge to make a decision. When the PS executes the plan (possibly mentally, leading to a protocol of verbalizations) and evaluates it, the result is an impasse. Another possibility is that the "execution" process has insufficient operators or heuristics. Then evaluation of the protocol will also come up with an impasse.

The *reaction* of the PS to *success* is: leave *"Goal Processing"* with a *solution*. The reaction to an *impasse* is the creation of subgoals to use weak heuristics for problem solving. Now there is a recursive call to "Problem Processing". "Goal Processing" and "Operational Goal Processing" are called again. This time, within Operational Goal Processing a plan to use heuristics is synthesized and executed. (Simple examples for these weak heuristics are to use a dictionary, to find an expert to consult, and so on.) A memory trace of the situation which led to the impasse is kept. If the use of heuristics is successful, the result is twofold:

- The heuristically based solution is transferred back further to the instance of the page "Goal Processing" where the impasse arose. Now the impasse is solved. The obtained solution is related to the memory trace of the impasse situation. Thus within *"Goal Processing"* new *domain specific* problem solving operators are inductively *acquired*.
- The obtained heuristically based solution is transferred back to "Problem Processing". Thus in *"Problem Processing"* the *domain-unspecific* heuristic knowledge is deductively *optimized*. So next time the PS encounters an impasse, he or she will be more skilled and efficient in using a dictionary, finding someone to consult, etc.

When *"Processing"* (Figure 4), the problem is decomposed and the subsolutions are composed into a final solution.

It is possible and necessary to refine the theory's transitions and places. For our purpose this simple theory is sufficient. Important for the rest of the paper are the theoretically and empirically validated statements:

- *New knowledge is acquired only at impasse time after the successful application of weak heuristics and on the basis of memory traces.*

- *Information is helpful only in impasses and if it is synchronized with the knowledge state of the PS.*

# 3 The ABSYNT Problem Solving Monitor

The visual language ABSYNT is based on ideas stated in an introductory computer science textbook [8]. ABSYNT is a tree representation of pure LISP without the list data structure (but we currently incorporate it) and is aimed at supporting the acquisition of basic functional programming skills, including abstraction and recursive systems. The motivation and analysis of ABSYNT with respect to properties of visual languages is described in [41]. The ABSYNT Problem Solving Monitor provides an *iconic programming environment* [12]. Its main components are a visual editor, trace, and a *help component: a hypotheses testing environment.*

In the editor (Figure 5) ABSYNT programs can be constructed. There is a head window and a body window. The left part of Figure 5 shows the tool bar of the editor: The bucket is for deleting nodes and links. The hand is for moving, the pen for naming, and the line for connecting nodes. Next, there is a constant, parameter and "higher" self-defined operator node (to be named by the learner, using the pen tool). Constant and parameter nodes are the *leaves* of ABSYNT trees. Then several primitive operator nodes follow ("if", "+", "-", "*", ...). Editing is done by selecting nodes with the mouse and placing them in the windows, and by linking, moving, naming, or deleting them. Nodes and links can be created *independently*: If a link is created before the to-be-linked nodes are edited, then shadows are automatically created at the link ends. They serve as place holders for nodes to be edited later. Shadows may also be created by clicking into a free region of a window. In Figure 5, a program is actually under development by a student. There are subtrees not yet linked and nodes not yet named or completely unspecified (shaded areas). The upper part of Figure 5 shows the Start window for calling programs. This is also where the visual trace starts if selected by the student. In the visual trace, each computational step is made visible by representing computation goals and results within the upper and lower region of operator nodes, and within the lower region of parameter nodes (see [38]).

In the *hypotheses testing environment* (Figure 6), the PS may state hypotheses (bold parts of the program in the upper worksheet in Figure 6) about the correctness of programs or parts thereof for given programming tasks. The hypothesis is: "It is possible to embed the boldly marked fragment of the program in a correct solution to the current task!". The PS then selects the current task from a menu, and the system analyzes the hypothesis. If the hypothesis can be confirmed, the PS is shown a copy of the hypothesis. If this information is not sufficient to resolve the impasse, the PS may ask for more information (completion proposals). If the hypothesis cannot be confirmed, the PS receives the message that the hypothesis cannot be completed to a solution known by the system.

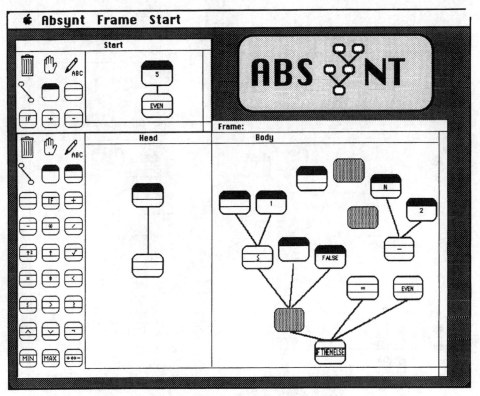

Figure 5: A snapshot of the visual editor of ABSYNT

The upper part of Figure 6 shows a proposed solution to the "even" problem just constructed by a student: "Construct a program that determines whether a number is even!" This solution does not terminate for odd arguments. In spite of that the *hypothesis* (bold program fragment in the upper part of Figure 6) is embeddable in a correct solution. So the hypothesis is returned as feedback to the student (thin program fragment in the middle part of Figure 6). The student then may ask for a completion proposal generated by the system. In the example the system completes the hypothesis successively with the constant "true" and with the "="-

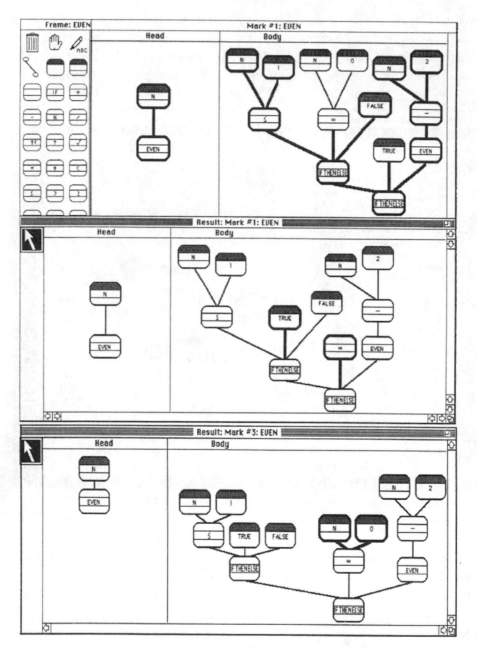

Figure 6: Snapshot of the ABSYNT hypotheses testing environment

operator (bold program fragments in the middle part of Figure 6). Internally, the system has generated a complete solution visible in the lower part of Figure 6. So the student's solution in the upper part of Figure 6 may be corrected by an interchange of program parts.

The hypotheses testing environment is the most significant aspect where the ABSYNT Problem Solving Monitor differs from other systems designed to support the acquisition of functional programming knowledge, like the LISP Tutor [6, 7, 14], the SCENT advisor [21, 33], and the ELM system [62]. One reason for the hypotheses testing approach is that in programming a bug usually *cannot be absolutely localized*, and there is a variety of ways to debug a wrong solution. Hypotheses testing leaves the decision which parts of a buggy solution proposal to keep to the PS and thereby provides a rich data source about the PS's knowledge state. Single subject sessions with the ABSYNT Problem Solving Monitor revealed that hypotheses testing was heavily used. It was almost the only means of debugging wrong solution proposals despite the fact that the subjects also had the visual trace available. This is partly due to the fact that in contrast to the trace, hypotheses testing does not require a complete ABSYNT program solution.

The answers to the learner's hypotheses are generated by rules defining a *goals-means-relation* A subset of these rules may be viewed as "pure" expert domain knowledge not influenced by learning. Thus we will call this set of rules EXPERT in the remainder of the paper. Currently, EXPERT contains about 650 rules and analyzes and synthesizes several million solutions for 40 tasks [36, 42]. One of them is the "even" task just introduced; more tasks will be presented later (see Figure 15). We think that such a large solution space is necessary because we observed that especially novices often construct unusual solutions due to local repairs. (This is exemplified by the clumsy-looking student proposal in the upper part of Figure 6.) Figure 7 depicts a hierarchy of types of rules in EXPERT. There are rules for programming (implementing), and rules for planning. The programming rules are split into rules implementing ABSYNT program heads (head rules), and rules implementing one ABSYNT node (node rules). The planning rules split into task plan rules and goal elaboration rules. Except for the task plan rules which will not be considered further, the following sections will provide definitions and examples of the different rule types.

The completions shown in the middle part of Figure 6 (bold program fragments) and the complete solution in the lower part of Figure 6 were generated by EXPERT rules. EXPERT analyzes and synthesizes solution proposals but is not *adaptive* to the learner's knowledge. Usually EXPERT is able to generate a large set of *possible* completions. Thus the main function of the *IM* (internal student model), which rules are derived from EXPERT, is to *select* a completion from this set which is maximally *consistent* with the learner's current knowledge state. This should minimize the learner's surprise to feedback and completion proposals.

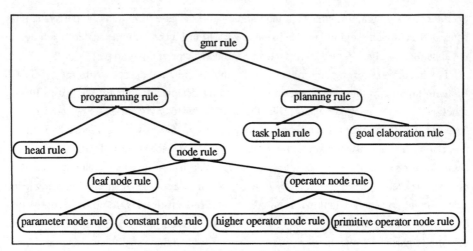

Figure 7: Hierarchy of types of rules in EXPERT

## 4 GMR Rules

This section describes the goals-means-relation GMR. The set of GMR rules may be split in two ways: *rule type* (simple, composed) vs. *database* of the rules (EXPERT, POSS, IM).

- As already indicated, there are three kinds of *simple rules*: *goal elaboration rules, rules implementing one ABSYNT node* (node rules), and *rules implementing ABSYNT program heads* (head rules).
- *Composite rules* are created by merging at least two successive rules parsing a solution. Composites may be produced from simple rules and composites. A composite is called a *schema* if it contains at least one pair of variables which can be bound to a goal tree and a corresponding ABSYNT program subtree. But if a composite is instantiated so that its variables can only be bound to node names or node values, then it is called a *case*.

The other way to partition the set GMR is the *data base* of the rules. EXPERT contains the ideal expert domain knowledge not changed by learning. So EXPERT contains only simple rules. The sets IM and POSS will be described below.

Figure 8 shows examples for simple rules depicted in their visual representations. Each rule has a *rule head* (left hand side, pointed to by the arrow) and a *rule body* (right hand side, where the arrow is pointing from). The rule head contains a *goals-means-pair* where the goal is contained in the ellipse and the means (implementation of the goal) is contained in the rectangle.

The rule body contains one goals-means-pair or a conjunction of pairs, or a primitive predicate (is_parm, is_const).

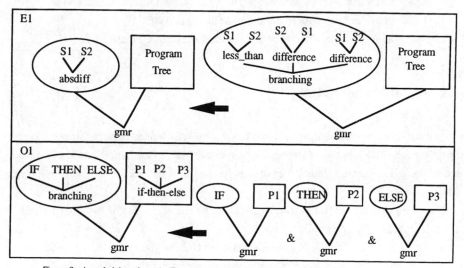

Figure 8: A goal elaboration rule (E1) and a rule (O1) implementing the ABSYNT node "if-then-else"

The first rule of Figure 8, E1, is a goal elaboration rule. It can be read:

If    (*rule head*):

        your main goal is "absdiff" with two subgoals S1 and S2,

then   leave space for a program tree yet to be implemented, and (*rule body*):

If    in the next planning step you create the new goal "branching" with the three
        subgoals "less_than (S1, S2)", "difference (S2, S1)", and "difference (S1,S2)",

then   the program tree solving this new goal will also be the solution for the main
goal"

O1 in Figure 8 is the "if-then-else" node rule (a primitive operator node rule), which is an example of a simple rule implementing one ABSYNT node (operator, parameter, or constant):

If    (*rule head*):

        your main goal is "branching" with three subgoals (IF, THEN, ELSE),

then   *implement* an "if-then-else"-node (or "if-"-node) with three links leaving from its
        input, and leave space above these links for three program trees P1, P2, P3 yet
        to be implemented; and (*rule body*):

if    in the next planning step you pursue the goal IF,

| then | its solution P1 will also be at P1 in the solution of the main goal, and |
|---|---|
| if | in the next planning step you pursue the goal THEN, |
| then | its solution P2 will also be at P2 in the solution of the main goal, and |
| if | in the next planning step you pursue the goal ELSE, |
| then | its solution P3 will also be at P3 in the solution of the main goal. |

# 5 Composition of Rules

In our theory, composites represent improved sped-up knowledge. Together with the simple rules, they constitute a partial order from simple rules ("micro rules") to solution schemata to specific cases representing solution examples for tasks. In this section we will define rule composition.

If we view the rules as Horn clauses [27], then the composite RIJ of two rules RI and RJ can be described by the inference rule:

$$\text{RI: } (F \leftarrow P \ \& \ C) \quad \text{RJ: } (P' \leftarrow A)$$

$$\overline{\qquad\qquad\qquad\qquad\qquad\qquad\qquad\qquad}$$

$$\text{RIJ: } (F \leftarrow A \ \& \ C)\sigma$$

The two clauses above the line resolve to the resolvent below the line. A, C are conjunctions of atomic formulas. P, P', and F are atomic formulas. $\sigma$ is the most general unifier of P and P'. RIJ is the result of unfolding RI and RJ - a sound operation [24].

For example we can compose the *schema* C7 (Figure 9) out of the set of simple rules {O1, O5, L1, L2}, where:

O1:     gmr(branching(IF,THEN,ELSE),if-pop(P1,P2,P3)):-
        gmr(IF,P1),gmr(THEN,P2),gmr(ELSE,P3).

O5:     gmr(equal(S1,S2), eq-pop(P1,P2)):- gmr(S1,P1),gmr(S2,P2).L1:
        gmr(parm(P), P-pl):- is_parm(P).

L2:     gmr(const(C), C-cl):- is_const(C).

C7:     gmr(branching(equal(parm(Y),const(C)),parm(X),ELSE),
                if-pop(eq-pop(Y-pl,C-cl),X-pl,P)):-
        is_parm(Y),is_const(C),is_parm(X),gmr(ELSE,P).

        where:

| if-pop | = | primitive ABSYNT operator "if-then-else" (or "if") |
|---|---|---|
| eq-pop | = | primitive ABSYNT operator "=" |
| P-pl, X-pl, Y-pl | = | unnamed ABSYNT parameter leaves |
| C-cl | = | empty ABSYNT constant leaf |

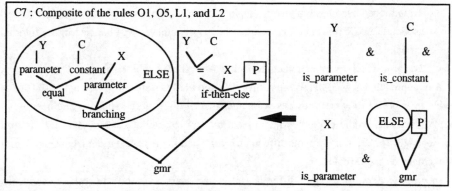

Figure 9: The composite C7

We also can describe the composition of node implementing rules RI and RJ with a shorthand notation:

$$RIJ = RI_k \bullet RJ$$

The index k denotes the place k in the goal tree of the head of RI. A place k is the k-th variable leaf numbered from left to right (eg.: O1$_3$ = ELSE). The semantics of "$\bullet$" can be described in three steps. First, the variable in place k in the goal term in the head of RI is substituted by the goal term in the head of RJ. Second the call term P in the body of RI which contains the to be substituted variable unifies with the head of RJ and is replaced by the body of RJ. Third the unifier $\sigma$ is applied to the term resulting from the second step, leading to the composed rule RIJ. Thus, the variables effected by the unification in step two are replaced by their bindings.

For example O1$_2$ $\bullet$ L1 = gmr(branching(IF, parm(P), ELSE), if-pop(P1,P-pl,P3)):-gmr(IF,P1), is_parm(P), gmr(ELSE, P3). C7 can be composed from the rule set {O1, O5, L1, L2} in 16 different ways. Two possibilities are:

$$C7 = (O1_2 \bullet L1)_1 \bullet ((O5_2 \bullet L2)_1 \bullet L1)$$
$$C7 = (((O1_1 \bullet O5)_3 \bullet L1)_2 \bullet L2)_1 \bullet L1$$

# 6 Empirical Constraints of Simple Rules, Chains, Schemata and Cases

Rules, rule chains and schemata give rise to different *empirical predictions*. The purpose of this section is twofold:

- To introduce hypotheses about the application of novice and expert knowledge, viewed as simple GMR rules and composites. These hypotheses will be used in the Internal Model.
- To show which specific predictions follow from these hypotheses.

Any approach designed to represent changing knowledge states must mirror the shift from novice to expert. In general, novices work *sequentially*, set more subgoals, and need more control decisions, while experts work in *parallel*, set less subgoals, and need less control decisions [13, 16, 23, 52]. Here this difference is reflected in the partial order from simple rules to schemata to specific cases.

In order to demonstrate this difference, it is necessary to specify hypotheses about the problem solving behavior. According to the ISP-DL Theory, a plan is synthesized from a goal, and execution of operators leads to a protocol of actions and verbalizations (Figure 3). Thus with respect to the theory we make a distinction between the problem solving phases of *planning* and *execution*: A *plan synthesizer* or *"planner"* synthesizes plans, and an *operator executor* or *"coder"* executes operators to implement the plans. The coder has implementation knowledge ("programming rules" according to Figure 7) for implementing ABSYNT trees, but no planning knowledge. The coder also has very limited execution knowledge: pattern matching without unification (except for parameter and higher operator names, and constant values). More complex processes are left to the planner whose job is to guide the coder, based on domain specific planning knowledge and on weak heuristics (to be specified by the External Model, as stated earlier. For such a model in a related domain see [48, 49]).

For illustration of a hypothetical interaction sequence between planner and coder, we assume that the goal "branching (equal (parm(y), const(0)), parm(x), ELSE)" is to be implemented, and that the coder has knowledge about the set of simple GMR rules {O1, O5, L1, L2}. Figure 10 shows how the interaction might proceed: At time $t_0$, the planner delivers the goal. The coder has no rule for it so he rejects the goal. So the planner chops the goal into subgoals. Next, he may present the subgoal "parm(y)" to the coder. The coder now has a rule, L1, instantiates it to L1', and edits an ABSYNT parameter node with the name "y". Next, the planner delivers the subgoal "parm(x)". The coder uses L1 again, leading to the instantiation L1", and programs a parameter x. Then the planner comes up with "const(0)". The coder uses L2, applying L2' and programming a constant node 0. Next, the subgoal "equal(S1, S2)" is given. The planner instantiates O5 to O5' and creates a "=" node with two open links: their upper ends are shadows (place holders for nodes). After time $t_j$, the planner tells the coder that "equal(S1, S2)" has "parm(y)" as its first subgoal. So the coder connects the first input link of the "=" node to the parameter y. Next, the planner tells the coder that "equal(S1, S2)" has "const(0)" as its second subgoal, so the coder connects the second input link of the "=" node to the constant 0. Thus it

Figure 10: Sequence of interactions between planner and coder while solving the goal "branching (equal (parm(y), const(0)), parm(x), ELSE)" with the set {O1, O5, L1, L2} of simple rules

may be possible that the coder has to rearrange the position of the nodes and/or the orientation of the links. This is symbolized by the hand in Figure 10. Next, the planner comes up with the "branching(IF, THEN, ELSE)" subgoal. The coder implements it, instantiating O1 to O1'. After time $t_m$, the planner tells the coder that "branching(IF, THEN, ELSE)" has "parm(x)" as its second subgoal and "equal(S1, S2)" as its first subgoal. So the coder connects the second and first input link of the "if-then-else" node to the parameter x and to the "=" node, respectively. Again, the position of links and/or nodes on the screen may have to be rearranged. Now the goal is solved.

Thus the planner does not know about the coder's knowledge, and vice versa. There is no fixed order of application of GMR rules. The order solely depends on how the goals are delivered to the coder by the planner. In the example the coder created the sequence of rule instantiations (L1', L1'', L2', O5', O1') depending on the goals delivered by the planner.

In contrast to this sequence, if the same goal "branching (equal (parm(y), const(0)), parm(x), ELSE)" is given and the coder knows the schema C7, then the interaction shown in Figure 11 will be produced. Again, at time $t_0$ the planner delivers the goal. This time the coder instantiates C7 to C7' and implements the ABSYNT tree contained in C7' without requiring subgoals and linking instructions from the planner.

If we compare the first interaction (Figure 10) where the coder knows {O1, O5, L1, L2} with the second one (Figure 11) where the coder knows C7, we observe:

- In the first sequence the coder implements five program fragments corresponding to the subgoals delivered by the planner. In the second sequence the coder implements just one program tree corresponding to the goal.
- In the first sequence the planner gives explicit information about linking program fragments, and the coder rearranges program fragments accordingly, if necessary. In the second sequence there is no such information.

In order to enable *empirical predictions*, we associate the following empirical claims with these observations:

- *Implementation* of ABSYNT program fragments:
  If the coder applies a certain GMR rule, then exactly the ABSYNT program fragment contained in it is implemented in an uninterrupted sequence of programming actions (like positioning a node, drawing a link, etc.). We do not postulate order constrains *within* this sequence, but we expect the sequence not to be interrupted by programming actions stemming from *different* rule instantiations.
- *Verbalization* of goals:
  Following the theoretically motivated distinction of a planner and a coder, selecting goals and subgoals for implementation by the coder is an act of planning involving control decisions. So it seems reasonable that at these decision points the selected goals may be verbalized [17]. The verbalizations explained by the selection of a certain GMR rule may be intermixed with the rule's programming actions, but not with verbalizations and actions stemming from different rule instantiations.

*Correction* of positions:

If the just implemented program fragment solves a dangling call or calls for another fragment already implemented, then it is to be connected with this existing fragment. Now corrective programming actions are likely: lengthening links, changing their orientation, and moving nodes.

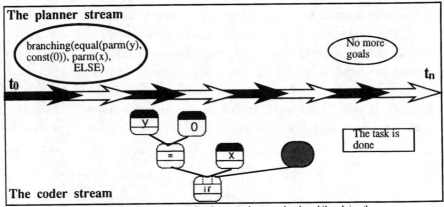

Figure 11: Sequence of interactions between planner and coder while solving the goal "branching (equal (parm(y), const(0)), parm(x), ELSE)" with the schema C7

If we compare the application of a single composite to the application of a set of simple rules (like C7 vs. {O1, O5, L1, L2}), then the following empirical consequences are assumed to result:

- *Implementation* of ABSYNT program fragments (*no-interleaving hypothesis*):
  For the set of simple rules, the order of rule applications is indeterminate, but the programming actions described by each rule should be continuous. *Actions of different rule instantiations should not interleave.* In contrast, when applying the composite there are no order constraints on the programming actions at all since just one rule is applied.

- *Verbalization* of goals (*verbalization hypothesis*):
  In the example, if the coder's knowledge contains C7 the planner has to make one control decision. If the coder knows only {O1, O5, L1, L2}, the planner has to make at least five control decisions (depending on how the goal is decomposed). Thus, we expect that applying composites is accompanied by *fewer goal verbalizations* than applying corresponding sets of simple rules.

- *Correction* of positions (*rearrangement hypothesis*):
  In case of the composite there are no open GMR calls to be implemented, and there are no to-be-linked program fragments left by earlier rule applications. Thus, we expect that applying composites leads to *fewer position corrections* of ABSYNT nodes and links than applying the corresponding sets of simple rules.
- Performance *time* (*time hypothesis*):
  Planning, selecting, and verbalizing goals, and correcting positions of nodes and links are internal or external actions that are expected to need time [46]. Thus, we expect that applying composites is *faster* than applying the corresponding sets of simple rules.

These relationships are illustrated in Figure 12 (suppressing the location information for composites) for the rule set {O1, O5, L1, L2}, the composite C7 which may be generated from it, and different sets in between, containing composites and simple rules. The rule sets are organized in a partial order which reflects the *degree of predictability of the order* of programming actions, the *degree of verbalization, position corrections,* and *performance time.*

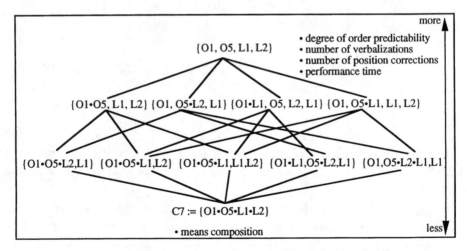

Figure 12: Rule sets partially ordered according to expected degree of order predictability, number of verbalizations, position corrections, and performance time

For example, if the rule set {O1, O5, L1, L2} is applied to the goal "branching (equal (parm(y), const(0)), parm(x),  ELSE)", the planner has to chop this goal tree because the coder's knowledge contained in the set {O1, O5, L1, L2} is not sufficient to implement this highly structured goal. If the goal tree is chopped to the stream of goals and goal-subgoal-relations (branching(IF, THEN, ELSE),

equal(S1, S2),

goal_subgoal_relation(branching(IF, THEN, ELSE), IF, equal(S1, S2)),

parm(y),

goal_subgoal_relation(equal(S1, S2), S1, parm(y)),

parm(x),

goal_subgoal_relation(branching(IF, THEN, ELSE), THEN, parm(x)),

const(0),

goal_subgoal_relation(equal(S1, S2), S2, const(0))),

then the stream of *event sets* (event-set(O1') < event-set(O5') < event-set(connect(O1', 1, O5')) < event-set(L1') < event-set(connect(O5', 1, L1')) < event-set(L1") < event-set(connect(O1', 2, L1")) < event-set(L2') < event-set(connect(O5', 2, L2'))) should be observed empirically, where:

- A < B means that the events in event-set A are followed by the events in set B
- event-set(O1')                  = {verb(branching(IF, THEN, ELSE), act(if-then-else),
                                       act(link(if-then-else, 1)), act(link(if-then-else, 2)),
                                       act(link(if-then-else, 3)))}
- event-set(O5')                  = {verb(equal(S1,S2)),act(=),act(link(=,1)), act(link(=,2))}
- event-set(connect(O1',1,O5'))   = {verb(connect(branching(IF,THEN,ELSE), IF,
                                       equal(S1,S2))),act(connect(link(if-then-else), 1, =))}
- event-set(L1')                  = {verb(parm(y)), act(parameter-node(y)),
                                       act(parameter-name(y))}
- event-set(connect(O5',1,L1')) = {verb(connect(equal(S1, S2), S1, parm(y))),
                                       act(connect(link(=), 1, parameter(y)))}
- event-set(L1")                  = {verb(parm(x)), act(parameter-node(x)),
                                       act(parameter-name(x))}
- event-set(connect(O1',2,L1"))    = {verb(connect(branching(IF,THEN,ELSE),THEN,parm(x))),
                                       act(connect(link(if-then-else),2, parameter(x)))}
- event-set(L2')                   ={verb(const(0)),act(constant-node(0)),act(constant value(0))}
- event-set(connect(O5',2, L2')) ={verb(connect(equal(S1, S2), S2, const(0))),
                                       act(connect(link(=), 2, constant(0)))}

The empirical meaning of the terms is:

- verb(Goal):              The Goal is possibly verbalized.
- verb(connect(Goal1,S,Goal2)): It is possibly verbalized that the subgoal S of Goal1 is
                            Goal2.

- act(Node): The Node is necessarily implemented in ABSYNT in a free region or on a link shadow.
- act(link(Node, I)): An ABSYNT link entering the I-th input of Node is necessarily implemented. Its other end is connected to another node or left as a shadow to be filled later.
- act(connect(link(N1),I,N2)): The ABSYNT link entering the I-th input of node N1 is connected to node N2. (That is, N2 is dragged onto the shadow at the upper end of the link, and/or the link is lengthened to N2.)

The planner may deliver the stream of goals and goal-subgoal-relations in a different order, like the one depicted in Figure 10. Then the order of the empirical event sets should change accordingly. But in any case, the actions and verbalizations *within* each event set should occur in an *uninterrupted sequence*. In contrast, there is no order predictability for the actions and verbalizations corresponding to the *schema* C7, and there is no information about goal-subgoal-relations. Just one set of events can be predicted:

- event-set(C7')  =  {verb(branching(IF, THEN, ELSE), verb(equal(S1, S2)),
  verb(parm(x)), verb(parm(y)), verb(const(0)), act(if-then
  else), act(=),  act(parameter-node(y)), act(parameter name(y)),
  act(parameter-node(x)), act(parameter-name(x)), act(constant-
  node(0)),  act(constant-value(0)), act(link(if-then-else, 1)),
  act(link(if-then-else, 2)), act(link(if-then-else, 3)),
  act(link(=, 1)), act(link(=, 2))}

We started to investigate some of these predictions empirically (see below). In addition, the no-interleaving hypothesis and the time hypothesis are used in the construction of the Internal Model to be described now.

## 7  The Internal Model (IM)

The IM is a set of domain specific knowledge fragments (simple GMR rules and composites) which are utilized and continuously updated. As stated earlier, the IM covers the subset of the ISP-DL Theory shaded in Figures 1 to 4. So before describing it in detail, we will sketch it in terms of the ISP-DL Theory.

- *Concerning Figure 1*: The PS is faced with a programming task (*goal*) and constructs a solution proposal (*solution*). The solution is parsed, using the *knowledge base* (rules in the IM and - as far as needed - in EXPERT). Subsequently, the rules just used for parsing are *optimized* by composition.

Since these new composites may be based on EXPERT rules, they are not directly inserted into the IM: according to ISP-DL Theory, a rule can only be improved after its successful application. This applies to the IM in that it cannot at the same time be augmented by a new simple rule (from EXPERT) and by composites built from the same simple rule. For this reason, in addition to the IM there is a set POSS of possible candidates for future composites of the IM. Composites of the rules used for parsing a solution proposal are generated and kept in POSS as candidates. Only those surviving a later test are moved into the IM.

- *Concerning Figure 2*: If parsing the solution is possible solely with rules in the IM, then the IM is considered as sufficient to construct the solution, and "Goal Processing" is terminated (*"reaction to success"*). But if parsing the solution requires additional EXPERT rules, then the IM may be augmented by these (simple) rules (*"inductive knowledge acquisition"*).

Thus, in accordance with ISP-DL-Theory, the IM contains *simple rules* representing newly acquired but not yet improved knowledge, and *composites* representing various degrees of expertise.

- *Concerning Figure 3*: The parse tree represents the student's hypothetical solution *plan*, whose *execution* led to a *protocol*: the sequence of programming actions, verbalizations, and corrections exhibited by the student. We call that part of the protocol consisting only of the student's programming actions (creating nodes and links, naming nodes) the student's *action sequence*. The action sequence is used to evaluate the parse rules:

  - Since knowledge improvement should result in sped-up performance (*time hypothesis*), a composite is moved from POSS to IM only if the PS shows a *speedup from an earlier to a later action sequence* where both sequences can be produced by the composite.

  - The IM contains only GMR rules (simple rules and composites) which proved to be *plausible* with respect to an action sequence at least once. This is defined now. With respect to some action sequence, GMR rules form four subsets:

    1. Rules not containing any program fragments ("goal elaboration rules") are *nondecisive* with respect to the action sequence. (But verbalizations can be related to the goal elaboration rules [42]).

    2. Rules whose head contains a program fragment which is part of the final result produced by the action sequence, and which was programmed in a

*noninterrupted*, temporally continuous subsequence (see the *no-interleaving hypothesis*). These rules are *plausible* with respect to the action sequence.

3. Rules also containing a program fragment which is part of the final result of the action sequence, but this fragment corresponds only to the result of a *non*continuous action subsequence *interrupted* by other action steps. These rules are *implausible* with respect to the action sequence.

4. Rules whose head contains a program fragment which is not part of the final result produced by the action sequence. These rules are *irrelevant* to the action sequence.

- A *credit* scheme rewards the usefulness of the rules in the IM. The credit of a rule is the total number of action steps explained by this rule in the problem solving process of the PS. It is the product of the length of the action sequence explained by the rule and the number of its successful applications. Thus the credit depends on the empirical evidence gathered for a rule.

During the knowledge acquisition process the IM is utilized and continuously updated according to a processing cycle shown in Figure 13:

- *Start* (Top of Figure 13): The first programming task is presented. Initially, both sets IM and POSS are empty.
- Now the learner solves the first task presented. Thus an *action sequence* is produced, leading to a *solution* to the task. The action sequence is saved in a log file.
- *First Test:* IM and POSS are empty, so nothing happens.
- *First Parse:* The learner's ABSYNT program solution to the actual task is parsed with the EXPERT rules, leading to a set of parse rules.
- *First Generate*: The EXPERT rules just used for parsing are compared to the action sequence. The *plausible* parse EXPERT rules are put into the IM and get credit. These rules are hypothesized as newly acquired and applied by the PS while solving the first task.

    Next, the composites of all parse rules are created and compared to the action sequence. The plausible composites are kept in POSS. These rules are hypothesized as newly created as a result of success-driven learning, but not yet actually used. Thus they are candidates of improved knowledge useful for future tasks. To each plausible composite, the time needed by the PS to perform the corresponding action sequence is attached.

    So the Generate phase results in an updated POSS and IM.

- Now the next task is presented to the PS. The PS creates an ABSYNT action sequence and solution to it.

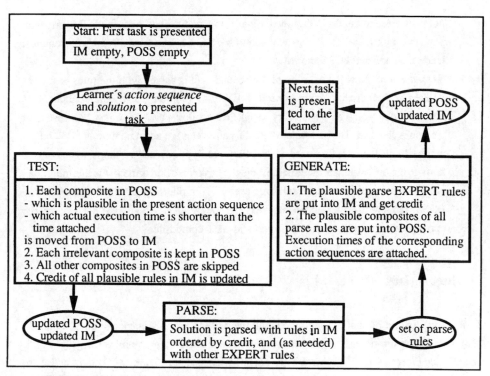

Figure 13: The utilizing and updating cycle of the IM during the knowledge acquisition process

- *Second Test*: Each composite in POSS is checked if
  a) it is plausible with respect to the action sequence, and
  b) the time needed by the PS to perform the respective continuous action sequence is shorter than the time attached to the composite. This means that the PS performs the action set *faster* than the previous corresponding action set which was shown by the PS before the hypothesized creation of the composite.

The composites meeting these requirements are put into the IM. Composites irrelevant to the action sequence of the solution just created are left in POSS. They might prove as useful composites on future tasks. All other composites violate the two requirements. They are skipped: that is, composites implausible to the actual sequence, or composites which predict a more speedy action sequence than observed. This means that the PS performs the action set *slower* than the previous corresponding action set which led to the creation of the composite. This slow-down is inconsistent with our model assumption that the PS prefers composites to simple rules; thus the composite is not transferred to the IM but skipped. Finally, the credits of all rules in the IM which are plausible with respect to the present action sequence are updated. Thus the second test leads to an updated POSS and IM.

- *Second Parse*: Now the solution of the second task is parsed with the rules of the IM ordered by their credits. As far as needed, EXPERT rules are also used for parsing.
- *Second Generate*: The plausibility of EXPERT rules which have just been used for parsing is checked. The plausible EXPERT parse rules are again put into the IM and get credit. As in the first Generate Phase, they are hypothesized as the newly acquired knowledge in response to impasses on the task just performed. Furthermore, the composites of all actual parse rules are created. The plausible composites are put into POSS, they will be tested on the next test phase. Again the time needed for the corresponding action sequence is stored with each composite.

# 8   Illustrations of the IM

To illustrate, Figure 14 shows a continuous fragment of the action sequence of a PS, Subject 2 (S2), on a programming task. Again we will restrict our attention to the rules O1, O5, L1, L2, and C7 (see Figures 8 and 9). When S2 performs the sequence of Figure 14, O1, L1 and L2 are already in the IM from earlier tasks. O5 is not yet in the IM but only in the set of EXPERT rules. C7 has not yet been created.

After S2 has solved the task, the *Test Phase* (Figure 13) starts. Since the only composite we look at here (C7) has not been created, we only consider the fourth subphase: Credit updating. O1 is *implausible* with respect to Figure 14 because the actions corresponding to the rule head of O1 are not continuous but *interrupted*. They are performed at 11:15:52, 11:15:58, 11:16:46, and 11:16:55 (Figure 14). Thus the action sequence corresponding to the rule head of O1 is interrupted at 11:16:42 and 11:16:50.

L1 and L2 are also implausible. Actions corresponding to L1 are performed the first time at 11:15:08 and 11:15:29. Thus this sequence is interrupted at 11:15:16 and 11:15:22. L1-like actions are shown a second time by the PS at 11:16:42 and 11:16:50. These are interrupted, too. Actions corresponding to L2 are performed at 11:15:16 and 11:15:34, with interruptions at 11:15:22 and 11:15:29. So since O1, L1, and L2 are implausible, their credits are not changed.

Now S2's solution is *parsed* with rules in the IM and, as needed, with additional EXPERT rules (Figure 13). O1, O5, L1, and L2 are among the parse rules in this case, as no other rules have a higher credit and are able to parse the solution.

After the Parse Phase, the *Generate Phase* (Figure 13) starts. O5 is an EXPERT rule used for parsing. But O5 is implausible, since its corresponding actions were performed at 11:15:22,

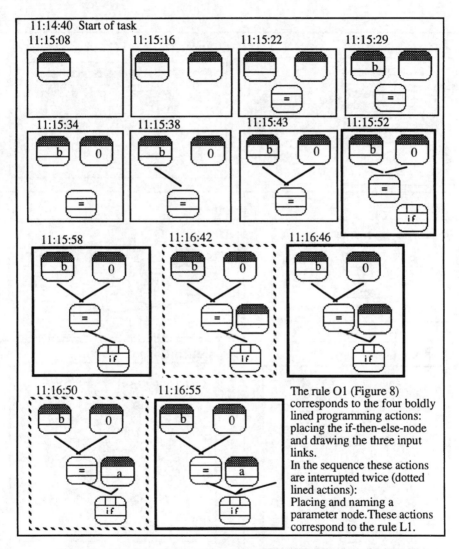

Figure 14: A continuous fragment of a sequence of programming actions of Subject S2

11:15:38, and 11:15:43, with interruptions at 11:15:29 and 11:15:34. So O5 is not put into the IM. Then the composites of the parse rules are formed. C7 (Figure 9) is a composite formed from O1, O5, L1 and L2. This composite is plausible because it describes the uninterrupted

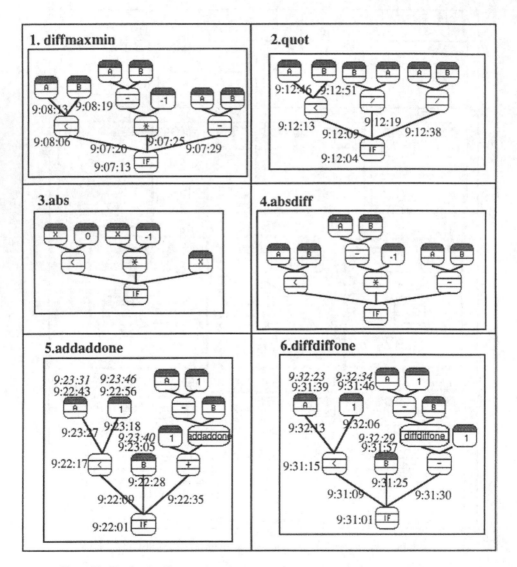

Figure 15: Simulated action streams and solution proposals to 6 ABSYNT programming tasks

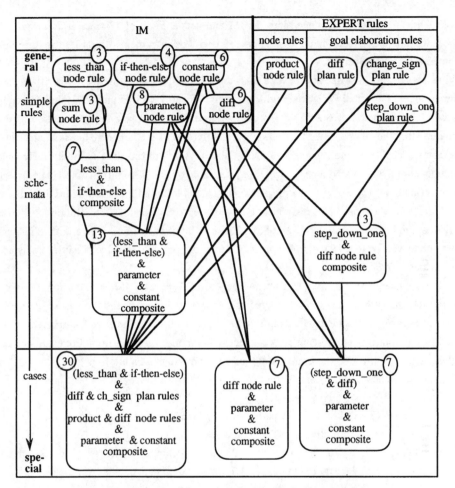

Figure 16: Specialization graph showing the partial order of simple rules, schemata, and cases as a result of the simulated programming sequence of Figure 15

sequence of programming actions from 11:15:08 to 11:16:55 (see Figure 14) - despite the fact that its components O1, O5, L1, and L2 are all implausible. Starting from the beginning of the task (at 11:14:40), the time for this action sequence is 135 seconds. Thus the composite C7 is stored in POSS with "135 seconds" attached to it.

After S2 has solved the next task, the following Test phase reveals that C7 is plausible again. The corresponding action sequence (not depicted) was performed in 92 seconds, which is less than 135. So C7 is moved into the IM and gets a credit of 13 since it describes 13 programming steps (see Figure 14). This credit will be incremented by 13 each time the composite is plausible again.

What does the IM look like after several tasks are solved? To give an impression we simulated the protocol of a virtual PS, starting with an empty IM and POSS. Figure 15 depicts the body trees of the solutions of 6 ABSYNT programming tasks: "diffmaxmin" (subtraction of the smaller from the larger of two numbers), "quot" (division of the larger by the smaller of two numbers), "abs" (absolute value of a number), "absdiff" (like "diffmaxmin": absolute difference of two numbers), "addaddone" (expressing addition by "+ 1"), "diffdiffone" (expressing subtraction by "- 1"). Some of the programming actions leading to these solutions are labeled with the time when they were performed. For example, the "<"-node in the solution to the task "diffmaxmin" was programmed at 9:08:06. The link between the "<"-node and the "if-then-else"-node was created at 9:07:20.The times of the actions of writing a value or name into a node are written in *italics*.

After solving the last task of this sequence, "diffdiffone", the IM contains simple rules, schemata, and cases. They can be ordered as a specialization graph, as shown in Figure 16. (The rules in Figure 16 are depicted in PROLOG in Appendix A.) The circled numbers are the credits. Each composite in Figure 16 is connected to the rules it is built from. For example, the "(less_than & if-then-else) & parameter & constant" composite in Figure 16 is:

gmr(branching (less_than (parm (Y), const (C)), parm (X), S),

if-pop (lt-pop (Y-pl, C-cl), X-pl, P)) :-

is_parm (Y), is_const (C), is_parm (X), gmr (S, P).

("lt-pop" is the primitive ABSYNT operator "<".)

According to Figure 16, this composite is the result of composing the "less_than & if-then-else" composite with the parameter node rule L1 and the constant node rule L2 presented earlier:

*"less_than & if-then-else" composite:*

gmr(branching(less_than(S1,S2), S3, S4), if-pop(lt-pop(P1, P2), P3, P4)) :-

gmr(S1, P1), gmr(S2, P2), gmr(S3, P3), gmr(S4, P4).

L1:     gmr(parm(P), P-pl):- is_parm(P).

L2:     gmr(const(C), C-cl):- is_const(C).

This composition can be expressed by

"(less_than & if-then-else) & parameter & constant" composite =

(("less_than & if-then-else" composite$_1$ • L1)$_1$ • L2)$_1$ • L1$_1$.

A few examples will demonstrate how the IM in Figure 16 develops for the simulated programming sequence of Figure 15:

- Initially the IM is empty, so the solution to the first task (diffmaxmin) is parsed with EXPERT simple rules. The if-then-else-node rule (rule O1 shown earlier) and the less_than node rule are among the parse rules of the solution of the first task. The times attached to the solution in Figure 15 show that these rules are plausible. For example, the "if-then-else"-node and the three links leaving it were programmed in a continuous uninterrupted sequence (four programming actions from 9:07:13 to 9:07:29). The same is true for the "<"-node and the two links leaving it (three programming actions from 9:08:06 to 9:08:19). So these two rules get into the IM and get the credits 4 and 3, respectively.

- Among the composites built from the parse rules of the solution to diffmaxmin, there is a schema, the "less_than & if-then-else composite". It is also plausible so it is moved into POSS. The action sequence explained by this composite starts at 9:07:13 and ends at 9:08:19, so the time "66 seconds" is attached to it.

- After solving "quot", the "less_than & if-then-else composite" is plausible again. Additionally, the corresponding action sequence is faster than 66 seconds (from 9:12:04 to 9:12:51, which is 47 seconds). So this composite is moved into the IM and gets a credit of 7 since it describes 7 programming actions.

- Another example is the "(less_than & if-then-else) & parameter & constant composite". The corresponding 13 actions are performed at the task "addaddone" in a continuous sequence (from 9:22:01 to 9:23:46, which is 105 seconds). Thus this schema is plausible and is put into POSS. On the next task, diffdiffone, this composite is plausible again, and the corresponding action sequence is sped up (from 9:31:01 to 9:32:34, which is 93 seconds). So the schema gets part of the IM with a credit of 13.

Figure 16 also shows that composites may be in the IM but not the simple rules they originate from. For example, the product node rule is not part of the IM but has been used for creating a case which is in the IM.


# 9 An Empirical Analysis of the IM

The IM represents the actual hypothetical knowledge of the PS. In this section we will investigate the no-interleaving hypothesis stating that the programming actions described by a rule in the IM are performed in a continuous uninterrupted temporal sequence. We will also take a look at some verbalizations, position corrections, and performance times. The analysis is based on the programming actions performed by a single subject, S2, solving seven consecutive nonrecursive ABSYNT programming tasks. The IM was run offline based on the action sequences exhibited by S2, because we had videotaped and categorized the session before.

- *Material and procedure.* In a "getting-started" phase, S2 constructed an ABSYNT Start tree for each primitive ABSYNT operator node, and reconstructed given programs. The purpose of this phase was to introduce S2 to the ABSYNT interface and language. Then she solved the following tasks: "diffmaxmin", "interval" (program that tests if a number lies between 1 and 2), "absdiff", "quot", "quotzero" (like quot, but preventing division by zero), "abs", and "volume" (program that computes the difference between the volume of a cube and a sphere, where the diameter of the sphere is equal to the length of the edge of the cube).

- *Creating subsequent states of the IM.* Subsequent states of the IM were created by generating an initial state of the IM and then running it on S2's solution sequence. We created an initial IM based on the following assumption: Since the subject was introduced to all ABSYNT nodes before she worked on the first programming task, "diffmaxmin", it seemed reasonable to put the primitive operator node rules, the constant node rule, and the parameter node rule into the IM. Then the IM was run on the sequence of solutions from "diffmaxmin" to "volume" constructed by S2. This produced a sequence of seven subsequent states of the IM.

- *Analyzing S2's protocol.* The protocol of S2's solutions to the seven programming tasks (S2's complete *subject trace*) was analyzed according to the following categories of events (actions and verbalizations):
  - placing a node
  - naming a parameter, constant, or higher operator node
  - creating a link
  - deleting a node or a link
  - replacing a node by another node, or changing a parameter name or a constant value
  - correcting the position of a node or a link
  - verbalizing a goal to place, name, or replace a node, or to create a link
  - verbalizing uncertainty ("maybe I should ...") or negations ("I don't know whether ...")

The actions and verbalizations of S2 while working in the Hypotheses Testing Environment were not included in this analysis because our hypotheses are not aimed at this activity.

- *Postdicting action and verbalization sequences* (event sequences). Based on
  - the state of the IM right before each task, and

- S2's event sequence leading to a solution of this task,

the following postdictions for this event sequence were made:

- *Sets* that contain actions of placing and naming nodes, creating links, and verbalizing respective goals *(model trace)*. Each set corresponds to the application of one IM rule. Thus the model trace is a set of sets where each set contains actions and verbalizations expected to occur in a continuous uninterrupted sequence within S2's subject trace *(no-interleaving hypothesis)*. The model trace contains no deletions of ABSYNT fragments (nodes, links) since our hypotheses do not cover deletions.
- *Position corrections*. If the position of a node is corrected, the IM rule explaining the corrected node should *not* explain the nodes connected to this node. Rather, these linked nodes should be explained by different rules. If the position of a link is corrected, the IM rule explaining it should not explain the node at the upper end of this link *(rearrangement hypothesis)*.
- *Performance times*. An event sequence explained by a composite should be shorter than the earlier event sequence which led to the creation of the composite *(time hypothesis)*.
- *Evaluation of the subject trace with respect to the model trace*. For two consecutive tasks of the task sequence, "absdiff" and "quot", Figures 17 and 18 show the actual state of the IM, S2's solution, the subject trace with correspondences (+) and contradictions (-) between model trace and subject trace, and the model trace. The assignment of "+" and "-" will be explained in a moment. More specifically, Figure 17 shows:
  a) a subset of the rules in the IM after solving the task "interval" (second task of the sequence). Here only the rule names are given. The actual rules are shown in Appendix B.
  b) S2's solution to "absdiff", which is the third task in the sequence.
  c) S2's subject trace of the solution to "absdiff" with correspondences (+) and contradictions (-) to the model trace.
  d) The postdicted model trace, given the subject trace and the state of the IM. (Dots in some of the model trace sets stand for actions expected according to the respective IM rule, but not occurring in the subject trace.)

  Figure 18 shows the same information for the next task, "quot". In Figures 17 and 18, the nodes are indexed if necessary in order to avoid ambiguities.

S2's subject trace was compared to the model trace in two equivalent ways. The first method better illustrates which events belong together according to the model trace. The first method leads to the "+" and "-" assignments on the left of the subject traces

(Figures 17c and 18c). The second method better illustrates the relations between adjacent subject trace events. It leads to the assignments on the right of Figures 17c and 18c.

*First method:*

- If *all* events within one set of the model trace occurred in an uninterrupted temporal sequence in the subject trace, then a "+" was assigned for *each* adjacent pair of this sequence. (Thus the IM rule corresponding to that model trace set is plausible.) For example, lines 5 to 7 of Figure 17c correspond to the third set of Figure 17d.

- If there was at least *one* interruption of this sequence by some other action or verbalization not in the respective model trace set, then a "-" was assigned for *each* pair of this sequence. (Thus the IM rule corresponding to that model trace set is not plausible.) For example, lines 1 and 3 of Figure 17c correspond to the first set of Figure 17d but they are interrupted by line 2. As another example, lines 18, 20, 21, 28, and 41 of Figure 17c correspond to the sixth model trace set of Figure 17d. These lines are not continuous, so *each* pair of them gets a "-".

"+" denote correspondences to the no-interleaving hypothesis, and "-" denote contradictions. This criterion is strong since a single interruption of an otherwise uninterrupted sequence causes *all* pairs of events of this sequence to be counted as "-". (For example, lines 20 and 21 of Figure 17c get a "-" although they are continuous. As another example, the pair of lines 8 and 9 of Figure 18c stem from the same model trace set, but this pair gets a "-" since the other events of this model trace set do not occur continuously, but at lines 18 and 24.) This is required by the no-interleaving hypothesis and the plausibility criterion of the IM.

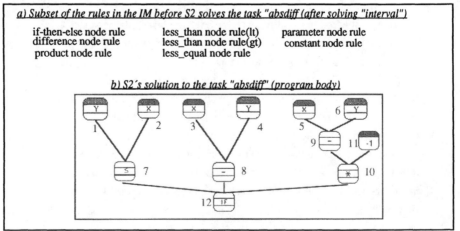

*a) Subset of the rules in the IM before S2 solves the task "absdiff (after solving "interval")*

| if-then-else node rule | less_than node rule(lt) | parameter node rule |
| difference node rule | less_than node rule(gt) | constant node rule |
| product node rule | less_equal node rule | |

*b) S2's solution to the task "absdiff" (program body)*

Figure 17 (continued on the next page): a) subset of the IM before solving "absdiff", b) S2's solution to "absdiff", c) subject trace with correspondences (+) and contradictions (-), and d) model trace

| | c) subject trace | | d) model trace |
|---|---|---|---|
| 1 | place node1 parameter | − | {place node1 parameter, name node1 X} |
| 2 | place node2 parameter | − | {place node2 parameter, name node2 Y} |
| 3 | name node1 X | | |
| 4 | name node2 Y | | |
| 5 | place node7 - | | {place node7 -, |
| 6 | create link from node7 - | + | create link from node7 - |
| | to node1 X | + | to node1 X, |
| 7 | create link from node7 - | | create link from node7 - |
| | to node2 Y | | to node2 Y} |
| 8 | verbalize uncertainty: > or < or | | {verbalize uncertainty: > or < or |
| | if-then-else for node7 - ? | | if-then-else for node7 - ?, |
| 9 | replace node7: - by ≤ | − | |
| 10 | place node12 if-then-else | | place node12 if-then-else, |
| 11 | create link from node12 | − | create link from node12 |
| | if-then-else to node7 - | | if-then-else to node7 -, ..., ...} |
| 12 | replace node7: ≤ by < | | |
| 13 | delete node12 if-then-else | | |
| 14 | delete node7 < | | |
| 15 | delete link from node12 to node7 | | |
| 16 | place node7 - | | |
| 17 | delete node7 - | | |
| 18 | verbalize goals: if-then-else, > | + | {verbalize goals: if-then-else, >, |
| 19 | place node7 > | | place node7 >, ..., ...} |
| 20 | place node12 if-then-else | − | {verb. goal if-th.-el., pl. node12 if-th.-el., |
| 21 | create link from node12 | − | create link from node12 |
| | if-then-else to node7 > | | if-then-else to node7 >, |
| 22 | place node3 constant | − | create link from node12 to node8 -, |
| | | | create link from node12 to node10 *} |
| 23 | replace node3: constant | | {replace node3: parameter for constant, |
| | by parameter | − | name node3 X} |
| 24 | place node4 parameter | − | {place node4 parameter, name node4 Y} |
| 25 | place node8 - | | {place node8 -, |
| 26 | create link from node8 - to node3 | + | create link from node8 - to node3, |
| 27 | create link from node8 - to node4 | + | create link from node8 - to node4} |
| 28 | create link from node12 if-then- | | |
| | else to node8 - | − | |
| 29 | name node3 X | | |
| 30 | name node4 Y | | |
| 31 | place node5 parameter | − | {place node5 parameter, name node5 X} |
| 32 | place node6 parameter | | {place node6 parameter, name node6 Y} |
| 33 | place operator9 - | + | {place operator9 -, |
| 34 | create link from node9 - to node5 | + | create link from node9 - to node5, |
| 35 | create link from node9 - to node6 | | create link from node9 - to node6} |
| 36 | place node11 constant | − | {place node11 constant, name node11 -1} |
| 37 | place node10 * | + | {place node10 *, |
| 38 | create link from node10 * to node9 - | + | create link from node10 * to node9 -, |
| 39 | create link from node10 * | | create link from node10 * |
| | to node11 constant | | to node11 constant} |
| 40 | name node11 -1 | | |
| 41 | create link from node12 to node10 * | | |
| 42 | name node5 X | | |
| 43 | name node6 Y | | |
| 44 | verbalize uncertainty: switch | | {verbalize uncertainty: switch |
| | names of node1 and node2? | + | names of node1 and node2?, |
| 45 | replace node1: X by Y | | replace node1: Y for X} |
| 46 | replace node2: Y by X | − | {verb. uncert., replace node2: X for Y} |
| 47 | replace node7: > by ≤ | | |

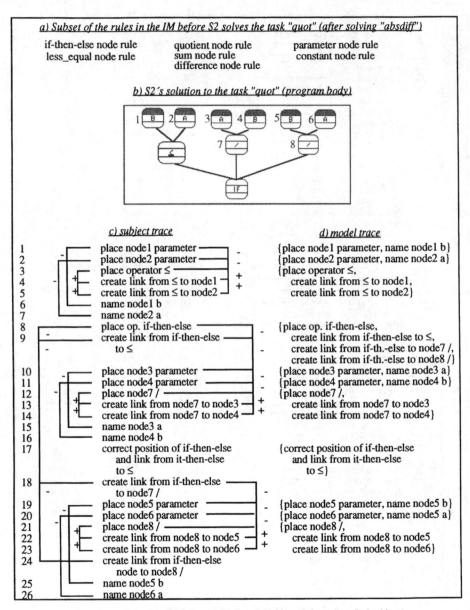

*a) Subset of the rules in the IM before S2 solves the task "quot" (after solving "absdiff")*

| if-then-else node rule | quotient node rule | parameter node rule |
|---|---|---|
| less_equal node rule | sum node rule | constant node rule |
| | difference node rule | |

*b) S2´s solution to the task "quot" (program body)*

| | *c) subject trace* | *d) model trace* |
|---|---|---|
| 1 | place node1 parameter | {place node1 parameter, name node1 b} |
| 2 | place node2 parameter | {place node2 parameter, name node2 a} |
| 3 | place operator ≤ | {place operator ≤, |
| 4 | create link from ≤ to node1 | create link from ≤ to node1, |
| 5 | create link from ≤ to node2 | create link from ≤ to node2} |
| 6 | name node1 b | |
| 7 | name node2 a | |
| 8 | place op. if-then-else | {place op. if-then-else, |
| 9 | create link from if-then-else to ≤ | create link from if-then-else to ≤, |
| | | create link from if-th.-else to node7 /, |
| | | create link from if-th.-else to node8 /} |
| 10 | place node3 parameter | {place node3 parameter, name node3 a} |
| 11 | place node4 parameter | {place node4 parameter, name node4 b} |
| 12 | place node7 / | {place node7 /, |
| 13 | create link from node7 to node3 | create link from node7 to node3 |
| 14 | create link from node7 to node4 | create link from node7 to node4} |
| 15 | name node3 a | |
| 16 | name node4 b | |
| 17 | correct position of if-then-else and link from it-then-else to ≤ | {correct position of if-then-else and link from it-then-else to ≤} |
| 18 | create link from if-then-else to node7 / | |
| 19 | place node5 parameter | {place node5 parameter, name node5 b} |
| 20 | place node6 parameter | {place node6 parameter, name node5 a} |
| 21 | place node8 / | {place node8 /, |
| 22 | create link from node8 to node5 | create link from node8 to node5 |
| 23 | create link from node8 to node6 | create link from node8 to node6} |
| 24 | create link from if-then-else node to node8 / | |
| 25 | name node5 b | |
| 26 | name node6 a | |

Figure 18: a) subset of the IM before solving "quot", b) S2´s solution to "quot", c) subject trace with correspondencies (+) and contradictions (-), and d) model trace

Instead of assigning "+" or "-" to *pairs* of events contained in the same model trace set, a "+" or "-" could be assigned only to *complete* sequences of the subject trace which correspond to a model trace set. But this does not account for the number of action steps explained by the supposed IM rule. (The parameter node rule explains two action steps, but composites can explain 30 or more.)

*Second method*: For each *adjacent* pair of events of the subject trace:

- If both events are contained in a model trace set which events occur in an uninterrupted sequence in the subject trace, then a "+" is assigned. For example, the pair of events in lines 3 and 4 of Figure 18c gets a "+", since all events of the corresponding model trace set (the third set of Figure 18d) are continuous in the subject trace.

- If both events are contained in the same model trace set but the events of this set do not occur in an uninterrupted sequence in the subject trace, then a "-" is assigned. For example, in Figure 18c a "-" is assigned to the pair of lines 8 and 9, because the events of the respective model trace set {place operator if-then-else, create link from if-then-else to ≤, create link from if-then-else to node7 /, create link from if-then-else to node8 /} do not form an uninterrupted sequence in the subject trace.

- If the two events are not contained in the same model trace set, and the first of these two events is contained in a model trace set having at least one more event later in the subject trace, then a "-" is assigned. For example, in Figure 18c a "-" is assigned to the pair of events in lines 1 and 2. The first action ("place node1 parameter") belongs to the model trace set {place node1 parameter, name node1 b} which contains another action ("name node1 b") occurring later in the subject trace.

- If the two events are not contained in the same model trace set, and the first one of these two events is the finishing event of the model trace set it belongs to (the last event of this set in the subject trace), then nothing is assigned. For example in Figure 18c nothing is assigned to the pair of lines 5 and 6, since the event of line 5 "create link from ≤ to node2" is in a model trace set whose other actions occurred earlier in the subject trace.

- *Results*
  - *Comparison of model trace and subject trace.* For S2's complete subject trace (for all seven tasks), there were 76 "+" and 60 "-" indicators. Since more "+" indicators should lead to longer and thus fewer runs (continuous sequences of "+" or "-", for example, the sequence "++---+" has three runs) than an equal distribution of "+" and "-", we applied the Runs-test to the sequence of "+" and "-" as obtained by the second method (on the right of Figures 17c and 18c). There were 42 runs in S2's complete subject trace, significantly less than to be expected by chance ($p < 0.001$). This confirms our no-interleaving hypothesis.

- *Position corrections*. S2's complete subject trace contained six position corrections. One of them occurs in the subject trace of "quot" (Figure 18c). There were three node corrections of parameters and constants. They were explained by different rules than the nodes connected to them. There were also three corrections of operator nodes and one of their input links. (In Figure 18c, the "if-then-else" node and its first input link are rearranged.) They were also explained by different rules than the node at the upper end of the respective link. (In Figure 18c, the "if-then-else" node and the "≤" node are explained by different IM rules.) So all position corrections are consistent with the rearrangement hypothesis.

- *Performance time*. Only one action sequence of S2's complete subject trace is explained by a composite. It shows a speedup (from 387 to 211 seconds) which is consistent with the time hypothesis.

- *Discussion*

The results indicate that the IM adequately describes more than half of the protocol of S2's actions and verbalizations with respect to the no-interleaving and rearrangement hypotheses. There was only one action sequence relevant to the time hypothesis. We will discuss several points raised by this analysis:

- *Time patterns*. There is another observation about time. The complete subject trace contained 29 event sequences denoted by a series of "+" indicators, thus, corresponding to a set of the model trace. (For example, in Figure 18c, lines 12 to 14 form such a sequence as expected by the set {place node7 /, create link from node7 to node3, create link from node7 to node4} of the model trace). For 23 of these 29 action sequences, their first action takes more time than each of the other actions. This is exactly what we would expect since according to our model, before the *first* action of an IM rule is executed, the planner has to generate a goal, and the coder has to look for and to select that rule.

- *Discrepancies*. There is of course a large amount of 60 discrepancies ("-"). How can they be explained?

    One possibility is that our criterion for assigning "+" and "-" is too strong because it does not allow for "partial" evidence for an IM rule. For a sequence of the subject trace corresponding to a model trace set, each pair of the sequence gets a "-" even if there is only one interruption. So an alternative is to weaken the no-interleaving hypothesis (and the plausibility concept used for IM creation as well) in the following way: a "+" is assigned to each pair of events which is contained within the same set of the model trace, and which is adjacent in the subject trace. (For example, in Figure 18c the pair of lines 8 and 9 "place operator if-then-else" and "create link from if-then-else to ≤" now gets a "+".) Correspondingly, a "-" is assigned to each pair within the same model trace set but interrupted by some other action(s). Using this criterion, there were 84 "+" and 52 "-" indicators in S2's complete subject trace. But this still leaves a lot of "-" indicators left to be explained.

Another observation with respect to the no-interleaving hypothesis is that a large portion of the discrepancies seems to be caused by parameters and constants. Table 1 shows the distribution of "+" and "-" across different types of rules in the IM:

| | Parameter node rule | Constant node rule | Primitive operator node rules | Composites |
|---|---|---|---|---|
| "+" cases | 3 | 4 | 46 | 23 |
| " -" cases | 28 | 8 | 24 | 0 |

Table 1: Distribution of "+" and "-" across different types of rules in the IM after solving the sequence of seven programming tasks

Thus the parameter node rule, for example, is responsible for 3 "+" and for 28 "-" indicators: S2 usually does not place and name a parameter node in sequence. The same seems true for the constant node rule. Given that this result will be reproduced with traces of other subjects, it seems that the no-interleaving hypothesis cannot be maintained for parameters and constants. There are two ways to cope with this:

1. to *split* the parameter node rule and the constant node rule into two new rules: one for positioning and one for naming a parameter node or constant node, respectively. Then the current parameter and constant node rule would be considered as a *composite* of more primitive rules explaining only one programming action.
2. to allow rule applications to be *interrupted*. Perhaps once S2 had acquired a rule, she was more flexible in applying it than stated by the no-interleaving hypothesis. This would mean that IM rule applications can be temporarily interrupted by the application of other rules. So if an IM rule is applied, some of the events of the corresponding model trace set might not be adjacent in the subject trace.

But this interruption hypothesis needs to be constrained further. Firstly, we would propose that interruptions of rule applications should not consist of deletions and replacements, since these actions indicate replanning which should cause the interrupted rule application to stop. Secondly, in terms of the planner-coder interaction, to interrupt a rule application means that the planner switches to another goal and the coder selects a rule to implement that goal. This should take additional time. So the times between adjacent events in the subject trace denoted by "-" should be longer than the times for pairs denoted by "+". These hypotheses will be investigated further when more information about the process of program planning is available by incorporating planning nodes into ABSYNT (see below).

- *Replacements.* Replacements were not considered in this analysis, but they could be handled in the following way. Several replacements occur in the subject trace of Figure 17c. For example, the first seven actions of subject S2 (lines 1 to 7) result in a program tree T1 consisting of two parameters, X and Y, and a "-" node linked to them. But then she feels uncertain (line 8), considers "if-then-else", ">", and "<", and then replaces the "-" node by a "≤" node (line 9). One might think of this replacement as a shortcut for deleting T1 and constructing a new tree T2 consisting of a "≤" node linked to two parameters, X and Y. In addition, we might assume that T2 would be constructed in the same manner as T1 before. So since the construction of T1 led to two "-" and two "+" indicators, two "-" and two "+" indicators should as well be assigned to the replacement action in line 9 ("-" by "≤") since this action is viewed as a shortcut for constructing T2.

    Altogether, S2's subject trace contains 13 replacements, 5 of them occurring at the task "interval" and 8 at "absdiff" (see Figure 17c. There are six immediate replacements, denoted as "replace node... ", and two delayed replacements where deletion of the to-be-replaced node and placing the new node are interrupted by another action. The first one of these two cases occurs in lines 14 and 16 of Figure 17c: "delete node7 <" ... "place node7 -", and the second, similar case consists of lines 17 and 19.) If we account for replacements in the way just described, we obtain 106 "+" and 90 "-" indicators for S2's complete subject trace.

- *Composites.* By the end of the last task ("volume"), there were only two composites in the IM. The virtually created programming sequence shown in the preceding section led to six composites (three schemata, three cases: Figure 16) after solving six tasks, and even more composites would have been possible. Thus according to the IM, subject S2 does not make much use of her own previous solutions but does much problem solving. This conclusion is supported by an inspection of the solutions of S2 to the seven tasks. For example, she solves "diffmaxmin" by "maximum of a and b minus minimum of a and b", but she solves the essentially identical task "absdiff" by "if b less than a then a minus b else (a minus b) times -1". (As can be expected by the large number of replacements, the "absdiff" task seems to be much harder for S2 than "diffmaxmin", even though "diffmaxmin" was solved earlier.) Subsequently, the task "quot" is solved in yet another way by interchanging parameters. Thus the diversity in solution approaches is reflected in the IM by the fact that it contains only few composites.

- *Impasses*. Based on S2's IM we cannot predict impasses because
  - the IM currently contains *only* implementation knowledge ("the coder's knowledge") but no planning knowledge. (We are working on extending the IM in this way.)
  - the IM contains *sufficient* implementation knowledge because, as stated, it contains all primitive node rules and parameter and constant rule from the beginning.

So there should be no impasses based on insufficient implementation knowledge. Consequently, all impasses in the protocol should be attributable to insufficient planning knowledge. If we propose verbalizations of uncertainty and negative comments as one empirical criterion for an impasse (similar to [57, 60]), then the protocol contains five impasses (without the hypotheses testing episodes). Four of them occur at the tasks "interval" and "absdiff" which seemed to be most difficult for S2. In three impasse situations S2 considers different implementations ("if-then-else" or a logic operator; ">" or "<", and so on) and is uncertain about them. (An example occurs at line 8 of Figure 17c). Thus there appears to be a planning problem. In the fourth case the impasse arises because S2 thinks that the solution just created will deliver a wrong result for a critical input value. In response to this, S2 switches parameter names. This does not seem to be an implementation problem either.

We are working on extending the ABSYNT Problem Solving Monitor and the IM by incorporating a planning level (see below). Then it should be possible also to predict impasses based on missing planning knowledge.

# 10 Discussion

We presented an approach to online diagnosis of students' knowledge states which is aimed at meeting the following requirements:

- to be based on a theoretical problem solving and learning framework,

- to be computationally effective and empirically valid,
- to support adaptive help generation.

We will now discuss how far the IM meets these requirements and how we plan to improve it.

- *Foundation on a theoretical framework.* In section 7 we showed how in our view the IM is related to the ISP-DL Theory. We tried to motivate the features of the IM by the theory. But still many aspects of the theory remain uncovered by the IM. Two of them are:
    - *Generalization* of knowledge. Our observations from single-subject sessions with ABSYNT indicated use of previous solutions and positive transfer especially for recursive tasks. Thus composites in the IM should be generalized. *Generalization of composites* may be viewed as another way of knowledge optimization (eg.[1, 65]) in response to the successful utilization of knowledge (Figure 1). Additionally, generalized knowledge should also result from *analogizing* as an alternative to synthesizing a plan (Figure 3).
    - Synthesizing a *plan.* Currently the IM takes only account of the implementation level, but there is no representation of planning knowledge within the IM.

We will sketch our current work on these two aspects:

- Concerning *generalization*, we will consider a simple example. We suppose that:
    a) The two fragments shown in Figure 19 were programmed on two consecutive tasks

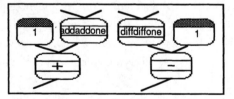

Figure 19: Two ABSYNT fragments

    b) The following two corresponding composites were plausible and thus moved into POSS:

C1: gmr (sum (const(C), addaddone (S1, S2)), add-pop (C-cl, Addaddone -hop (P1, P2))):-
is_const (C), gmr (S1, P1), gmr (S2, P2).

C2: gmr (diff (diffdiffone (S1, S2), const(C)), sub-pop (Diffdiffone-hop (P1, P2), C-cl)) :-
gmr (S1, P1), gmr (S2, P2), is_const (C).

("add-pop" is the primitive ABSYNT operator "+",

> "sub-pop" is the primitive ABSYNT operator "-",
> "Addaddone-hop" and "Diffdiffone-hop" are self-defined "higher"
> ABSYNT operators with names given by the user.)

Furthermore, C1 was composed from the node rules:

O2:     gmr(sum(S1, S2), add-pop(P1, P2)) :- gmr(S1, P1), gmr(S2, P2).

L2:     gmr(const(C), C-cl) :- is_const(C).

O3:     gmr(addaddone(S1, S2), Addaddone-hop(P1, P2)) :-
        gmr(S1, P1), gmr(S2, P2).

The composite C1 can be described by the formula $(O2_1 \cdot L2)_1 \cdot O3$.

In order to obtain a generalization of these two composites, first the two solution fragments have to be syntactically aligned by goal elaboration rules. For example, by using the goal elaboration rule

> E2: gmr (sum (S1, S2), P) :- gmr (sum (S2, S1), P).

expressing commutativity of addition, together with O2, L2, and O3 the program fragment on the left of Figure 20 can be generated. This syntactically aligned program fragment corresponds to the composite $C1_{ex}$ ("ex" for exchange):

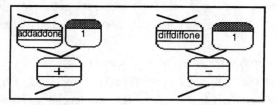

Figure 20: Syntactically aligned solution fragments of Figure 19

$C1_{ex}$: gmr (sum (addaddone (S1, S2), const(C)), add-pop(Addaddone-hop(P1, P2),C-cl)):-
        gmr (S1, P1), gmr (S2, P2), is_const (C).

which is based on the same node rules as C1 and can be described by $(O2_1 \cdot O3)_1 \cdot L2$.

Now a new generalized rule $G_{msg}$ can be created from C2 and $C1_{ex}$ by replacing the different goals and operators corresponding to the two program fragments (Figure 20) by variables. The possible values of the new variables are restricted by constraints. These constraints are built from the constants and their relations of the two original rules C2 and $C1_{ex}$.:

$G_{msg}$: gmr (Goal_1 (Goal_2 (S1, S2), const(C)),
        Op_Name_1-pop (Op_Name_2-hop (P1, P2), C-cl)) :-
        constraints([on(Goal_1, [sum, diff]),
        on (Goal_2, [diffdiffone, addaddone]),
        on(Op_Name_1, [add, sub]),

$$\text{gmr(Goal\_1(\_,\_), Op\_Name\_1(\_,\_)),}$$
$$\text{gmr(Goal\_2(\_,\_), Op\_Name\_2(\_,\_))]),}$$
$$\text{gmr (S1, P1), gmr (S2, P2), is\_const (C).}$$

This is an example for a most specific generalization ("$G_{msg}$"). The rule $G_{msg}$ is not able to parse or to generate similar problems. For example if the root goal is the goal to program a product the rule $G_{msg}$ will fail, because the constraints are not satisfied. If the problem solver has no knowledge to program a product then there will be an impasse. One way to overcome this impasse would be to extend the constraints of the rule $G_{msg}$ accordingly by inserting the "product" goal into the list [sum, diff] and the "mult" node into the list [add, sub].

It is also possible to generate another rule $G_{mgg}$ from C2 and C1$_{ex}$. This most general generalization of the constraints differs from the example above by the missing variable restrictions:

$$G_{mgg}: \text{gmr (Goal\_1 (Goal\_2 (S1, S2), const(C)),}$$
$$\text{Op\_Name\_1-pop (Op\_Name\_2-hop (P1, P2), C-cl)) :-}$$
$$\text{gmr (S1, P1), gmr (S2, P2), is\_const (C).}$$

This rule is an overgeneralization so it may produce errors. Remedial information (ie. error feedback to hypotheses) may lead to a stepwise restriction of the variables by constraints.

- As mentioned, introducing a *planning level* is another topic of our current research. Currently the learner's hypothetical solution plan is the parse tree of the solution. It is reconstructed retrospectively by the system after the solution is complete. We want the learner to be able to construct plans with an extension of the ABSYNT language by new goal nodes so that *mixed* ABSYNT programs containing operator nodes and goal nodes will be possible. The learner will be able to test hypotheses and to receive error and completion feedback at this *planning* level even if the learner has no idea yet about the implementation. Thus the learner may first *plan* a goal tree for the task at hand, test hypotheses about it, and debug it, if necessary. Afterwards the learner may *implement* the goals by replacing them with operator nodes or subtrees.

For the user's point of view, the benefit of using goal nodes will be that hypotheses testing will be possible at the *planning stage*, not just at the implementation stage. From a psychological point of view, the benefit is that *objective* data about the planning process can be obtained in addition to the verbalizations. Finally, from a help system design point of view, the benefit is that in addition to hypotheses testing it will be possible to offer *planning rules* as help to the learner. The planning rules will be visual representations of GMR goal elaboration rules.

*Computational feasibility and empirical validity.* A current problem with the IM is that composites are first generated, based on the parse rules of a solution, and then tested for plausibility. Generation of composites can be time-consuming for very complicated ABSYNT program solutions. It is possible to change this situation by generating composites only for program fragments which were created by the student in temporal sequence. In this way many composites which would not pass the plausibility test would not be created in the first place.

Another problem is that the creation of the IM currently does not deal with program modifications performed by the student, like deleting and replacing nodes and links (although in the *evaluation* of the IM we were able to account for these data). Despite these shortcomings, we think that it is possible to extend the IM in appropriate ways. As we have also shown, it is possible to put the IM to empirical test and to draw conclusions for its improvement. For example, the study described above suggested changing simple parameter node rules. Some more testable hypotheses will be presented below. Thus advance towards an empirically validated knowledge diagnosis seems possible.

*Adaptive help generation.* The ultimate goal of the IM is to provide *adaptive* help or, more generally, to have an impact on the user-system-interaction in a way that takes account of the individual. In the ABSYNT Problem Solving Monitor, the need for the IM is very clear:

- There is a large solution space (the system is able to analyze and generate many solutions to given tasks) which is necessary because we want to be able to take care of novices' often unusual or unnecessarily complicated solutions (as illustrated in Figure 6).
- Because of the large solution space, there is usually a large amount of completion proposals that can be generated by the system. So the problem is which one to select. The task of the IM is to enable *user-centered* selection.

But as indicated, the role of the IM will not be restricted to the completion of ABSYNT nodes. Extending completion to the planning level and offering visual planning rules as help will impose additional demands on the IM. Additionally, the IM does more than just help selection. The information provided to the student may be varied in several ways, and this gives rise to empirical predictions which in turn might support or weaken the IM. Figure 21 illustrates how information intended as help can be varied, and what can be predicted. Basically, when the student is caught in an impasse and asks for a completion proposal, according to the IM there are two possible situations:

- The student has implementation knowledge but does not make use of it. Thus with respect to the interaction of planning and coding described earlier, there is a *planning* problem.
- The student lacks implementation knowledge, so there is a *coding* problem.

The latter, hypothetical situation is depicted in Figure 21: the student has just performed some programming actions, then gets stuck, and asks for completion proposals. According to the IM, there is a knowledge gap on the coding level, and after filling it the student would be able to proceed (shaded part of the horizontal arrow in the upper right of Figure 21). Now there are several possibilities to react to the gap: the information provided might vary in *grain size* and *amount* (on the left of Figure 21).

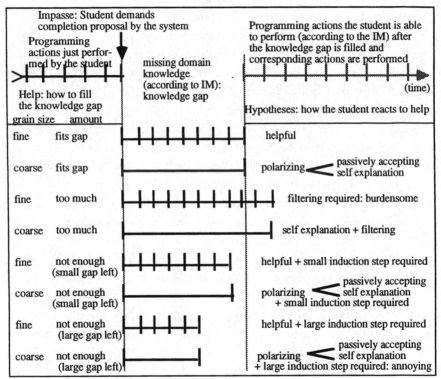

Figure 21: Types of information possibly provided in response to a knowledge gap diagnosed by the IM, and hypotheses concerning the student's reaction to this information

- *Grain size* concerns the rules underlying the completion proposal. If the grain size is *fine*, then the completion proposal may rest on a chain of simple rules which covers the gap. In this case the completion proposal may consist of an ABSYNT subtree with an explanation of each programming step needed to construct this subtree, where the explanation is based on the goal structure of the chain of simple rules. If the grain size is *coarse*, then the completion proposal may rest on a single composite (to take the other extreme). Thus the same subtree may be provided, but only with an explanation of the root goal.

- *Amount* concerns the relation between the completion and the gap. The completion proposal might *exactly fill* the gap, so subsequently the student can proceed by relying on her / his own knowledge. Alternatively, the completion proposal may contain *too much* information (more than necessary) or *not enough* information (the gap is not completely covered).

On the left and middle part of Figure 21, the different combinations of grain size and amount of information are shown. They lead to different hypotheses (on the right of Figure 21). We will describe some of them:

- If the information is fine-grained and exactly fills the gap (first row in Figure 21), then we would expect that the student considers this information as *helpful*.
- If the information is coarse-grained and exactly fills the gap (second row), then the student misses explanations. So s/he might either *passively accept* what is being offered, or engage in *self-explanation* [59].
- If the information is fine-grained but exceeds the knowledge gap (third row), then the student has to "*filter*" the content relevant to the current situation. This might be experienced as *burdensome*.
- If the information leaves a small knowledge gap (fifth and sixth row), then the student might try to induce one new simple rule and thereby cover the rest of the gap. (This situation seems similar to the induction of one subprocedure at a time by van Lehn's SIERRA program [55].)
- Finally, the last case to be considered here is that there is a large gap left, and the information offered is too coarse (last row). The student should experience such information as very inadequate to his current problem. Thus she or he should feel annoyed or even upset.

There remains much work, of course, to work out these hypotheses and put them to empirical test. But we think we have shown that the IM is an empirically fruitful approach to knowledge diagnosis and adaptive help generation which is testable and also touches upon further important research problems, like motivation and emotion.

# Appendix A: GMR Rules of Figure 16 (PROLOG notation)

<u>IM rules</u>

*Simple rules:*

> *if-then-else node rule*
>> gmr(branching(IF, THEN, ELSE), if-pop(P1, P2, P3)) :-
>> gmr(IF, P1), gmr(THEN, P2), gmr(ELSE, P3).
>
> *less_than node rule*
>> gmr(less_than(S1, S2), lt-pop(P1, P2)) :- gmr(S1, P1), gmr(S2, P2).
>
> *sum node rule*
>> gmr(sum(S1, S2), add-pop(P1, P2)) :- gmr(S1, P1), gmr(S2, P2).
>
> *difference node rule*
>> gmr(diff(S1, S2), sub-pop(P1, P2)) :- gmr(S1, P1), gmr(S2, P2).
>
> *parameter node rule*
>> gmr(parm(P), P-pl) :- is_parm(P).
>
> *constant node rule*
>> gmr(const(C), C-cl) :- is_const(C).

*Schemata:*

> *less_than & if-then-else composite*
>> gmr(branching(less_than(S1,S2), S3, S4), if-pop(lt-pop(P1, P2), P3, P4)) :-
>> gmr(S1, P1), gmr(S2, P2), gmr(S3, P3), gmr(S4, P4).
>
> *(less_than & if-then-else) & parameter & constant composite*
>> gmr(branching(less_than(parm(Y), const(C)), parm(X), S),
>> if-pop(lt-pop(Y-pl, C-cl), X-pl, P)) :-
>> is_parm(Y), is_const(C), is_parm(X), gmr(S, P).
>
> *step_down_one & difference node-rule composite*
>> gmr(step_down_one(S), sub-pop(P1,P2)) :- gmr(S,P1), gmr(const(1), P2).

*Cases:*

> *(less_than & if-then-else) & difference & change_sign plan-rules & product & difference node-rules & parameter & constant composite*
>> gmr(branching(less_than(parm(A), parm(B)), diff(parm(C), parm(D)),
>> diff(parm(E), parm(F))),
>>
>> if-pop(lt-pop(A-pl, B-pl), mult-pop(sub-pop(D-pl, C-pl), -1-cl),
>> sub-pop(E-pl, F-pl))) :-
>>
>>> is_parm(A), is_parm(B), is_parm(D), is_parm(C),is_const(-1),
>>> is_parm(E), is_parm(F).
>
> *difference node-rule & parameter & constant composite*
>> gmr(diff(parm(X), const(C)), sub-pop(X-pl, C-cl)) :- is_parm(X), is_const(C).
>
> *(step_down_one & difference) & parameter & constant composite*
>> gmr(step_down_one(parm(X)), sub-pop(X-pl, 1-cl)) :- is_parm(X), is_const(1).

## EXPERT rules

*product node rule*

    gmr(product(S1, S2), mult-pop(P1, P2)) :- gmr(S1, P1), gmr(S2, P2).

*difference plan rule*

    gmr(diff(S1, S2), ProgTree) :- gmr(ch_sign(diff(S2, S1))).

*change_sign plan rule*

    gmr(ch_sign(S), ProgTree) :- gmr(product(S, const(-1))).

*step_down_one plan rule*

    gmr(step_down_one(S), ProgTree) :- gmr(diff(S, const(-1))).

# Appendix B: GMR Rules of Figures 17 and 18 (Visual and PROLOG notation)

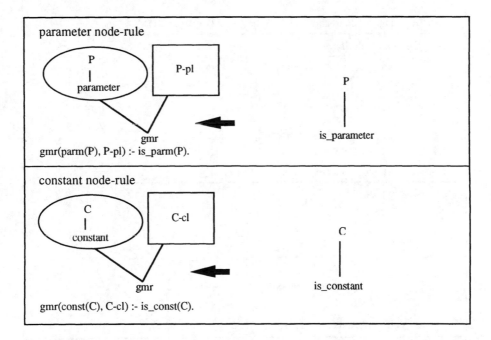

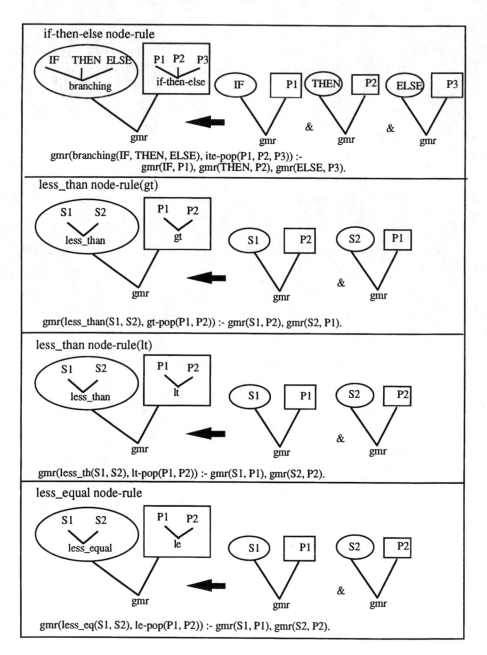

**if-then-else node-rule**

gmr(branching(IF, THEN, ELSE), ite-pop(P1, P2, P3)) :-
    gmr(IF, P1), gmr(THEN, P2), gmr(ELSE, P3).

**less_than node-rule(gt)**

gmr(less_than(S1, S2), gt-pop(P1, P2)) :- gmr(S1, P2), gmr(S2, P1).

**less_than node-rule(lt)**

gmr(less_th(S1, S2), lt-pop(P1, P2)) :- gmr(S1, P1), gmr(S2, P2).

**less_equal node-rule**

gmr(less_eq(S1, S2), le-pop(P1, P2)) :- gmr(S1, P1), gmr(S2, P2).

261

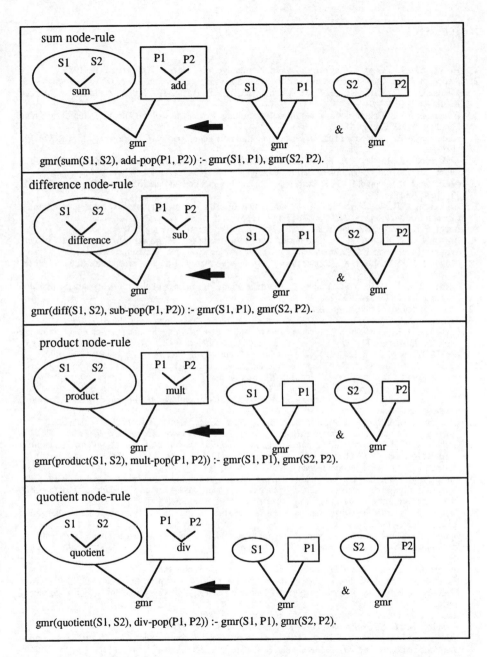

sum node-rule

gmr(sum(S1, S2), add-pop(P1, P2)) :- gmr(S1, P1), gmr(S2, P2).

difference node-rule

gmr(diff(S1, S2), sub-pop(P1, P2)) :- gmr(S1, P1), gmr(S2, P2).

product node-rule

gmr(product(S1, S2), mult-pop(P1, P2)) :- gmr(S1, P1), gmr(S2, P2).

quotient node-rule

gmr(quotient(S1, S2), div-pop(P1, P2)) :- gmr(S1, P1), gmr(S2, P2).

# References

1. Anderson, J. R.: *The Architecture of Cognition.* Cambridge, MA: Harvard University Press 1983
2. Anderson, J. R.: Knowledge compilation: the general learning mechanism. In: *Machine Learning* (R. S. Michalski, J. G. Carbonell, & T. M. Mitchell, eds.). Vol. II, pp. 289-310. Los Altos, CA: Morgan Kaufmann 1986
3. Anderson, J. R.: Causal analysis and inductive learning. Proceedings of the 4th Workshop on Machine Learning, Irvine, CA, pp. 288-299 1987
4. Anderson, J. R.: A theory of the origins of human knowledge. *Artificial Intelligence*, 40, pp. 313-351 (1989)
5. Anderson, J. R., Boyle, C. F., Farrell, R., & Reiser, B. J.: Cognitive principles in the design of computer tutors. In: *Modelling Cognition* (P. Morris, ed.), pp. 93-133. New York, NY: Wiley 1987
6. Anderson, J. R., Conrad, F. G., & Corbett, A. T.: Skill acquisition and the LISP tutor. *Cognitive Science*, 13, pp. 467-505 (1989)
7. Anderson, J. R. & Swarecki, E.: The automated tutoring of introductory computer programming. *Communications of the ACM*, 29, pp. 842-849 (1986)
8. Bauer, F. L. & Goos, G.: *Informatik, Vol. 1.* 3rd ed. Berlin: Springer-Verlag 1982
9. Brown, J. S. & Burton, R. R.: Diagnosing bugs in a simple procedural skill. In: *Intelligent Tutoring Systems* (D. Sleeman & J. S. Brown, eds.). pp. 157-183. New York, NY: Academic Press 1982
10. Brown, J. S. & VanLehn, K.: Repair theory: a generative theory of bugs in procedural skills. *Cognitive Science*, 4, pp. 379-426 (1980)
11. Carbonell, J. G. & Gil, Y.: Learning by experimentation. Proceedings of the 4th Workshop on Machine Learning, Irvine, CA, pp. 256-266, 1987
12. Chang, S. K.(ed): *Principles of Visual Programming Systems.* Englewood Cliffs: Prentice Hall 1990
13. Chase, N. G. & Simon, H. A.: Perception in chess. *Cognitive Psychology*, 4, pp. 55-81 (1973)
14. Corbett, A. T. & Anderson, J. R.: Student modeling and mastery learning in a computer-based programming tutor. In: *Intelligent Tutoring Systems* (C. Frasson, G. Gauthier, & G. I. McCalla, eds.). Proceedings of the ITS 92, pp. 413-420, Lecture Notes in Computer Science, Vol. 608, Berlin: Springer-Verlag 1992
15. Egan, D. E. & Greeno, J. G.: Theory of rule induction: knowledge acquired in concept learning, serial pattern learning, and problem solving. In: *Knowledge and Cognition* (L. W. Gregg, ed.). pp. 43-103. Potomac: Lawrence Erlbaum Associates 1974
16. Elio, R. & Scharf, P. B.: Modeling novice-to-expert shifts in problem solving strategy and knowledge organization. *Cognitive Science*, 14, 579-639 (1990)
17. Ericsson, K. A. & Simon, H. A.: *Protocol Analysis.* Cambridge, MA: MIT Press 1984
18. Frasson, C. & Gauthier, G. (eds): *Intelligent Tutoring Systems.* Norwood, NJ: Ablex 1990
19. Gollwitzer, P. M.: Action phases and mind sets. In: *Handbook of Motivation and Cognition: Foundations of Social Behavior* (E. T. Higgins & R. M. Sorrentino, eds.). Vol. 2, pp. 53-92. 1990
20. Gollwitzer, P. M.: *Abwägen und planen.* Göttingen: Verlag für Psychologie 1991
21. Greer, J., McCalla, G. I., & Mark, M. A.: Incorporating granularity-based recognition into SCENT. In: *Proceedings of the 4th International Conference on Artificial Intelligence and Education*, Amsterdam (D. Bierman, J. Breuker & J. Sandberg, eds.), pp. 107-115, Amsterdam: IOS 1989
22. Gregory, S.: *Parallel logic Programming in PARLOG: The language and its Implementation.* Wokingham: Addison-Wesley 1987
23. Gugerty, L. & Olson, G. M.: Comprehension differences in debugging by skilled and novice programmers. In: *Empirical Studies of Programmers* (E. Soloway & S. Iyengar, eds.). pp. 13-27. Norwood, NJ: Ablex 1986
24. Hogger, Ch. J.: *Essentials of Logic Programming.* Oxford University Press 1990
25. Huber, P., Jensen, K., & Shapiro, R. M.: Hierarchies in colored petri nets. In: *Advances in Petri Nets 1990* (G. Rozenberg, ed.), Lecture Notes in Computer Science, Vol. 483, pp. 373-341, Berlin: Springer-Verlag 1991
26. Kearsley, G.: *Online Help Systems.* Norwood, NJ: Ablex 1988
27. Kowalski, R.: *Logic for Problem Solving.* Amsterdam: Elsevier 1979
28. Laird, J. E., Rosenbloom, P. S., & Newell, A.: *Universal Subgoaling and Chunking: The Automatic Generation and Learning of Goal Hierarchies.* Boston, MA: Kluwer 1986
29. Laird, J. E., Rosenbloom, P. S., & Newell, A.: SOAR: an architecture for general intelligence, *Artificial Intelligence*, 33, pp. 1-64 (1987)
30. Lanzetta, J. T. & Driscoll, J. M.: Effects of uncertainty and importance on information search in decision making. *Journal of Personality and Social Psychology*, 10, pp. 479-486 (1968)

263

31. Lehnert, W. G.: *The Process of Question Answering*. Hillsdale, NJ: Lawrence Erlbaum Associates 1978
32. Lewis, C.: Composition of productions. In: *Production System Models of Learning and Development* (D. Klahr, P. Langley, & R. Neches, eds.). pp. 329-358. Cambridge, MA: MIT Press 1987
33. McCalla, G. I., Greer, J., and the SCENT Research Team: Intelligent advising in problem solving domains: the SCENT-3 architecture. *Proceedings of the 2nd International Conference on Intelligent Tutoring Systems*, Montreal, Quebec (C. Frasson, G. Gauthier & G. McCalla, eds.), pp. 124-131, Lecture Notes in Computer Science, Vol. 608, Berlin: Springer-Verlag 1992
34. McCalla, G. I., Greer, J., & Coulman, R.: Enhancing the robustness of model-based recognition. *Proceedings of the 3rd International Workshop on User Modeling*, Wadern, Germany (E. Andre, R. Cohen, W. Graf, B. Kass, C. Paris, & W. Wahlster, eds.). pp. 240-248, Kaiserslautern: DFKI 1992
35. Minton, S. & Carbonell, J. G.: Strategies for learning search control rules: an explanation-based approach. Proceedings of the IJCAI 1987, pp. 228-235, Milan, Italy 1987
36. Möbus, C.: Toward the design of adaptive instructions and help for knowledge communication with the problem solving monitor ABSYNT. In: *Artificial Intelligence in Higher Education*, (V. Marik, O. Stepankova, & Z. Zdrahal, eds.), pp. 138-145, Lecture Notes in Computer Science, Vol. 451, Berlin: Springer-Verlag 1990
37. Möbus, C.: The relevance of computational models of knowledge acquisition for the design of helps in the problem solving monitor ABSYNT. Proceedings of the Conference on Advanced Research on Computers in Education (ARCE '90), pp. 137-144, (R. Lewis & O. Setsuko, eds.). Amsterdam: North-Holland 1991
38. Möbus, C. & Schröder, O.: Representing semantic knowledge with 2-dimensional rules in the domain of functional programming. In: *Visualization in Human-Computer Interaction, 7th Interdisciplinary Workshop in Informatics and Psychology*, Schärding. Austria, 1988 (P. Gorny & M. Tauber, eds.). pp. 47-81, Lecture Notes in Computer Science, Vol. 439, Berlin: Springer-Verlag 1990
39. Möbus, C., Schröder, O., & Thole, H. J.: Runtime modeling the novice-expert shift in programming skills on a rule-schema-case continuum. Proceedings of the IJCAI Workshop W.4 Agent Modelling for Intelligent Interaction, 12th International Joint Conference on Artificial Intelligence, (J. Kay & A. Quilici, eds.). pp. 137-143, Darling Harbour, Sydney, Australia, 1991
40. Möbus, C., Schröder, O., & Thole, H. J.: Online modelling the novice-expert shift in programming skills on a rule-schema-case partial order. In: *Working Notes of the AAAI Spring Symposium Series: Cognitive Aspects of Knowledge Acquisition*, pp. 155-161. Stanford University, 1992
41. Möbus, C. & Thole, H. J.: Tutors, instructions and helps. In: *Künstliche Intelligenz KIFS 1987* (Th. Christaller, ed.). pp. 336-385. Informatik-Fachberichte 202, Berlin: Springer-Verlag 1989
42. Möbus, C. & Thole, H. J.: Interactive support for planning visual programs in the problem solving monitor ABSYNT: giving feedback to user hypotheses on the language level. In: *Computer Assisted Learning*. Proceedings of the 3rd International Conference on Computer-Assisted Learning (ICCAL 90), Hagen, Germany, 1990. (D. H. Norrie & H. W. Six, eds.). pp. 36-49, Lecture Notes in Computer Science, Vol. 438, Berlin: Springer-Verlag 1990
43. Neves, D. M. & Anderson, J. R.: Knowledge compilation: mechanisms for the automatization of cognitive skills. In: *Cognitive Skills and their Acquisition* (J. R. Anderson, ed.). pp. 57-84. Hillsdale, NJ: Lawrence Erlbaum Associates 1981
44. Newell, A.: The knowledge level. *Artificial Intelligence*, 18, pp. 87-127 (1982)
45. Rosenbloom, P. S., Laird, J. E., Newell, A., & McCarl, R.: A preliminary analysis of the SOAR architecture as a basis for general intelligence. *Artificial Intelligence*, 47, pp. 289-305 (1991)
46. Rosenbloom, P. S. & Newell, A.: Learning by chunking: a production system model of practice. In: *Production System Models of Learning and Development* (D. Klahr, P. Langley, & R. Neches, eds.). pp. 221-286. Cambridge, MA: MIT Press 1987
47. Schank, R. C.: *Dynamic Memory*. London: Cambridge University Press 1982
48. Schröder, O.: A model of the acquisition of rule knowledge with visual helps: the operational knowledge for a functional, visual programming language. In: *Computer Assisted Learning*, Proceedings of the 3rd International Conference on Computer-Assisted Learning (ICCAL 90), Hagen, Germany 1990 (D. H. Norrie & H. W. Six, eds.). pp. 142-157, Lecture Notes in Computer Science, Vol. 438, Berlin: Springer-Verlag 1990
49. Schröder, O.: *Erwerb von regelwissen mit visuellen hilfen: das semantikwissen für eine graphische funktionale programmiersprache*. Frankfurt: Lang 1992
50. Self, J. A.: Bypassing the intractable problem of student modeling. In: *Intelligent Tutoring Systems : at the Crossroads of Artificial Intelligence and Education* (C. Frasson & G. Gauthier, eds.). pp. 107-123. Norwood, NJ: Ablex 1990
51. Self, J. A.: Formal Approaches to Learner Modelling. Technical Report AI-59, Department of Computing, Lancaster University, Lancaster, UK 1991

52. Simon, H. A. & Simon, D. P.: Individual differences in solving physics problems. In: *Childrens' Thinking: What Develops?* (R. S. Siegler, ed.). pp. 325-348. Hillsdale, NJ: Lawrence Erlbaum Associates 1978
53. Sleeman, D.: An attempt to understand students' understanding of basic algebra. *Cognitive Science*, 8, pp. 387-412 (1984)
54. Sleeman, D. & Brown, J. S.: *Intelligent Tutoring Systems*. New York, NY: Academic Press 1982
55. VanLehn, K.: Learning one subprocedure per lesson. *Artificial Intelligence*, 31, pp. 1-40 (1987)
56. VanLehn, K.: Toward a theory of impasse-driven learning. In: *Learning Issues for Intelligent Tutoring Systems* (H. Mandl & A. Lesgold, eds.). pp. 19-41. New York, NY: Springer-Verlag 1988
57. VanLehn, K.: Learning events in the acquisition of three skills. Proceedings of the 11th Conference of the Cognitive Science Society, Ann Arbor, MI, pp. 434-441, 1989
58. VanLehn, K.: *Mind Bugs: The Origins of Procedural Misconceptions*. Cambridge,MA: MIT Press 1990
59. VanLehn, K.: Two pseudo-students: applications of machine learning to formative evaluation. In: *Advanced Research on Computers in Education*, (R. Lewis & S. Otsuki, eds.). pp 17-25. Amsterdam: Elsevier/IFIP 1991
60. VanLehn, K.: Rule acquisition events in the discovery of problem solving strategies. *Cognitive Science*, 15, pp. 1-47 (1991)
61. Vere, S. A.: Relational production systems. *Artificial Intelligence*, 8, pp. 47-68 (1977)
62. Weber, G.: Cognitive diagnosis and episodic modeling in an intelligent LISP tutor. *Proceedings of the 2nd International Conference on Intelligent Tutoring Systems*, Montreal, Quebec (C. Frasson, G. Gauthier & G. McCalla, eds.), pp. 207-214, Lecture Notes in Computer Science, Vol. 608, Berlin: Springer-Verlag 1992
63. Weber, G.: Explanation-based retrieval in a case-based learning model. Proceedings of the 13th Annual Meeting of the Cognitive Science Society, Chicago, IL, pp. 522-527, Hillsdale, NJ: Lawrence Erlbaum Associates 1991
64. Wenger, E.: *Artificial Intelligence and Tutoring Systems*. Los Altos, CA 1987
65. Wolff, J. G.: Cognitive development as optimization. In: *Computational Models of Learning* (L. Bolc, ed.). pp. 161-205. Berlin: Springer-Verlag 1987

Part 4

Formalizing Student Modelling

# Modelling a Student's Inconsistent Beliefs and Attention[1]

Xueming Huang

Knowledge Systems Laboratory, Institute for Information Technology, National Research Council Canada, Ottawa, Canada

**Abstract:** A student may hold inconsistent beliefs, but has a tendency to avoid those inconsistencies that have been recognized. In this research we assume that a student can recognize inconsistencies in the beliefs under attention, so a tutor can lead the student to remove the inconsistencies and the misconceptions behind them by bringing the inconsistent subset of beliefs to the student's attention. We present a logic of attention to capture the student's inconsistent beliefs and attention, and show how the logic could be used to model multiple viewpoints of a student and be used in a Socratic tutoring system.

**Keywords:** inconsistent beliefs, attention, logic, student modelling, intelligent tutoring

## 1 Introduction

Recently, there has been interest among ITS researchers in studying the formal aspects of student modelling [19, 20, 21]. In this research, a student model is viewed as the intelligent tutor's beliefs about a student's beliefs. Thus, building a student modelling system requires dealing with many knowledge representation issues, such as incomplete knowledge, inconsistent knowledge, and belief revision [15]. In recent research [9], we developed a belief revision system for student modelling. Here we study the issue of reasoning about inconsistent beliefs in student modelling.

A student model contains two levels of beliefs. The object level beliefs represent the student's beliefs. The meta-beliefs are the tutoring system's beliefs. Such a belief system may be

---

[1] This is a revised version of a paper entitled "Inconsistent Beliefs, Attention, and Student Modelling" that first appeared in the *Journal of Artificial Intelligence in Education*, 3(4), pp. 417. Reprinted with permission of the Association for the Advancement of Computing in Education (AACE, P.O. Box 2966, Charlottesville, VA 22902 USA).

represented using a modal logic. The logic has two operators: $B_t$ that denotes the tutor's beliefs and $B_s$ that denotes the student's beliefs. Thus, the modal proposition $B_t(\alpha)$ represents that the tutor believes $\alpha$, and $B_t(B_s(\varphi))$ represents that the tutor believes that the student believes $\varphi$. But since all knowledge in the tutoring system is actually the tutor's beliefs, every logical sentence in the student model would have an operator $B_t$ at the outmost level. To simplify the knowledge representation, we could strip this outmost $B_t$ from every sentence. Then, we could use $\alpha$ and $B_s(\varphi)$, instead of $B_t(\alpha)$ and $B_t(B_s(\varphi))$, to represent that the tutor believes $\alpha$ and that the tutor believes that the student believes $\varphi$, respectively.

A student may hold inconsistent beliefs. As students learn new knowledge, they also obtain misconceptions. Thus, it is desirable that the logical system allows inconsistencies at the object level beliefs. That is, it should allow the student model to contain the logical formula $B_s(\varphi) \wedge B_s(\neg \varphi)$. On the other hand, ideally the tutor's beliefs are consistent,[2] so inconsistencies at the meta-level beliefs should not be allowed. That is, the student model should not contain the formula $B_s(\varphi) \wedge \neg B_s(\varphi)$.

The purpose of representing a student's inconsistent beliefs in an ITS is to guide the student to remove the inconsistencies. One way of doing this is to bring the student's inconsistent beliefs to his or her attention, leading him or her to remove misconceptions. This approach is used in the Socratic tutor [3] and recent research into "learning by teaching" [18]. The goal of our research is to develop a formal knowledge representation for inconsistent beliefs and attention in a student model. Here we propose a *logic of attention* as such a knowledge representation and show how the logic could be used in intelligent tutoring. The chapter is organized as follows: Section 2 introduces the "society of mind" approach related to the logic of attention; Section 3 discusses the intuition behind the logic and presents the semantics and an axiomatization of the logic; Section 4 and Section 5 discuss how the logic could be used to model multiple viewpoints and be used in a Socratic tutoring system; and Section 6 gives conclusions.

# 2 The "Society of Mind" Approach

One reason that people hold inconsistent beliefs is because they don't pay attention to all issues simultaneously. At each particular moment, one focuses on only a small subset of beliefs relevant to the problem at hand. This type of local reasoning can be captured by the so-called "society of mind" approach [4, 17] in which each agent consists of many independent *frames of*

---

2  Here we say that such a student modelling system is idealized since in practice maintaining consistency of the tutor's beliefs is usually inefficient. For an approach to overcoming inefficiency in belief revision see [9].

*mind*. In fact, Fagin and Halpern [5] have used this approach to develop a *logic of local reasoning* that models inconsistent beliefs. In their logic, an agent may hold two types of beliefs: *explicit beliefs* and *implicit beliefs*. Agent a holds an explicit belief p (ie., $B_a(p)$ is true) if it believes p in some frame of mind. It holds an implicit belief p (ie., $L_a(p)$ is true) if it believes p when information in all frames is put together. An agent may hold inconsistent beliefs, that is, it may hold an explicit belief p in one frame and an explicit belief $\neg p$ in another since the two beliefs may not be put together. Thus, $B_a(p) \wedge B_a(\neg p)$ does not imply $B_a(false)$, but it implies $L_a(false)$.

Although explicit beliefs in the logic of local reasoning capture people's inconsistent global beliefs,[3] the logic has no syntactic notion to represent one's consistent local beliefs and it provides no mechanism for doing local reasoning in a frame. This limitation causes difficulties in using the logic in student modelling systems since students are generally expected to make some, although they may not make all, inferences, and their beliefs are generally expected to be consistent at some local level.

# 3  Logic of Attention

## 3.1  Motivation

Harman [6] claims that although people's beliefs are inconsistent, they have a tendency to avoid those inconsistencies that have been recognized in their beliefs. A problem that arises here is that people's abilities to recognize inconsistent beliefs differ from one another, so building a general model for such partially consistent beliefs is difficult.

Here we present a *logic of attention* to attack this problem. We assume that people are able to recognize logical inconsistencies in the beliefs under their attention, but they may not recognize inconsistencies in the beliefs not under attention. The logic of attention extends the logic of local reasoning by distinguishing the frame of mind under the agent's current attention from the other frames. The idea behind the logic also partly comes from Cherniak's [1] recent research in philosophical psychology where he proposed a model for human beliefs based on the standard duplex structure of *short-term memory* and *long-term memory*. In his model, the short-term memory is active. Logical inferences can be made in it (so it is also called the *working memory*). Thus, beliefs in the short-term memory are closed under implication and consistent. On the other

---

[3]  Explicit beliefs in the logic of local reasoning are regarded as local beliefs in Fagin and Halpern's paper since each of them is believed in one frame of mind. We regard them as global beliefs from the viewpoint that they form the global belief base of an agent.

hand, the long-term memory is passive. It is merely storage organized for efficient retrieval of beliefs into the short-term memory.

Our logic combines the duplex structure in Cherniak's model and the frames of mind from the logic of local reasoning. In the logic of attention, *working memory (WM) beliefs* are explicit beliefs in the frame (of mind) under current attention. They are relevant to the problem in hand. *Global memory(GM) beliefs* are defined in the same way as the explicit beliefs in the logic of local reasoning. They form the agent's global belief base. The logic may be extended to include implicit beliefs that are propositions derivable from the student's GM beliefs. The student may not actually hold an implicit belief since he or she may not have made the inference to derive it.

Two other logics of Fagin and Halpern [5], the *logic of awareness* and the *logic of general awareness*, also distinguish a subset of beliefs (the *explicit beliefs*) from the global beliefs (the *implicit beliefs*). The set of explicit beliefs is the conjunction of the set of implicit beliefs and a set called *awareness*. But awareness is an arbitrary set of formulas that may be inconsistent, which is different from our notion of attention, which distinguishes a consistent, independent subset of beliefs. More importantly, both explicit beliefs and implicit beliefs must be consistent, so the logic of (general) awareness does not capture inconsistent beliefs. In contrast, our logic of attention allows inconsistent global beliefs, so it is more useful for student modelling systems.

## 3.2  A Formal Semantics

The formal language of attention **AL** is formed from a set of primitive propositions **P**, a special formula, *true,* two standard connectives, $\neg$ and $\wedge$, from propositional logic, and two modal operators, W and B, to denote WM beliefs and GM beliefs, respectively. We also define boolean connectives, $\vee$, $\Rightarrow$ and $\equiv$, in terms of $\neg$ and $\wedge$ as usual. The formula *false* is an abbreviation of $\neg$ *true*.

Sentences of **AL** are interpreted semantically using a Kripke [13] structure M that is a tuple $(\mathcal{S}, \pi, \mathcal{B})$ where $\mathcal{S}$ is a set of (epistemic) states, $\pi(s, \cdot)$ is a function from primitive propositions for each state $s \in \mathcal{S}$ into the set of truth values $\{true, false\}$, and $\mathcal{B}$ is a function applied to states such that for each state s, $\mathcal{B}(s) = \{T_1, ..., T_k\}$ is a nonempty set where each element $T_i$ is a nonempty subset of $\mathcal{S}$. In particular, $T^*(s) \in \mathcal{B}(s)$ is a distinguished element. Intuitively, each $T_i$ is a frame of mind that the agent may hold in state s. $T^*(s)$ is the frame that is in the focus of attention. In each state, there is at least one frame of mind that the agent may hold, and in each frame of mind there is at least one state that it considers possible. The standard truth relation $\models$ for the logic of attention is defined as follows:

M, s $\models$ *true;*

M, s $\models$ p, where p is a primitive proposition, iff $\pi(s, p) = $ *true;*

M, s $\models \neg \varphi$ iff M, s $\not\models \varphi$;

M, s $\models \varphi \wedge \psi$ iff both M, s $\models \varphi$ and M, s $\models \psi$;

M, s $\models B(\varphi)$ iff there is some $T \in \mathcal{B}(s)$ such that M, s' $\models \varphi$ for every s' $\in$ T;

M, s $\models W(\varphi)$ iff M, s' $\models \varphi$ for every s' $\in T^*(s)$.

As usual, we say that $\varphi$ is *valid* if M, s $\models \varphi$ for all structures M and all states s in every M; and that $\varphi$ is *satisfiable* if M, s $\models \varphi$ for some state of some structure. This completes the semantics of **AL**.

Here we show that **AL** indeed captures some important properties of beliefs in the WM and in the GM as well as the relations between them. First, $W(\varphi) \wedge W(\varphi \Rightarrow \psi) \wedge \neg W(\psi)$ is not satisfiable, but $B(\varphi) \wedge B(\varphi \Rightarrow \psi) \wedge \neg B(\psi)$ is. This shows that WM beliefs are closed under implication, but GM beliefs are not. Also, $B(\varphi) \wedge B(\neg \varphi)$ is satisfiable, while $W(\varphi) \wedge W(\neg \varphi)$ is not. This shows that WM beliefs are consistent, but GM beliefs may not be. Moreover, $W(\varphi) \Rightarrow B(\varphi)$ is valid, showing that everything believed in the WM is also believed in the GM, since the frame of mind under attention is indeed one of the frames of mind of the agent. But $B(\varphi) \Rightarrow W(\varphi)$ is not valid since the frame of mind in which $\varphi$ is believed may not be the one under attention.

Note that using the results from Fagen and Halpern [5], it is straightforward to extend **AL** to cope with a multi-agent structure by replacing $\mathcal{B}$ in the Kripke structure with n elements $\mathcal{B}_1, ...,$ $\mathcal{B}_n$. Also the notion of implicit belief can be included in **AL** by defining a new modal operator L such that

$$M, s \models L(\varphi) \text{ iff } M, s' \models \varphi \text{ for all } s' \in \bigcap_{T \in \mathcal{B}(s)} T.$$

That is, $L(\varphi)$ is true if $\varphi$ is true in every state that is considered possible in all frames of mind.

## 3.3 An Axiomatization

This section provides an axiomatization for the logic of attention. The axiomatization contains four axioms and three rules of inference:

| | |
|---|---|
| A1. | All instances of propositional tautologies; |
| A2. | $\neg B(false)$; |
| A3. | $W(\varphi) \wedge W(\varphi \Rightarrow \psi) \Rightarrow W(\psi)$; |
| A4. | $W(\varphi) \Rightarrow B(\varphi)$; |
| R1. | From $\varphi, \varphi \Rightarrow \psi$, infer $\psi$; |
| R2. | From $\varphi$, infer $W(\varphi)$; |
| R3. | From $\varphi \Rightarrow \psi$, infer $B(\varphi) \Rightarrow B(\psi)$. |

The following thesis and derived rule that we will use in the later discussions are derivable from the above axiomatization ([11], p. 33-34):

T1.                    $W(\varphi) \wedge W(\psi) \equiv W(\varphi \wedge \psi)$;

DR1.                   From $\varphi \Rightarrow \psi$, infer $W(\varphi) \Rightarrow W(\psi)$.

The axiomatization provides another way to understand the logic. Axiom A3 clearly shows that beliefs in the WM are consistent and closed under implication, but beliefs in the GM may not be so since the GM may contain more beliefs than the WM (as shown in axiom A4). The axiomatization also states that incoherence (*false*) is never believed in either the GM or the WM (by axioms A2 and A4), and different lexical notations for the same proposition have the same belief status in the WM (by derived rule DR1) and in the GM (by rule R3).

**Theorem 1:**[4] The above axiomatization is sound and complete for the logic of attention.

If the logic is extended to include the modal operator L to represent implicit beliefs, as mentioned in Section 3.1, then a sound and complete axiomatization also includes the following two axioms:[5]

A5.                    $B(\varphi) \Rightarrow L(\varphi)$;

A6.                    $L(\varphi) \wedge L(\varphi \Rightarrow \psi) \Rightarrow L(\psi)$.

Fagin and Halpern ([5], Theorem 8.1) have shown that the problems of deciding whether a formula is satisfiable and whether it is provable in the logic of local reasoning are PSPACE-complete. Their proof also applies to the logic of attention. That is, although we have introduced extra machinery, the complexities of the problems in our logic remain the same as theirs.

# 4  Multiple Viewpoints

In this and the next sections we show how the logic of attention could be used in the applications of student modelling. One such potential application is to model multiple "viewpoints". A student may have different views on a matter. For example, a second grade student may view a multiplication operation as a sequence of addition operations or as a look up operation in the multiplication table. In some situations different viewpoints on a matter result in the same conclusion, but in the other situations they don't. The viewpoints that "Nixon is a Quaker" and that "Nixon is a republican" may lead to different conclusions regarding the proposition "Nixon

---

[4]  A proof of the theorem is included in the Appendix.
[5]  A proof of the soundness and completeness of this extended axiomatization for the extended logic of attention can be easily obtained by combining the proof in the Appendix and the relevant part of the proof of Theorem 8.5 (the soundness and completeness of logic of local reasoning) in [5].

was a war-monger" [20]. These mutually inconsistent viewpoints can be represented by the explicit beliefs of the logic of local reasoning or by the LTM beliefs of the logic of attention. Suppose we use the following propositions to represent the above statements:

| a: | Nixon is a Quaker; |
| b: | Nixon is a Republican; |
| c: | A Quaker loves peace; |
| d: | A Republican likes war; |
| e: | Nixon is a war-monger. |

Then we have the knowledge base:

$$\{ B(a), B(b), B(c), B(d), B(a \wedge c \Rightarrow \neg e), B(b \wedge d \Rightarrow e) \}.$$

However, from this knowledge base we can neither derive $B(e)$ (the student believes that Nixon is a war-monger) or $B(\neg e)$ (the students believes that Nixon is not a war-monger). This inference can only be drawn if we have a mechanism to do local reasoning. The WM beliefs of the logic of attention provide such a mechanism. If the student's currently active viewpoint is "Nixon is a Quaker", then the beliefs related to this viewpoint are in the WM, so we have the knowledge base:

$$\{ B(a), B(b), B(c), B(d), B(a \wedge c \Rightarrow \neg e), B(b \wedge d \Rightarrow e),$$
$$W(a), W(c), W(a \wedge c \Rightarrow \neg e) \}.$$

Using the axiomatization provided in Section 2.3, we can derive $W(\neg e)$, $\neg W(e)$ and $B(\neg e)$ from this knowledge base.

# 5 Socratic Tutoring

Now we use an example to show another potential application of the logic of attention, Socratic tutoring [3]. In the example, we use the extended version of the logic that includes the modal operator L.

A Socratic tutor does not teach a subject by direct exposition, but leads students by successive questions to formulate general principles on the basis of individual cases, to validate their own hypotheses, and to discover contradictions. For instance, the tutor may ask a question that brings a subset of inconsistent beliefs to the student's attention, leading the student to discover the inconsistency and to remove the misconception(s) behind the inconsistency. Here we show how to use the logic of attention in a Socratic tutoring session.

Consider the example of the dialog between the Socratic tutor and a student on grain growing shown in Figure 1. In the example, the student made a prediction, "Oregon does not grow rice", based on an unnecessary factor, "Oregon does not have flat land". The student seems to believe a malrule, "A place that grows rice must have flat land", and use the malrule in the prediction. In order to give an appropriate counterexample that can lead the student to remove the misconception, the tutor must know what the student believes. It must also be able to identify the inconsistent subsubset of the student's beliefs containing the misconception and the subset of beliefs in this inconsistent subset that were not under the student's attention. The counterexample should be able to bring this subsubset to the student's attention.

---

*Student:* (In response to why they can not grow rice in Oregon) I don't think the land is flat enough. You've got to have flat land so that you can flood a lot of it.
*Tutor:* What about Japan? (Pick a counterexample for an unnecessary factor.)
(Japan grows rice but does not have much flat land.)

---

Figure 1: A dialog excerpt of socratic tutoring (from [2])

In the example, the tutor used the question "What about Japan?" to lead the student to discover an inconsistency in beliefs. The tutor seems to believe that the student believed "Japan grows rice" and "Japan does not have flat land" and that these two beliefs are not under the student's attention. It also inferred that these two beliefs are inconsistent with the malrule. Here, we show that the logic of attention is indeed a mechanism that allows the tutor to do this kind of reasoning. We use the following propositional formulas to represent the above statements:

| | |
|---|---|
| $p_1$: | Oregon does not grow rice; |
| $p_2$: | Oregon does not have flat land; |
| r: | A place that grows rice must have flat land. |
| $p_3$: | Japan grows rice; |
| $p_4$: | Japan does not have flat land; |

From the student's utterances in the dialog, the tutor could recognize that the student was using beliefs $p_1$, $p_2$ and r, so it inferred that these beliefs were under the student's attention. But beliefs about $p_3$ and $p_4$ were not under attention, for otherwise the student would have discovered the inconsistency. Thus, the student model contains the following set of sentences of the logic of attention:

$$\{ W_s(p_1), W_s(p_2), W_s(r), B_s(p_3), B_s(p_4), B_s(p_3 \wedge r \Rightarrow \neg p_4) \}.$$

The last belief in the set above shows that the tutor expected that the student would be able to infer $\neg p_4$ if both $p_3$ and r were under the student's attention.

Using axioms A4, A5 and rule R1, the tutor can derive the following sentences from the student model:

$$B_s(r), L_s(r), L_s(p_3), L_s(p_4), L_s(p_3 \wedge r \Rightarrow \neg p_4).$$

Then, using axiom A6 and rule R1, the tutor can derive $L_s$(false), that is, the student's beliefs were inconsistent! By examining the belief subset involved in the inferences, it can identify that the beliefs about $p_3$, $p_4$ and $p_3 \wedge r \Rightarrow \neg p_4$ were in the inconsistent subset and not under the student's attention. Suppose the tutor believed that asking the question "What about Japan?" at that time could bring these beliefs to the student's attention (ie., the Socratic tutor has rules $q \wedge B_s(p_3) \Rightarrow W_s(p_3)$, $q \wedge B_s(p_4) \Rightarrow W_s(p_4)$, $q \wedge B_s(p_3 \wedge r \Rightarrow \neg p_4) \Rightarrow W_s(p_3 \wedge r \Rightarrow \neg p_4)$, where q represents the question). Then after the question the student model contains the following new WM beliefs:

$W_s(p_3)$, $W_s(p_4)$, $W_s(p_3 \wedge r \Rightarrow \neg p_4)$.

But either the old beliefs $W_s(r)$ or one of these new beliefs must be removed, for otherwise the tutor's beliefs would be inconsistent (using axioms A2, A3, A4, thesis T1 and rule R1, *false* would be derived from the above four sentences) which is prohibited in the system. Thus, a belief revision process must be carried out in the student model.

In [9], we developed a *student model maintenance system* (*SMMS*) that carries out belief revision whenever the tutor's beliefs are found inconsistent. The SMMS uses a *reason maintenance system* (*RMS*) [14] to deal with beliefs from direct observation and deductive inferences [12] and a stereotype algorithm to handle default beliefs. We [9] also developed an *attention-shifting belief revision system* (*ABRS*) that uses a limited reasoning approach to overcome the inefficiency problem in the RMS. The ABRS has been shown to be potentially very useful in student model revision and instructional planning [10]. The underlying intuitions of the logic of attention and the ABRS are very similar. Important follow up research is to extend and modify the logic of attention to formalize the ABRS and the SMMS.

Now we return to the example. Suppose after the question, the student did discover the inconsistency and remove the malrule from the belief set, as was expected by the tutor, and suppose the tutor carried out a belief revision process that removed the sentence $W_s(r)$ from the student model. Then the updated consistent student model becomes:

{ $W_s(p_1)$, $W_s(p_2)$, $W_s(p_3)$, $W_s(p_4)$, $W_s(p_3 \wedge r \Rightarrow \neg p_4)$,

$B_s(p_1)$, $B_s(p_2)$, $B_s(p_3)$, $B_s(p_4)$, $B_s(p_3 \wedge r \Rightarrow \neg p_4)$ }.

# 6  Conclusions

We have investigated the issue of reasoning about a student's inconsistent beliefs and attention. A new logic has been proposed as a knowledge representation for student modelling systems doing this kind of reasoning. An axiomatization of the logic has been designed and proven to be sound and complete with respect to the proposed semantics. As an example, we have shown how the logic could be used to model multiple viewpoints of a student and used in a Socratic tutoring system to reason about a student's inconsistent beliefs and attention, which allows the system to ask appropriate questions that leads the student to discover inconsistent beliefs and to remove the misconceptions behind them.

It is not clear whether the logic can handle multiple levels of nested beliefs such as the tutor's beliefs about the student's beliefs about the tutor's beliefs, or the tutor's beliefs about the student's beliefs about the student's beliefs, etc. However, most current student modelling systems [22] are only concerned with the tutor's beliefs about the student's domain knowledge. Since the tutor's beliefs at the outmost level need not to be explicitly represented (see Section 1), our logic can well handle these kinds of two-level "nested" beliefs, as shown in the above example.

We are considering two extensions to this research. One extension is to focus on belief revision, which has been discussed in Section 5. The other extension is to deal with modal predicate logical formulas. This extension would give the logic more expressive power and allow the student model to be represented more efficiently (using fewer logical sentences) and more naturally. For example, we may use the predicates g for "grows rice" and f for "has flat land". Thus, $p_3$, $p_4$ and r becomes g(Japan), $\neg$ f(Japan) and $\forall$ (x)g(x) $\Rightarrow$ f(x), respectively. Then we can naturally derive $L_s$(f(Japan)) from $B_s$(g(Japan)) and $B_s$($\forall$ (x)g(x) $\Rightarrow$ f(x)) and discover the contradiction in the student's beliefs, without introducing the "odd" belief $B_s$($p_3 \wedge$ r $\Rightarrow \neg p_4$). A difficulty of this extension is that the satisfiability of the logic would then become undecidable [11]. However, the logic may be used as a theoretical framework, on which a student modelling language may be based, similar to the way Prolog was developed based on predicate logic.

# Appendix:  A Proof of the Soundness and Completeness of Logic of Attention

## (1)  A proof of the soundness of the logic

We prove the soundness of the logic by showing that all axioms and rules of inference in the axiomatization are valid, but we omit the validity proofs for axiom A1 and rule R1 since they can be found in any standard textbook of mathematical logic, such as [16]. We use T*(s), without further definition, throughout the following proofs to denote the distinguished element of $\mathcal{B}$(s) for the s in the particular proof.

*Validity of A2:*  Assume the contrary that $\neg$ B(false) is not valid. Then B(false) is satisfiable, so there is some model M and some $s \in S$ s.t. M, s $\models$ B(false). This means that there is some T $\in \mathcal{B}$(s) s.t. for all s' $\in$ T, M, s' $\models$ *false,* a contradiction.  ∎

*Validity of A3:* For any model M and any state s,

$$M, s \models (W(\varphi) \wedge W(\varphi \Rightarrow \psi)) \Rightarrow W(\psi)$$

$$\Leftrightarrow \qquad M, s \models \neg W(\varphi) \vee \neg W(\neg \varphi \vee \psi) \vee W(\psi).$$

We exhaust all three cases: (1) if there is a state $s' \in T^*(s)$ s.t. $M, s' \not\models \varphi$, then $M, s \not\models W(\varphi)$ and $M, s \models \neg W(\varphi)$, so the formula is true; (2) if for every $s' \in T^*(s)$, $M, s' \models \psi$, then $M, s \models W(\psi)$, so the formula is also true; (3) finally, if for every $s' \in T^*(s)$, $M, s' \models \varphi$ and there is a state $s'' \in T^*(s)$ s.t. $M, s'' \not\models \psi$, then $M, s'' \not\models \neg \varphi \vee \psi$. ($M, s'' \models \varphi$ since $s''$ is an $s'$). Thus, $M, s \not\models W(\neg \varphi \vee \psi)$ and $M, s \models \neg W(\neg \varphi \vee \psi)$. The formula is still true. ∎

*Validity of A4:* For any model M and any state s,

$$M, s \models W(\varphi) \Rightarrow B(\varphi)$$

$$\Leftrightarrow \qquad M, s \models \neg W(\varphi) \vee B(\varphi).$$

If there is a state $s' \in T^*(s)$ s.t. $M, s' \not\models \varphi$, then $M, s \not\models W(\varphi)$ and $M, s \models \neg W(\varphi)$. The formula is true. Otherwise, for every $s' \in T^*(s)$, $M, s' \models \varphi$, so $s \models B(\varphi)$. The formula is also true. ∎

*R2 preserves validity:* Let $\models \varphi$. Then $\varphi$ is true in every state and every model. Thus, for any model M and any state s, we have $T^*(s) \in \mathcal{B}(s)$ s.t. for every $s' \in T^*(s)$, $M, s' \models \varphi$, so $M, s \models W(\varphi)$. Thus, $\models W(\varphi)$. ∎

*R3 preserves validity:* This can be shown in the same way as the proof for R3 except that we use "some $T \in \mathcal{B}(s)$" here to replace "$T^*(s)$" there. ∎

## (2) A proof of the completeness of the logic

**Definition 1** [7]: A formula $\varphi$ is *consistent* (with respect to an axiom system) if $\neg \varphi$ is not provable. A finite set $\{\varphi_1, ..., \varphi_k\}$ is consistent iff the formula $\varphi_1 \wedge ... \wedge \varphi_k$ is consistent. An infinite set of formula is consistent if every finite subset of it is consistent. A set F of formula is a *maximal consistent set* if it is consistent and any proper superset of it is inconsistent. ∎

Using standard techniques of propositional reasoning we can show

**Lemma 1** [5]: In any axiom system that includes axiom A1 and rule R1:

(1)   Any consistent set can be extended to a maximal consistent set.

(2)   If F is a maximal consistent set, then for all formula $\varphi$ and $\psi$:

   (a)   either $\varphi \in F$ or $\neg \varphi \in F$;

   (b)   $\varphi \wedge \psi \in F$ iff $\varphi \in F$ and $\psi \in F$;

   (c)   if $\varphi \in F$ and $\varphi \Rightarrow \psi \in F$, then $\psi \in F$;

   (d)   if $\varphi$ is provable, then $\varphi \in F$. ∎

Now we define a canonical Kripke structure for attention $M^c = (\mathbf{S}, \pi, \mathbf{B})$ by taking

$\mathbf{S} = \{s_F \mid F$ is a maximal consistent subset$\}$

$\pi(s_F, p) = \begin{cases} true, & \text{if } p \in F \\ false, & \text{if } p \notin F \end{cases}$

$\mathbf{B}(s_F) = \{T_{\psi,F} \mid B(\psi) \in F\}$, where $T_{\psi,F} = \{s_G \mid \psi \in G\}$

In particular, $T^*(s) = T_{\omega,F}$ is the distinguished element of $\mathbf{B}(s_F)$, where $\omega = \bigwedge_{W(\varphi) \in F} \varphi$.
Note that since $W(\omega) \in F$, by axiom A4 and Lemma 1 (2c), $B(\omega) \in F$. Thus, $T_{\omega,F}$ is automatically contained in $\mathbf{B}(s_F)$. To show that $M^c$ is indeed a Kripke structure for attention, we must show that $\mathbf{B}(s_F)$ is a nonempty set of nonempty subsets of $\mathbf{S}$. Since $true$ is provable by axiom A1, $W(true)$ is provable by rule R2 and $B(true)$ is provable by axiom A4 and rule R2, so we have $B(true) \in F$ for every maximal consistent set F by Lemma 1 (2d). Thus, $T_{true,F} \in \mathbf{B}(s_F)$ and $\mathbf{B}(s_F)$ is nonempty. To see that each set in $\mathbf{B}(s_F)$ is nonempty, suppose $B(\psi) \in F$. Then $\psi$ must be consistent; for if not, $\psi \Rightarrow false$ would be provable by axiom A1, and by rule R3 and Lemma 1 (2d) we would have $B(false) \in F$, contradicting the consistency of F by axiom A2. Since $\psi$ is consistent, there must be some maximal consistent set G containing $\psi$, so $s_G \in T_{\psi,F}$.

Next we show by induction on structure of formulas that $M^c$, $s_F \models \varphi$ if $\varphi \in F$. This will show that all consistent formulas are satisfiable, which is equivalent to that all valid formulas are provable, and thus gives us completeness of the axiomatization. The basis of the induction that $\varphi$ is a primitive proposition is proved by definition of $M^c$. For the inductive part of the proof, the cases that $\varphi$ is of the form $\neg \varphi'$ or $\varphi' \wedge \psi''$ are obvious. Thus, the only interesting cases arise when $\varphi$ is of the form $B(\varphi')$ or $W(\varphi')$.

For $B(\varphi')$, note that if $B(\varphi') \in F$, then $T_{\varphi',F} \in \mathbf{B}(s_F)$. By construction, if $s_G \in T_{\varphi',F}$, then $\varphi' \in G$. Using the inductive hypothesis, it follows that $M^c$, $s' \models \varphi'$ for all $s' \in T_{\varphi',F}$. Thus, $M^c$, $s_F \models B(\varphi')$. For the converse, suppose $B(\varphi') \notin F$. We want to show that $M^c$, $s_F \not\models B(\varphi')$, so we must show that for all $T_{\varphi'',F} \in \mathbf{B}(s_F)$, there is some $s' \in T_{\varphi'',F}$ such that $M^c$, $s' \models \neg \varphi'$. Now if $T_{\varphi'',F} \in \mathbf{B}(s_F)$, then we must have $B(\varphi'') \in F$. It must be the case that $\varphi'' \wedge \neg \varphi'$ is consistent; for if not, then $\varphi'' \Rightarrow \varphi'$ is provable, so by rule R3 and Lemma 1 (2c), we must have $B(\varphi') \in F$, a contradiction. Since $\varphi'' \wedge \neg \varphi'$ is consistent, there must be some maximal consistent set G such that $\varphi''$, $\neg \varphi' \in G$. But by construction, $s_G \in T_{\varphi'',F}$, and by the inductive hypothesis we have $M^c$, $s_G \models \neg \varphi'$. Thus, $s_G$ is the desired state.

For $W(\varphi')$, note that if $W(\varphi') \in F$, then for $\omega = \bigwedge_{W(\varphi) \in F} \varphi$, there must be some $B(\varphi'') \in F$ such that $\varphi' \wedge \varphi'' = \omega$ by the definition of $\omega$. Thus, by Lemma 1 (2b), $W(\omega) \in F$, and by axiom A4 and Lemma 1 (2c), $B(\omega) \in F$. By construction, if $s_G \in T_{\omega,F}$, then $\omega \in G$. By Lemma 1 (2b), $\varphi' \in G$. Using the inductive hypothesis, it follows that $M^c$, $s' \models \varphi'$ for all $s' \in T_{\omega,F}$. Thus, $M^c$, $s_F \models W(\varphi')$. For the converse, suppose $W(\varphi') \notin F$. We want to show that $M^c$, $s_F \not\models W(\varphi')$, so we must show that there is some $s' \in T_{\omega,F}$ such that $M^c$, $s' \models \neg \varphi'$. Now since $T_{\omega,F} \in \mathbf{B}(s_F)$ by construction, we have $W(\omega) \in F$. It must be the case that $\omega \wedge \neg \varphi'$ is consistent; for if not, then $\omega \Rightarrow \varphi'$ is provable, so by derived rule DR1 and Lemma 1 (2c), we must have $W(\varphi') \in F$, a contradiction. Since $\omega \wedge \neg \varphi'$ is consistent, there must be some maximal consistent set G such that $\omega, \neg \varphi' \in G$. But by construction, $S_G \in T_{\omega,F}$, and by the inductive hypothesis we have $M^c, s_G \models \neg \varphi'$. Thus, $s_G$ is the desired state. ∎

## Acknowledgements

Thanks to Eric Neufeld for his valuable input to this research and Gordon McCalla and Jim Greer for their discussions on the ideas in this paper. Peter Turney, Rob Wylie, Randy Coulman, Greg Adams, and Jack Brahan read and commented on the draft of the paper. The University of Saskatchewan, the Natural Science and Engineering Research Council of Canada and the Institute for Robotics and Intelligent Systems have provided financial support for this research.

## References

1. Cherniak, C.: *Minimal Rationality*. Cambridge, MA: MIT Press 1986
2. Collins, A.: Processes in acquiring knowledge. In: *Schooling and the Acquisition of Knowledge* (R. C. Anderson, R. J. Spiro & W. E. Montague, eds.), pp. 339-364 Hillsdale, NJ: Lawrence Erlbaum Associates 1977
3. Collins, A. & Stevens, A. L.: Goals and strategies of inquiry teachers. In: *Advances in Instructional Psychology, Vol. 2* (R. Glaser, ed.), pp. 65-120, Hillsdale, NJ: Lawrence Erlbaum Associates 1982
4. Doyle, D.: A society of mind. Proceedings of the IJCAI-83, Karlsruhe, Germany, pp. 309-314 1983
5. Fagin, R. & Halpern, J. Y.: Belief, awareness, and limited reasoning. *Artificial Intelligence*, 34 (1), pp. 39-76 (1988)
6. Harman, G.: *Change in View: Principles of Reasoning*. Cambridge, MA: MIT Press 1986
7. Helpern, J. Y. & Moses, Y.: A guide to the modal logics of knowledge and belief: preliminary draft. Proceedings of the IJCAI 85, Los Angeles, CA, pp. 480-490, 1985
8. Huang, X., McCalla, G. I., Greer, J. E. & Neufeld, E.: Revising deductive knowledge and stereotypical knowledge in a student model. *User Modeling and User-Adapted Interaction*, 1(1), pp. 87-115 (1991)
9. Huang, X., McCalla, G. I. & Neufeld, E.: *Using attention in belief revision*. Proceedings of the AAAI-91, Anaheim, CA, pp. 275-280 1991
10. Huang, X. & McCalla, G. I.: Instructional planning using focus of attention. *Proceedings of the 2nd International Conference on Intelligent Tutoring Systems*, Montreal, Quebec (C. Frasson, G. Gauthier & G. McCalla, eds.), pp. 433-450, Lecture Notes in Computer Science, Vol. 608, Berlin: Springer-Verlag 1992
11. Hughes, G. E. & Cresswell, M. J.: *An Introduction to Modal Logic*. London: Methuen 1968
12. Kass, R.: Building a user model implicitly from a cooperative advisory dialog. Paper presented at the 2nd International Workshop on User Modeling, Honolulu, HI 1990
13. Kripke, S.: Semantical analysis of modal logic. *Z. Math. Logik Grundl. Math*, 9, pp. 67-96 (1963)
14. McAllester, D. A.: *Truth maintenance*. Proceedings of the AAAI-90, Boston, MA, pp. 1109-1115, 1990
15. McCalla, G. I.: Knowledge Representation Issues in Automated Tutoring. Research Report 87-4, Department of Computational Science, University of Saskatchewan, Canada 1987
16. Mendelson, E.: *Introduction to Mathematical Logic*. Princeton, NJ: Van Nostrand 1979
17. Minsky, M.: *The Society of Mind*. New York, NY: Simon and Schuster 1985

18. Palthepu, S., Greer, J. & McCalla, G.: Learning by teaching. In: *The International Conference on the Learning Science: Proceedings of the 1991 Conference* Evanston, IL (L. Birnbaum, ed.). pp. 357-363, Charlottesville, VA: AACE 1991
19. Self, J. A.: The case for formalizing student models (and intelligent tutoring systems generally). In: *Proceedings of the 4th International Conference on Artificial Intelligence and Education*, Amsterdam, (D. Bierman, J. Breuker & J. Sandberg eds.), pp. 244, Amsterdam: IOS 1989
20. Self, J. A.: Formal Approaches to Learner Modelling. Technical Report AI-59, Department of Computing, Lancaster University, UK 1991
21. Villano, M.: Probabilistic student model: bayesian belief networks and knowledge space theory. *Proceedings of the 2nd International Conference on Intelligent Tutoring Systems*, Montreal, Quebec (C. Frasson, G. Gauthier & G. McCalla, eds.), pp. 491-498, Lecture Notes in Computer Science, Vol. 608, Berlin: Springer-Verlag 1992
22. Wenger, E.: *Artificial Intelligence and Tutoring Systems.* Los Altos, CA: Morgan Kaufmann 1987

# A Formal Approach To ILEs

Ernesto Costa[1], Graça Gaspar[2], and Helder Coelho[3]

[1] Laboratório de Informática e Sistemas, Universidade de Coimbra, Quinta da Boavista, Coimbra, Portugal
[2] Departamento de Informática, Universidade de Lisboa, Lisboa, Portugal
[3] Departamento de Matemática,, Universidade Técnica de Lisboa, Lisboa, Portugal

**Abstract:** In the field of AI and Education, Intelligent Tutoring Systems (ITS) were replaced by Intelligent Learning Environments (ILE). This name transformation embodies a radical change concerning the role of such artificial agents and the possible ways they can be used to promote human learning. Recently some researchers (eg. J. Self) have pointed out the need for a formal characterization of these ILE systems. The goal of this article is to show one possible way of formalization. It will be based on a modification of the idea of deductive structures (DS) first proposed by Konolige. These DS will be accompanied by heuristic principles and criteria that define different types of societies and agents. We will show how this technical apparatus can be adopted in distinct educational scenarios.

**Keywords:** belief revision, formal models, learning scenarios, multi-agent interaction, intelligent learning environments, intelligent tutoring systems

## 1 Introduction

In his most influential paper J. Self [11] advocated the need for a new discipline he called *Computational Mathetics* (C.M.) defined as "the study of learning, and how it may be promoted, using the techniques, concepts and methodologies of computer science and artificial intelligence". Contrary to most of today's practices Computational Mathetics is placed at a level which is abstract, independent of applications and psychologically neutral. As a consequence it is clear that if we accept the new paradigm of C. M. we must shift our research focus in the direction of formal theories for Intelligent Learning Environments (ILEs) [13].

One possible way of formalization, which we will pursue here, is based on the two following hypotheses:

> _Hypothesis 1_: Learning and teaching are particular cases of interaction between autonomous rational agents (RA);
>
> _Hypothesis 2_: Rational Agents can be modelled in terms of belief states and how they change as a consequence of interactions with other RA and the environment.

Before continuing some clarification is needed in order to explain the terminology used. First, when we say that an agent is _rational_ we mean that the agent chooses, from among the actions it believes will contribute to the satisfaction of its goals, the one(s) that more closely matches its preferences; second, by _autonomous_ we mean that an agent is an open system [9] and so its behavior cannot always be anticipated; third, a _belief_ is a logic concept, that is a belief is just a formula of a logical language. (For the different possible uses of the term belief see [8], where Hadley points out six usages of the word belief).

From the two hypotheses above it is clear that one important research direction is, on one hand, the construction of a formal theory about the dynamics of belief systems and, on the other hand, its evaluation in a learning context. These are the main objectives of this paper.

Our approach is based on a modification of the idea of deductive structures (DS) proposed first by Konolige [10], and is presented in section 2. In section 3, we discuss how these DS, accompanied by heuristic principles and criteria, define different types of societies and agents. In section 4, we will show how this apparatus can be used to construct distinct educational scenarios. Finally, in section 5, we summarize the main aspects of the paper and mention the points that deserve future attention.

## 2 The Model of an Agent

### 2.1 The Model

Informally, an autonomous rational agent's (hereafter called simply agent) belief state can be characterized by several structures: one that determines his own beliefs about the world, and one for each one of the other agents whose existence he is aware of which define this agent's beliefs about the beliefs of the other agents. So each agent will have at a particular moment a base set of beliefs which is in fact an indexed set of sets of beliefs, $B_A$, where A is a set of agent identifiers. The set A includes the special identifier _own_ denoting the agent itself. Each element of a set $B_a$, where a is the name of an agent, is a sentence in the internal language of that agent. We will assume, for the sake of simplicity, that the internal language is the same for all agents and that it is a first order language. It will be denoted by $L^1$.

An agent must have some inferential capability in order to reason. This will be expressed by a set of deduction rules. As with the base set of beliefs what we have in fact, for each agent, is an indexed set of sets of deduction rules denoted by $R_A$, where A is a set of identifier names of agents.

We will assume also that our agents are imperfect reasoners [10]. This means that the set of deduction rules an agent has is not necessarily complete or sound. Moreover the whole set of beliefs explicitly held by the agent may be inconsistent. This situation leads us to introduce a partial order relation on the base set of formulas (candidate beliefs) of an agent, $<_a$, allowing us to define at each moment the preferred subtheories T of agent a.

> Definition. T is a preferred subtheory of $B_a$ if there is a total ordering of formulas
> $(f1, f2, ... , fn)$ respecting $<_a$ such that T is the deductive closure of Tn where:
> - $T0 = \{ \}$ and, for $0 \leq i < n$
> - $Ti+1 = Ti$      if fi+1 is contradictory with Ti else
>   $Ti » \{fi+1\}$
>
> that is, T is a maximal non-contradictory subtheory of $B_a$ relative to $<_a$.

By non-contradictory we mean the incapacity to derive false using the set of beliefs and the deduction rules of the agent. This definition is different from the one presented by Brewka [1] in the sense that the preferred subtheory depends not only on the priorities among formulas but also on the deductive capacity of the agent.

> *Definition* A deduction structure of an agent a, $D_a$, is a triple formed by a set of
> formulas (candidate beliefs), a partial order on that set, and a set of deduction
> rules. It is denoted by $< B_a, <_a, R_a >$.

We can now define the belief set associated with a deduction structure $D_a$, denoted by $bel(D_a)$:

> *Definition*. $f \in bel(D_a)$ iff f belongs to a preferred subtheory T of $D_a$.

If $<_a$ is a partial order, several total orders may exist that respect $<_a$, leading therefore to several possible preferred subtheories. From those the agent will choose one, T (according to heuristic criteria presented below or arbitrarily).

---

[1] As we will see later each belief (each first-order formula) has attached two more bits of information. One relates to the justification for believing the formula and the other relates to the time the formula start being believed.

Let us consider the deductive structure of a general agent called $\underline{a}$:

$B_a$ =    {quaker(nixon), republican(nixon), quaker(X) fi pacifist(X),
         republican(X) fi not pacifist(X)}

$<_a$ =    {(quaker(X) $\Rightarrow$ pacifist(X) $<_a$ republican(X) $\Rightarrow$ not pacifist(X)}

$R_a$ =    {modus-ponens}

To obtain a preferred subtheory of $\underline{a}$ (his beliefs) we start by building the sequence Ti:

T0 =    { }

T1 =    {quaker(nixon)}

T2 =    {quaker(nixon), republican(nixon)}

T3 =    {quaker(nixon), republican(nixon), quaker(X) $\Rightarrow$ pacifist(X)}

T4 =    {quaker(nixon), republican(nixon), quaker(X) $\Rightarrow$ pacifist(X)}

Now T, a maximal non-contradictory subset of $B_a$ relative to $<_a$ and $R_a$, is:

T =    {quaker(nixon), republican(nixon), quaker(X) $\Rightarrow$ pacifist(X),
       pacifist(nixon)}.

pacifist(nixon) results from considering the deductive closure of T4 using the rules in $R_a$.

---

Example 1

It is reasonable to assume that the set of beliefs held by an agent is structured. This means that an agent has a tendency to group together beliefs that are related in some way. The whole set of beliefs may be viewed as divided into several (possibly intersecting) spaces, each one defining a context or a viewpoint [4, 12]. To define this we introduce a relation:

$$\text{rel: F * C}$$

where F is the set of wff of L and C is the set of names of contexts[2]. In practice there is more than one way to define *rel*. We can define it intentionally: instead of formulas we use the names of the predicates and define the criteria, for instance syntactic criteria, that establish when a formula belongs to a context. We can also define *rel* extensionally: the formulas themselves are linked to a context.

Agents have tendency to ascribe some credibility for the fact that another agent is reasoning in a certain context. This aspect can be formally defined by introducing the function:

$$\text{cred: A * C} \rightarrow \text{N}$$

where N is the set of the natural numbers[3].

---

[2] Contexts are not necessary disjoint. So the same formula may belong to different contexts.

[3] It is clear that credibility ratings will change as communication between the agent and the others agents he is aware of goes on.

If we put all these pieces together we arrive at the notion of a model of the belief state of an agent.

*Definition.* The belief state of an agent a is the tuple $m_a$ = < A, C, cred, rel, $D_A$>.

---

Let us give a concrete example of a belief state of an agent.

A =     {own, ernesto}

C =     {politics, commerce}

cred:     {(ernesto, politics, 4), (ernesto, commerce, 2)}

rel:     {( P, politics), (C, commerce)}

where P, the set of formulas associated with context "politics" is:

P =     {social_class(nobless), social_class(bourgeoisie), social_class(clergy), social_class(people), opposite(people, bourgeoisie), un_occupied(portuguese_noble), goal(portuguese_noble, fight), un_occupied(X) $\Lambda$ enemy(X, Y) $\Rightarrow$ fight(X, Y), religion(X, Y) $\Lambda$ religion(Z, W) $\Lambda$ different(Y, W) $\Rightarrow$ enemy(X, Z)}

and C, the set of formulas associated with context "commerce" is:

C =     {social_class(nobless), social_class(people), goal(bourgeoisie, make_money), rich(bourgeoisie), goal(people, make_money), poor(people), country(portugal), medium(portugal), poor(portugal), discover(vasco_da_gama, way_to_india), country(india), large(india), rich(india)}

$D_{own}$=< $B_{own}$, <$_{own}$, $R_{own}$>

where

$B_{own}$={social_class(nobless), social_class(bourgeoisie), social_class(clergy), social_class(people), opposite(people, bourgeoisie), un_occupied(portuguese_noble), goal(portuguese_noble,fight), un_occupied(X) $\Lambda$ enemy(X,Y) $\Rightarrow$ fight(X,Y), religion(X, Y) $\Lambda$ religion(Z, W) $\Lambda$ different(Y, W) $\Rightarrow$ enemy(X, Z), goal(bourgeoisie, make_money) , rich(bourgeoisie), goal(people, make_money), poor(people), country(portugal), small(portugal), poor(portugal), discover(vasco_da_gama, way_to_india), country(india), large(india), rich(india)},

<$_{own}$={people < bourgeoisie, nobless < bourgeoisie, poor($\bullet$) < rich($\bullet$)},

$R_{own}$={modus_ponens, universal instantiation, and-introduction}

$D_{ernesto}$=<$B_{ernesto}$, <$_{ernesto}$, $R_{ernesto}$>

where

$B_{ernesto}=\{$un_occupied(portuguese_noble), goal(portuguese_noble, fight),
un_occupied(X) $\wedge$ enemy(X, Y) $\Rightarrow$ fight(X, Y), religion(X, Y) $\wedge$
religion(Z, W) $\wedge$ different(Y, W)$\Rightarrow$enemy(X, Z), religion(portugal,
catholicism), social_class(nobless), social_class(bourgeoisie),
social_class(people), goal(bourgeoisie, make_money), rich(bourgeoisie),
poor(portuguese_bourgeosie), isa(portuguese_bourgeosie, bourgeoisie),
goal(people, make_money), poor(people), goal(X, Y) $\wedge$ goal(Z, Y) $\Rightarrow$
collaborate(X, Z)$\}$,
$<_{ernesto}=\{$bourgeoisie $<$ nobless , rich($\bullet$) $<$ poor($\bullet$)$\}$,
$R_{ernesto}=\{$modus_ponens$\}\}$

---

Example 2

From the example above we can see that contexts may intersect each other, and that we can have contradictory beliefs in different contexts and even inconsistent information inside the same context.

## 2.2 The External Language

If we want to talk about an agent's beliefs in a given state, a new language (external) will be needed. It will be denoted by $L^B$ and will be based on L augmented with a belief operator [$\bullet$]. In particular [a]f will be used with the intended meaning that the agent under consideration believes that agent a believes formula f. If we use f alone this relates to the fact that the agent himself believes in f. In the external language we also need the operators for conjunction and negation, distinct from those in the internal language. Notice that an agent may believe in f and believe in g without believing in f $\wedge$ g.

Syntax

$L^B$ is recursively defined by the following rules:

1. $L^B$ includes the formulas of L;
2. If f is a formula of L and a is an agent's identifier then [a]f is a formula of $L^B$;
3. If f is a formula of $L^B$ then ~f is a formula of $L^B$;
4. If f and g are formulas of $L^B$ then f & g is a formula of $L^B$.

Semantics

The validity of a sentence of $L^B$ in a model $m_a = <$ A, C, cred, rel, $D_A>$ of an agent's belief state , represented by $\models_{m_a}$ f, is defined in the following way:

1. If f $\in$ L then $\models_{m_a}$ f iff f $\in$ bel($D_{own}$);

2.  $\models_{m_a} [\ b]\ f$ iff $b \in A$ and $f \in bel(D_b)$;
3.  $\models_{m_a} \sim f$ iff $\not\models_m f$;
4.  $\models_{m_a} f\ \&\ g$ iff $\models_m f$ and $\models_m g$.

It is clear that defined in this way, $L^B$ is the simplest possible language to speak about the beliefs of an agent. It only allows us to express the fact that a certain formula belongs to the belief set of an agent. We cannot express, for instance, dependencies and preferences among beliefs. Also in the same way as the internal language all agents follow the same rules of formation of the external language formulas.

## 3  Agents and Belief Revision

### 3.1  Structure of Messages

Agents communicate among each other by a mechanism of message passing [14]. It is thus important to see how this communicative process can affect their epistemic state [6]. In particular we have to introduce a function called *Assimilation* that, given a model of an agent and a message, shows how its belief state is modified:

$$\text{Assimil: M * Mess} \rightarrow \text{M}.$$

Let us look more closely to the structure of messages. First of all messages can have a different nature and a distinct type. In nature they can be *public* or (exclusively) *private*. *Public* messages are those addressed to a particular agent or agents but that can be accessed by other agents[4]. *Private* messages, in contrast, can only be "used" by the recipients of the message.

Concerning the types of possible messages agents can exchange we may have:
- *presentation* messages, sent by an agent to introduce himself to other agents;
- *request* messages, that essentially state questions about the receiving agent's belief state (whether a given formula is believed or not) or ask the agent to perform some action;
- *reply* messages, that send back answers to previous request messages; and
- *information* messages, that communicate some information about the belief state of the sending agent.

A message itself has six components: the nature of the message, the type of the message, the sending agent, the receiving agent (or agents), the content of the message, and the time of occurrence[5]. The content of a message can be a formula or a sequence of formulas of L. In

---

[4] In our society there will be a particular agent also called public which behaves like a mail-box receiving and keeping all public messages sent by the other agents. It never takes the initiative of communication, limiting itself to reply to request messages.

[5] The importance of the time parameter will be discussed later on.

conclusion, a message is a sextuple:

mess(<nature>, <type>, <send_agent>, <receive_agents>, <content>, <time>)

The way the content of a message is interpreted depends on the nature and type of the message. For instance the content of a private reply message can be the sequence (A, A → B, B). In that case the content has the role of an explanation.

---

- presentation message:

    mess(public, presentation, ernesto, patricia, name(ernesto), 50)
- request message:

    mess(private, request, ernesto, [patricia, paulo] , $\exists$X, Date:

    kingofPortugal(X, Date) and year(Date, 1498), 123 )
- reply message:

    mess(private, reply, patricia, ernesto, kingofPortugal(joãoII), 140)
- information message:

    mess(public, information, ernesto, discover(india, vascodeGama), 5)

---

Example 3

## 3.2 Situations and Assimilation

In order to see how communication affects the belief state of an agent we must introduce some basic principles that define possible attitudes of agents in particular situations. These principles cannot be justified on purely logical grounds as being only "reasonable" principles [7]. For instance, if we want to model a society based on the idea of honesty we can introduce the two following principles:

*Principle 1* - Sincerity of the sending agent

If an agent a at a given belief state $m_a$ sends a message of type *presentation*, *request* or *information* with content f then a believes in f, that is f $\in$ bel($D_a$).

In an educational scenario, if the sending agent is the teacher and the message is of type *request* this means that the teacher is able to solve the problem he/she put to the student.

*Principle 2* - Confidence of the receiving agent

If an agent a, at a given belief state $m_a$, receives a message from agent b of type *presentation*, *reply* or *information* with content f then he/she believes that the sender believes in f, that is f $\in$ bel($D_b$).

Again using the learning metaphor this means that the student believes the information message sent to him by the teacher.

These principles are certainly not always applicable. For instance if we are trying to model the process of negotiation in a political society, we usually do not assume either sincerity nor confidence.

Another possible principle could be:

*Principle 3* - Credulity of the receiving agent
   If an agent a, at a given belief state $m_a$, receives a message from an agent b of type *presentation, reply* or *information* with content f and if he/she does not believe f to be false he/she enters a new belief state where he/she believes in f, that is in the new model $m'_a$ $f \in bel(D_a)$.

Principle 3 says that an agent will adopt as his own beliefs all beliefs of the other agents that he cannot contradict. This implies that the agents being not cautious can accept wrong beliefs with all the bad consequences of that fact.

The analogy of this principle in education has to do with students who ascribe an unquestionable authority to their teachers.

It is clear that these principles (and other, alternative or complementary) define the behavior of agents in particular situations, that is they define different types of societies. They give us simple mechanisms for implementing the assimilation function. For instance, with principle 2, after receiving an information message with content f from agent a, agent b will introduce in its $B_a$ the formula f. Using Principle 3 he will include f in $D_b$.

## 3.3 Types of Agents and Assimilation

Until now we have not discussed the possibility that incoming messages may contradict the beliefs that an agent has himself or those that he/she has about the other agents. This problem will again be treated at an heuristic level. The heuristics we are going to present reflect the existence in the society of distinct types of agents or, in other words, the existence of agents with different personalities. In the discussion below we assume that we are only concerned with messages of type information and with their effects in $D_{own}$. We can easily generalize to other types of messages and to the possible modifications in the deductive structure of the sending agent included in the model of the receiving agent.

Let us suppose that Cont is the set of formulas belonging to $D_{own}$ that participate in the proof of the contradiction.

A   Arrogant agent;

An *arrogant* agent is the one which uses:

   *Criteria 1* - Highest support given by $<_{own}$

That is, he will order the formulas in Cont according with $<_{own}$ and will choose accordingly.

B   Shy agent;

A *shy* agent will look to the support that the other agents give to the contradictory formulas in Cont and will decide using the:

   *Criteria 2* - Highest support given by context

We consider that all agents, other than own, that believe in a formula f of Cont are the sources of knowledge represented in that formula. Each one will support f with a strength corresponding to their credibility in the formula topics. For each of the formulas in Cont we calculate its maximal support and we order Cont according to that measure. The maximal support is defined as[6]:

$$\text{max\_support}(f) = \max \{\text{support}(f,b) : \models m[b] \; f\}$$

$$\text{support}(f,b) = \max \{\text{cred}(b,c) : \text{rel}(f,c)\}$$

C   Lazy agent;

This is the simplest criteria:

   *Criteria 3* - Recency

Whenever two formulas contradict each other the last received is given higher priority.

One can think of many other types of agents that may use other criteria (for instance: a "simpler" formula will be preferred over a more "complex" one) or a combination of the criteria presented above.

As before these or other alternative or complementary criteria cannot be justified in logical terms. Another aspect has to do with the fact that, as happens with human agents, we must also admit that agents may change their personality through time, starting at a certain moment using different criteria. This is a difficult aspect to model that will not be discussed in this paper.


# 4   Different Learning Scenarios

The model of agents plus the assimilation function just presented are the nucleus of a model of agents in a communicative society. Using this framework we can model different educational situations.

---

[6] Remember that contexts are not necessarily disjoint and so a formula may belong to different contexts.

## 4.1 One-to-One Tutoring

In one-to-one tutoring our society has only two agents: the teacher and the learner. Their abstract models will be very simple. We can use Example 1 where own is the teacher and ernesto is the student. The preferred subtheory associated with $D_{ernesto}$ is the teacher model, and the set of beliefs of ernesto is the student model. Symmetrically the student will also have a teacher's model! $D_{own}$ contains both the domain module and the pedagogical module of a typical ITS architecture[7]. In this case there are no *public* messages. Messages will be typically of type *information*, *request*, and *reply*. We can think of a more restrictive educational setting by disabling the student's capability to send *request* messages to the teacher. This corresponds to a classical computer-aided instruction program where the student remains passive during the educational process.

Within this framework student modelling corresponds to how the teacher assimilates the messages he receives from the student.

## 4.2 One-to-Many Tutoring

This is the typical classroom situation. In our set of agents we have the teacher, the students and a particular agent called public.

---

Let us look at another example that expands and slightly modifies the previous one. Own is the teacher and ernesto and patricia are students. The society as seen by the teacher can be described by:

A = {own, ernesto, patricia, public}

C = {politics, science, religion, commerce}

cred: {(ernesto, science, 4), (ernesto, religion, 2), (patricia, religion, 5), (patricia, commerce, 10)}

rel: {(({social_class(nobless), social_class(bourgeoisie), social_class(clergy), social_class(people), opposite(people, bourgeoisie), un_occupied(portuguese_noble), goal(portuguese_noble, fight), un_occupied(X)∧enemy(X, Y) ⇒ fight(X, Y), religion(X, Y) ∧ religion(Z, W) ∧ different(Y, W) ⇒ enemy(X, Z)}, politics), ({discover(portuguese, astrolabe), discover(portuguese, way_to_india), discover(vasco_da_gama, way_to_india)}, science), ({religion(X, Y) ∧ religion(Z, W) ∧ different(Y, W) ⇒ enemy(X, Z),

---

[7] In a more elaborate model we can conceive the separation of these two modules by introducing in the model a new structure similar to a DS. The first component will be the goals of the teacher, the second component a partial order the goals, and the third component the set of pedagogical strategies used by the teacher.

goal(priest, expand_religion), religion(portugal, catholicism),
religion(india, hinduism)}, religion),
({new_markets(new_world), goal(bourgeoisie, make_money),
rich(bourgeoisie), goal(people, make_money), poor(people),
country(portugal), small(portugal), poor(portugal), religion(portugal,
catholicism), discover(vasco_da_gama, way_to_india), country(india),
large(india), rich(india), in(new_world, india) , religion(india,
hinduism)}, commerce)}

$D_{own}$={{discover(portuguese, astrolabe), discover(portuguese, way_to_india),
social_class(nobless), social_class(bourgeoisie), social_class(clergy),
social_class(people), un_occupied(portuguese_noble),
goal(portuguese_noble, fight), un_occupied(X)∧enemy(X, Y)⇒fight(X,
Y), religion(X, Y)∧religion(Z, W)∧different(Y, W)⇒enemy(X, Z),
new_markets(new_world), goal(bourgeoisie, make_money) ,
rich(bourgeoisie),  goal(people, make_money), poor(people),
opposite(people, bourgeoisie), goal(priest, expand_religion),
country(portugal), small(portugal), poor(portugal), religion(portugal,
catholicism), discover(vasco_da_gama, way_to_india), country(india),
large(india), rich(india), in(new_world, india) , religion(india,
hinduism)},
{people < bourgeoisie, portuguese_noble < bourgeoisie, poor(•) <
rich(•)}, {modus_ponens}}

$D_{ernesto}$={{discover(portuguese, astrolabe), discover(portuguese,
way_to_india), goal(bourgeoisie, make_money), rich(bourgeoisie),
goal(people, make_money), poor(people), goal(X, Y) ∧ goal(Z, Y) ⇒
collaborate(X, Z),  goal(priest, expand_religion), country(portugal),
small(portugal), poor(portugal), religion(portugal, catholicism), poor(X)
∧ rich(Y) ⇒ fight(X, Y)},
{collaborate(•, •) < fight(•, •), rich(•) < poor(•)},
{modus_ponens}}

$D_{patricia}$={{un_occupied(portuguese_noble), goal(portuguese_noble, fight),
un_occupied(X) ∧ enemy(X, Y) ⇒ fight(X, Y), religion(X, Y) ∧
religion(Z, W) ∧ different(Y, W) ⇒ enemy(X, Z), social_class(nobless),
social_class(bourgeoisie), social_class(clergy), social_class(people)},
{bourgeoisie < clergy, nobless < clergy},
{modus_ponens}}

Example 4

In this situation the teacher has a model of each student. The students in turn have a teacher's model plus a model of each one of their colleagues.

This society works as follows: at a particular moment the teacher may address the whole classroom with *public informative* messages. *Request* messages can be sent to a particular student concerning the subject matter being taught but, being *public*, they can be answered by another student. For this to be possible, students send *request* and receive *reply* messages from the agent public. The assimilation process proceeds in the same way as before.

## 4.3 Many-to-Many Learning

In this case the teacher is not absolutely necessary and we can model the situation where students are trying to solve a problem in collaboration. We can also conceive of the situation where the teacher divides his students into groups each one trying to solve the same problem. In that case each group only knows about the existence of the agents belonging to the group and the teacher. Within the group all messages will be *public*. If we want to model the situation where groups are put into competition by the teacher this can be done by electing one element of each group as "leader" and enabling him to send *public* messages addressed to the teacher or to the other group leaders.

## 5 Conclusions and Future Work

We have presented a first tentative of a formalization of Intelligent Learning Environments (ILEs) based on a formal model of an autonomous rational agent. The dynamics of the epistemic state of an agent were captured by the notion of an assimilation function which is supported by heuristic principles. We hope it is clear from the discussion above that our approach is general enough to deal with different educational scenarios. Moreover, being based on a formal model helps in clarifying some concepts used in the field of Artificial Intelligence and Education like, for instance, what a *student model* really is. Currently we are starting an implementation using an object oriented programming approach.

There is of course a lot of work to be done in the future. In particular, we are interested in exploring at least two aspects:

The first aspect is to effectively use the time dimension present in the messages. To that end each formula in the deductive structure of an agent will have information attached concerning the time when it was believed (or not believed) plus the corresponding justification. With that information we will be able to build histories for each formula. A History Management System (an ATMS [5] working in the time dimension) [2] will be responsible for determining what is consistent in a particular moment.

The second aspect, already mentioned in the text, is related to the introduction of a new component in the agent's model similar to the deductive structure. It will have three components: the goals of the agent, a partial order over these goals, and a set of meta-rules. With this new element we will able to define more clearly the intentions of an agent and how they can be achieved. In educational terms this means having the goals of the teacher and the students together with the strategies they prefer to use to attain these goals.

# References

1. Brewka, G.: Preferred subtheories: an extended logical framework for default reasoning. Proceedings of the 11th International Joint Conference on Artificial Intelligence, Detroit, MI, pp. 1043-1048 1989
2. Cardoso, A.: *Histories Management* (draft, in Portuguese) 1992
3. Costa, E., (ed.): *New Directions for Intelligent Tutoring Systems*, NATO ASI Series F, Vol. 91, Berlin: Springer-Verlag 1992
4. Costa, E., Duchénoy, S. & Kodratoff, Y.: A resolution-based method for discovering student's misconceptions. In: *Artificial Intelligence and Human Learning* (J. Self, ed.), pp. 156-164 Chapman and Hall 1988
5. de Kleer, J.: An assumption-based TMS, *Artificial Intelligence*, 28(2), pp. 127-162 (1986)
6. Galliers, J.: Belief Revision and a Theory of Communication. Technical Report 193, Computer Laboratory, University of Cambridge, UK 1990
7. Gaspar, G.: Communication and belief changes in a society of agents: towards a formal model of an autonomous agent. Proceedings of the 5th Rocky Mountains Conference on AI, Pragmatics in AI, Las Cruces, pp. 28-30. 1990
8. Hadley, R.: The many uses of "belief" in AI. *Minds and Machines*, 1, pp. 55-73 (1991)
9. Hewitt, C.: Open information systems semantics for distributed artificial intelligence. *Artificial Intelligence*, 47, pp. 79-106 (1991)
10. Konolige, K.: *A Deduction Model of Belief*. London: Pitman 1986
11. Self, J. A.: Computational mathetics: the missing link in Intelligent Tutoring Systems research? In: *New Directions for Intelligent Tutoring Systems* (E. Costa, ed.), pp. 38-56, NATO ASI Series F, Vol. 91, Berlin: Springer-Verlag 1992
12. Self, J. A.: Computational Viewpoints. Technical report AI-44, Department of Computing, University of Lancaster, UK, 1990
13. Self, J. A.: Formal Approaches to Learner Modelling. Technical report AI-59 Department of Computing, University of Lancaster, UK, 1991
14. Sernadas, A, Coelho, H. & Gaspar, G.: Communicating knowledge systems: big talk among small systems. *Applied Artificial Intelligence*, 1, pp. 3-4 (1987)

# Formal Approaches to Student Modelling

John A. Self

Department of Computing, Lancaster University, Lancaster, UK

**Abstract:**  This paper considers student modelling from the point of view of the formal techniques that are involved. It attempts to provide a theoretical, computational basis for student modelling which is psychologically neutral and independent of applications. It is derived mainly from various areas of theoretical artificial intelligence. Because of the intrinsic difficulty of the student modelling problem, these links to AI are often merely pointed out and not pursued in depth.

**Keywords:**  diagnosis, belief revision, machine learning

## 1  Introduction

Like all models, a *student model* is intended to provide information about the object modelled, in this case, the individual student who is using a computer-based learning system. The system uses the student model to help determine actions appropriate for that student. *Student modelling* is the process of creating a student model. Student modelling necessarily occurs mainly at run-time, when the student uses the system, since it is mainly through the evidence provided by the student's inputs to the system that the student model is created. This evidence is usually scanty, making student modelling a difficult process.

The aim of this paper is to review various formal approaches to student modelling. Before embarking on this, some words of justification are required, on why student modelling is important and why formal approaches are necessary. Without a student model a computer-based learning system will perform in exactly the same way with all users, since there is no basis for determining otherwise. But obviously, students are different:  they have different prior knowledge, different interests, different learning aptitudes, and so on. An *intelligent learning environment* (or *ILE)* is primarily one which understands the individual student well enough to be able to determine individualised actions. A student model does not have to be completely accurate to be useful. Indeed, it is not the case that a more accurate student model is necessarily better: the computational effort to improve accuracy may not justify the extra pedagogical leverage obtained. Computational utility, not cognitive fidelity, is the measure for student models. Thus, we will need to consider how student models are used in ILEs. For the moment, we will simply assume that the student model is data for the instructional component of an ILE.

A number of student modelling techniques have been developed [16]. Generally, these techniques are embedded within more-or-less complete ILEs making it difficult to analyze them in isolation. In order to determine the properties of such techniques (so that we may compare them, specify when each is appropriate, develop refinements, etc.) some formalization of them may help. It may not - because, as we will see, many of the techniques skirt difficult issues in theoretical artificial intelligence and it may be better to rely on the pragmatic approach of implementation and empirical evaluation. Also, premature formalization may focus on what is formalizable rather than what is important. However, most sciences progress through formalization and we may hope that student modelling will as well, in due course. Such a formalization should be psychologically and educationally neutral, that is, independent of particular psychological theories and educational discussions of student-model-based ILEs.

The remainder of this paper is organized as follows. First, we introduce a general foundation for formal student modelling and a simple example to illustrate it. We then review methods for creating student models, by initializing them and subsequently revising them in the light of system-student interactions. We first imagine an 'ideal student', that is, one who holds no misconceptions and who reasons and learns rationally. We then consider 'real students' who are naturally less considerate and who therefore present considerably more problems to the formalization effort. The different kinds of content of student models are described. Finally, we re-consider the potential uses of student models in ILEs, in order to re-emphasize that student models are not independent, autonomous components of ILEs but must be fully integrated with other components.

## 2   Foundations

Our starting point of view is that an ILE is intended to support productive interactions between the belief systems of the student and the system ('productive' in this case meaning that they lead to an 'improvement' in these belief systems, especially that of the student, of course). We will use $B_a p$ to denote that an agent $a$ believes proposition $p$ (we will omit the subscript when the agent is irrelevant). The belief-set $\mathcal{B}_a$ of the agent $a$ is the set of propositions believed by

$a:\mathbf{B}_a=\{p\mid B_ap\}$. We will consider the expression $B_ap$ to be itself a proposition and thus that such expressions can be nested: $B_bB_ap$ denotes that agent b believes agent a believes proposition p.

Our basic framework is shown in Figure 1 - we emphasize that this is only a starting point, with the concepts of belief, proposition, etc. to be elaborated in the following. We have three components:

$\mathbf{B}_S$ denotes the student's belief-set;

$\mathbf{B}_C$ denotes the computer system's belief-set;

$\mathcal{LM}$ denotes that subset of the system's belief-set which are beliefs that the system has about the student. The set of propositions which the system believes are believed by the student will be denoted by $B_{cs}$, ie. $B_{cs}=\{p\mid B_cB_sp\}$. The set $\{B_sp\mid B_cB_sp\}$ is a subset of $\mathcal{LM}$.

The computer system has no direct access to $\mathbf{B}_S$: all its reasoning about the student has to be through the analysis of $\mathcal{LM}$

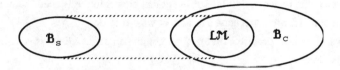

Figure 1: The basic framework

This is intended to be an abstract foundation so general that it can encompass any view of student modelling. It will be made more concrete through examples later. But first we have to say something about the basic concepts of belief and proposition. Philosophers have laboured for millennia over the meaning of such terms, and associated concepts such as knowledge and truth. We will just summarize the main points of relevance to student modelling.

Regarding *belief*, we can make the following points:

1. We can distinguish between the belief itself and the object of the belief, here called the proposition. Thus, we can say "The student's belief that momentum depends only on velocity is reasonable given the examples she[1] has seen", where we are commenting on the belief, not on the proposition itself, that "momentum depends only on velocity".

2. A belief, unlike other attitudes such as regret, wish, etc., can be assessed as true or false, ie. (to keep it simple!) in accordance with the facts. (We will not consider the everyday use of "belief" in phrases such as "I believe in democracy" - the extent to which such non-propositional beliefs can be reduced to beliefs that certain propositions

---

[1]For simplicity we will use 'she' to refer to the learner and 'it' to refer to an agent in general.

are true is a matter of controversy.)

3. Beliefs are held (usually) for reasons, and often changes in beliefs are a function of an analysis of the reasons that they are held. Thus, our student models will rarely be an unstructured set of beliefs as suggested above but may maintain, for each derived belief, some justification for it.

4. Beliefs are related to behaviour: if an agent believes p then it is disposed to act as if p were true. Of course, there is no guaranteed mapping between belief and behaviour (and vice versa): if there were, student modelling would be straightforward. However, some beliefs (eg. that Neptune is cold) do not appear to have much influence on behaviour (except to enable us to respond "yes" to the question "Is Neptune cold?"). Also, a belief may be 'quiescent', ie. even though we may consider it to be possessed by an agent (because of previous behaviour perhaps) it may not be manifested in behaviour when one might expect it, perhaps because the agent has for some reason not considered it relevant to the situation at hand.

5. It does not matter whether or not beliefs have any kind of real existence in the mind (whatever that may mean): it is sufficient that agents find it is useful to attribute beliefs to others in order to understand and predict what they do.

*Knowledge* is usually described in terms of belief - an agent a knows p, $K_a p$, under the following conditions:

$$K_a p \equiv (1)\ B_a p,\ (2)\ p \text{ is true, and } (3) \text{ there is an account for } p .$$

As usual, there is much philosophical debate about this definition, but it will serve our purposes. The third condition is necessary because we would not want to consider that, for example, "I know it is snowing in Moscow" just because I believe it is and it happens to be true, unless I can give a convincing account of why I believe it (eg. that I have just seen a live television broadcast from Red Square). This raises the question of when an account is to be considered convincing and thus the belief to be justified Empiricists claim that all knowledge is acquired through the use of the senses, and hence that no empirical proposition is ever certain, and therefore that we cannot properly claim to know the truth of such propositions. Rationalists, however, consider that it is possible to acquire knowledge by means independent of empirical investigation. In student modelling, part of the computer system's belief set $B_c$ is often considered to represent knowledge, although the fact that it is true is only implicit and the justifications may be absent. The system may consider the student to possess knowledge if parts of $B_{cs}$ correspond to entries in $B_c$:

$$K_c p \ \& \ B_c B_s p \ \rightarrow \ B_c K_s p$$

although this axiom overlooks the role of the account of p, mentioned above.

Computationalists will be happy with the concept of a *proposition*. Clearly, if an Englishman were to assert "I believe that Neptune is cold" and a Frenchman that "Je crois que Neptune est froide" then we would prefer to say that they believe not the sentences "Neptune is cold" and "Neptune est froide" but some language-independent, mind-independent, abstract, symbolic representation of the meaning of the sentences. (We will continue to use sentences to represent propositions where the representation is irrelevant.) Knowledge representation (really, belief representation) in AI is concerned with devising just such representations. There is no assumption that a proposition is an expression in propositional logic or even predicate logic, eg. Cold(neptune). We will be very liberal in considering what may count as a proposition - we will include procedures ("I believe that the way to do subtraction is ..."), goals ("I believe that I want to ..."), plans ("I believe that I will ..."), maybe even attributes ("I believe that I am reliable"). (Note that these sentences in brackets are not meant to imply that agents only possess beliefs if they assert that they do!) Naturally, the representation and processing of these more complex propositions is difficult.

We can usefully distinguish between *object-level propositions* and what for the moment we will simply call non-object-level propositions. Any given ILE is concerned with some domain, say, elementary physics: true propositions contained in $\mathfrak{B}_c$ about that domain (eg. "momentum = mass x velocity"), which it is intended that the student acquire, are object-level propositions. In general, $\mathfrak{B}_c$ contains a set of object-level propositions $O_c$, plus non-object-level propositions of various kinds, for example:

- further propositions about the domain (eg. "momentum is often confused with impetus") - the union of these propositions and $O_c$ we will call the system's domain knowledge $\mathfrak{D}_c$;
- 'meta-level' propositions which are to some extent domain-independent (eg. "it is best to vary one variable at a time");
- propositions in the student model $\mathcal{LM}$ (eg. "the student has fallen asleep", "the student knows what velocity is", etc.).

Unless the ILE's objectives are very precisely specified, the borderline between object-level propositions and domain-related non-object-level propositions is not clear-cut. For example, if an ILE decides to help the student learn that "it is best to vary one variable at a time" then that proposition becomes an object-level one. Usually, the student model focuses on domain-related propositions - of course, this is a simplification: the student will believe non-domain-related propositions, too.

Few ILEs explicitly represent their beliefs as beliefs, that is, they do not use representations such as Believe(computer, author(macbeth, shakespeare)). There is no need to if the beliefs are not to be processed as beliefs - and if all expressions begin with $B_c$ as they have so far, then that part may be left implicit. However, we include it in our formalization as a constant reminder of the empiricist's skepticism about the nature of knowledge and to retain the impression of a 'symmetrical' interaction between two belief-holding agents.

# 3 An Example

Rather than present the various formal approaches in a dry, domain-independent fashion, we will use various example ILEs in order to help describe and illustrate ideas more concretely. This first ILE is as simple as possible: we have no commitment to this particular ILE or the models presented to describe it. We imagine a student using a simulation of two colliding balls. She can vary the masses and velocities of the two balls. Her aim is to predict the resultant velocity (or velocities, for elastic collisions) and thus to develop some understanding of the concept of momentum (and energy).

The student modelling problem is to build a representation of the student which may be useful for instructional interventions. (Whether such interventions are desirable is a separate issue, but few students have no difficulty even with this simple problem.) Building a student model on the basis of a student's inputs alone is difficult, as an empirical study soon indicates. The ILE may, of course, initiate interactions specifically to clarify the content of the student model, and in general this is to be recommended - however, there are difficulties:

1. An appropriate language for such interactions needs to be devised (natural language being too vague and verbose).
2. Such interactions need to be non-intrusive. To avoid a lengthy interrogation about all possible beliefs, system questions need to be maximally informative: a student model is needed to determine such questions.
3. Students' assertions about their beliefs are not wholly reliable. They may not fully understand the terms used ("I know what momentum is") or may be mistaken.

Some illustrative entries in the belief-sets might be:

$B_c = \{$     "momentum = mass * velocity",
          "momentum is conserved",
          "mass cannot be negative",
          "students often think the velocity is the average of the previous velocities",
          "if you increase the masses, the velocity will decrease", ...$\}$

$LM = \{$    "the student believes that mass cannot be negative",
          "the student believes that if you halve one mass, the velocity will double",
          "the student is a novice physicist",
          "the student believes that velocity cannot be negative", ... $\}$

$B_{cs} = \{$    "mass cannot be negative",
          "if you halve one mass, the velocity will double",
          "velocity cannot be negative", ... $\}$

$B_s = \{$    "mass cannot be negative",
          "velocity can be negative",
          "energy has got something to do with where the ball is on the screen",...$\}$

Where we are not concerned with the content of the propositions, we may write, eg.

$$\textbf{B}_s = \{p_1, p_2, p_3, \ldots\}.$$

We can, of course, express relations between propositions, thus:

$$P_6 = B_1p_3,$$
$$P_{12} = B_1 \sim P_{14}.$$

# 4 Initializing the Student Model

When a student first uses the ILE $LM$ is empty. It can be initialized in two ways: by explicit questioning or by default assumptions.

## 4.1 Explicit Questioning

If there is a finite set of independent propositions $\{p_1, p_2, p_3, \ldots\}$ such that $B_sp_i$ may be true, we may ask the student "Do you believe $p_1$?" etc. Clearly this is tedious in the extreme. If the propositions are not independent, then some optimum sequence of questions may be determined. For example, if we use $K_aC$ to denote that an agent a knows a concept C if it believes all the relevant true propositions concerning that concept, then we may express a prerequisite structure in terms of a set of rules of inference (where we use italics to denote a concept):

$$BcKs \; momentum \rightarrow BcKs \; velocity$$
$$BcKs \; velocity \rightarrow BcKs \; speed, \text{ etc.}$$

Given such a set of inference rules, an optimum (or at least sensible) order of questions can be determined. In general, concepts in the middle of the structure should be asked first, since if a student says she knows that concept, the rules say she knows all the prerequisites, whereas if she doesn't then she also does not know all the concepts of which it is a prerequisite, assuming we also have the rules of the form:

$$Bc \sim Ks \; velocity \rightarrow Bc \sim Ks \; momentum$$

In addition to asking the student about object-level propositions, we may also ask about certain non-object-level propositions. For example, we may ask the user to assign herself to one of a set of classes (usually called *stereotypes*): "Do you believe yourself to be an expert, novice or beginner?" Associated with each such class may be a set of inferences:

$$B_c \text{ "student is a novice"} \rightarrow BcKs \; velocity \; \& \; Bc \sim Ks \; momentum, \text{ etc.}$$

## 4.2 Default Assumptions

Normally, the stereotypes are arranged into a hierarchical structure (eg. Figure 2), which permits some ordering of such questions to be determined and the inheritance of inferences. However, because the stereotypes are broad, the inferences they provide for the student model are generally considered to be default assumptions, liable to be over-ridden by later evidence. A set of propositions is associated with each node, representing a stereotype, such that if the student is (believed to be) a member of that stereotype then the system believes that she believes those propositions, together with those propositions attached to any encompassing stereotypes. We might also assume that a student does not believe those propositions attached to sub-stereotypes. In general, a student may be assigned to stereotypes along several dimensions, leading to the possibility of inconsistencies in the default assumptions (considered later).

In the absence of information about the student, she might be assigned to the 'any fool' stereotype, such that she is assumed to believe only those things which any fool believes, that is, so-called common knowledge. Some subset of $\mathcal{B}_c$ might be distinguished as common knowledge and hence assigned to $\mathcal{B}_{cs}$ We might also attempt to make some *a priori* ascriptions of beliefs to the student. For example, the system might assume that she knows nothing of what she is to learn: $\forall p \ ( \ p \ \& \ O_c \ \rightarrow \ B_c \sim B_s p \ )$.

Wilks and Ballim [63] suggest a general default belief ascription axiom:

$$B_a p \ \& \ \sim \exists q \ (B_a q \ \& \ q \ \rightarrow \ B_a \sim B_b p) \ \rightarrow \ B_a B_b p$$

ie. if an agent believes a proposition p and believes there is no reason q why a second agent should not believe it then assume that it does. However, they also point out that there are several 'special cases' (eg. secrets) where almost the opposite applies, ie. the default is to assume that the second agent does not believe it. An ILE is an intermediate case: some but not all (otherwise the learning interaction would be redundant) of the system's beliefs are to be ascribed to the student (but we cannot know which ones).

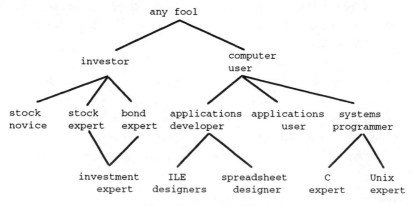

Figure 2: A stereotype hierarchy

Stereotypes are useful for initializing user models generally, especially for systems which do not anticipate much subsequent change in the content of the model (which is the case in most other user modelling contexts). But, for student modelling, where the focus is on the subsequent dynamic tracking of changes in the user (ie. student), stereotypes are not of much use beyond the initialization stage because they do not permit the necessary fine-grained analysis.

# 5  Updating the Student Model

## 5.1  Diagnosis

If the ILE encounters evidence that the current student model is inaccurate, for example, by observing that the student acts differently (eg. when solving problems) to the way the student model would predict, then the system may try to diagnose the student model, that is, find and alter those components necessary to enable the model to correspond to observed behaviour.

## 5.1.1  Reconstruction

After the student model has been initialized there are two further sources of information on the basis of which the student model may be updated: (1) the student's inputs to the ILE, and (2) the current contents of the student model. In general terms, our problem is to map the inputs into a set of propositions:

$$\text{Interpret } (\{i_1,\ i_2,\ i_3,\ldots,\ i_n\}\ ) \rightarrow \{p_1,\ p_2,\ p_3,\ \ldots,\ p_m\}$$

such that we can assert $B_cB_sp_j$ for $j = 1$ to $m$. An answer to a direct question is the simplest such interpretation:

$$\text{Interpret } (\{\text{"yes, I know that force = mass x acceleration"}\})$$
$$\rightarrow \{\text{"force = mass x acceleration"}\}.$$

Usually, the interpretation is much more complex, for example:

$$\text{Interpret}(\{\ \text{student sets } m_1 \text{ to 3 and } v_1 \text{ to 6,}$$
$$\text{student sets } m_1 \text{ to 2 and } v_1 \text{ to 9 }\})$$
$$\rightarrow\{\text{"the product m x v is a useful concept"}\}$$

Interpret has to do much more than just identify the propositions explicit in the student's inputs: it must reason about what the inputs mean in terms of the student's beliefs. Kass [32] gives a set of 'acquisition rules' which makes default interpretations of students' inputs. Two such rules, for example, state (adapting to the student modelling context):

$$\text{Tells}(s,c,p) \rightarrow B_cB_sp\ \&\ \forall q\ (\text{Component}(q,p) \rightarrow B_cB_sq)$$

ie. if the student states a proposition then the system believes that she believes it and all components of it:

Problem(c,p) & Subproblem(q,p) & ~Do(s,q)

→ B_C(~B_S(Problem(c,p)) v ~B_S(Subproblem(q,p)) v B_S(~Can-do(q)))

ie. if the computer sets a problem p for which a subproblem q must be solved but the student does not attempt to solve the subproblem then the computer believes that either the student does not believe that p is the problem or she does not believe that q is a subproblem or she believes that she cannot solve the subproblem. If (as is likely) the system cannot resolve this indeterminacy it might form the basis for the subsequent dialogue with the student.

Often the set of inputs is the student's solution to a problem posed by the ILE. Let us consider first the case where the solution is just the answer A to the problem (with no intermediate steps). The process of inferring the student's derivation of A is called *reconstruction*. If A is correct, according to $\mathbf{D}_c$ we might assume that

$$\{p_1, p_2, p_3, \ldots, p_m\} \rightarrow A \text{ and } p_i \in \mathbf{D}_c \text{ for } i = 1 \text{ to } m$$

$$\rightarrow B_C B_S p_i \text{ for } i = 1 \text{ to } m$$

provided that there is a unique such set $\{p_i\}$. Of course, this is only an assumption because the student may have used beliefs not in $\mathbf{D}_c$. Normally, however, there is no such unique set.

If there are several such sets serving as potential explanations of the student's answer we may attempt to disambiguate them by using intermediate steps and the technique of *model tracing*. If we have some intermediate steps, our problem is to

$$\text{Interpret}(\{step_1, step_2, step_3, \ldots, A\})$$

given that we have several ordered sets $\{p_i\}$ such that

$$\{p_1, p_2, p_3, \ldots, p_m\} \rightarrow A$$

Usually here each $p_i$ is a rule in a production:system - the application of the rules transforms the problem P into the answer A. The sequence of applications yields a sequence of sub-problems $P_1, P_2, P_3, \ldots$ For each of the candidate sets $\{p_i\}$ we can compare the system-derived sequence $\{P_i\}$ with the student-input sequence $\{step_i\}$. In general, there will be no exact match - for one thing, the lengths of the two sequences may not be equal. The lengths can be forced to be equal (as in GREATERP [50]) by:

1. Ensuring that the grain of each rule is such that it corresponds to a single problem solving step, eg. in GREATERP a rule determines the next Lisp symbol to be input, and

2. Requiring the student to specify the corresponding step (which raises pedagogical issues of no concern here).

It is not necessary to wait for the complete input sequence to be available before beginning this analysis. At each intermediate stage, the ILE may determine the potentially relevant rules and hence the potential next steps. These predicted steps can be compared to the student's input step: non-corresponding steps can be eliminated from the search (ideally there should be only one step, and hence only one rule, left). This 'model tracing' process yields no computational benefit unless the student makes mistakes, as considered below. (Here we are not comparing with the attempted analysis of solutions where the sequence information has been lost, such as a completed Lisp program.)

The outcome of this process, if it is successful, is the addition to the student model of a set of propositions of the form $B_CB_Sp_i$ where each $p_i \in \mathbf{D}_c$. If:

$$\forall i \ (B_CB_Sp_i \ \rightarrow \ p_i \in \mathbf{D}_c))$$

the student model is called an *overlay* .

In an overlay the propositions $p_i$ act as the unjustified *basic beliefs* of a *foundation theory* of knowledge [47]. Indeed, in an overlay there are *only* such basic beliefs. For example, if

$$\mathbf{D}_c = \{ \ a{\rightarrow}b, \ b{\rightarrow}c, \ c{\rightarrow}d, \ \dots \ \}$$

then

$$\text{Interpret} \ (\{\,\text{"a}{\rightarrow}\text{d"}\})$$

might yield $\{a{\rightarrow}b, b{\rightarrow}c, c{\rightarrow}d\}$ but it would not, by the process as described, result in $B_CB_S(a{\rightarrow}d)$ , or indeed $B_CB_S(a{\rightarrow}c)$ or $B_CB_S(b{\rightarrow}d)$, being added to the student model. Thus the student model would contain no derived beliefs and hence, of course, no derivations of them. However, if we were to consider $\mathbf{D}_c$ to contain not only the explicitly mentioned propositions but also any proposition derivable from them, then we could extend the interpretation to yield also any derived propositions (and their derivations). The implicit axiom

$$B_ap \ \& \ B_a\,(p{\rightarrow}q) \ \rightarrow \ B_aq$$

may be safe for the system, which we may desire to be a rational agent, but perhaps not for the student, as we consider further below.

So far, we have assumed that a proposition p which the system now believes the student believes previously existed only in $\mathbf{D}_c$. But if the student model is not empty, then we may already have $B_CB_Sp$. Reasserting the same proposition does no harm, but the question arises as to whether the system should attempt to reconstruct the student's derivation of A from the student model or from its own domain knowledge. Let us define the student's domain knowledge $\mathbf{D}_s$ by:

$$\mathbf{D}_s = \{ \ p \ | \ B_CB_Sp \ \& \ p \in \mathbf{D}_c \ \}$$

If the system is able to reconstruct A using $\mathbf{D}_s$ then the system may believe that the student already believes the necessary propositions (but of course the student may have been guessing) and hence that there is no need to update the student model.

### 5.1.2 Cognitive Diagnosis

However, if the student's answer is incorrect, ie. A cannot be derived from $\mathbf{D}_c$ and if the student model is an overlay then one or more of the propositions necessary (according to $\mathbf{D}_c$) to solve the problem posed by the ILE must be missing from $\mathbf{D}_S$. The general problem of reconciling the student's answer $A_S$ with the computer system's (correct) answer $A_C$, derived from $\mathbf{D}_C$ using propositions $p_1$, $p_2$, $p_3$, ..., $p_m$ is an instance of *diagnosis*. Indeed, some authors use the term 'cognitive diagnosis' interchangeably with 'student modelling'.

Reiter [51] has developed a general theory of diagnosis from first principles, that is, by reasoning not dependent on domain-dependent heuristics representing compiled experience. The system (eg. an electrical circuit, or a medical patient) to be diagnosed is described by means of a set SD of axioms defining the behaviour of the components of the system if they are not faulty, eg.

$$\text{and-gate}(x) \ \& \ {\sim}\text{faulty}(x) \ \rightarrow \text{out}(x) \ = \ \text{in1}(x) \ \text{and} \ \text{in2}(x)$$

ie. if an and-gate is not faulty, its output is the conjunction of its inputs. If all the components are not faulty the axioms determine the expected behaviour of the system, ie.

$$\text{SD} \ \& \ {\sim}\text{faulty}(c_1) \ \& \ {\sim}\text{faulty}(c_2) \ ... \ \rightarrow \text{expected behaviour}$$

where $c_1$, $c_2$, .. are the components of the system. Diagnosis begins if the observed behaviour OBS differs from the expected behaviour.

Diagnosis involves retracting one or more assumptions that a component is not faulty to restore the consistency between expected and observed behaviour. Clearly we would tend to prefer a diagnosis which conjectures that some minimal set of components is faulty. Thus, a diagnosis D is a minimal set such that

$$D \subseteq \{c_1, c_2, ...\} \ \&$$
$$\text{SD} \cup \text{OBS} \cup (\text{faulty}(c) \mid c \in D) \cup ({\sim}\text{faulty}(c) \mid c \in \{c_1, c_2, ...\} - D)$$

is consistent. Re-expressing this in our previous notation, we have a cognitive diagnosis D being a minimal set such that

$$\mathbf{D}_C \cup A_S \cup (\text{faulty}(p) \mid p \in D) \cup ({\sim}\text{faulty}(p) \mid p \in \{p_1, p_2, ..\} - D)$$

is consistent, where

$$\mathbf{D}_C \ \& \ {\sim}\text{faulty}(p_1) \ \& \ \text{faulty}(p_2) \ ... \ \rightarrow A_C$$

As a result of such a diagnosis, the ILE may assert $B_C{\sim}B_S p$ for each $p \in D$.

To determine a diagnosis we may systematically postulate that each component (proposition or rule) in turn is faulty, and then that each pair of components is faulty, and so on. Obviously, this method is too inefficient for systems with large numbers of components when a number of them may be faulty. Reiter [51] gives a more efficient algorithm, later modified by Greiner, Smith and Wilkerson [27], for computing diagnoses. In the student modelling context, however, we may have little confidence in a diagnosis that postulated that several components were faulty, and hence a simple generate-and-test algorithm may be adequate. Huang, McCalla, Greer and Neufeld [30] describe an application of Reiter's diagnosis procedure to student modelling.

In fact, a rather similar procedure to Reiter's had been proposed by Young and O'Shea [65] in their production system analysis of subtraction. The postulate $\text{faulty}(c_i)$ effectively disables the definition of the component $c_i$ from SD: similarly, Young and O'Shea suggested that an ILE could diagnose many of a student's subtraction mistakes by removing one or more rules from the system describing the component sub-procedures of a correct subtraction algorithm. Thus, the rules of their production system:

> CM:   processcolumn $\rightarrow$ compare, finddiff, nextcolumn.
>
>          B2a:   S>M $\rightarrow$ borrow.
>
>                 etc.

can be re-expressed as 'component axioms' in Prolog, eg.

```
rule(cm):- not faulty(cm), processcolumn, compare, finddiff, nextcolumn.
rule(b2a):- not faulty(b2a), gr(S,M), borrow.
etc.
```

Running the rules (using an interpreter with the required conflict resolution strategies) with no assertions that a rule is faulty gives the expected (correct) output, because of Prolog's closed-world assumption. But if we assert, for example, $\text{faulty}(b2a)$, then the output is not as expected because $\text{rule}(b2a)$ no longer fires.

Deleting a rule (for example, the one which decrements the preceding digit when borrowing) from a production system does sometimes produce output behaviour which corresponds to standard students' mistakes. But sometimes it is known that when a component is faulty then it doesn't merely not work at all but it often works in some other predictable way. So in addition to deleting a rule by assuming it faulty we may add further rules which may correspond to the faulty behaviour (as suggested by Young and O'Shea). For example, we might add the rule:

```
rule(cm):- faulty(cm), processcolumn, finddiff, nextcolumn.
```

which says that a faulty version of the cm rule omits to carry out the compare operation (leading to the common mistake that 46 - 29 = 23). We could add a number of such rules to correspond to known faulty versions of the 'correct' rule.

The status of such faulty rules (or, more generally, beliefs) in the ILE needs to be carefully described. If $f$ is such a rule, we cannot say $B_c f$ (since the computer system does not believe it to be true) nor $B_c B_s f$ (since the system cannot assume that the student believes it). Rather, we can assert $B_c \sim f$ and, more usefully, that the system believes that a typical hypothetical student may believe it, which we will denote by $B_c B_h f$. We will define a *fault* to be a proposition $f$ such that $B_c \sim f$ & $B_c B_h f$. Faults are sometimes called *bugs* or *mal-rules* (if the proposition is expressed as a production rule). A set of faults $\{f_1, f_2, ..\}$ is sometimes called a *bug catalogue*. It is common to extend the definition of the student's domain knowledge $\mathbf{D}_s$ to include propositions $f$ such that $B_c B_s f$ & $f \in \text{bug-catalogue}$, although strictly 'knowledge' here is a misnomer.

A *fault-diagnosis* F is a minimal set of paired terms {<p, f>} such that

$$p \in \{p_1, p_2, ..\} \ \&$$
$$f \in \{f_1, f_2, ..\} \ \&$$
$$\mathbf{D}_c \cup A_s \cup (\text{faulty}(p_i) \ \& \ f_i \mid p_i \in D) \cup$$
$$(\sim\text{faulty}(p) \mid p \ \& \ \{p_1, p_2, ..\} - D)$$

is consistent, where

$$\mathbf{D}_c \ \& \ \sim\text{faulty}(p_1) \ \& \ \sim\text{faulty}(p_2) \ ... \rightarrow A_c$$

that is, a fault-diagnosis is a minimal set such that if the description of a component $p_i$ is replaced by that of an associated faulty component $f_i$. then the system may derive the student's answer. It is conjectured that a fault-diagnosis (which describes *how* a component is faulty) provides more pedagogical leverage than a diagnosis (which says *that* a component is faulty) - this conjecture is considered below.

A revised diagnostic procedure for an ILE might be as follows: first, attempt to derive $A_s$ using $\mathbf{D}_c$ and $\mathbf{D}_s$ - if this is successful, then the system may postulate that the student believes those propositions used in the derivation; if it fails, then use a diagnosis procedure (such as Reiter's algorithm) to isolate missing or faulty components; then, for those components isolated, use a fault-diagnosis procedure to determine associated faults. An exhaustive fault-diagnosis procedure, in which each faulty component is systematically replaced by a member of the set of faults, is clearly not feasible in general. Instead, all ILEs which make use of a set of faults contain explicit pre-determined links between a component and its associated faults. Thus, identifying the faulty component leads directly to a small set of potential faults which can be exhaustively searched. In the case of GREATERP's model tracing algorithm these steps are combined: the propositions (or rules) such that $B_c p$ or $B_c B_h f$ are merged and this merged set is used to make predictions about the student's next step - some correct, corresponding to the $B_c p$ propositions, some faulty, corresponding to the $B_c B_h f$ propositions.

## 5.1.3  Generative Mechanisms

Prespecifying a set of faults is a laborious process (there are hundreds of such faults in GREATERP). Moreover, most of the faults are irrelevant for any particular student. It may be more efficient to generate them as needed, if it is possible. A few such generative techniques have been proposed:

1. Syntactic transformations of a 'correct' proposition, eg. by removing parts of a production rule (so that it sometimes applies when it should not, or sometimes does not do all that it should), or by replacing constants by variables (or vice versa) to make the proposition more general or more specific. The number of such transformations is clearly very large.

2. The use of 'meta-rules', ie. rules which define likely faulty transformations of other rules, for example, in language learning a meta-rule which says that it is common to overlook gender agreement permits the generation of a number of specific faults.

3. The use of 'repairs' to overcome impasses during problem-solving. If when using $\mathcal{LM}$ to model the student's attempt to solve a problem, the interpreter cannot proceed (because no rules apply), then a simple, local patch may be attempted, eg. to skip a step, back up to a previous point, or find an analogous operation. The cognitive issues involved in such repairs are thoroughly discussed in VanLehn [58]. Technically, two complications may be pointed out. First, the interpreter needs to be able to detect an impasse - a non-trivial problem - and enter a repair-generating phase, and is thus not the normal problem-solving interpreter. Secondly, when an impasse is encountered it is rarely clear where the repair should be attempted. When parsing a typical incorrect foreign language sentence literally hundreds of apparent impasses are met, where a parser will back up to try to find alternatives - any one of these impasses may indicate the real reason for the eventual unsuccessful parse.

4. The inference of a fault to bridge the gap in an analysis of a problem solution. If when using $\mathcal{LM}$ the system can reason from the problem to a point q and from the answer backwards to a point q' and the gap between q and q' is small, then the system may hypothesize a rule to transform q into q'. In general, however, there will be a large search tree and hence a large number of such gaps - it will not be obvious which gap should be filled.

It is somewhat strange that researchers have emphasized the use of generative procedures to generate faults without emphasizing that these procedures do not just generate faults. Occasionally they generate correct beliefs. Indeed, they all correspond to perfectly reasonable learning procedures, which inevitably (because of the complexity of what is to be learned) lead to faults from time to time.

Thus, in order to formalize procedures for generating beliefs (whether faulty or not) we may look to the large body of machine learning research. For the moment, we will consider the implications for student modelling.

Instead of labelling a belief as categorically correct or faulty (as we have so far), we may begin to recognize that what is considered faulty depends on the context. In a certain context, a belief may be considered 'applicable', that is, correct for the purposes of this context but perhaps faulty in another one. Thus, instead of implicitly viewing the situation as one in which the ILE aims to move a student from a 'faulty' context to a 'correct' one, we may consider that there is a sequence of contexts and that the applicable rules in one context may form the 'faulty' rules of another context. For example, in learning French, we might have the following rules:

1. the possessive pronoun agrees with the gender of the possessor → "son table" (for "his table"): this rule may have been acquired by transfer from English.

2. the possessive pronoun agrees with the gender of the thing possessed → "sa table", "sa adresse" (for "his/her table", etc.).

3. as above except when the following noun begins with a vowel → "son adresse" (for "her address").

4. as 2 except when the following noun begins with a vowel or a mute "h" → "son horloge" (for "her clock"), and, in principle, so on.

In any context, a faulty rule may be accepted as correct, at least temporarily. While teachers often give students 'rules' of language they are rarely strictly correct. In most domains, in fact, there are degrees of correctness rather than the clear-cut correct-incorrect division of typical ILE domains (subtraction, Lisp programming, etc.), and in some domains (eg. economics) there may be considerable disagreement about what the 'correct' rules are. Of course, the previous view may be regarded as just one snapshot from the new view: at any instant the student is in context i and the system is in context (i+1), and indeed many ILEs function by helping a student move through increasingly complex contexts. However, several refinements to our view of ILE student modelling are now possible:

1. There may be more than one sequence of contexts which leads to the 'target context'. Maybe these sequences can be dynamically generated rather than pre-ordained by the system.

2. There may be no 'target context', that is, the system may seek to help a student move from a given context but not necessarily towards a target known to the system. The building and use of a student model in such a situation is obviously a more subtle process.

3. Even if there is a target context, we are reminded that most knowledge is not categorically correct or not but appropriate or not for a context - this may be reflected in the style of interaction adopted by the ILE.

4. The same representation may not be appropriate for beliefs in different contexts; for example, in one context beliefs may be semi-qualitative, in other quantitative. Therefore, there is a potential problem in relating beliefs in different contexts.

## 5.2   Revising Beliefs

If we now regard an ILE as seeking to cause a student to revise her beliefs (possibly toward some target beliefs), rather than aiming to replace a faulty belief by a correct one, then we need to consider when and how a student revises her belief-set, because the student model will need to be revised similarly. In general terms, a student may revise her belief-set if she perceives it to lead to inconsistencies, or if it appears to be inefficient or inadequate in some respect. The former situation tends to lead to the discarding of beliefs, the latter to the creation of new beliefs.

## 5.2.1  Discarding Beliefs

Imagine that $\mathfrak{D}_s$ contains the following propositions:

$p_1$  "Fire rises."

$p_2$  "The higher regions of the universe are more fiery than lower ones."

$p_3$  "Fire produces light."

$p_4$  "The sun produces more light than the stars."

$p_5$  "The sun is more fiery than the stars."

$p_6$  "The sun is higher than the stars."

and the student is made aware of a new piece of evidence:

$p_7$  "The stars are higher than the sun."

If the new proposition were simply added to $\mathfrak{D}_s$ then the student modelling process would be complicated by the contradiction between $p_6$ and $p_7$, which under normal inference rules would enable any proposition at all to be inferred. One solution is to discard one or more propositions from the set $\{p_1, \ .. \ p_7\}$.

There are two different bases for deciding which proposition(s) to discard. First, we must recall that $\mathfrak{D}_s$ is derived from the system's beliefs about the student's beliefs. The system may be mistaken in its beliefs about the student. Therefore the system may analyze its reasons for asserting $B_c B_s p_i$ and decide, for example, to discard the 'weakest' default assumption.

Secondly, the system may consider $\mathfrak{D}_s$ to be an accurate description of the student's beliefs and must then concern itself with how the student would actually resolve the conflict. There are several possibilities:

1.  The student may continue to believe all seven propositions (as Anaximander (550 BC) apparently did in this situation). She may be able to reason with inconsistent belief-sets using methods different to those of classical logic, as considered below.

2.  She may disbelieve the new proposition: there is a natural reluctance to overthrow an existing belief-set on scanty evidence, especially if no simple modification of the existing belief-set overcomes the problem.

3.  She may discard one or more old propositions. In order to determine which propositions to discard, she (and the system) may analyze the reasons why they are held. To permit this, we distinguish between *basic beliefs* (or premises or assumptions or hypotheses)

and *derived beliefs*. In the above example, $p_1$, $p_3$, $p_4$, and $p_7$ may be basic beliefs and $p_2$, $p_5$ and $p_6$ derived beliefs. Those beliefs from which a derived belief is derived constitute a *justification* for that belief. For example, $\{p_2, p_5\}$ may be a justification of $p_6$. In general (but not here), there may be several justifications for the same derived belief. We denote the justifications $j_1$, $j_2$, $j_3$, .. for a proposition $p$ as follows:

$$p: \quad \{j_1, j_2, j_3, ..\}$$

For example:

$$p_6: \{\{p_2, p_5\}\}$$
$$p_5: \{\{p_3, p_4\}\}$$
$$p_2: \{\{p_1\}\}$$

For completeness, we may consider a basic belief to be its own justification, eg.:

$$p_1: \{\{p_1\}\}$$

A justification is thus in terms of the propositions from which a belief is immediately derived. In assumption-based approaches to belief revision, the system maintains a list of the basic beliefs upon which the belief ultimately depends - in this case, we would have:

$$p_6: \{\{p_1, p_3, p_4\}\}$$
$$p_5: \{\{p_3, p_4\}\}, \text{ etc.}$$

Discarding a derived belief (eg. $p_6$) may overcome the immediate problem but if the basic beliefs from which it was derived remain then the discarded belief may be re-derived. To prevent this, we must discard one or more basic beliefs from its justification (in this case, one or more members of the set $\{p_1, p_3, p_4\}$ ). In general, when there is a set $J$ of justifications, we must find a hitting set, that is, a set of propositions that contains at least one element of each set in $J$. If we then discard the propositions in the hitting set then no justifications for the original belief remain. In general, there will be a number of such hitting sets and we would aim to select that which is in some sense minimal, ie. causes the least disruption to the existing belief-set.

Once a basic belief is discarded, we may also discard any derived belief which is justified only by that basic belief. With a foundation theory of knowledge, beliefs no longer justified are abandoned; with a coherence theory, beliefs are retained in the absence of any challenge to them. Work on this and associated problems in AI goes under the name of *belief revision* (although really it is belief-sets that are revised, beliefs being merely discarded). Psychological studies are relevant only to the second of the two bases mentioned above for discarding beliefs, modelling belief revision by the student. In a student modelling context (as in fact in most belief revision work), it may not be possible or necessary for the system alone to select which proposition(s) to discard: rather, the set of potential amendments may be used to focus subsequent clarification dialogues with the student.

As we have seen, the basic requirement for any belief-discarding scheme is that whenever a new belief is added to a belief-set the system records how that belief depends upon other beliefs.

Various refinements to the basic scheme have been investigated (and some of them will be discussed in later sections):

1. The use of non-classical logics - it is not essential that the dependencies between beliefs correspond to standard logical implication.
2. The recording of a set of basic beliefs as inconsistent once they have been found to be so - to avoid subsequent consideration or to permit the system to be aware that the set is inconsistent, if it is considered later.
3. The use of non-monotonic reasoning, by recording with each proposition not only the justifications for believing it but also any propositions that have to be disbelieved in order for the proposition to be believed.
4. The use of *labels* to mark a proposition as disbelieved rather than the erasing of it - this improves efficiency if the system subsequently wishes to re-consider its disbeliefs, and also enables the system to work within limited contexts.

## 5.2.2   Creating Beliefs Through Reasoning

An agent may derive further beliefs by reasoning about the propositions in a belief-set. The reasoning processes are described or defined by a *logic* $L$, expressed as a set of axiom schemata. (The word 'logic' is not meant to imply that reasoning is necessarily sound or complete.) Student modelling is difficult partly because a number of different kinds of logic are potentially relevant. Here are a few illustrations:

$$L_1 = \{\ B(p \lor q)\ \&\ B(\neg p \lor r)\ \rightarrow\ B(q \lor r)\ \}\ .$$

This logic, with a single axiom schema (the rule of inference called resolution, which is known to be sound and complete in predicate logic), might be used by the system to reason about its domain knowledge, for example, to determine whether the student's answer accords with the system's knowledge. A standard heorem-prover or a language such as Prolog could be used for this purpose.

$$L_2 = \{\ B(p\ \&\ q)\ \rightarrow\ B_p\ ,$$
$$B(p \rightarrow q)\ \&\ B_p\ \rightarrow\ B_q\ ,$$
$$B(p \rightarrow q)\ \&\ B(q \rightarrow p)\ \rightarrow\ B(p = q)\ ,\ \dots\ \}$$

This might be intended to define a logic of 'natural deduction'. $L_2$ might be more useful than $L_1$ when the system is carrying out the process of reconstruction (section 5.1.1), since the intermediate steps passed through when using $L_2$ might correspond better with the steps which a rational student might pass through. $L_1$ is a computationally oriented logic; $L_2$ is intended to have some psychological validity.

$$L_3 = \{\ B(p \rightarrow q)\ \&\ B_q\ \rightarrow\ B_p\ ,$$
$$B(p \rightarrow q)\ \&\ B \neg p\ \rightarrow\ B \neg q\ ,\ \dots\ \} \cup L_2$$

Whereas $L_2$ might be intended to describe the reasoning of an ideal rational student, $L_3$ might be intended to describe that of an actual student, since it contains some 'irrational' schemata in addition to the axiom schemata of $L_2$. Since real students may have faulty reasoning schemata, the process of reconstruction may perhaps be better carried out with $L_3$ than with $L_2$. Also, of course, the student may be lacking some of the 'ideal rational student's' schemata. In other words, the same kinds of issues as discussed in section 5.1 with respect to object-level propositions arise also at the level of reasoning schemata. If it is necessary for the system to handle a student's difficulties at the reasoning level, the explicit axiom schemata need to be provided.

$$L_4 = \{ \ B(p,\alpha) \ \& \ B(q,\alpha) \ \rightarrow \ B(p \ \& \ q,\alpha) \ ,$$
$$B(p,\alpha) \ \& \ B(q,\alpha \cup \beta) \rightarrow \ B(p{\rightarrow}q,\beta) \ , \ \dots \ \}$$

This example illustrates that the logic of our axiom schemata does not have to be classical logic with it standard notion of validity. This particular case (*relevance logic* [2]) denies the so-called paradoxes of implication: $p{\rightarrow}(q{\rightarrow}p)$ and $(p \ \& \ {\sim}p){\rightarrow}q$. Instead, in relevance logic, one proposition entails another only if there is an element of causality that relevantly connects them. Each wff p is associated with an *origin set* $\alpha$ containing all the basic beliefs used in its derivation. This is written p, $\alpha$. The first axiom scheme in $L_4$ says that if p and q are wffs with the same origin set, then we can deduce p & q and associate it with the same origin set. Relevance logic has been used in work on belief revision [39] and is presumably partly motivated by a feeling that human reasoning follows such schemata rather than those of classical logic.

$$L_5 = \{ \ B(goal(x)) \ \& \ B(precondition(x,y))$$
$$\rightarrow \ B(must\text{-}satisfy(y)) \ ,$$
$$B(goal(x)) \ \& \ B(precondition(x,y)) \ \& \ B(can't\text{-}satisfy(y))$$
$$\rightarrow \ B(can't\text{-}do(x)) \ , \ \dots \ \}$$

$L_5$ indicates that our logics may include 'pragmatic reasoning schemata' [29]. Such schemata are intermediate between domain-specific rules and the abstract rules of standard formal logic (as illustrated above). Pragmatic reasoning schemata are abstract rules in that they apply to a wide range of content domains but they are constrained by particular inferential goals and event relationships. The extent to which students use such pragmatic schemata is a matter of debate.

$$L_6 = \{ \ K_cp \ \& \ Tells(c,s,p) \ \rightarrow \ B_cB_sp \ ,$$
$$p \in O_c \ \rightarrow \ B_c{\sim}B_sp,$$
$$\dots$$
$$B_cB_s(p{\rightarrow}q) \ \& \ B_cB_s{\sim}p \ \rightarrow \ B_cB_s{\sim}q \ ,$$
$$B_cB_s(p{\rightarrow}q) \ \& \ B_cB_sq \ \rightarrow \ B_cB_sp \ , \ \dots \ \}$$

The logics $L_1$ to $L_5$ all considered the case of a single agent deriving new beliefs. In student modelling, however, we are deriving nested beliefs of the form $B_cB_sp$. The appropriate axiom schemata here will be of two forms: one defining how the system reasons about instructional events and its own beliefs and the other defining how the system believes the student reasons about her beliefs. Thus, in $L_6$ the earlier schemata are of the first form and the later schemata of the second form. For example, the first schema says that if the system knows a proposition and tells it to the student then the system believes the student believes that proposition. The last schema given in $L_6$ denotes that the system believes the student reasons using an axiom schema from $L_3$ (of course, we could also use schemata from $L_4$, $L_5$ and other logics).

It is clearly difficult to define a satisfactory set of such schemata for student modelling purposes and indeed no existing ILEs make use of explicit schemata of this kind. However, they do use ad-hoc, implicit schemata, for otherwise the student model would never be updated. Advantages that might follow from making them explicit include:

1. As with any formalization, it might be easier to understand and analyze the processes being formalized.

2. As we have seen, belief revision is facilitated by recording the justifications for beliefs. But merely listing the justifications, as in $p_6:\{\{p_1, p_3, p_4\}\}$, does not enable the system to reason about the validity of the justifications. If we also recorded the axiom schemata which enabled the belief to be derived, the system could, for example, take account of faulty derivations.

3. With explicit reasoning schemata, the system may be able to discuss the reasoning processes themselves, and thus move beyond domain-related issues, as advocated by many educationalists.

4. We may customize the reasoning process, ie. we may adopt different logics for different students, or for the same student at different times. Thus, we have additional scope for individualizing instructional interactions.

5. By identifying distinct reasoning schemata appropriate for different aspects of the student modelling problem, we may be able to separate computational and cognitive issues which are currently inter-mingled. Student modelling may be "unabashedly psychological" [9] but, as stated earlier, the primary aim is computational utility, not cognitive validity. By isolating where cognitive issues are important, we may develop computational frameworks which are independent of them.

## 5.2.3 Limited Reasoning

Defining a set of schemata does not define how those schemata will be interpreted by the system. For example, for $L_1$, the standard rule of resolution, a large number of theorem-proving strategies have been devised. The simplest mechanism - that all axiom schemata are repeatedly applied until no further conclusions can be drawn - is inadequate computationally (in general, it would take much too long), psychologically (human agents do not normally draw all possible conclusions from their beliefs) and philosophically (it seems strange to say that an agent believes a proposition if it takes it ten minutes of intense reasoning before it avers that it does). Therefore, the system's interpreter of axiom schemata will carry out some 'limited reasoning' process. However, we ought not to bury those limitations in the interpreter but to make them explicit so that they too may become a possible focus for student modelling.

The starting point for discussions of limited reasoning mechanisms for knowledge and belief is the *possible world semantics* of modal logic [28]. The intuitive idea is that besides the true state of affairs there are a number of other possible states of affair, or possible worlds. The worlds are connected by an accessibility relation R which may be defined to satisfy various constraints, eg. it may be transitive, ie. $uRv$ and $vRw$ implies $uRw$, where $u$, $v$ and $w$ are worlds. In each world, a proposition is given a truth value. An agent in a world $w$ is said to believe a proposition if it is true in all worlds accessible to $w$.

The modal logic based on a transitive accessibility relation (called weak S4) can be given a sound and complete proof theory comprising the following rules of inference and axioms:

| | | |
|---|---|---|
| $R_1$ | Necessity | $p \Rightarrow Bp$ |
| $R_2$ | Modus ponens | $p \ \& \ p{\rightarrow}q \Rightarrow q$ |
| $A_1$ | Tautologies | $p$, where $p$ is valid in propositional logic |
| $A_2$ | Distribution | $Bp \ \& \ B(p{\rightarrow}q) \rightarrow Bq$ |
| $A_3$ | Positive introspection | $Bp \rightarrow BBq$ |

Other logics, perhaps less suitable for representing belief, have different accessibility relations and use one or more of the following axioms:

| | | |
|---|---|---|
| $A_4$ | Knowledge | $Bp \rightarrow p$ |
| $A_5$ | Negative introspection | $\sim Bp \rightarrow B(\sim Bp)$ |
| $A_6$ | Consistency | $Bp \rightarrow \sim B{\sim}p$ |

Any modal logic which includes $A_1$ and $A_2$ (as does every modal logic using the possible worlds approach) suffers from the problem of *logical omniscience*, that is, the agent believes all tautologies and all implications of its beliefs. This is considered a problem for the reasons given above - that it is computationally intractable and psychologically implausible. There are basically two ways in which the problem may be overcome and hence some element of limited reasoning introduced: we may adopt a 'semantic approach' in which we use a modified notion of truth compared to the classical one used in possible world semantics; or we may follow a 'syntactic approach' in which beliefs are sentences in some syntactically specified set and sentences are distinguished by syntax (thus, for example, we may have $B(p \ v \ q)$ and yet not necessarily $B(q \ v \ p)$).

Levesque [36] adopted the former approach in developing the distinction between *explicit belief* and *implicit belief*. We use $I_p$ to denote that an agent implicitly believes a proposition - i.e., that it is a logical consequence of its explicit beliefs - and $E_p$ to denote that it explicitly believes it. Informally, the explicit beliefs are intended to be that subset of the implicit beliefs which the agent considers relevant or which have been 'activated' within the agent. Formally, implicit belief may be modelled by classical possible world semantics but explicit belief requires a modified version. Levesque used the idea of a situation, in which a proposition may be true, false, both or neither. A complete, coherent situation - ie. one in which propositions are true or false - corresponds to the standard possible world, but we may also have a 'partial world' in which a proposition may be nether true nor false and an 'incoherent world' in which it may be both.

By specifying a semantics similar to that for relevance logic, Levesque showed that, while implicit belief retains the properties of belief in possible world semantics, explicit belief does not suffer from the problem of logical omniscience. For example, all the following formulas are satisfiable:

```
1.      Ep & E(p→q) & ~Eq
2.      Ep & ~E(p & (q v ~q))
3.      ~E(p v ~p)
4.      Ep & E~p
5.      E(p & ~p)
```

The properties of explicit belief follow from the incoherence and incompleteness introduced in situations - the former leads to the possibility of believing unsatisfiable propositions (eg. 5 above), the latter to the possible lack of belief of valid propositions (eg. 3 above).

Thus, it is possible to define formal logics to express some aspects of the inconsistencies and incompletenesses which students display. However, many subtle issues remain. For example, if reasoning is considered to be carried out with respect to the situations thought possible by the agent, is it reasonable to allow incoherent situations as being possible? Also, the effect of imperfect reasoning in a classical logic is achieved by assuming perfect reasoning in a non-classical logic (relevance logic). Moreover, the formal logic of explicit belief does not cover the expression of nested, multi-agent beliefs which we have seen that we need for student modelling.

The syntactic approach to overcoming the limitations of possible world modal logics emphasizes the role of syntactic form in determining the truth of a belief. However, the semantics of belief logics must differ from those of classical logic because, unlike the ordinary logical operators, the modal operators of belief are referentially opaque, ie. if $p$ is equivalent to $q$ then we cannot substitute $q$ for $p$ in any expression within the scope of B (for example, if largest-planet=neptune then we cannot infer B(Cold(largest-planet)) from

B(Cold(neptune))))). Instead, we may define a sentential semantics in which, for each agent i, we associate a belief-set $\mathcal{B}_i$ and a logic (a set of inference rules) $L_i$ The theory formed by the closure of $\mathcal{B}_i$ under $L_i$ is denoted by $\mathcal{T}_i$. A proposition $p \in \mathcal{T}_i$ if and only if $p$ is provable in i's theory using i's inference rules. Then $B_ip$ has the value true if and only if $p$ is in the theory associated with i. (This semantics is referentially opaque, as desired, because an equivalent (in our theory) expression may not be in the agent's theory.)

Fagin and Halpern [23] attempted to isolate the advantages given by Levesque's notion of incomplete situations by defining a syntactic *awareness* function. The intuition is that an agent cannot believe a proposition if it is not aware of it, and that we might say that an agent is aware of p if it explicitly believes p or its negation:

$$Ap = E(p \lor \sim p)$$

Instead of using incoherent or partial worlds, Fagin and Halpern use standard possible worlds with the awareness function to filter out those formulae of which the agent is unaware. A world w supports the truth of Ep if all the worlds the agent considers possible in w support the truth of p relative to the set of primitive propositions of which the agent is aware in world w. Implicit belief is as before and explicit belief is similar to Levesque's except that (1) an agent's set of explicit beliefs is closed under implication and (2) an agent cannot hold inconsistent beliefs, eg. $E(p \And \sim p)$ is not satisfiable.

Consider the following belief-set:

$E_c$ (Foreigner(s))

$E_c$ (Foreigner(x) $\rightarrow$ $\sim A_x$(sconce))

$E_c$ (Prerequisite(sconce,college-etiquette))

$E_c$ ($\sim A_s$(c) & Prerequisite(c,g) $\rightarrow$ $\sim$Infer(s,g))

ie. the system believes the student to be a foreigner, that all foreigners are unaware of the concept of a sconce (a fine imposed at Oxbridge), which is a prerequisite for understanding Oxbridge college dining etiquette, and that a student cannot infer propositions if she is unaware of a prerequisite concept. In such a case the system cannot show (for example) that the student can infer (college-etiquette $\lor$ $\sim$college-etiquette) even although the tautology follows from the system's facts (indeed any facts) because s, a foreigner, is unaware of a prerequisite concept (this example is considered further below).

A major benefit, for student modelling purposes, offered by this logic of awareness is that, as we see above, it allows nested beliefsbelief:nested which Levesque's logic of implicit belief does not. From the definitions, we can derive various relationships between implicit belief, explicit belief and awareness, eg.

$$E_cE_s(p \lor q) \equiv (A_cp \And I_c(A_sp \And I_sp))$$

Nested multi-agent beliefs enable us to describe the system's reasoning about the student's beliefs, and nested single-agent beliefs provide us with a basic notation for discussing self-reflection and metacognitive processes (as pursued in section 5.3.4)

Fagin and Halpern's logic of *general awareness* goes further in defining an essentially syntactic operator $A_i$ (for 'agent $i$ is aware of') in addition to $E_i$ and $I_i$ which is not limited to primitive propositions, as the previous logic of awareness is. Since an agent explicitly believes a proposition if it implicitly believes it and it is aware of it, we have:

$$E_ip \equiv I_ip \sim A_ip$$

Thus, explicit belief retains many of the properties of implicit belief, relativised to awareness. For example, the rules and axioms $R_1$, $A_2$ and $A_3$ in the weak S4 logic become:

| $R_1$ | Necessity | $p \Rightarrow (Ap \rightarrow Ep)$ |
|---|---|---|
| $A_2$ | Distribution | $Ep$ & $E(p \rightarrow q)$ & $Aq \rightarrow Eq$ |
| $A_3$ | Positive introspection | $Ep$ & $AEp \rightarrow EEp$ |

To these general axioms, we might wish to add restrictions to provide desired properties of the logic - for example, we might specify that an agent $i$ is unaware of (any proposition that mentioned) agent $j$, or that an agent is aware only of a certain subset of primitive propositions.

This last restriction can be elaborated to provide a logic of *local* reasoning which differs from the logic of general awareness in that it enables an agent to hold inconsistent beliefs. The idea is that an agent's belief-set may be partitioned into a set of non-interacting clusters such that any cluster is internally consistent but may contradict a different one. In this logic we use $E_ip$ to denote that agent $i$ explicitly locally believes p, ie. believes p in some 'frame of mind', and $I_ip$ to denote that agent $i$ implicitly believes p, ie. believes p if all its frames of mind are pooled.

This version of implicit belief satisfies axioms $A_1$ and $A_2$ of weak S4 but not axiom $A_3$, and the version of explicit belief is not closed under implication and hence not subject to the problem of logical omniscience. The formula $E_ip$ & $E_i$ $(p \rightarrow q)$ $\rightarrow$ $E_iq$ is satisfiable because $i$ might believe p in one frame of mind and $p \rightarrow q$ in another but never be in a frame of mind where it puts these facts together. Moreover, an agent may hold inconsistent beliefs, ie. $E_ip$ & $E_i \sim p$, because it might believe p and $\sim$p in different frames of mind. However, agents do not believe in incoherent worlds, ie. $E_i (p$ & $\sim p)$ is impossible. As with the logic of general awareness, we may impose conditions to capture various properties. For example, Fagin and Halpern define a narrow-minded agent to be one who when in one frame of mind refuses to admit it may occasionally be in another. For such an agent $E_i (\sim (E_ip$ & $E_i \sim p))$ is valid even though $E_ip$ & $E_i \sim p$ is consistent. In addition, although the logic of local reasoning assumes an agent can do perfect reasoning within each cluster, we can add an awareness function to the structure for local reasoning to provide a model of belief which is not closed under valid implication.

It should be emphasized at this stage that it is not the aim to develop from among this great variety of limited reasoning mechanisms one which is 'correct'. This is an unattainable aim: some philosophical or computational objection can assuredly be raised against any proposed scheme. Rather, the aim is to develop a general framework within which any such scheme can be explicitly defined and theoretically analysed. The problems of student modelling, involving a limited agent (the computer system) reasoning about the beliefs of another limited agent (the student), are complex but it is no long-term solution to bury techniques within opaque algorithms.

## 5.2.4 Meta-Reasoning

In section 5.2.2, we pointed out that an agent may use different logics (sets of axiom schemata) for reasoning about beliefs and that there are potential benefits in making those logics explicit. In section 5.2.3, it was described how different interpretations of the logics can lead to different kinds of limited reasoning. Similarly, we may expect there to be benefits from making such interpretations explicit. In other words, we are suggesting an explicit meta-logic $\mathcal{M}$ which interprets a logic $L$ with respect to a belief-set $\mathcal{B}$ to derive new propositions. (In this section, we will ignore the considerations of explicitness, implicitness and awareness, discussed in the previous section.)

For example, consider:

$$\mathcal{B} \quad = \quad \{ \quad \text{Cold(neptune) ,}$$
$$\text{Cold(pluto) ,}$$
$$\forall x \ \text{Cold(x)} \rightarrow \text{Lifeless(x) ,}$$
$$\sim \text{Lifeless(mars) ,}$$
$$-\text{Lifeless(earth) }\}$$

$$L \quad = \quad \{ \quad \text{B(p \& q)} \rightarrow \text{Bp ,}$$
$$\text{B(p} \rightarrow \text{q) \& Bp} \rightarrow \text{Bq ,}$$
$$\text{B(}\sim\text{q) \& B(p} \rightarrow \text{q)} \rightarrow \text{B(}\sim\text{p) }\}$$

$$\mathcal{M} \quad = \quad \{ \quad \text{Difficult('B(}\sim\text{q) \& B(p} \rightarrow \text{q)} \rightarrow \text{B(}\sim\text{p)') ,}$$
$$\forall s \ \sim\text{Difficult(s)} \rightarrow \text{Easy(s) ,}$$
$$\forall s \ \text{Difficult(s)} \rightarrow \text{Apply-at-most(s,1) ,}$$
$$\forall s \ \text{Easy(s)} \rightarrow \text{Apply-at-most(s,3) }\}$$

Ignoring for the moment the considerable technical problems, the intention is that the metalogic express that the third schema in the logic is a difficult one, that all schemata that aren't difficult are easy, and that difficult schemata are only applied once at most and easy schemata three times at most. Applying $\mathcal{M}$ to $L$ and $\mathcal{B}$, we obtain the derived beliefs:

$$\text{Lifeless(neptune)}$$
$$\text{Lifeless(pluto)}$$
$$\sim\text{Cold(mars)}$$

but not ~Cold (earth), assuming that the schemata are applied from the beginning of the belief-set.

We will refer to $\mathcal{M}$ as the meta-level and $L$ and $\mathcal{B}$ as the base-level. The general idea, then, is that the meta-level specifies properties of the base-level logic which determine how it is interpreted with respect to a belief-set. The aim, for student modelling purposes, is to enable the system to explicitly model and reason about different aspects of the student's competence. Unless these components are declaratively specified, they cannot be dynamically changed by the system (to model changes in the student or to adapt the general framework to an individual student) and they cannot form the focus of instructional interactions.

The above example is in terms of a single agent, and thus could correspond to the system (or the student) reasoning about its (or her) own beliefs, but as we have seen (eg. in $L_6$) student modelling is already at a meta-level, since it concerns the system reasoning about the student's beliefs. This 'level-shift' is one of the things that makes student modelling formally complex.

The idea of a metalanguage has been much studied in AI and in mathematics (for example, to overcome logical paradoxes). At first in AI, meta-reasoning was used to shorten proofs obtained using simple, uniform deduction strategies such as those based on resolution (our $L_1$ above), by for example looking at syntactic structure rather than repeatedly applying inference rules. Meta-reasoning has since been applied to many areas of AI. We will illustrate the method by two examples related to student modelling, addressing the two different kinds of axiom schemata given in $L_6$, ie. those related to the system interpreting instructional events in terms of student beliefs and those related to the system reasoning about the student's reasoning.

The first example is adapted from Cialdea et al. [8] who describe a system called SEDAF to help students learn how to graph mathematical functions by solving for characteristics of the function. They describe a system belief-set:

$$\mathcal{B}_c = \{ \quad \texttt{Stationary(x,f) \& Decreasing-left(x,f) \&}$$
$$\texttt{Increasing-right(x,f)} \rightarrow \texttt{Minimum(x,f)} ,$$
$$\texttt{Denominator-zero(x,f)} \rightarrow \texttt{Pole(x,f)} , \ldots \}$$

and a system mal-rule belief-set:

$$\mathcal{B}_h = \{ \quad \texttt{Decreasing-left(x,f) \& Increasing-right(x,f)}$$
$$\rightarrow \texttt{Minimum(x,f)} ,$$
$$\texttt{Numerator-one(x,f)} \rightarrow \texttt{Singular(x,f)} , \ldots \}$$

The system's logic of schemata is not stated explicitly but is in fact equivalent to resolution (ie. our $L_1$).

In order to link a meta-level with the logic, a meta-level predicate $\texttt{Proof}(\mathcal{B}, L, \texttt{p}, \texttt{d})$ is defined which asserts that d is a derivation or proof of proposition p using logic $L$ on belief-set $\mathcal{B}$. It is assumed that $\texttt{Proof}$ is defined by a suitable set of meta-axioms, so that if $\texttt{Proof}(\mathcal{B}, L, \texttt{'p'}, \texttt{'d'})$ is a theorem of the meta-theory then d is a derivation of p using $L$ and

$\mathfrak{B}$, where 'p' and 'd' are the representations of p and d at the meta-level [60]. Cialdea et al.then provide the following five meta-level axioms (adapted slightly):

```
M = {    Answers (p,dontknow) & Proof(Bc,L1,p,d) & q ∈ d → Bc~Bcq ,
         Answers (p,dontknow) & Proof(Bc,L1,not(p),d) & q ∈ d
         → Bc~Bsq ,
         Answers (p,yes) & Proof (Bc,L1,not(p),d) & q ∈ d → Bc~Bsq,
         Answers( p,yes) & Proof(Bc∪ Bh,L1,p,d) & q ∈ d
         & Acceptable-proof(d) → BcBsq ,
         Answers (p,yes) & Proof(Bc,L1,p,d) & q ∈ d → BcBsq }
```

The first axiom specifies that if the student does not know the answer to a problem which the system can solve (using $\mathfrak{B}_c$ and $L_1$) then the system believes the student does not know propositions used in the derivation of the answer. (In general, of course, she would not know one or more of those propositions - as discussed with reference to reconstruction in section 5.1.1 - and the system might begin some dialogue to work out which.) The predicate Acceptable-proof verifies whether it is plausible to believe that the student has constructed the derivation d (either by interrogating the student or by analysing the current student model). Note that the same logic $L_1$ is used throughout, which is not necessary formally.

These two meta-level predicates (Proof and Acceptable-proof) just ask questions about derivations in the base-level. In general, $\mathfrak{M}$ can also impose restrictions (such as those discussed in the previous section) on what can be derived from $L$ and $\mathfrak{B}$. The meta-level could, for example, assume that the base-level will draw the inferences it is capable of, unless the meta-level knows of constraints which prevent them being drawn. This approach is independent of the underlying base-level reasoning procedure - but to actually design such a meta-level we have to commit ourselves to a particular underlying procedure.

Van Arragon [57] describes a system called LNT in which the underlying reasoning is based upon linear resolution, for which we need the meta-level predicate

$$\text{Infer}(\mathfrak{B}_a,b{\rightarrow}g)$$

as used in the 'foreigner' example of section 5.2.3, where b→g is a fact in $\mathfrak{B}_a$ where b is a conjunction of literals. (For clarity, we omit the quotes which are strictly necessary for the meta-level.) To reason about limitations in the base-level, the meta-level includes propositions of the form

$$\ldots \rightarrow \text{~Infer}(\mathfrak{B}_a,L_a,\text{~}b{\rightarrow}g)$$

where the ... defines the conditions under which the inference b→g cannot be made, and where we include the logic $L_a$ to make it clear that different such logics may be defined.

For example, the following $\mathcal{M}$ specifies that the student can infer no more than three steps:

$$\mathcal{M} = \{ \quad \text{Infer}(\mathcal{B}_s, \mathcal{L}_s, b1 \rightarrow g1) \ \&$$
$$\text{Infer}(\mathcal{B}_s, \mathcal{L}_s, b2 \rightarrow g2) \ \&$$
$$\text{Infer}(\mathcal{B}_s, \mathcal{L}_s, b3 \rightarrow g3) \ \&$$
$$g \neq g1 \ \& \ \dots \ \& \ g2 \neq g3 \ \rightarrow \ \sim\text{Infer}(\mathcal{B}_s, \mathcal{L}_s, b \rightarrow g) \ \}$$

Given the following belief-set:

$$\mathcal{B}_s = \{ \quad \text{true} \rightarrow p_1, \ p_1 \rightarrow p_2, \ p_2 \rightarrow p_3, \ p_3 \rightarrow p_4 \ \}$$

follows from $\mathcal{B}_s$ it requires four instances of $\text{Infer}(\mathcal{B}_s, \mathcal{L}_s, b \rightarrow g)$. Thus, the system may handle $\mathcal{B}_s$s which are potentially inconsistent - for example, if we had:

$$\mathcal{B}_s = \{ \quad \text{true} \rightarrow p_1, \ p_1 \rightarrow p_2, \ p_2 \rightarrow p_3, \ p_3 \rightarrow p_4, \ \sim p_4 \ \}$$

then the system could, using $\mathcal{M}$, consider that the student's reasoning is too limited to realize the inconsistency.

This was the basic idea used in the foreigner example to handle a more interesting case of limited reasoning, that of lack of awareness. Other types of limitation can be similarly expressed. For example, a particular reasoning step may be too difficult for novices to carry out:

$$\mathcal{M} = \{ \quad \text{Difficult}(b \rightarrow g) \ \& \ \text{Novice}(\text{student}) \ \rightarrow \ \sim\text{Infer}(\mathcal{B}_s, \mathcal{L}_s, b \rightarrow g) \ \}$$

Both SEDAF and LNT have been implemented in Prolog, in which it is relatively easy to write a meta-interpreter to define meta-level predicates such as Proof and Infer. Such implementations demonstrate both the methodological advantages of having a formal specification and the practical advantages of concise, rapid prototyping. However, the extra layer of interpretation may lead to inefficiency although techniques are being developed to help overcome this [18].

## 5.2.5 Non-Monotonic Reasoning

Non-monotonic reasoning and limited reasoning present orthogonal dimensions of complexity of the student modelling problem - they are orthogonal in the sense that it is possible to have either without the other. Usually they are considered together since reasoning that is limited often leads to non-monotonicity. Non-monotonic reasoning refers to reasoning in which a conclusion made at one time may no longer be valid at a later time because of information acquired in the interim.

Non-monotonic reasoning is usually discussed with respect to a single agent, and we need to consider that aspect too. But student modelling itself, involving two agents, is deeply and unavoidably non-monotonic, for three reasons:

1. The system's beliefs about the student's beliefs can never be confirmed as correct and must therefore always be considered subject to revision. Even apparently objective facts such as students' assertions about what they know or descriptions of students' actions need to be regarded as provisional (because they may not fully understand terms they use, or they may make slips in performing tasks, for example).

2. Because of the 'bandwidth problem' systems will rarely have access to sufficient data to permit reliable inferences about students' beliefs, and consequently will have to make default assumptions which may later have to be withdrawn.

3. Students do occasionally learn (and forget) and therefore what the system believes of the student at one time will not necessarily hold at a later time.

Within AI generally, the field of non-monotonic reasoning is vast and active, but there has been little explicit linking to the student modelling problem. In this section, we will just summarize the main approaches and point out the potential relevance to student modelling. Of course, the effect of non-monotonic reasoning may be achieved through computational techniques (such as semantic networks) which are efficient but not completely understood, rather than through the use of formal systems which are generally intractable. However, formal approaches to non-monotonic reasoning may yield benefits in terms of clarity and correctness, and provide useful tools for specifying and describing non-monotonic systems, in particular for that limited class which are actually covered by relatively ad-hoc techniques [21].

There are two basic approaches to non-monotonic reasoning: model-theoretic and proof-theoretic. Model-theoretic approaches are based on the idea that anything that does not follow is assumed to be false ('model' here is used in the mathematical sense: a model of a theory $T$ is any structure $M$ such that $T$ is true in $M$). Proof-theoretic approaches use non-standard (non-monotonic) logics to derive conclusions through inference rules.

The closed-world assumption (as used in Prolog) is the simplest example of a model-theoretic approach and the various formalizations of *circumscription* the most comprehensive. The basic idea of circumscription is that one considers not all models of $T$ but only those which are minimal with respect to a specific property $P$. For example, if we have:

$$\mathcal{B}_s = \{ \quad \texttt{Prime-minister(Thatcher)} \ \& $$

$$\texttt{Prime-minister(Major)} \ \& $$

$$\texttt{Female(Thatcher)} \ \& $$

$$\texttt{Prime-minister(x))} \ \& \ \texttt{~Female x))} \ \rightarrow \ \texttt{Public-school(x)} \ \}$$

which says that a student believes the three facts indicated and believes that prime-ministers who are not female went to a public-school, then we cannot logically conclude from $\mathcal{B}_s$ that Public-School(Major), since we do not have ~Female(Major) or, more generally, that the student believes that all prime-ministers except Thatcher are not female. Assuming the equality axioms, applying circumscription to minimize the predicate Female we obtain:

$\text{Circum}(\textbf{B}_s,\text{Female}) = \textbf{B}_s \ \& \ (\text{Female}(x) \rightarrow (x = \text{Thatcher}))$

from which the conclusion Public-school(Major) now follows.

Circumscription is achieved by means of a second order axiom schema:

$\text{Circum}(T,P): \ T(\phi) \ \& \ \forall x(\phi(x)->P(x)) \ \rightarrow \ \forall x(P(x) \rightarrow \phi(x))$

where $T(\phi)$ is the result of replacing all occurrences of P in T by the predicate expression $\phi$, P is an n-ary relation and x abbreviates $x_1, \ldots x_x$ Informally, this states that if $\phi$ satisfies the conditions satisfied by p and every n-tuple that satisfies $\phi$ also satisfies p, then the only n-tuples which satisfy P are those which satisfy $\phi$. For the simple example above, the outcome is the same as for the closed-world assumption. More complex forms of circumscription have been defined, for example, prioritized circumscription allows the predicates which are to be minimized to be placed in an order of relative importance: this, for example, could be used to allow us to conclude ~Public-school(Thatcher), which does not follow from $\text{Circum}(\textbf{B}_s,\text{Female})$ as above. The precise relationships between these forms of circumscription and other forms of the closed-world assumption have been the subject of many studies.

Any student model which purports to represent what a student believes is bound to make implicit use of some circumscription-like scheme since it would be unreasonable to require the student model to represent explicitly all that which the student does not believe. However, formally, the matter is more complex than even circumscription can handle. For, if there is no proposition of the form $B_cB_sp$ then is the missing default assumption ~$B_cB_sp$ or $B_c$~$B_sp$ or $B_cB_s$~$p$, all of which mean subtly different things? The four possibilities almost correspond to the values 'yes' ($B_cB_sp$), 'no' ($B_cB_s$~$p$), 'unknown' ($B_c$~$B_sp$, although these last two should probably include the ~$p$ case as well) and 'fail' (~$B_cB_sp$) of the four-valued logic for student modelling suggested by Mizoguchi et al.[41].

The use of second-order axioms as in circumscription obviously allows the first-order mechanisms to stay unchanged. Proof-theoretic approaches to non-monotonic reasoning, on the other hand, include within the first-order logic extra rules which allow non-monotonic inferences to be drawn. For such logics, a new semantics must be defined. These non-monotonic logics focus on the notion of normality, ie. on rules which tend to apply unless there are exceptions.

For example, *default logic* allows a theory to contain ordinary first-order formulas plus defaults, ie. expressions of the form

$$p : q \rightarrow r$$

which may be read as "if p is derivable and the formula q is consistent (ie. its negation is not provable) with the theory, then the default rule is applicable and the conclusion r may be drawn." This is non-monotonic because a formula q, previously consistent with a theory, may become inconsistent if new formulas are added to the theory. The two most common forms of default are where q=r or q=r&s, for example:

$B_C$(Physics-graduate(s)) : $B_C$(Knows-about-momentum(s))

      → $B_C$(Knows-about-momentum(s))

Prime-minister(x) : Male(x) & ~Eq(x = Thatcher) → Male(x)

Such defaults act as rules of 'conjecture', allowing inferences which would not be possible under ordinary first-order logic rules. The conclusion has the status of a belief which may need to be withdrawn (as discussed in section 5.2.1) if the assumption becomes inconsistent. The potential circularity (arising from the fact that what is provable in a default logic both determines and is determined by what is not provable) is avoided by requiring that an *extension* of a particular theory (1) contain all the known facts, (2) be closed under the implication rules, and (3) contain the consequents of all defaults which apply within that extension. In general, there are many possible extensions for a given default theory. Informally, an extension describes an acceptable set of beliefs that an agent may have about an incompletely specified world and thus is similar to the concept of a possible world. Since determining whether a formula is within an extension is undecidable, the implementation of default logic seems problematic, although for most practical cases (eg. the kinds of default illustrated above) implementations are possible, for example, the LNT system discussed above has an underlying default logic written in Prolog [48].

Default logic involves an agent reflecting upon its own knowledge, in particular, in considering whether a proposition is consistent with what it believes. The notion of consistency is, however, outside the language of default logic. We could instead attempt to capture the notion within the logic, as is done in an *autoepistemic logic*. For example, we could rephrase:

$$p : q → r$$

by the sentence:

$$B_a p \ \& \ \sim B_a \sim q → r$$

ie. "if p belongs to the agent's belief-set and ~q does not, then r is true." Not surprisingly, given this translation, various formal equivalences between variations of default logic and autoepistemic logic can be established. The main point here, however, is that we have a link through belief logics to other aspects of the student modelling problem, such as limited reasoning, as discussed above, and thus a prospect of being able to tie together all the threads of student modelling, in due course.

Unfortunately, as discussed by Levesque [37], this link is weakened by the fact that work on autoepistemic logics and default logics has defined different semantics for the notion of belief to that used in belief logics. Levesque attempts to overcome this by defining a second modal operator, in addition to B, namely O, such that $O_a p$ is to be read as "p is *all* that is believed" or perhaps "*only* p is believed", and then by developing a semantics for a language with two such operators. Subsequently, this operator is modified to $O_a [n] p$ for "only p is believed about n", just as circumscription takes place with respect to a predicate and not the whole belief-set.

Clearly, difficult technical issues remain and most work in this area continues to focus on the detailed properties of different formalizations rather than on considering possible applications to areas such as student modelling. However, some general implications for student modelling may be listed:

1. Although some formalizations are theoretically intractable, practical implementations for realistic applications are possible and are beginning to be developed [18].

2. Since non-monotonicity often arises through an agent reasoning about its (or other's) beliefs, the meaning of the belief operator depends on the context (ie. the other beliefs). Thus, B functions as an indexical and expressions in the student model should ideally be indexed. Formally, this is an aspect which has not been considered.

3. Non-monotonicity is intimately related with other aspects of the student modelling problem: for example, determining which belief(s) to withdraw (section 5.2.1) is likely to depend to some extent on which beliefs were derived by ordinary inferences and which by defaults; similarly, limited reasoning may be achieved by not reflecting too deeply about a set of beliefs and hence leading to the derivation of default assumptions.

4. We can use logical notations to describe non-monotonic reasoning without making any psychological claims, or, as Levesque [37] puts it, we can use logics objectively rather than subjectively.

5. To repeat a general point, formal characterizations of non-monotonic reasoning begin to provide us with a way of precisely describing and analysing aspects of student modelling which at present are proposed, described and implemented in an ad-hoc manner.

## 5.2.6 Creating Beliefs Through Learning

In so far as they may be distinguished, reasoning leads (through deductive processes) to the creation of relatively temporary beliefs for solving a particular problem, whereas learning leads (through inductive processes) to the creation of relatively permanent beliefs for solving problems in general. If reasoning leads straightforwardly to a problem solution, then learning may well not occur since the agent may re-generate the temporary beliefs by the same deductive processes. If the reasoning process is inadequate in some way then learning processes may be activated to analyze the results of reasoning.

As with reasoning, work on machine learning is relevant to student modelling in two ways: (a) to enable the system to learn about aspects of the student modelling problem, and (b) to model how the student learns. Again as with reasoning, the aim in the latter case is not to seek the unattainable, that is, fully reliable predictions about the student's learning processes, but to develop a theoretical framework within which such processes may be described and to hope that particular instantiations lead to useful analyses which can form the basis for instructional interactions. In fact, we can repeat with respect to learning many of the points made in the previous sections about reasoning:

- the potential benefits of developing explicit representations of learning processes;
- the recognition that, for both human and system agents, learning processes will be limited;
- the need to distinguish situations where psychological validity is important from those where it is not;
- the fact that the computational intractability of many techniques imposes limitations on what may be possible as far as dynamic student modelling is concerned; and so on.

There is a rich machine learning literature from which to elaborate these points, and there has been considerable work within student modelling which applies machine learning ideas: for example, Langley and Ohlsson [35] describe a system which aims to induce a student's problem-solving procedure from observations of her solutions by using psychological heuristics to guide hypothesis formation; VanLehn [58] develops a theory of inductive learning which is intended to model the process whereby students learn from examples, the theory relying heavily on 'felicity conditions', that is, tacit conventions about the teaching-learning process; Costa et al. [13] describe an application of explanation based learning to the problem of reconstruction, using the technique to disambiguate between possible contexts which a student may have adopted to solve problems.

All these examples, and almost all others from machine learning, are concerned with learning by a single agent (be it system or human student). Rather than expand on these examples, we will discuss one which illustrates the potential of machine learning research to support the view that learning may occur through an interaction between two agents (system and human student, or two human students). Imagine we have two agents, a and b, who are both trying to learn the same concept but do so by studying different examples and by describing the examples in different ways. How can the two agents make sense of what the other agent learns, in order perhaps to integrate the two different learned concepts (in order to develop a richer joint one) or to be able to discuss the differences between the learned concepts?

Brazdil [4] gives the following illustration. Each agent has a vocabulary v (a list of predicates used to describe the world), a set of observed examples E, and a knowledge base K describing what the agent knows about the examples in terms of its vocabulary v. For example,

| Agent a | Agent b |
|---------|---------|
| $V_a$ = { father,mother } | $V_b$ = { parent,male,female } |
| $E_a$ = { gfather(oscar,steve), | $E_b$ = { gfather(william,steve), |
| gfather(paul,louis), | gfather(oscar,peter) } |
| gfather(oscar,andrew) } | |
| $K_a$ = { father(paul,oscar), | $K_b$ = { parent(william,sylvia), |
| father(oscar,louis), | parent(sylvia,steve), |
| father(louis,steve), | parent(oscar,helen), |
| father(louis,andrew) } | parent(helen,peter), |
| | male(william), male(oscar), |
| | male(steve),female(sylvia), |
| | male(peter),female(helen) } |

Applying an inductive procedure (eg. GOLEM [43]), here assumed the same for both agents, to $E_i$ and $K_i$ the agents might induce, in Prolog notation:

```
gfather(X,Y): -                 gfather(X,Y) : -
       father(X,Z),father(Z,Y).        parent(X,Z),male(X),
                                        female(Z),parent(Z,Y).
```

Neither agent's rule applies to the other's knowledge base, since the vocabularies are different. Moreover, even if an agent comes to know both rules (say b tells a its rule), then the combined rule:

```
gfather(X,Y): -
       father(X,Z),father(Z,Y);
       parent(X,Z),male(X),female(Z),parent(Z,Y)
```

is of no use unless an agent has access to the other agent's description of its world. For example, if a describes using its vocabulary the world from which b derived $K_b$, we have:

```
Ka' = {      father(william,sylvia),
             mother(sylvia,steve),
             father(oscar,helen),
             mother(helen,peter)}
```

for which the combined rule fails. In order to fully integrate b's knowledge, a needs to learn b's vocabulary as well, ie. the concepts parent, male, female. This is possible if b conveys its description to a, so that a can compare the two descriptions $K_b$ and $K_a'$. Since $K_b$ contains examples of the concepts to be learned, a could apply an inductive procedure to $K_b$ and $K_a'$, to learn:

```
parent(X,Y):- father(X,Y).
male(X):- father(X,_).
female(X):- mother(X,_).
```

Thus, using standard machine learning techniques, we can enable an agent to understand another agent's theory. If we regard one of the agents to be the system, then we could imagine such a procedure being applied to handle situations where the student has a different viewpoint about the domain to that of the system. If we imagine both agents to be human students, then the above kind of analysis might be adapted to enable a system to help the students work collaborative to come up with an agreed integrated theory of the domain.


## 5.3   Beyond Belief

So far we have adhered to the original definition of the student model in terms of a belief set, ie. an unstructured set of beliefs held by the system about the student (including her beliefs), where the object of a belief was taken to be a simple proposition. However, this adherence has been strained in several ways, for example, in the need to associate links between beliefs to facilitate belief revision, and in the need to consider a production rule as a kind of proposition. In this section, we will review several extensions to the simple belief-set. Again, this is related to the broad area of knowledge representation research in AI and we will only discuss aspects particularly relevant to student modelling.


### 5.3.1   Belief Structures


A belief-set may become structured, and hence a 'belief-structure' rather than a belief-set, in basically two ways: by specifying relationships between pairs of elements and by partitioning the elements into subsets. The former is needed, for example, to indicate that one belief is derived from or is a generalization of another one; the latter, for example, to deal with local reasoning (section 5.2.3).

Two of the most useful relationships to specify are those of abstraction (isa) and aggregation, ie. part-whole relationships (partof). Greer and McCalla [26] structure their belief space as a lattice based on these two relationships. One dimension specifies abstractions - for example, in their domain of Lisp programming strategies:

```
{ function-definition isa lisp-program,
  recursion isa function-definition,
  cdr-recursion isa recursion,
  car-recursion isa recursion, ... }
```

The other dimension specifies part-whole relationships, for example:

```
{  null-base-case partof cdr-recursion,
   recursive-cdr-reduction-case partof cdr-recursion,
   some-test-default partof recursive-cdr-reduction-case, ... }
```

Those elements which are not partof of any other element may be shown in a 'principal abstraction hierarchy'. If there are no abstraction relationships between elements not in the principal abstraction hierarchy then one can picture 'slicing' the space into objects at different 'grain sizes'.

Such a structuring is useful for student modelling because it enables diagnosis to be carried out at an appropriate level of detail. For example, given a particular student solution, such as:

```
(defun findb (lst)
    (cond ((null lst) nil)
        ((atom 'b) t)
           (t (cons nil (findb (cdr lst))))))
```

then it may be difficult to identify specific mal-rules, if any, but we may be able to at least recognize the solution as an example of cdr-recursion. We can imagine searching the abstraction hierarchy from the root (lisp-program) seeking the lowest node (cdr-recursion) for which the specified parts are present (here we have a null-base-case and a recursive-cdr-reduction-case). Pedagogically useful information may be determined by analysing why the solution is not recognized as an instance of lower nodes (eg. cdr-tail-end-recursion) in the abstraction hierarchy on the path from the recognized node to the 'preferred solution' node. Thus, it may be possible to limit some of the problems discussed in section 5.2 (such as belief revision) which may arise because of a premature commitment to a default assumption, for example. Instead, the system may maintain an appropriately vague student model, which is refined only when it is possible to do so. In this sense, Greer and McCalla's granularity scheme is similar to the bounded model approach of Elsom-Cook [20] where a version space maintains upper and lower bounds on the possible states of the student.

A student-model oriented structuring of the domain concepts is not necessarily the same as a curriculum-oriented one. For example, Greer and McCalla's abstraction hierarchy may not carry pedagogical implications, such as that the general concept of recursion should be taught before the more specific concept of cdr-recursion, or vice versa. While the actual structures may turn out to be quite similar, their purposes are very different. Here we are concerned only with the aim of enabling 'imprecise' student modelling. The progression of causal models from qualitative to quantitative developed by White and Frederiksen [62] appears similar to Greer and McCalla's abstraction hierarchy, but the former's aim is to eliminate most student modelling problems by building systems which enable students to build their own models. Student modelling then becomes a matter of the system identifying which of the pre-specified sequence of causal models the student has acquired, and thus is a version of overlay modelling - "the students are assumed to have the current model when they can correctly solve problems that the current model can solve but the previous model could not" ([62], p. 150).

## 5.3.2   Viewpoints

Specifying relationships between elements of a belief-set is useful when the student modelling component needs to adjust its focus on the student: partitioning the elements into subsets is useful when a different pair of spectacles is needed altogether. For example, imagine (from [13]) that:

$$\mathcal{B}_{cs} = \{ \; \texttt{Man(x) \& Noble(x) \& Live(x,17th-century)} \rightarrow \texttt{Wig(x)},$$
$$\texttt{Man(Louis-XIV)} ,$$
$$\texttt{Lived(Louis-XIV,17th-century)},$$
$$\texttt{Wig(Louis-XIV)}, \; \ldots \; \}$$

and the system asks the student why Louis-XIV wore a wig, expecting the answer "because he was a noble" since this may be derived from the student model. If instead the student answers "because he liked having fun" then the system may seek a context different to the 'Louis-XIV as a 17th-century noble' context to make sense of this answer. It may, for example, replace the first proposition above by one or more axioms in the system's belief-set defining alternative contexts:

$$\mathcal{B}_c = \{ \; \{ \; \texttt{Man(x) \& Criminal(x)} \rightarrow \texttt{Disguise(x)},$$
$$\texttt{Disguise(x)} \rightarrow \texttt{Wig(x)} \; \}, \; \ldots$$
$$\{ \; \texttt{Man(x) \& Bald(x)} \rightarrow \texttt{Wig(x)} \; \}, \; \ldots$$
$$\{ \; \texttt{Man(x) \& Farceur(x)} \rightarrow \texttt{Have-fun(x)},$$
$$\texttt{Have-fun(x)} \rightarrow \texttt{Wig(x)} \; \}, \; \ldots \; \}$$

Finding a context, eg. 'Louis-XIV as a farceur', from which $\texttt{Wig(Louis-XIV)}$ may be derived enables the student model to be revised and an appropriate response to be generated.

We provisionally define a *viewpoint* $\mathcal{V}_a$ to be a triple $\langle \mathcal{B}_a, \mathcal{L}_a, \mathcal{M}_a \rangle$, where each element is a subset of the agent's complete belief, logic and meta-logic space, respectively. The above example is just concerned with the belief-set but in general we might imagine different viewpoints to involve different reasoning processes. If the agent is the system then we are emphasizing the fact that there may be many different ways of looking at one domain, rather than just one definitively correct one: if the agent is the student then we are recognizing that students may well have different views about the domain to the system. Both aspects have been emphasized recently in attempts to move intelligent tutoring systems beyond straightforward knowledge communication systems. Wenger [61] identifies 'viewpoints' as a topic ripe for more research and as a means of shifting from "what is wrong to what is right".

However, the notion of a viewpoint is rather diffuse despite, or perhaps because of, being studied under various guises within many branches of AI and computer science [53]. In distributed AI, for example, there are discussions of different agents (or nodes in a network) holding different views about some problem and the need to divide a problem between agents and to coordinate the behaviour of them. They emphasize the role of *negotiation* to reconcile potentially conflicting views (section 6.3). Similarly, in ITS research, we find an increasing emphasis on the student's ability to negotiate both about the concepts to be discussed and about the meaning of the concepts themselves [42].

To illustrate the potential relevance of viewpoints to student modelling we may adapt an example from Wilks and Ballim [63] who consider a 'viewpoint' to be an agent's set of beliefs about some topic. The example emphasizes that such viewpoints need to be nested. Imagine the system is mediating an interaction between two medical students a and b. We might have:

$$\mathcal{B}_c \;=\; \{\; \text{Type(thalassemia,genetic-disorder)},$$

$$\text{Medically-informed(x)}$$
$$\rightarrow B_x(\text{Type(thalassemia,genetic-disorder)}),$$

$$\text{Average-person(x)}$$
$$\rightarrow B_x(\text{Type(thalassemia,disease)}),$$

$$\text{Type(x,genetic-disorder) \& Suffers(a1,x)}$$
$$\text{\& Suffers(a2,x) \& Child(a1,a2,a3)}$$
$$\rightarrow \text{Suffers(a3,x)}, \dots \}$$

The system's might have the following two student models:

$$\mathcal{LM}_a \;=\; \{\; B_a(\text{Suffers(fred,thalassemia)}),$$
$$B_a(\text{Suffers(mary,thalassemia)}),$$
$$\text{Medically-informed(a)}, \dots \}$$

$$\mathcal{LM}_b \;=\; \{\; B_b(\text{Suffers(fred,thalassemia)}),$$
$$B_b(\text{Suffers(mary,thalassemia)}), \dots \}$$

ie. the system believes a to be medically-informed but not b. From such student models, the system might reason that:

$$\mathcal{LM}_a \;=\; \{\; \dots,$$
$$B_a(\text{Type(thalassemia,genetic-disorder)}),$$
$$B_a(\text{Child(fred,mary,a3)} \rightarrow \text{Suffers(a3,thalassemia)}),$$
$$\dots \}$$

$$\mathcal{LM}_b \;=\; \{\; \dots,$$
$$B_b(\text{Type(thalassemia,disease)}), \dots \}$$

ie. that a will reason that a child of Fred and Mary will suffer from thalassemia but that b will not (on the default assumption that b is an average person). The system could then carry out independent dialogues with the two students but neither such dialogue would be of much interest to the other student. Instead, the system could take account of what one student believes the other student believes. For example, the system might consider that a believes b is also medically-informed (making the default assumption that b is the same as a unless a has evidence otherwise) and thus that:

$$\mathbf{B}_{cab} = \{ \ldots,$$

$$\text{Type(thalassemia,genetic-disorder)},$$
$$\text{Child(fred,mary,a3)} \rightarrow \text{Suffers(a3,thalassemia)}, \ldots \}$$

Then, for example, the system might engage a in discussing with b why b's conclusions differ from those expected by a of b. In general, the point is that in any interaction between two or more agents it may help for an agent to hold beliefs about what may be believed by the other agent(s).

There are many theoretical and practical difficulties to be overcome before the idea of viewpoints can be fully used in student modelling. For example, it is clear that viewpoints are not entirely independent but that some beliefs may be shared between even radically different viewpoints, although perhaps some core set of beliefs may be unique to one viewpoint. Practically feasible ways of handling multiply-overlapping belief sets need to be developed. Also, we need efficient ways of identifying the student's working viewpoint - will it suffice to work systematically through potential viewpoints (as implied in the 'wig example') since there may not be many of them, or will we need to reason about mismatches with the previously assumed viewpoint? And, do all the potential viewpoints need to be anticipated or may they be generated, as needed, by the system?

### 5.3.3 Plans

In section 5.1.1 we defined reconstruction as the interpretation of a set of student inputs in terms of the propositions which the student may be held to believe. Often, however, the system is concerned to interpret the inputs in terms of what the student is doing rather than what she believes or knows, because the system may intend to discuss plans and goals directly or because by re-directing the student's plans the system may lead her more effectively to the desired beliefs. The problem of identifying the student's plans is unfortunately complex for the following reasons:

1. Unlike planning itself, plan recognition is inherently a multi-agent process since it involves one agent (the system) reasoning about the plans of another (the student) - except in those situations where an agent is trying to reconstruct its own planning.

2. It invariably involves uncertain reasoning since a set of observed actions rarely uniquely identifies a plan (yet definite conclusions may still be drawn even after uncertain reasoning).

3. Students are particularly prone to leave out actions, insert faulty actions, interleave actions from some other plan, and often to have no plan anyway!

Many approaches to plan recognition transform it into a parsing problem. A grammar specifies how plans are decomposed into actions and sub-actions, and a particular sequence of observations is regarded as a sentence to be parsed with respect to this grammar. Formally, this is no doubt a sufficient characterization of the problem, but we will instead describe a method developed by Kautz and Allen [33] which is closer to our view of student modelling.

The method requires the specification of three kinds of information:

1. The observations, eg.

    Occurs(e9,make-pasta)
    ∃e Occurs(e,make-noodles) & T(e)=17

    ie. event e9 is an instance of type make-pasta, and an event of type make-noodles occurred at time 17. Such a description is based on a general theory of action and time [1] and inherits from it axioms such as

    ∀e,i During(T(S(i,e)),T(e))

    ie. the time of the i-th subaction of event e occurs during the time of event e. (We might imagine a student using a simulation to learn how to cook or to perform some similar activity.)

2. An action hierarchy, ie. an exhaustive description of the ways in which an action can be performed and of the ways in which an action can be used as a step of a more complex action. These are specified as axioms of specialization and decomposition (which are just the inverses of Greer and McCalla's abstraction and aggregation):

    ∀e Occurs(e,make-pasta) → Occurs(e,prepare-meal)
    ∀e Occurs(e,make-fettucini) → Occurs(e,make-noodles)
    ∀e Occurs(e,make-spaghetti) → Occurs(e,make-noodles)

    . . .

    ∀e Occurs(e,make-pasta) →
        ∃t    Occurs(S(1,e),make-noodles) &
              Occurs(S(2,e),boil) & Occurs(S(3,e),make-sauce) &
              Object(S(2,e)) = Result(S(1,e)) &
              Hold(Noodle(Result(S(1,e))),t) &
              Overlap(T(S(1,e)),t) & During(T(S(2,e)),t)

    . . .

The decomposition axioms specify the subactions, their preconditions and effects, and constraints on temporal relationships. Of course, subactions may also be decomposed. In addition, the system needs a set of disjointedness axioms, eg.:

$\forall$e Occurs(e,make-fettucini-alfredo) not-and

Occurs(e,make-fettucini-marinara)

3. A set of 'simplicity constraints' to choose between interpretations, eg. "minimize the number of top-level actions". These are represented as second-order logical formulae, which are instantiated to first-order formulae for any particular case.

Before recognizing a plan, the action hierarchy is supplemented by axioms derived by applying circumscription to make the assumptions that (a) the known ways of performing an action are the only ways and that (b) all the possible reasons for performing an action are known:

$\forall$e Occurs(e,prepare-meal) $\rightarrow$

Occurs(e,make-pasta) exc-or Occurs(e,make-meat)

. . .

$\forall$e Occurs(e,make-noodles) $\rightarrow$

$\exists$a      Occurs(a,make-pasta) & e = S(1,a)

$\forall$e Occurs(e,make-marinara) $\rightarrow$

$\exists$a      (Occurs(a,make-fettucini-marinara) & e = S(3,a)) v

(Occurs(a,make-chicken-marinara) & e = S(3,a))

Although there is no general method for carrying out circumscription, these axioms are easily derivable by special-purpose algorithms which retain the benefits of having a formal semantics for the process.

Now, given an observation, eg.:

Occurs(el,make-fettucini) v Occurs(el,make-spaghetti)

ie. that the student is making fettucini or spaghetti (but we're not such which), we may infer:

$\exists$e Occurs(e,make-pasta)                              ..(1)

and hence that, for example:

$\exists$e Occurs(S(2,e),boil)

So, even though particular actions and plans may not be identified, specific predictions may be made. If we now observe:

Occurs(e2,make-marinara)

then the system can infer, from the specialization axioms, that:

$\exists$e Occurs(e,make-pasta) v Occurs(e,make-meat)

Given the previous inference (1), the simplicity constraint mentioned above would eliminate the second disjunct of this inference.

Thus, the system may monitor the student's actions and attempt to derive the student's plans. The virtues of this approach are that it provides a formal theory with a precise semantics for the plan recognition process by specifying axioms (supplemented by circumscription) from which conclusions are derived deductively and it thus integrates plan recognition with other aspects of student modelling discussed previously (instead of regarding plan recognition as a rather specialist sub-problem for which different techniques are needed).

## 5.3.4   Meta-Beliefs

Planning is but one of a set of "mysterious mechanisms" [5] denoted by the terms *metacognition* and *metaknowledge*. We might distinguish, for example, between problem-solving itself and reasoning before, during and after problem-solving (planning, monitoring and reflecting, perhaps). The issues are complex and no attempt will be made here to solve any mysteries - simply, some links to student modelling will be discussed.

Whatever they are precisely, metacognitive abilities are considered important in both education and AI. Dewey, Vygotsky and Piaget all emphasized various aspects of metacognition, and more recently Schoenfeld [52] has stressed their role in mathematics education. In AI, metaknowledge, meta-reasoning and meta-level architectures have been extensively discussed (eg. [38, 25]), and, although there has been no explicit link to such AI research, ILE design has increasingly emphasized metacognitive aspects (eg. [11, 55]).

However, metacognition is not an unqualified benefit. Its alleged importance derives from a view that it is necessary for an agent not only to know more than a set of facts (namely, how to apply them to solve problems) but also to be able to reason rationally about the problem-solving process itself. This, it is assumed, will enable the agent to improve problem-solving performance (ie. to learn), to develop transferrable metacognitive skills, and to engage in discussions (eg. tutorial interactions) about such processes. These may sound like platitudes but they are questioned by those who doubt that activity derives, or should derive, from a rational reasoning process: instead, it might follow in response to the situation in which the agent finds itself. Others may even question the implicit educational aim of fostering rationality. We cannot resolve such issues, but we can concede that metacognitive mechanisms must be applied with caution: an agent that spent too much time at the meta-level might accomplish less at the object-level.

Some computational mechanisms for addressing metacognitive issues have already been introduced, for example, axioms of introspection in modal logics (section 5.2.3) meta-level reasoning (section 5.2.4), and autoepistemic logics (section 5.2.5). As usual, our aim is not to develop such mechanisms per se but to apply them to student modelling. For example, the axioms of positive and negative introspection and their inverses (and corresponding axioms for knowledge):

$$B_a p \rightarrow B_a B_a p$$
$$\sim B_a p \rightarrow B_a (\sim B_a p)$$
$$B_a B_a p \rightarrow B_a p \text{ , etc.}$$

are clearly inadequate as a basis for deriving reliable conclusions concerning a student's beliefs about her own beliefs but rather than embark on a probably futile attempt to 'correct' them we may seek to indicate how they may be used to build student models adequate to support instructional interactions. For example, imagine a student attempting to solve fraction problems $(f_1 - f_2 = f_3)$ who asserts that she believes that it is always the case that $f_1 > f_3$ From an axiom such as:

$$\text{Asserts}_s(p) \rightarrow B_s B_s p$$

and the third rule above, the system might infer $B_s(f_1 > f_3)$. If however her problem-solving performance leads to $B_c B_s q$, where $q \rightarrow (f_1 < f_3)$ - for example, the student may appear to believe the mal-rule that one subtracts both numerators and denominators and thus obtains 7/8 - 3/4 = 4/4 - then the system might initiate a dialogue about the apparent contradiction, but in terms of general beliefs about the problem domain not the specific problem.

In general terms, an intelligent agent should be able to reason about its own problem-solving performance, for example, to consider the merits of alternatives, and should be able to use the results of such deliberations in subsequent problem-solving. This requires a metalanguage in which to formalize the process of problem-solving. Genesereth and Nilsson [25] show how predicate logic, extended with a quoting mechanism to overcome quantification problems, can be used to formalize the process of resolution theorem-proving. The same method can be used (as we assumed in section 5.2.4) to describe other inference procedures, such as limited or even unsound ones. We might in fact define what it means for an agent to believe a proposition in terms of a meta-level predicate Provable, defined as appropriate:

$$\forall a \forall p \ B_a p \Leftrightarrow \text{Provable } (\mathbf{B}_a, p)$$

In AI there are (at least) two kinds of metaknowledge - knowledge about how to use knowledge, and knowledge about the contents of one's own knowledge. The former has been thoroughly studied in the form of expert system meta-rules, which generally help determine rule selection, but we will look instead at the more subtle issue of *reflection*. The latter kind of metaknowledge, which has been less studied, is concerned with issues of *introspection*, which is clearly of relevance to student modelling and will be considered below.

Dewey [15] defined reflection as the "active, persistent and careful consideration of any belief or supposed form of knowledge in the light of the grounds that support it". Genesereth and Nilsson [25] are more specific - reflection is "the process of suspending the process of reasoning, reasoning about that process, and using the results to control subsequent reasoning" -

and they also provide a computational realization of the definition. The basic idea is to include within the meta-level a specification of the conditions under which a 'reflection phase' is entered. For example, we might have:

$$\mathcal{M} \quad = \quad \{ \quad \mathtt{Infer}(\mathcal{B}, \{p_1, p_2, \quad , p_n\}) \;\&\; n < d \to \{p_1, p_2, \quad p_n\} \;,$$
$$\mathtt{Infer}(\mathcal{B}, \{p_1, p_2, \ldots, p_n\}) \;\&\; n >= d \to \mathtt{Reflect}(\mathcal{B}) \; \}$$

to indicate that if the number of inferences which could be made from a belief-set is less than some threshold $d$ then they are made, otherwise some reflection process is begun. Obviously, $\mathtt{Reflect}(\mathcal{B})$ is intended to lead to some change in $\mathcal{B}$ and hence to changes in subsequent processing. Various other conditions which promote reflection could also be defined, for example, a 'compulsively reflective' agent might be one who reflects during every inference step. (We are glossing over many subtle technical and philosophical issues. For example, on what basis are the steps of $\mathtt{Reflect}$ separated from those of $\mathtt{Infer}$ and considered to be at a different level? - exactly the same result could be achieved by redefining $\mathtt{Infer}$ if we wished.)

Such a mechanism could be used to lend precision to attempts at the cognitive modelling of reflective processes. For example, Foss [24] tried to specify conditions under which students abandoned a solution path when using the AlgebraLand system conditions such as 'the result of an operation is longer than the previous expression' or 'an unreasonably complicated piece of arithmetic is required'. At the moment, however, as Genesereth and Nilsson [25] admit "little is known about when a procedure should reflect", nor indeed about what the results of reflection should be. Nonetheless, we may anticipate that research on computational reflection will lead to some much-needed precision in discussions of such metacognitive aspects and eventually enable ILEs to make some predictions about which kinds of instructional event may promote reflection and about when to intervene to suggest that the student might reflect (ie. pause from problem-solving and reason about her progress).

It is sometimes argued that what a student knows is less important than what she knows she knows (or does not know) - which is what the work on introspection is attempting to formalize. Knowledge of one's own limitations can be a reason for acting, to acquire knowledge, and for not acting, to avoid contemplated actions outside one's competence. We would like to be able to handle common situations such as a student asserting that she believes she knows nothing about art:

$$\forall p \; \mathtt{About}(p, \mathtt{art}) \; \to . \; B_s \!\sim\! K_s p$$

and to make reasonable inferences from such expressions, eg.:

$$\forall p \; B_s \!\sim\! K_s p \; \to \; B_s (\mathtt{Not\text{-}worth\text{-}knowing\text{-}about}(p))$$

and to use more general axioms, such as those of 'arrogance' and 'coherence' [14]:

$$B_a (B_a p \; \to \; p)$$
$$B_a \!\sim\! B_a p \; \to \; \sim\! B_a p$$

The last of these is logically equivalent to:

$$\sim\!B_a\,(p\ \&\ \sim\!B_ap)$$

which holds, according to Davis [14], for any agent who is not "seriously confused" - unfortunately, our students often are. These kinds of axiom, over-simple though they are, are closely related to methods developed for non-monotonic reasoning, as discussed by Konolige [34]. For example, the closed-world assumption may be re-expressed as:

$$B_a\!\sim\!K_ap\ \rightarrow\ B_a\!\sim\!p$$

(anything that is not known is believed to be false), and default logic can be represented in autoepistemic terms, as we saw in section 5.2.5.

But we must pause to reflect on what this research may contribute to student modelling. If reflection "is the transferral of argumentation to an internal level" [59] then there is little chance that an ILE would be able to monitor or reconstruct a student's reflective processes in the way that we have imagined for problem-solving processes (which is difficult enough). 'Internal reflection' is not an activity for which moment-to-moment student modelling is possible or appropriate - rather like reading from a hypertext system, where we found that minutes of apparent inactivity separated flurries of activity [56]. ILE interruptions to "tell me what you are thinking" may well be counter-productive, since they will interfere with on-going cognitive activity.

However, in some situations, it may be beneficial to make the reflection 'external'. The ILE's role might then be to determine when it is appropriate to externalize reflection and other meta-level processes and to share in its execution. For example, if the student model indicates that $B_cB_sp$ and $B_cB_s\!\sim\!p$, then it may be more rational for the ILE to conclude nothing (let alone embark on a risky reason maintenance exercise) except perhaps that one or both is wrong and to discuss the issue with the student. Similarly, if the student model indicates that in the current problem-solving situation one of a number of rules could have been applied, rather than attempting to second-guess which (if any) has in fact been applied, an ILE might do better to enter a meta-level where it is discussed explicitly. Often, such a discussion may bring into the open issues of which a student is only implicitly aware. For example, in algebra problem-solving, performance might lead to $B_cB_sf$, ie. to the system believing that the student 'believes' a particular fault. Whether or not the student 'really believes' such a fault is debatable: perhaps it should be debated with the student. Payne and Squibb [45] show that students do have sufficient metacognitive awareness that they are able reliably to assign levels of confidence to their answers: in some cases, a wrong answer (which is actually believed to be wrong by the student) is evidence that the student believes that she does not know something ($B_s(\exists p\!\sim\!B_sp)$), not that she genuinely believes something which is in fact incorrect. Different pedagogic interactions are surely needed for such different situations.

### 5.3.5   Attributes

The idea of using student attributes, ie. properties or qualities which can be predicated of the student, in student modelling is intuitively appealing but has proved to be of limited practicality, possibly because the exorbitant effort required to build an ILE capable of dealing with a single content in a single way has precluded attempts to build systems capable of dynamically varying content and teaching strategy, for which student attributes may be more relevant. Our aim in this section is not to argue the case for or against the use of student attributes but to consider how they might be encompassed within our theoretical framework.

Our general approach is to associate an 'attribute' with a meta-level description of a component of a student model, although our comments are necessarily speculative. As we have seen, some components of a student model are domain-dependent and some are not (and some are intermediate): attributes tend to be associated with domain-independent components.

We are naturally only concerned with attributes (sometimes referred to as *aptitudes*) which have some bearing on learning. Corno and Snow [12] identify three kinds of aptitude:

1. Cognitive; eg. (prior) knowledge and intellectual abilities. ILE design has tended to emphasize the role of knowledge, implicitly agreeing with Chi, Glaser and Rees [7] that students' difficulties "can be attributed mainly to inadequacies of their knowledge base and not to limitations in either the architecture of their cognitive systems or processing capabilities". This kind of attribute is similar to that of a stereotype (section 4.2): to say that a student is a 'Unix-expert', for example, is to say that she knows a certain set of propositions. Attributes referring to intellectual abilities describe the reasoning and learning components of the student model. For example, a student with good 'visual analogic intelligence' would be modelled by including a component good at visual analogy.

2. Conative, ie. concerned with wants, intentions, etc. and, in the educational context, cognitive and learning styles. Many such styles have been studied, usually in terms of contrasts: holist vs. serialist, reflective vs. impulsive, convergent vs. divergent, etc. These attributes seem to refer to global properties (rather than the performance properties, as with cognitive attributes) of the meta-level of a student model. Thus a 'holist' style refers to the general strategy of the learning component. Similarly, 'reflective' refers to the number and type of meta-level interruptions on the base-level problem-solving.

3. Affective, ie. concerned with values. This includes the difficult issue of 'motivation', for which many attributes such as anxiety, autonomy, self-concept, etc. remain to be disentangled. It is hard to imagine how such attributes may be modelled other than by simple labels but 'self-concept', for example, is presumably concerned with what a student believes about the model she has of herself.

The permanence or otherwise of such attributes is also a concern. Some attributes (eg. knowledge of a particular law of physics) are transient and it may be the ILE's aim to change them, some (eg. blindness) may be permanent but nonetheless of pedagogic concern if not focus, but many (eg. anxiety) may be situation-dependent. The value of relatively permanent attributes may be determined off-line, through psychological tests which are outside the scope of this review. On-line interrogation concerning attributes is of little use since the technical terms used in educational research are rarely used by students in the same sense. The on-line assignment of a particular event (or series of events) to student attributes can be problematic: for example, a student may neglect to try to disconfirm her hypotheses - is this evidence for certain cognitive, conative or affective attributes?

The use of a simple label for attributes ("student is a Unix-expert", "student is reflective") may not be theoretically insightful but may be practically adequate, if that is all the instructional component needs to know. Ideally, however, such attributes should be defined in terms of other contents of the student model:

$$\text{"student is a Unix-expert"} \leftrightarrow K_s\{p_1, p_2, \ldots, p_n\}$$

Perhaps, in general, we could say that the system believes the student possesses an attribute $A_s$ iff the student model possesses certain properties $\{p_1, p_2, \ldots, p_n\}$, to be defined (which is difficult, of course):

$$B_c A_s \leftrightarrow \{p_1, p_2, \ldots, p_n\} \quad (\mathcal{LM})$$

For the attribute to be more than a shorthand summary, however, the set $\{p_1, p_2, \ldots, p_n\}$ needs to be partitionable into two subsets: those properties which enable the attribute to be recognized and those which follow from its recognition. If either subset is empty then the attribute serves no student modelling purpose.

Maybe, as has happened with learning processes, the necessary formal precision will evolve from computational descriptions rather than through attempted analyses of informal educational and psychological literature. Previously, we have seen formal definitions of terms such as 'narrow-minded', 'compulsively reflective', and 'arrogant', and other definitions, for example, of 'persistent' and 'cooperative', exist in the AI literature. Such terms are used without necessarily any psychological claims (and perhaps even semi-seriously), but at least they provide a benchmark against which educational psychologists can try to define the terms when they use them.

# 6 Using the Student Model

Describing student modelling, as we have, virtually independently of other ILE activities creates the impression that that is how student modelling should actually be carried out. In fact, only if student modelling is tightly coupled with, in particular, the instructional component of the ILE is the task likely to prove tractable. Analyzing the current event becomes much more feasible if it is not done in ignorance of the instructional context and of previous analyses of the agents' plans and goals. Unfortunately, this coupling has not been addressed in any formal way. In this section, we will not attempt a thorough review of instructional activities but just describe some that impinge upon student modelling.

## 6.1 Prediction and Planning

An ILE needs to be capable of *dynamic planning,* that is, the on-line creation and revision of instructional plans, since for any significant learning context the pre-specification of a plan to be strictly followed is not possible. In order to plan, an agent needs to be able to evaluate the states which it predicts that it could reach. In our case, since the ILE's goals concern what the student learns, the evaluation is determined by a function of $LM$. This function could be defined in many ways, with respect to pre-specified objectives or intrinsic properties of the student model.

This evaluation is not of the current student model but of ones which might exist after a sequence of instructional events. These hypothesized student models need to be predicted by the reasoning and learning components of the student model (section 5). Thus, components of the current student model map the student model and the sequence of events onto a new student model:

$$LM \times \{o_1, i_1, o_2, i_2, \ldots, o_n, i_n\} \rightarrow LM'$$

where $\{o_1, i_1, o_2, i_2, \ldots, o_n, i_n\}$ is a sequence of system outputs and student inputs. Because of the indeterminacy and cost of the mapping and the large number of potential events, $n$ is usually kept small (giving the opportunism often considered characteristic of instructional planning). Of course, the actual student inputs are not known at the time when the plan needs to be created: but they are to some extent predictable by the student model, otherwise the mapping would need to take account of all possible student inputs. In general, for any contemplated system output $o_j$ one of a small number of student inputs may be anticipated. This small set of anticipated inputs greatly eases the reconstruction problem (section 5.1.1), since often the desired analysis has been 'preconstructed'.

The plan created depends on more than the student model. For example, it may depend on any curricular organization of the subject matter and on any resource constraints, which are outside our scope. But the plan itself is to be regarded not as a recipe for system action but as a context to support interpretation by the student modelling process. Clearly, an ILE that merely reacts to (as opposed to interacts with) a student does not need to predict or plan, but any ILE that takes any kind of instructional initiative must base its decision concerning the initiative to take on some kind of instructional plan, possibly implicit.

Since no plan can be created in a vacuum, plans are 'dynamic' only to a degree. Most current ILEs plan only to the extent of dynamically choosing between pre-specified skeletal plans (eg. Meno-Tutor [64]) or between pre-specified problem sets (eg. GREATERP [50]). ILEs which come closer to planning as the term is understood in AI - that is, constructing an explicit plan representation, subject to constraints, which is interpreted, monitored and revised - include those of Murray [44] and Peachey and McCalla [46], the latter explicitly representing expected changes to the student model.

## 6.2 Diagnosis and Remediation

The phases of planning and diagnosis need to be interleaved in order to minimize the problems of both, but how precisely this may be done is not known. The results of diagnosis are represented by the contents of the student model and thus are in general terms the system's understanding of the student. More narrowly, diagnosis is often construed as the process of finding faults (as in section 5.1.2), which may then be subject to remediation.

Remediation may take many forms (it is for educational psychology to determine which form is appropriate when - our task here is to relate the forms to student modelling):

1. Reteaching. If we have that $B_c \sim B_s p$ then the system may reteach the proposition $p$ (in the same or a different fashion to previously). More generally, if:

$$B_c \ (\exists p \ p \ \in \ \{p_1, \ p_2, \ \ldots, \ p_n\} \ \& \ \sim B_s p)$$

ie. the system believes the student does not know one of a set of propositions but cannot determine which, the system may reteach the whole set. A priori, we might expect reteaching to be more effective if the student model enables it to focus on specific gaps in knowledge. But, in general, reteaching is an option whenever the student model indicates that the student has some difficulty but the system cannot identify it. For example, Ikeda, Mizoguchi and Kakusho [31], rather despairingly, consider that when a student has a "nonlogical belief structure" then "the task of constructing a model is not only difficult but futile ... in such cases ... the only possible instruction ... is to give elementary explanation of the teaching material".

2. Emendation. If the system is able to carry out a fault-diagnosis (section 5.1.2) and has identified one or more paired terms $<p, \ f>$, where $f$ is a faulty version of a proposition $p$, then the system may seek to emend the fault. For example, McCoy [40] suggests that misconceptions (of expert system users rather than students) may be emended by a three part system output: (i) a denial of $f$, (ii) an assertion of $p$, and (iii) a 'justification', often based on a refutation of the user's support for $f$. She also emphasizes the role of the user's viewpoint or domain perspective in determining the

user's support for a misconception. Various frames are specified for addressing certain kinds of misconception - for example, for a 'misattribution':

$B_CB_S$ (f: x has attribute y with value v) &

$B_C$ (p: x has attribute y with value w) &

$\exists z\ B_C$ (z has attribute y with value v) & $B_C$ (Similar (x,z))

$\rightarrow$ Deny(f) & Assert(p) &

Comment ("have you confused x and z, etc")

It should also be pointed out that emendation may also address difficulties not at the object level. If the student model has a sufficiently explicit representation of the student's reasoning, meta-reasoning and learning abilities then shortcomings here may also be focussed upon. For example, if the student is developing mal-rules through some impasse-repair mechanism then it may well be more productive to address this mechanism rather than some specific mal-rule that results, that is, to point out that 'syntactic patches' to overcome local difficulties is not always a productive strategy..

3. Counter-examples. A counter-example is a problem p such that:

$$D_c (p)\ \rightarrow A_c\ \&\ D_s (p)\ \rightarrow A_s\ \&\ not\ (A_c=A_s),$$

where the domain knowledge is represented procedurally, for example, as a production system. Evertsz [22] describes techniques for generating counter-examples, given two production systems (representing the system's and the student's knowledge). Of the set of potential counter-examples, the system might prefer one that generates an $A_s$ which violates any beliefs the student may have about answers in general (for example, a fraction problem for which $A_s=0$). Different instructional interactions may then ensue depending on whether or not the student realizes that the example is in fact a counter-example.

4. Garden-path problems. Among many more subtle remediations, we briefly mention just one, the use of 'garden-path problems', that is, problems which (according to the student model) the student can solve but only in such a tortuous fashion that she may realize that her current knowledge, while not actually incorrect, is inadequate. Methods for the automatic generation of such problems have yet to be developed. Formally, it would appear to be related to the conditions which promote reflection and to the results of any reflective process.

When discussing diagnosis, we should distinguish carefully between situations in which the system attempts to lead the student to diagnose her own (mis)understanding such as the above - and those in which the system attempts to diagnose its own (mis)understanding about the student. The former case may be characterized as the student resolving $B_CB_S$ (p v q); the latter as the system resolving $B_C$ ($B_S$p v $B_S$q). Similar techniques (eg. the generation of counter-examples) may be used in both cases, although the aims and instructional interactions are different. Work on formal theories of diagnosis (eg. [51]) has considered the general problem of automatically determining which 'measurements' to take when attempting to differentiate between multiple potential diagnoses of a faulty system.

ILE diagnosis is a rather richer concept than the diagnosis of formal AI theories. The former is more concerned with understanding the student than with identifying her difficulties. Moreover, the student is considered to be an active participant in the diagnostic process (and not just a system to be observed), with the consequence that the diagnostic process itself may change the student being diagnosed. Such aspects have not been incorporated in formal theories of diagnosis.

## 6.3  Negotiation and Collaboration

The role of a student model in a dogmatic intelligent tutoring system seems clear cut: it is mainly to identify misunderstandings which the system may remediate. In other styles of ILE, however, where the student may have greater scope for following her own goals and developing her own understanding, the role of the student model is more subtle (but not non-existent). No longer is the emphasis on developing detailed object-level models, defined with respect to specified domain knowledge, but on representing the student's beliefs and goals on their intrinsic merits, in order that the system may offer (fallible) comment and advice in the role of a cooperative partner rather than a knowledgeable tutor.

Such a role may be achieved by a disingenuous concealment of its domain knowledge by the system - but the role is likely to be more appropriate in situations where computational representations of domain knowledge are unattainable or controversial. If the system's domain knowledge is not complete or necessarily correct, then the system may need reasoning and learning capabilities commensurate with those of the student. With such capabilities, the system may maintain a student model, which together with the system's model, represents some joint understanding of the domain. Naturally, in such a context, the student model is less an internal component of the ILE but becomes an 'external' focus of discussion, as indeed does the system's model of the domain. Thus the student model may be built by a more direct interaction with the student rather than through some internal analysis by the system.

The view that a system-student interaction is just one instance of the class of multiagent interactions leads us to consider distributed AI, where concepts such as *negotiation* and *cooperation* have been much studied but have yet to take clear formal shape. Durfee and Lesser [19] consider that there is "confusion and misunderstanding among researchers who are studying different aspects of the same phenomenon". They urge that we distinguish carefully between negotiations which are about the shared construction of meaning and those which are about task-sharing or planning. Both are of course central to the philosophy of ILEs, the former being concerned with the nature of knowledge and the latter with the issue of student control, and both being the subject of preliminary investigations in the ILE context by, respectively, Dillenbourg and Self [16] and Baker [3]. Baker ventures a definition of negotiation as "a sequence of dialogue exchanges during which the mental states of the interlocutors are changed from the postures of indifference or conflict with respect to one or more propositions to one of cooperation, and where one or more interlocutor possesses the goal that this posture should be achieved". An agent x is said to cooperate with y's goal that p be eventually true, Coop (x, y, p), if:

$$B_x \ (\mathrm{Goal}(y,\mathrm{possibly}(p))) \ \& \ \mathrm{Prefer} \ (x,p,\sim p)$$
$$\rightarrow \mathrm{Persistent\text{-}goal}(x,p,\mathrm{Goal}(y,\mathrm{possibly}(p)))$$

ie. if x's recognition of y's goal that p be true and x's preference of p over ~p results in the generation of a persistent goal for p, relative to y's possession of the goal.

## 6.4  Interaction and Communication

In order to handle interactions beyond the straightforward single-question-single-answer format we need some theory of dialogue. This again is a research field in its own right and one which is of more concern to the instructional component of ILEs than to student modelling. However, such theories have implications for student modelling, as we illustrate here with two examples.

Dialogue game theory is a formal device for generating well-formed sequences of locutionary acts. It is semi-empirical in that it is based partly on analyses of discourse and partly on abstract specifications of valid processes of reasoning, discussion and argumentation. The theory has three components:

1. A set of 'issue spaces' [49] or 'commitment stores' describing what each participant believes or is committed to at any given stage of the dialogue;
2. A definition of the set of locutionary events (moves in the dialogue game), with a definition of the changes to the issue spaces when such an event occurs;
3. A set of constraints on the sequence of events, from which is intended to emerge the coherent episodic structure of rational dialogue.

Thus, in an ILE context, dialogue game theory posits a central role for the student model (or issue space) and considers that student model updating occurs as an on-going part of the instructional dialogue, not as a result of some separate diagnostic process. The goals of the 'dialogue game' must of course be generated by the student or the instructional component, which is not of concern here.

Dialogue game theory goes same way - maybe far enough to manage ILE interactions towards showing how Gricean maxims of conversation "fall out from a general characterization of the aims and means of linguistic exchanges together with obvious assumptions of rationality of the participants" [6]. We may also attempt to make these "obvious assumptions" explicit, to provide a deeper theory of communication and, in an ILE context, to confirm the need for detailed student models. For example, Cohen and Levesque [10] present a four-stage derivation of the basis of a theory of communication. The four stages define:

1. Primitives: a set of modal operators intended to define the mental states of the participants. These operators are expressed in a modal logic based on a possible world semantics of knowledge and a situation calculus model of action. The four operators defined are:

    $Bel(x,p)$ – p follows from x's beliefs (this is thus an implicit belief);

    $Goal(x,p)$ – p follows from x's goals;

    $Bmb(x,y,p)$ – p follows from x's beliefs about what is mutually believed by x and y;

    $After(a,p)$ – p is true in all courses of events that obtain from act a's happening.

    These operators are defined through a set of propositions and lemmas, for example, that of 'shared recognition':

    $$Bmb(y,x,Goal(x,p)) \ \& \ Bmb(y,x,Bel(x,Always(p \rightarrow \xi q)))$$
    $$\rightarrow Bmb(y,x,Goal(x,q))$$

2. A theory of rational action: a set of propositions defining the properties of ideally rational individual agents with persistent goals, for example, to specify that agents do not knowingly and deliberately make their persistent goals impossible for them to achieve. Theorems may then be derived from such propositions, eg.:

    $$\forall p \ Persistent\text{-}goal(y,p) \ \& \ Always(Competent(y,p))$$
    $$\rightarrow Eventually(p \ v \ Bel(y,Always(y,p))$$

    ie. if an agent has a persistent goal that it is able to bring about then eventually p becomes true or it believes that nothing can be done to achieve it.

3. A theory of rational interaction: a set of definitions and propositions intended to characterize interactions between agents. For example, an agent x may be said to be sincere or expert with respect to y and a proposition p under the following conditions:

    $$Sincere(x,y,p): \ Goal(x,Bel(y,p)) \ \rightarrow Goal(x,Know(y,p))$$
    $$Expert(x,y,p): \ Bel(y,Bel(x,p)) \ \rightarrow Bel(y,p))$$

    Such definitions of cooperative agents provide formal descriptions of the kinds of behaviour summarized by conversational maxims. No doubt, similar definitions for uncooperative agents could be ventured.

4. A theory of communication: descriptions of communicative acts such as questioning, requesting, etc. derived from general principles of belief and goal adoption between agents. These descriptions enable a distinction between, for example, real questions,

rhetorical questions and teacher-student questions. In principle, multi-act utterances and multi-utterance acts can be handled in the same scheme.

Thus, the derivation of communicative acts could be based ultimately upon the kinds of representation of agents' beliefs that we have adopted for student models. Of course, the definition of the content of the various levels is complex, but the intention is that each level be independently motivated, that is, for example, that the notion of a cooperative agent be developed independent of that of communication, and that of rational action be independent of that of interaction. The extent to which such a deep analysis is necessary to support adequate ILE-student interactions in practice remains to be seen.

# 7 Conclusions

We have reviewed a substantial body of techniques and theories from computer science and AI which may be applied to and adapted for student modelling. We have tried to indicate what particular techniques and theories may contribute by developing a view of student modelling within ILEs seen as systems to support and promote interactions between the belief systems of the agents involved.

We have not considered student modelling to be just a special case of cognitive modelling, emphasizing instead that computational utility not cognitive validity provides the main motivation for student modelling. Of course, the techniques and theories considered are justified to some extent by cognitive concerns but they can be developed and analysed independently of their cognitive content - just as a computational linguist may analyze grammars without commitment to their content or any view of human language use: an analogy which led to the coining of the term 'computational mathetics' for the kind of study presented here [54].

Implicit in this analysis is a bias towards 'traditional' symbolic AI as the appropriate basis for student modelling (as opposed to, say, connectionist or situationist approaches). This results from an emphasis on the meta-aspects of ILE interactions, deriving from an assumption that students should not just be able to use knowledge but also be able to reflect upon it, to discuss it, to explain it, etc. For an ILE to participate in such an interaction it would seem to need explicit symbolic representations of that knowledge.

As we have seen, student modelling calls upon many active areas of modern AI. In many cases, student modelling imposes currently unsatisfiable demands on formal AI - for example, to describe the non-monotonic reasoning of the system about the non-monotonic reasoning of the student, to take just one case. Nonetheless, the attempt to clarify what student modelling involves may lead to theoretical and practical benefits in due course.

# References

1. Allen, J F.: Towards a general theory of action and time, *Artificial Intelligence*, 23(2), pp. 123-154 (1984)
2. Anderson, A. & Belnap, N.: *Entailment: the Logic of Relevance and Necessity*. Princeton, NJ: Princeton University Press 1975
3. Baker, M. J.: Negotiating goals in intelligent tutoring dialogues. In: *New Directions for Intelligent Tutoring Systems*, (E. Costa, ed.), pp. 229-255, NATO ASI Series F, Vol. 91, Berlin: Springer-Verlag 1992
4. Brazdil, P. B.: Integration of knowledge in multi-agent environments. In: *New Directions for Intelligent Tutoring Systems*, (E. Costa, ed.), pp. 256-275, NATO ASI Series F, Vol. 91, Berlin: Springer-Verlag 1992
5. Brown, A.: Metacognition, executive control, self-regulation and other more mysterious mechanisms. In: *Metacognition, Motivation and Understanding*, (F. E. Weinert & R. H. Kluwe, eds.). Hillsdale, NJ: Lawrence Erlbaum Associates 1987
6. Carlson, L.: *Dialogue Games: an Approach to Discourse Analysis*. Dordrecht: Reidel 1983
7. Chi, M., Glaser, R. & Rees, E.: Expertise in problem solving. In: *Advances in the Psychology of Human Intelligence*, (R. Sternberg, ed.). Hillsdale, NJ: Lawrence Erlbaum Associates 1982
8. Cialdea, M., Micarelli, A., Nardi, D., Spohrer, J. & Aiello, L.: Meta-Level Reasoning for Diagnosis, ITS Technical Report DIS, University of Rome "La Sapienza" 1990
9. Clancey, W. J.: Qualitative student models. *Annual Reviews of Computer Science*, 1, pp. 381-450 (1986)
10. Cohen, P. R. & Levesque, H. J.: Rational interaction as the basis for communication. In: *Intentions in Communication*, (P. R. Cohen, J. Morgan & M. E. Pollack, eds.), pp. 221-256 Cambridge, MA: MIT Press 1990
11. Collins, A. & Brown, J. S.: The computer as a tool for learning through reflection. In: *Learning Issues for Intelligent Tutoring Systems*. (H. Mandl & A. Lesgold, eds.), New York, NY: Springer-Verlag 1988
12. Corno, L. & Snow, R.: Adapting teaching to individual differences among learners. In: *Handbook of Research on Teaching*, (M. Wittrock, ed.), pp. 605-629 New York, NY: Macmillan 1986
13. Costa, E., Duchenoy, S. & Kodratoff, Y.: A resolution based method for discovering students' misconceptions. In: *Artificial Intelligence and Human Learning* (J. A. Self, ed.), pp. 156-164 Chapman & Hall 1988.
14. Davis, E.: *Representations of Commonsense Knowledge*. Palo Alto, CA: Morgan Kaufmann 1990
15. Dewey, J.: *Experience and Education*. New York, NY: Collier 1990
16. Dillenbourg, P. & Self, J. A.: A Framework for Learner Modelling, Technical Report A1-49, Department of Computing, Lancaster University 1990
17. Dillenbourg, P. & Self, J. A.: Designing human-computer collaborative learning. To appear in: *Computer-Supported Collaborative Learning*, (C. O'Malley, ed.), NATO ASI Series F, Berlin: Springer-Verlag 1994
18. Donini, F. M., Lenzerini, M., Nardi, D., Pirri, F. & Schaerf, M.: Nonmonotonic reasoning, *Artificial Intelligence Review*, 4, pp. 163-210 (1990)
19. Durfee, E. H. & Lesser, V. R.: Negotiating task decomposition and allocation using partial global planning. In: *Distributed Artificial Intelligence II*, (L. Gasser & M. N. Huhns, eds.), pp. 229-244 San Mateo, CA: Morgan Kaufmann 1989
20. Elsom-Cook, M.: Guided discovery tutoring and bounded user modelling. In: *Artificial Intelligence and Human Learning*, (J. A. Self, ed.). pp. 165-178 London: Chapman & Hall 1988
21. Etherington, D. W.: Formalizing nonmonotonic reasoning systems, *Artificial Intelligence*, 31, pp. 41-85 (1987)
22. Evertsz, R.: Refining the student's procedural knowledge through abstract interpretations. In: *Proceedings of the 4th International Conference on Artificial Intelligence and Education*, Amsterdam, ND (D. Bierman, J. Breuker & J. Sandberg, eds.)., pp. 101-106. Amsterdam, ND: IOS 1989
23. Fagin, R. & Halpern, J. Y.: Belief, awareness, and limited reasoning, *Artificial Intelligence*, 34, pp. 39-76 (1987)
24. Foss, C. L.: Learning From Errors in Algebraland, Technical Report IR1-87-003, Institute for Research on Learning, Palo Alto 1987
25. Genesereth, M. R. & Nilsson, N. J.: *Logical Foundations of Artificial Intelligence*, Los Altos, CA: Morgan Kaufmann 1987
26. Greer, J. E. & McCalla, G. I.: A computational framework for granularity and its application to educational diagnosis. Proceedings of the 11th International Joint Conference on Artificial Intelligence, Detroit, MI, pp. 477-482, 1989
27. Greiner, R., Smith, B. A. & Wilkerson, R. W.: A correction to the algorithm in Reiter's theory of diagnosis, *Artificial Intelligence*, 41, pp. 79-88 (1989)
28. Hintikkca, J.: *Knowledge and Belief*. Ithaca: Cornell University Press 1962

29. Holland, J. H., Holyoak, K. J., Nisbett, R. E. & Thagard, P. R.: *Induction: Processes of Inference, Learning and Discovery.* Cambridge, MA: MIT Press 1986
30. Huang, X., McCalla, G. I., Greer, J. E. & Neufeld, E.: Revising deductive knowledge and stereotypical knowledge in a student model. In: *User Modeling and User-Adapted Interaction,* 1(1), pp. 87-116 (1991)
31. Ikeda, M., Mizoguchi, R. & Kakusho, O.: Design of a general framework for intelligent tutoring systems. *Proceedings of the 2nd International Conference on Intelligent Tutoring Systems,* Montreal, Quebec (C. Frasson, G. Gauthier & G. McCalla, eds.), pp. 433-450, Lecture Notes in Computer Science, Vol. 608, Berlin: Springer-Verlag 1992
32. Kass, R.: Building a user model implicitly from a cooperative advisory dialogue. Paper presented at the 2nd International Workshop on User Modelling, Honolulu, HI 1989
33. Kautz, H. A. & Allen, J. F.: Generalized plan recognition, Proceedings of AAAI 86, 32-37 (1986)
34. Konolige, K.: Reasoning by introspection. In: *MetaLevel Architectures and Reflection,* (P. Maes & D. Nardi, eds.). Amsterdam: North-Holland 1988
35. Langley, P. & Ohlsson, S.: Automated cognitive modelling. Proceedings of the National Conference on Artificial Intelligence, Austin, TX, pp. 193-197 1984
36. Levesque, H.: A Logic of Implicit and Explicit Belief. Fairchild FLAIR Technical Report No. 32, Palo Alto 1984
37. Levesque, H.: All I know: a study in autoepistemic logic, *Artificial Intelligence,* 42, pp. 263-309 (1990)
38. Maes, P. & Nardi, D., eds.: *Meta-Level Architectures and Reflection,* Amsterdam: North-Holland 1988
39. Martins, J. P. & Shapiro, S. C.: A model for belief revision, *Artificial Intelligence,* 35, pp. 25-79 (1988)
40. McCoy, K. F.: Generating context-sensitive responses to object-related misconceptions, *Artificial Intelligence,* 41, pp. 157-195 (1989)
41. Mizoguchi, R., Ikeda, M,. & Kakusho, O.: An innovative framework for intelligent tutoring systems. In: *Artificial Intelligence Tools in Education,* (P. Ercoli & R. Lewis, eds.), pp. 105-120. Amsterdam: North-Holland 1988
42. Moyse, R. & Elsom-Cook, M., eds.: *Knowledge Negotiation.* London: Academic Press 1992
43. Muggleton, S. & Feng, C.: Efficient induction of logic programs. Proceedings of the 1st Conference on Algorithmic Learning, Tokyo 1990
44. Murray, W. R.: Control for intelligent tutoring systems: a blackboard-based dynamic instructional planner, *AI Communications,* 2, pp. 41-57 (1989)
45. Payne, S. J. & Squibb, H. R.: Algebra mal-rules and cognitive accounts of error, *Cognitive Science,* 14, pp. 445-481 (1990)
46. Peachey, D. R. & McCalla, G. I.: Using planning techniques in intelligent tutoring systems, *International Journal of Man-Machine Studies,* 24, pp. 77-98 (1986)
47. Pollock, J. L.: *Contemporary Theories of Knowledge,* London: Hutchinson 1986
48. Poole, D. L.: A logical framework for default reasoning, *Artificial Intelligence,* 36, pp. 27-47 (1988)
49. Reichman, R.: *Getting Computers to Talk Like You and Me.* Cambridge, MA: MIT Press 1985
50. Reiser, B., Anderson, J. & Farrell, G.: Dynamic student modelling in an intelligent tutor for LISP programming. Proceedings of the 9th International Joint Conference on Artificial Intelligence, Los Angeles, CA, pp. 8-14 1985
51. Reiter, R.: A theory of diagnosis from first principles, *Artificial Intelligence,* 32, pp. 57-95 (1987)
52. Schoenfeld, A. H., ed.: *Cognitive Science and Mathematics Education,* Hillsdale, NJ: Lawrence Erlbaum Associates 1987
53. Self, J. A.: Computational viewpoints In: *Knowledge Negotiation,* (R. Moyse & M. Elsom-Cook, eds.), pp. 21-40 London: Academic Press 1992
54. Self, J. A.: Computational mathetics: the missing link in intelligent tutoring systems research. In: *New Directions in Intelligent Tutoring Systerns,* (E. Costa, ed.), pp. 38-56, NATO ASI Series F, Vol. 91, Berlin: Springer-Verlag 1992
55. Shute, V. J. & Glaser, R.: A large-scale evaluation of an intelligent discovery world: Smithtown. *Interactive Learning Environments,* 1, pp. 51-77 (1990)
56. Taylor, C. D. & Self, J. A.: Monitoring hypertext users, *Interacting with Computers,* 2, pp. 297-312 (1990)
57. van Arragon, P.: Modeling default reasoning using defaults,*User Modeling and User-Adapted Interaction.* 1(3), pp. 259-288 (1991)
58. VanLehn, K.: *Mind Bugs: the Origins of Procedural Misconceptions,* Cambridge, MA: MIT Press 1989
59. Vygotsky, L. S.: *Mind in Society.* Cambridge, MA: Harvard University Press 1978
60. Weyhrauch, R.: Prolegomena to a theory of mechanized formal reasoning, *Artificial Intelligence,* 13, pp. 133-170 (1980).
61. Wenger, E.: *Artificial Intelligence and Tutoring System.* Los Altos, CA: Morgan Kaufmann 1987
62. White, B. Y. & Frederiksen, J. R.: Causal model progressions as a foundation for intelligent learning environments, *Artificial Intelligence,* 42, pp. 99-157 (1990)

63. Wilks, Y. & Ballim, A.: Multiple agents and the heuristic ascription of beliefs. Proceedings of the 10th International Joint Conference on Artificial Intelligence, Milan, Italy, pp. 118-124, 1987
64. Woolf, B. P.: Representing complex knowledge in an intelligent tutor, *Computational Intelligence*, 3, pp. 45-55 (1987)
65. Young, R. M. & O'Shea, T.: Errors in children's subtraction, *Cognitive Science*, 5, pp. 153-177 (1981)

Part 5

Epilogue

# Re-Writing Cartesian Student Models[1]

Warren Sack[2], Elliot Soloway[3], and Peri Weingrad[3]

[2]MIT Media Laboratory, Cambridge, MA USA
[3]Highly-Interactive Computing Environments (HiCE) Group, Department of EECS, University of Michigan, Ann Arbor, MI USA

**Abstract**: A variety of research and technologies for programming education, in particular, and design, in general, has been produced by the laboratories of Elliot Soloway during the past decade: the Highly Interactive Computing Environments (HiCE) Group at the University of Michigan, Ann Arbor (1988 - present); and, the Cognition and Programming Project (CAPP) at Yale University (1981 - 1988). Central to the work produced by HiCE and CAPP have been discussions with and about students. Some of our efforts have gone into describing or modelling students. Some of our efforts have gone into getting students to describe themselves. These descriptions have been videotaped, catalogued, refined into computational cognitive model, transformed into academic papers on computers and education and been used, implicitly and explicitly, to build educational computer systems. Over the last ten years our models of students have moved away from mainstream artificial intelligence, objectivist formulations towards a more community-responsive, constructivist understanding of students. Starting with two issues that motivated many years of student modelling work -- "bugs" and "transfer" -- we tell our story of how, as our work with computers in the classroom has changed, our theories about student knowledge and learning have been forced to change and so, reflectively, has our understanding of "bugs", "transfer", and student models changed. Central to our story are philosophical discussions detailing our shift in position from objectivist to constructivist.

## 1 Introduction: Preunderstandings and the *Dasein* of our Current Research

Two recently published books surprised the computer science community: Lucy Suchman's *Plans and Situated Actions* and Terry Winograd and Fernando Flores' *Understanding*

---

[1]This chapter also appeared in the *Journal of Artificial Intelligence in Education*, 3(4), pp. 381, (1993). Reprinted with the permission of the Association for the Advancement of Computing in Education (AACE, P.O. Box 2966, Charolettesville, VA 22902 USA).

*Computers and Cognition.* These books are among the handful of sites where the terminology of phenomenology has been injected into the literature of computer science. The appearance of phenomenology *per se* was not the surprise. After all, esteemed phenomenologists like Hubert Dreyfus have been criticizing us, of the artificial intelligence community, for years. Winograd, Flores and Suchman do indeed provide critiques of computer science. However, two other aspects of their use of the phenomenologist's lexicon were the surprises.

First of all, distinctions made by phenomenologists (eg., the difference between the *ready-to-hand* and the *present-at-hand*) are now being championed as indispensable working assumptions for the design of practical computer systems. Using the considerations of phenomenology, Dreyfus told us what he thought impossible to do while the "computational phenomenologists" are now using the same kind of considerations to help sort out pipe dreams from practical projects.

Secondly, the appearance of terminology from phenomenology marks one of the first forays computer scientists have made out of the known territory of analytic philosophy into the wilderness of continental philosophy. This "jump across the Channel" is virtually unprecedented. While computer scientists have readily mined the ideas of Boole, Russell, Whitehead, Turing, even the young Wittgenstein, most of us have been oblivious to, if not outright contemptuous of, much of nineteenth and twentieth century, French and German philosophy that falls outside of what Winograd and Flores have termed the "rationalistic" tradition.

For many this "jump across the Channel" was shocking. At a departmental meeting at Yale, soon after the appearance of Winograd and Flores' book, one well known artificial-intelligence researcher hissed that the work was "traitorous." This remark throws a very harsh light on the issues at stake. For many, artificial intelligence (even computer science as a whole) is the "first son" of logical empiricism and continuing the family feuds is a matter of honor. Even though the centuries old clash between empiricists and rationalists is no longer the war to be fought, the English Channel is still a border to be defended.

It is perhaps ironic that we, the more pragmatic, didn't understand why the positivists were so upset. After all if the affairs these authors had with Heidegger bettered their work, allowed them to design better computer systems, then why be so hasty about the divorce proceedings?

Of course if we'd been prescient enough to heed the ideologues we might have been able to nip these diseased, philosophical notions in the bud. As it is, the continental explosion has erupted even within our own familiar group: computers and education. The situated learning theorists have brought the seeds home with them. At first we were concerned that our turf was contaminated, but, as we continue to till, we now realize how much more fertile our field has become. By concentrating on the production of practical systems for education we have found that "cavorting with the enemy" can be both constructiv(ist) and challenging.

In what follows we trace the kicking and screaming we did to cross the Channel and meet the other: to rethink our work from a more continental perspective. Our discussion is focussed around the thinking we have done over the past decade on "student modelling", "bugs", and "transfer."

In retrospect one can identify a sort of cartesian split in our thinking about computers and education: we have tended to separate the issues of *conception* and *use* of knowledge. With respect to mis-*conceptions* we have been concerned with student errors or "bugs." Differences between expert and student understanding have been termed "bugs" and it has been our claim that one can identify misconceptions that underlie students' bugs.

On the other hand, our concerns with students' *use* of knowledge have revolved around our interest in "transfer." In particular we have been curious to discover whether in learning computer programming students learn skills applicable to related types of problem solving (like the solution of algebra word problems) [61].

Of course, bifurcations like concept/use and bugs/transfer are exactly the no-no that Wittgenstein, in his later years, worked so hard to tear down in his *Philosophical Investigations*. The meaning of a word is exactly its use. This sort of insight is what J. L. Austin used in the 1950's to explode the logical positivist's definition of meaning. We have had to go through a similar sort of violence to learn how to design better computer systems for education. In our case, we have had to realize that the significance of a bug is the role it plays in facilitating or preventing transfer.

The path we have followed is somewhat different than the one that has been described by some of the situated learning theorists (eg.[10, 15]) and which might be described as more directly influenced by the philosophies of phenomenology. In contrast to these philosophies, we are working towards a *constructivist* understanding of knowledge, power, and community in order to re-examine our previous work and describe our more recent research on the design of educational, computer technologies.

Constructivism, especially as it has been employed in the study of the history of science (eg.[43]) and education (eg.[48]) contrasts the notion of socially constructed meanings with the objectivist preference that meaning exists independently of the act of interpretation. The constructivist view is that knowledge and meaning are created by a (perhaps) identifiable group of people for strategic, practical purposes. In other words, knowledge does not have some sort of independent existence that allows it to be "discovered" or "communicated." Instead, activities of knowledge production (eg. science) and reproduction (eg. education) are about convincing, recruiting and enculturing others. In short, a constructivist analysis of knowledge foregrounds *rhetoric*: the powers of persuasion and the difficulties of dispute.

Transfer, from a constructivist point of view, is the appropriation of knowledge or technology from one community for use in another. This understanding of transfer allows us not only to rethink student errors, or bugs, but can also be applied recursively to re-examine our own research agenda. Adopting a constructivist view of the technologies that we build and test has allowed us to more clearly see how our technologies fit into the larger, national and international debates about education. It can be argued that our previous work on student models, transfer, and bugs contributed towards an educational technology that is complicit with a reactionary, educational philosophy that, in the United States, is known as the back-to-basics movement [6, 35]. In fact, we will point out how back-to-basics adherents have explicitly appropriated artificial intelligence research to argue for their educational reforms.

The point of this paper, however, is not simply to point out how our previous work on "bugs" and "transfer" can be appropriated for educational programmes that we do not support.[2] Rather, our point in this paper is to emphasis the central role that knowledge of community should play in the development of educational technologies. Currently, we are trying to consciously support particular educational communities by working closely with teachers and students in those communities. For example, we have a close relationship with and "field test" our educational software in a local high school in Ann Arbor, Michigan. We are engaged in providing the means and media through which community members can communicate and express themselves to one another. Specifically, we are engaged in the production of tools that students can use to create *transitional objects*, artifacts created by students and used by students to represent themselves to a larger community. Furthermore, we are trying to rethink our older ITS work to see if we can reappropriate it to make it serve the needs of our community high school, rather than serving the needs of the back-to-basics faction. In this paper we will present a constructivist exegesis of our previous work on "bugs", "transfer"; and "student models." In so doing we hope to illustrate some of the differences between our previous work and our newer work on educational technologies.

## 2  Bug Catalogs and Mechanisms of Critique

When we started cataloging students' programming errors our purpose was to construct a library of non-syntactic bugs that could be used by a critiquing system [38, 62]. The library was to be articulated as a collection of patterns that could be matched against student programs. Each bug pattern had an English language description attached to it such that, if a pattern was matched by the critiquing system against a student's program, the attached description could be output to the student.

---

[2]See [46] for an interesting discussion on how artificial intelligence (AI) technologies for education serve, or are appropriated to serve, the political purposes of various organizations, especially the military.

Contemporary software engineering practice encouraged bug categorization according to textual differences. Many of our colleagues in software engineering were (and still are) categorizing programming errors according to surface features (eg., missing parentheses, misspelled variable names, misplaced line of code, etc.).

Research done by Rich, Waters and Shrobe at MIT [51] showed how programs could be profitably viewed as sets of textually interwoven, functional units "glued" together with control and data flow connections. Rich, Waters and Shrobe called their functional units "plans." Viewing programs as plan composites seemed vastly superior to descriptions that could only appeal to a syntactic structure.

## 3 The Cognitive Connection

Furthermore, the name "plans" connoted relationships to research being done in other domains by artificial intelligence researchers. Specifically, we saw connections to work being done on the mechanical "understanding" of intention in stories, texts and conversations (eg. [1, 56]). In the view of many researchers the intentions of a speaker/author could be recovered by reconstructing the underlying plans and goals that were implied by the utterance/text.

The combined interest in goals, plans, intentions and programs produced the hypothesis that student programs should be parsed into sets of *intended* goals and plans. Under this model, bugs are differences between the structure and functionality of the student's code and the structure and functionality of the intended goals and plans [39].

Our colleagues, Jim Spohrer [63] and Jeffrey Bonar [7] refined this notion of bug as difference between the intended and the implemented. They each offer a different explanation of the origin of bugs. Both of their explanations propose a set of knowledge structures (plans and goals) coupled with a problem solving method. Both propose a structure of knowledge which mates two predominant families: (1) non-programming goals and plans to describe step-by-step procedures, and (2) programming goals and plans to describe the implementation of step-by-step procedures. Programming errors are due to either the use of non-programming knowledge for programming tasks or translation difficulties from non-programming to programming structures.

Spohrer's and Bonar's digenistic models of knowledge exclude a more richly textured polygenistic understanding of students. One might counter that the exclusions of the models could be ameliorated by grafting more types of knowledges onto their non-programming categories enriching the models' breadth, but not diminishing their explanatory powers: translation from non-programming to programming knowledge is a complex and difficult task because of the distinctive nature of the programming media. Both models enriched our understanding of intended programming goals and plans by articulating their relationships to some non-programming goals and plans.

## 4   Educational Impact

By encoding programming knowledge as patterns we have developed a practical technology to critique student programs. Each pattern can be matched against parts of a student program. To evaluate the pedagogical effects of a critiquing system based upon this technology, PROUST [38], we found it convenient to divide the curriculum into units similar to our patterns. In this way we were able to compare

- the contents of our mechanical critic's knowledge base (the patterns) with
- parts of the homework done by students (pieces of the student programs that could be matched against the patterns) with
- sections of the final examination (parts of the exam that were analogous to pieces of code that we had seen students generate in the course of their homework).

By tracing these pattern-homework-test connections one can transform the question "Is PROUST educationally effective?" into the question "If, during homework, a student sees and understands the message associated with a given pattern in PROUST will that student do better on parts of the final exam that might also be matched by the given pattern?" In 1986, we did a transformation of this sort in our evaluation of PROUST [55] and the answer was yes, students who received good advice from PROUST might be said to have done somewhat better on the final exam. John Anderson has done much more elegant sorts of studies of the same nature in which he shows how learning specific programming skills can be correlated to learning particular sets of patterns (production rules) encoded in his system [2].

## 5   Schemas as Canon

One might base a programming curriculum on a set of knowledge base patterns (goals and plans) from PROUST, or one of our other critiquing programs. We have argued this point elsewhere [58].

Cognitive scientific studies conducted across a large number of domains have been done to show the key role that schemata play in expert thinking (chess [19]; physics [42]; programming [59]; etc.) It would be consistent with the findings of cognitive science and artificial intelligence to make schema acquisition the aim of education. A national education reform has been proposed on this insight. Basing his case on recent work in cognitive science and artificial intelligence, E. D. Hirsch makes this point in his book *Cultural Literacy: What Every American needs to know.*

> Good reading, like good chess, requires the rapid deployment of schemata that have already been acquired and do not have to be worked out on the spot. Good readers, like good chess players, quickly recognize typical patterns,... ([35], p. 63)

Hirsch goes on to outline a set of schemata that he and his colleagues think "every American needs to know." The philosophy of education embodied in our previous models of programming knowledge, bugs and mechanical analysis of student programs is in concordance with E. D. Hirsch's proposal at an epistemological level. Seen from Hirsch's perspective our efforts to articulate a database of non-programming and programming knowledge was essentially an effort aimed at the establishment of a canon. The evaluations we have done can be seen as investigations to see if our defined canon survived intact into the students' texts/programs.

## 6 The Process Bid

The notion of "process" has been used to differentiate back-to-basics proposals for education (like Hirsch's) from the education proposals generated by us and others within the computer and cognitive science communities. The argument is made that computers can present not only descriptive information, but also information about process and usually runs as follows:

> With a computational medium it becomes possible, and often, easy, to capture directly the processes by which a novice or an expert carries out a complex task. Properly abstracted and structured, this process trace or audit trail can become a useful object of study for students who are trying to learn how to improve their performance on a task. ([16], p.1)

Ironically, process becomes subordinated to a *description* of process once a trace has been "properly abstracted." Our models of student programming knowledge and misconceptions have been characterized by a virtual explosion of neologisms created to describe the processes of program generation. Explaining a process model's contents to students (and colleagues for that matter) forces one to define the neologisms which, via a sort of dialectic circle, returns us to face the problems of exporting a canon of knowledge to a student body.

## 7 Distinguishing Process from Description of Process

> The psychologist or educator who formulates pedagogical theory without regard to the political, economic, and social setting of the educational process courts triviality and merits being ignored in the community and in the classroom. ([12], p. 115)

Precollegians often ask "Why do we have to learn this?" and "Will this be on the test?" These are healthy questions. They are attempts to connect classroom activity to larger personal goals and cultural aims. Information -- texts, programs, schemas, "process traces", etc. -- does not have invariant value outside of specific social, political, or economic contexts.

Winograd and Flores compare artificial intelligence work on natural language understanding with the opposing viewpoint:

> For the objectivist school of hermeneutics [to which, among others, Emilio Betti and E. D. Hirsch belong], the text must have a meaning that exists independently of the act of interpretation. The goal of a hermeneutic theory (a theory of interpretation) is to develop methods by which we rid ourselves of all prejudices and produce an objective analysis of what is really there. The ideal is to completely 'decontextualize' the text. ([75], p. 28)

Up until very recently, cognitive science and artificial intelligence work on learning, understanding and problem solving has been predominantly concerned with the performance of individuals "decontextualized" from their friends, colleagues, and, in general, the social fabric that surrounds and contains them. The only reason that Simon's ant had to wander is because it lost the trail and its companions [57].

Key to any philosophy of education superior to the transmission paradigm implicit in Hirsch's proposal is a rich understanding of the processes of learning and interpretation that situates the learner in a larger social and political context. Perhaps John Seely Brown says it best:

> . . . learning is at core a process of enculturation, of entry into a culture or community of practice. ([11], p. 277)

Thus we might say that the stronger definition of process that we need in order to distinguish a process-oriented education from an education characterized by the memorization of vast libraries of schemata is a definition of *process as culturally situated praxis* [8, 44].

Responding to the insights of learning as enculturation and process as praxis is problematic. Brown, Collins and their colleagues have proposed reformulating the teacher/student relationship into one of master/apprentice [10]. Papert has a vision of students as practicing engineers and mathematicians [48]. Investigations like the Acid Rain Project [67] allow students to become real scientists. If these sorts of efforts are to become more than simply resurrections of Dewey's programme to make schools into "embryonic societies" [36] students must be trusted with real projects and real tools instead of just toys.

## 8  Non-Objectivist Student Models

Rearticulating the process of learning as enculturation pushes one to a new understanding of the roles of student and teacher. The "new" teacher/student roles discussed by Brown, Collins and Papert are indicative of a non-objectivist way of defining students.

Objectivist student models are those models which attempt to define, what Wenger [72] has termed, *knowledge states*. With an objectivist methodology, a student is characterized according to a canon of knowledge (of rules, procedures, schemas, etc.) that either the student is missing (eg., *overlay* models), possesses, or possesses in partial or corrupted form (eg., *malrule* models). An objectivist student model is defined around a *canon*.

In contrast, a non-objectivist student model is defined around a *community*. Bugs in an objectivist student model are deviations from the expected answers. Bugs in a non-objectivist student model are, instead, deviations from the community and are, thus, issues of debate and intrinsic interest to the parties involved the community. Transfer;, from an objectivist perspective, is the correct application of knowledge -- acquired in one domain -- to the solution of a problem -- from another domain. Transfer, from a non-objectivist perspective, is the use of knowledge -- of one community -- to address the concerns -- of another community. The shift, from an objectivist point of view to a non-objectivist point of view, is primarily a shift of attention away from an understanding of knowledge as an inert, acquirable commodity towards an understanding of knowledge as the ongoing concerns of a given community.

By adopting the perspective that learning is a process of enculturation, we are forced to pay close attention to issues of culture, community and the social, political, and economic roles played by community members. Consequently, it is no surprise that Brown, Collins and Papert have all described new roles for students: non-objectivist student models are defined by the social, political, and economic roles that students will play within their communities.

## 9 Sociolinguistics : Linguistics :: Non-Objectivist Students Models : Student Models

> The key to a rational concept of language change is the possibility of describing orderly
> differentiation in a language serving a community. ([41], p. xv)

To better envision what sort of impact a community-oriented approach will have on the field of student modelling one can look at how an objectivist to non-objectivist shift in perspective has affected other fields. For example, twenty years ago William Labov started to look at the social, political, and economic causes of language change. His investigations into the community basis for linguistic process provided him with concrete explanations where other linguistics could only formulate guesses as sets of abstract rules.

> By studying the frequency and distribution of phonetic variants of /ay/ and /aw/ in the
> several regions, age levels, occupational and ethnic groups with the island [Manhattan],
> it will be possible to reconstruct the recent history of this sound change; by correlating
> the complex linguistic pattern with parallel differences in social structure, it will be

possible to isolate the social factors which bear directly upon the linguistic process. ([41], p. 1)

Labov's work in sociolinguistics explains the cultural causes of particular differences in linguistic knowledge. Similarly, to pursue research based upon an understanding of learning as enculturation, it will be necessary to focus on the sociologics of bugs and transfer.

# 10  Constructivism

Our newer educational software is based upon a non-objectivist, constructivist understanding of knowledge creation and sharing which gives central focus to learning as enculturation and process as praxis. By adopting a constructivist design philosophy we have been forced to rethink our original, objectivist-inspired ideas of who and what students are. We are rethinking the ontology of *student models* and by so doing we are also reevaluating our preconceptions of *model students*.

Perhaps it would be helpful to clarify what we mean by constructivism by presenting, here, a short description of its origins. Phenomenology and constructivism are both influenced by continental, or non-analytic philosophies, but they are two distinctly different intellectual traditions. One might trace contemporary constructivism back to the Russian constructivism of the early part of the twentieth century [4]. Russian constructivists were active in a number of fields including art, architecture, literature and the nascent -- at that time -- area of industrial design. The Russian constructivists were not only concerned with the technical nature of their work; much of their focus was devoted to articulating the ways and means by which the products of art, science and technology can impact social, political, and economic dimensions of society [45].

An aestheticized version of constructivism was exported to Western Europe at the beginning of the 1920s when the constructivists lost favor with the Soviet government and many of their leaders emigrated to join various artistic communities in the West like the Bauhaus in Weimar, the De Stijl group in Amsterdam, the Circle Group in London, and the Abstraction-Creation movement in Paris [14].

However, perhaps the most direct link between the Russian constructivists and contemporary, computer technologists who call themselves constructivists can be found by examining the influence that friends and collaborators of the constructivists, Russian formalist critics, had on French-speaking structuralists like Roland Barthes, Jacques Lacan, Jean Piaget, and Claude Lévi-Strauss [4, 37].

... part of the structuralist approaches that emerged in the 1960s, mainly in France, are rooted in so-called Russian formalism [23]. The Russian formalists, who started publishing around the time of the Russian Revolution, counted among them important linguists, such as Roman Jakobson, and literary theorists, such as Sklovskij, Tynjanov, and Eixenbaum. ([71], p 18).

The Russian formalists were introduced to French structuralists [33] by, among others, Tsvetan Todorov with his translation of some of their works into French [68], and through the work of the Russian emigrant Julia Kristeva [28].

Structuralists, like Jean Piaget, from time-to-time, used the term constructivism in explaining their work on learning and education [32]. One could say that it is through the former students and junior colleagues of French structuralists that constructivism has made its way into contemporary design philosophies for educational, computer technologies. For example, Sherry Turkle [69, 70] worked with Jacques Lacan; Seymour Papert [48] worked with Jean Piaget.

It is also the case that constructivist ideas, in the form of social constructivist studies of science and technology (eg., [5, 43]), have had an influence on other areas of computer science, and specifically, on the field of distributed artificial intelligence (DAI) (see [27, 34]). A genealogy that could bridge the work of the Russian constructivists with contemporary work in DAI would, of course, include a slightly different cast of characters than the cursory one we have described for constructivist, computer technologies for education.

Not all of our colleagues who design constructivist technologies for education would draw out a constructivist genealogy that reaches as far back into the past as the one we have sketched here. (For example, most of the contributors to a recent special issue of the journal *Educational Technology* [22] go back only as far as the work of Jean Piaget.) However, we share with our constructivist colleagues a belief that it is important to investigate how technology and society mutually impact one another and a recurrent fascination with the tropes of "construction" and "structure" to explain the constitutions and histories of the psychologies of individuals and the sociologies of institutions and technologies.

One might be tempted to equate constructivism to the sorts of technologies produced by constructivists. For example, researchers in intelligent tutoring systems (ITS) have often made the mistake of equating constructivist work and computer-based microworlds (like the LOGO programming environment). However, constructivism is more than just microworlds, it is also a discursive practice that provides the means through which one can describe the social, political and economic circumstances that surround and give meaning to a given piece of educational technology.

## 11 The Debatable Nature of Bugs

For example, our constructivist emphasis takes us away from our original concerns of defining bugs as differences between the intended and actual code. Of course, we still recognize that such discrepancies exist. However, the primary concern now becomes the differentiation of *stated* intentions and actual code. We adopt the concerns of the everyday world of software engineering where what is of issue is whether the code meets the specifications. Students must not only write workable code, but also author convincing explanations to show that the code does indeed meet the specifications.

We want to understand bugs as disputes: contestable differences between coded implementation and specified design. Pedagogically what we want to do is make bugs a point of debate that forces students to expand their explanations and, possibly, change their mechanisms.

Consequently, "bugs" for constructivists are a very different species than "bugs" for rationalistic, objectivist student model builders. Several years ago, while we were building PROUST, we made large catalogs of bugs we observed in student programs, gave them very long and complicated names, and then organized them into taxonomies [40, 64]. Unfortunately, these lists of bugs with formal identities never made it out of the laboratory and into the classroom because our taxonomies were nothing that either teachers or students were interested in arguing about. Our bug catalogs were mainly of interest to other specialists in our immediate research community because, in the rationalistic, objectivist tradition, we could argue (in that community) that the bugs catalogued did, actually exist "in the heads of students."

However, from our present constructivist perspective we would argue that our old bug taxonomies are of no educational interest. Nevertheless, any bug that we observed *could* be of interest to the extent that it constitutes a disputable difference between the student's concerns and the concerns of a larger community (usually "represented" by a teacher). From this point of view, a bug is what separates a student from a larger community, or, more profoundly, what separates a student's community from another community.

Interestingly, this is exactly the effect that bugs have on a student's life even in an educational setting where bugs are assumed to be "in the student's head." For example, a bug, or mistake, on a standardized test can cause a student to be refused admission to a university, thus, effectively, barring the student from the university community. Some standardized tests have been found to effectively discriminate against women and people of color [47]. Mistakes or bugs on tests and problem sets are of interest to the extent that they reveal the cultural imperatives of the test makers and the test takers.

A constructivist technology of education has to be built with the understanding that bugs are debatable entities because they reflect individual and/or cultural differences between the teacher and the student. Indeed, one can accept this constructivist assumption without, necessarily, falling into the Relativist's trap of thinking that there is no difference between "right" and "wrong." For example, in the "real" world it is mostly the "customer" (or rather the person with money) that is "right." Thus, it is usually the case that students of well financed school districts make fewer bugs on, for example, standardized tests than students from poor school districts [18].

## 12 Discipline and Disciplines

For years educators have complained about the disjunction which exists between school and the "real" world (eg. [50]). However, to see this as a problem that can be isolated to the schools is to overlook the cultural values which encourage specialization (and thus isolation) in many non-educational institutions as well. Several educationalists have pointed out that twentieth century American schools are based upon a nineteenth century industrial model (eg. [24]). Taylorist management practices like centralized, hierarchical management; a rigid sense of time; strict division of work into simple, repetitive tasks; and an overvaluation of the virtues of standardization are all organizing principles that are alive and well in the late-twentieth century school systems of the United States.

In his review of discipline and disciplines (two concepts central to the structure of public education) Michel Foucault [25] points out that, in fact, strict separation of the school from the "real" world, one subject matter from another, and the regimentation of students' time and assigned tasks all had their genesis in training techniques for religious orders and the military of the seventeenth and eighteenth centuries.

Thus, the practices of dividing disciplines one from another (thereby discouraging "transfer") and separating students from the "real" world have historically deep roots in Western culture. They are not recent problems of the current educational system. Indeed, these sorts of separations now seem almost a matter of common sense. Mixing disciplines by, for example, testing for knowledge of chemistry on an English exam sounds nonsensical, or, at the very least, unfair to students. In situations that count (eg., testing situations) students are encouraged, and rewarded, to forget everything except that which their instructor has told them within the past few days or weeks [52].

## 13 Technologies for the Construction of Artifacts and Explanations

Obviously, "fixing" education, making school activities more relevant to the larger communities from which students come, is not going to be achieved simply by adding a few well designed computer programs into the existing educational system. However, one can design software that *facilitates* the "fixing" of schools; that encourages students to produce inter- or multi-disciplinary artifacts: artifacts like films, essays, architectural designs, and software.

Of primary concern to us is the means by which students can be supported to design and author artifacts and explanations that will have political, social and economic currency in the communities that they currently participate in (eg. the school) and in communities that they may soon want to be a part of (eg. the profession of software engineering). In order to accommodate our new understanding of bugs as points of debate we are building educational technologies which engender and support debate, argumentation and explanation. These technologies are constructivist to the extent that they are used by teachers and students to cross academic, disciplinary boundaries and produce socially relevant artifacts.

Over the last four years, the Highly Interactive Computing Environments (HiCE) research group at the University of Michigan, Ann Arbor has built and classroom tested (in both the high school and the university) a range of computer aided design (CAD) systems that were designed expressly to support students and teachers in both the learning and the doing of design in a variety of domains [60].

- *GPC editor* (Goal, Plan, Code Editor) supports students learning to design software.
- *Emile* ; is an adaptable support environment for developing Hypercard scripts [29].
- *MediaText* supports students as they compose documents that include video, audio, graphics, animations, and other media, as well as text [9].
- *IByD* (Instruction By Design) supports students (teachers-in-training) learning unit and lesson design.
- *PSE* (A Project-Support Environment for Teachers) is a multimedia learning environment that will assist teachers in making the transition to the new form of teaching demanded by a project-based curriculum.
- *ProgramCritic* is an intelligent tutoring system for novice programmers [53, 54].

The sampling of systems listed above is divided into two sorts: (1) tools for students, and (2) tools for teachers. All of the systems are designed for particular communities. Each of the systems provides a medium within which users can build some sort of artifact (program, video, etc.) that they can exchange or share with their colleagues.

# 14 Tools for Students

For example, the GPCeditor allows students to build libraries of Pascal programs and program components (ie., programming "plans"). When students exchange plans with one another, plan names acquire the status of a more abstract, descriptive, documentation language for the Pascal programs. Students begin to talk to one another about their programs in terms of plans and plan compositions. Ideally, these sort of descriptions will "scale up" to the demands of describing software in a professional environment. Indeed, our colleague, Luke Hohmann, is currently building an "industrial-strength" version of the GPCeditor for professional programmers. In short, the GPCeditor project is aimed at strengthening two dimensions of communication in the community of programmers: students-to-students and students-to-professionals.

The Emile and MediaText systems are strengthening interdisciplinary ties. Within these environments students author multimedia documents that combine text, films, pictures and graphics. Both of these systems have been used in, for example, high school physics classes. Multimedia documents composed by students using these environments constitute a new sort of interdisciplinary genre for expression comparable to the *essay* that was perfected by intellectuals in the eighteenth century and that is a genre still used today by many academics in the humanities. The French etymological root of *essay* ties it to the process of *trying something out*. Similarly, multimedia documents are typically a place where new ideas and combinations of physics, software design, and graphical illustration are tried out by students.

Using Emile a student can do things like write a HyperCard program to present an animated movie of projectile motion thus combining together their knowledge of software design, graphics, film production, and physics all in one project. Projects like these obviously bridge the gaps that exist between the subject matter of different fields like physics and film studies. However, we are finding that multimedia documents constructed in the Emile and MediaText environments also build new bridges of communication between teachers and students. One student used a short, animated movie to illustrate his discussion of kinetic energy. However, the movie that the student produced was a movie showing "impossible physics." Of course the "real" literature of physics abounds with examples of physicists trying out "impossible" worlds. But hypotheticals of this sort are usually out-of-bounds for high school physics students engaged in grinding through equations to solve problem sets. At first, the student's physics teacher thought the movie clip was just a reflection of the student's misconceptions. However, the "buggy" movie opened up a dialog between the teacher and the student that allowed the teacher to see the students "bugs" as interesting contributions.

This sort of new understanding between a teacher and student is the first step towards new forms of student assessment. By providing students with the means to produce interesting, multimedia documents we are engineering some of the technological underpinnings necessary to support what is beginning to be known as "portfolio analysis" [49]. Students can be evaluated according to a week's, a month's, or a semester's worth of work constituted as a collection of multimedia documents and assembled together in a portfolio.

## 15  Tools for Teachers

HiCE has produced the IByD system that provides teachers-in-training at a college of education with an environment in which they can plan out curricula and lesson sequences. IByD gives teachers-in-training a medium in which they can exchange lesson designs with one another (by storing and retrieving lessons from an electronic library). The system also has facilitated the merging of a "teaching methods" class with various "subject" classes required of the teachers-in-training (eg., classes on the subject matter of elementary school science) because the IByD design environment makes it easy for the teachers-in-training to plan out detailed subject-matter-specific, lesson plans.

On the level of supporting the learning of the teachers-in-training IByD is a successful, constructivist environment. However, paradoxically, the skill that the teachers-in-training learn through using IByD, lesson planning, is not necessarily a constructivist skill.

One can, however, create a constructivist learning environment for teachers-in-training that encourages the teachers to learn skills for creating constructivist environments for their own students. PSE is a multimedia learning environment for project-based teaching; it provides teachers-in-training with tools for constructing and evaluating videotaped portfolios of themselves and others in the classroom. PSE is intended to help teachers communicate with one another about, and develop evaluation procedures for, project-based curricula.

IByD allows teachers to create and share lesson plans. PSE allows them to share multimedia-based, video portfolios with one another. What is crucial to these constructivist learning environments is that they provide a group of people a medium in which information can be shared that would not normally be shared.

It is even possible to make a "knowledge base" a medium of exchange. In work that we are doing with colleagues at the Educational Testing Service (Princeton, NJ) we have developed an intelligent tutoring system (ITS) for teaching novices to computer program, the ProgramCritic. We have also developed a tool which automates some of the work necessary to create new knowledge bases for the tutoring system; this tool, the ExampleCompiler, allows a user to generate a new rule for a knowledge base by pointing and clicking a mouse [54]. Consequently, we hope to give teachers and students the means to create and modify knowledge bases so that they can be used as a medium to exchange ideas about program construction and analysis. This use of knowledge bases and ITSs as vehicles of communication, and not as delivery devices, effectively appropriates ITS research for constructivist purposes in a manner parallel to the way Idit Harel [32] used computer aided instruction (CAI) for constructivist purposes.

Harel asked her students, not to use CAI software, but rather to design and implement CAI software for other students. Harel's students engaged in interdisciplinary work combining knowledge of Logo programming, fractions and pedagogy to create their CAI systems. Thus, the students' CAI programs were objects to think with that challenged classroom discipline and disciplines. Hopefully, the knowledge bases created by students and teachers with the ExampleCompiler will be equally challenging.

# 16 The Transitional Object

Each of our systems provides facilities for constructing, annotating and archiving artifacts that are of potential interest beyond the school walls. The "currency" of an artifact is of vital interest. Seymour Papert has developed a notion of *transitional object* [48] by which he means an object under the student's control (an object adapted, appropriated or created by the student) that can be used by the student to become interested in, think though, or reinvent the ideas of a domain.[3] Papert says that, in his own childhood, it was gears which served as a transitional object that opened his mind to the ideas of mathematics [48]. In this manner, the artifacts producible with the GPCeditor, MediaText, and Emile can act as transitional objects for students.

However, Papert's notion of a transitional object is not very well thought out from a constructivist point of view. The "ideas of mathematics" are not simply "there" to be found by students with an appropriate object. While Papert says that a transitional object carries math into the mind we would say the transitional object provides the means by which the student can be carried into the community of mathematicians. By inventing an object that has currency with, for example, mathematicians, students shape, or model, their own image in a larger community that extends beyond the boundaries of the classroom. In other words, transitional objects are self-articulated models of students insofar as they reflect the image of the student/creators.

# 17 The Question of Transfer

Transitional objects invert the "question" of *transfer*. No longer is it necessarily of interest to determine whether or not students can solve problems in two arbitrary domains (like programming and algebra). Instead, the question of transfer is this: Which domains (ie., communities of knowledge) are bridged by a student's transitional object? If it is deemed necessary for a student to produce artifacts that are equivaluable in two particular domains (eg., the communities of the algebraist and the computer programmer), then producing transfer can be pursued using a straightforward pedagogical programme: introduce the student the the world of the algebraists and their artifacts (equations, proofs, etc.), introduce the student to the world of the computer programmer (and software, machines, etc.) and then introduce the student to

---

[3] Actually, Papert did not develop the notion of transitional object. He has appropriated this notion from an area of psychoanalytic theory known as object-relations theory (see, especially, [73, 74]). In comparison to Papert, Sherry Turkle has a much more sophisticated articulation of the role of transitional objects in computer science learning (see [70]). Both Turkle and Evelyn Fox Keller, among others, explain the important function that transitional objects serve in both science education and scientific research.

the concerns of those people who feel that the worlds of the algebraist and the computer programmer overlap to a significant and arguable degree. If the student becomes engaged with the issues of the overlap, then "transfer" should occur. Unfortunately, most work in cognitive science that has focussed on the elusive "transfer" effect has used extraordinarily boring and irrelevant problems as source material for discussion with students. No wonder transfer is so rare in the literature of psychology!

## 18 Project-Oriented Education in the Classroom

Project-oriented or transitional-object-centered education is difficult to facilitate in a standard classroom. Students and teachers acquire new roles in their efforts to understand one another and their respective communities. For example, Brown and Collins point out that a project-oriented education can engender a master/apprenticeship relationship between teacher and student. We believe that this is just one of many possible new relationships that a project-oriented education can encourage. The transitional objects shared between students and teachers can constitute a two-way, give-and-take relationship as opposed to a one-way education that Paolo Freire calls a "banking education": teachers make "deposits" which students must receive, file, store, and repeat.

Liberating education consists in acts of cognition, not transferrals of information. It is a learning situation in which the cognizable [ie., transitional] object (far from being the end of the cognitive act) intermediates the cognitive actors -- teacher on the one hand and students on the other. Accordingly, the practice of problem-posing education [what we have been calling a "project-oriented education"] entails at the outset that the teacher-student contradiction be resolved. Dialogical relations -- indispensable to the capacity of cognitive actors to cooperate in perceiving the same cognizable object -- are otherwise impossible.

Indeed, problem-posing education, which breaks with the vertical patterns characteristic of banking education, can fulfill its function as the practice of freedom only if it can overcome the above contradiction. Through dialogue, the teacher-of-the-students and the students-of-the-teacher cease to exist and a new term emerges: teacher-student with student-teachers. The teacher is no longer merely the-one-who-teaches, but one who is himself [sic] taught in dialogue with the students, who in turn while being taught also teach. They become jointly responsible for a process in which all grow. In this process, arguments based upon "authority" are no longer valid; ...([26], p. 67)

While Freire's analysis may sound too idealistic to many it is useful in that it makes clear a startlingly different student model than the models we have been developing in mainstream

American education. It is also useful to keep in mind that Freire's model works: he has taught adult literacy for decades and is currently minister of education for one of Brazil's largest metropolises, Rio de Janeiro.

## 19  Conclusion

Over the last ten years our models of students have moved away from mainstream artificial intelligence, objectivist formulations towards a more community-responsive, constructivist understanding of students. For years we and our colleagues compiled catalogues of student errors, built computational models of students and did studies to see if knowledge "transferred" from one domain to the next: all of these endeavors were based upon an understanding of student knowledge as an reified, pseudo-economic commodity. Discourse about knowledge acquisition, transfer, and bugs is firmly grounded in objectivist/rationalistic traditions which are overly Materialist (and matériel-ist too).

Change came when we tried to employ our intelligent tutoring systems in real classrooms. It was then that we realized the overwhelming weight of the social dynamics of the school and larger community. Driven to rethink our original conception of students and learning we have accepted a position which might be summarized as *learning is a process of enculturation.* Seen in this light, "bugs" and "transfer" are issues of enculturation and thus *community.* Student models are also issues of community: a given student model is, in a certain sense, a record or an example of a student's reputation and abilities in a given community; student models, in general, are the sorts of values and attributes that one might impose on the ideal, or *model* student.

Although we understand and respect the difficulties involved in student evaluation, we would like to see that students are able to model, or rather, represent, themselves in an uncompromised fashion. Our newer educational systems (eg., GPCeditor, MediaText, and Emile) are built to allow students to work on projects which are more ambitious (and so, hopefully, more representative of students) than standard classroom exercises. We realize that our wishes to support a constructivist technology for education may simply look like another effort to resurrect some old ideas by Dewey. However, we think our efforts are different: we aren't so much trying to recreate a micro-society within the school that reflects what is outside, but, rather we want to put powerful, real-world tools in the hands of students so that they might have the opportunity to create transitional objects which will serve to introduce them to the society-at-large. Transitional objects are students' models of themselves that can be used to represent them in communities beyond the walls of the school.

In short, instead of trying to model students, we are now trying to provide students with the tools, facilities and communities they need to support the development of models for their own uses.

374

# Acknowledgements

We would like to thank Mark Guzdial, Jennifer González, Sherry Turkle, Edith Ackermann, Scott Mobley, Gordon McCalla, Jim Greer, and the anonymous reviewers for reading and commenting on earlier versions of this article.

# References

1. Allen, J.: Recognizing intentions from natural language utterances. In: *Computational Models of Discourse*. (J. M. Brady & R. C. Berwick, eds.), pp. 107-166, Cambridge, MA: MIT Press 1983
2. Anderson, J.: Production systems, leaning and tutoring. In: *Production System Model of Learning and Development*. (D. Klahr, P. Langley & R. Neches, eds.). Cambridge, MA: MIT Press 1987
3. Austin, J. L.: *How to do Things With Words*. (J. O. Urmson & M. Sbisà, eds.). Cambridge, MA: Harvard University Press 1962
4. Bann, S (ed.): *The Tradition of Constructivism*. New York, NY: Da Capo Press 1974
5. Bijker, Wiebe E., Hughes, T. P., & Pinch, T. (eds.): *The Social Construction of Technological Systems: New Directions in the Sociology and History of Technology* Cambridge, MA: MIT Press 1987
6. Bloom, A.: *The Closing of the American Mind*, New York, NY: Simon and Schuster 1987
7. Bonar, J. & Soloway, E.: Pre-programming knowledge: A major source of misconceptions in novice programmers *Human-Computer Interaction*, 1, pp. 133-161 (1985)
8. Bourdieu, P.: *Outline of a Theory of Practice*, Cambridge, MA: Cambridge University Press 1977
9. Boyle, R. A., Weingrad, P., & Soloway, E.: Multimedia composition: writing with words, pictures, and sounds. Paper presented at the Annual Meeting of the American Educational Research Association, San Francisco, CA, 1992
10. Brown, J. S., Collins, A., & Duguid, P.: Situated cognition and the culture of learning, *Educational Researcher*, 18, pp. 32-42 (1989)
11. Brown, J. S.: Toward a new epistemology for learning. In: *Intelligent Tutoring Systems* (C. Frasson & G. Gauthier, eds.), pp. 266-282 Norwood, NJ: Ablex Publishing Corporation 1990
12. Bruner, J.: *The Relevance of Education*. New York, NY: Norton 1973
13. Chase, W. G. & Simon, H. A.: Perception in chess, *Cognitive Psychology*, 4, pp. 55-81 (1973)
14. Chipp, H. B.: *Theories of Modern Art*. Berkeley, CA: University of California Press 1968
15. Clancey, W.: Situated cognition: stepping out of representational flatland. *AI Communications -- The European Journal on Artificial Intelligence* , 4(2/3), pp. 109-112 (1991)
16. Collins, A., Brown, J. S.: The Computer as a Tool for Learning Through Reflection, Technical Report #376, University of Illinois, Center for the Study of Learning, Champaign, Illinois: University of Illinois at Urbana-Champaign; Cambridge, MA: Bolt, Beranek and Newman 1986
17. Collins, A., Brown, J. S., & Newman, S. E.: Cognitive apprenticeship: teaching the craft of reading, writing and mathematics. In: *Condition and Instruction: Issues and Agendas*, (L. B. Resnick, ed.). Hillsdale, NJ: Lawrence Erlbaum Associates (in press)
18. Crouse, J.: *The Case Against the SAT*, Chicago, IL: University of Chicago Press 1988
19. de Groot, A.: *Thought and Choice in Chess*. The Hague: Mouton 1965
20. Dewey, J.: *Experience and Education*. New York, NY: Collier Books 1963
21. Dreyfus, H. L.: *What Computers Can't Do: A Critique of Artificial Intelligence Reason*. New York, NY: Harper & Row 1972
22. Duffy, T. M. & Jonassen, D. H. (eds.): *Educational Technology*, special issue on Constructivism: New Implications for Instructional Technology? May 1991.
23. Erlich, V.: *Russian Formalism: History, Doctrine, 2nd revised edition*. The Hague: Mouton 1965
24. Fiske, E. B.: *Smart Schools, Smart Kids: Why do some schools work?*, New York, NY: Simon and Schuster 1991
25. Foucault, M.: *Discipline and Punish: The Birth of the Prison*, New York, NY: Vintage Books 1979
26. Freire, P.: *Pedagogy of the Oppressed*. (M. B. Ramos, translator). New York, NY: Continuum 1990
27. Gasser, L.: Social conceptions of knowledge and action: DAI foundations and open systems semantics, *Artificial Intelligence*, 47, pp. 107-138 (1991)
28. Grosz, E.: *Sexual Subversions: Three French Feminists*. Sydney: Allen and Unwin 1989

29. Guzdial, M.: *Emile: an Adaptable Support Environment for Developing Hypercard Scripting Expertise*, Doctoral Dissertation, University of Michigan, Ann Arbor: Department of Electrical Engineering and Computer Science and Department of Education
30. Haraway, D.: *Primate Visions* New York, NY: Routledge 1989
31. Harel, I. & Papert, S.: Software design as a learning environment, *Interactive Learning Environments*, 1(1), pp. 1-32 (1990)
32. Harel, I. & Papert, S. (eds.): *Constructionism* Norwood, NJ: Ablex 1991
33. Hawkes, T.: *Structuralism and Semiotics*. Berkeley, CA: University of California Press 1977
34. Hewitt, C.: Open information systems semantics for distributed artificial intelligence, *Artificial Intelligence*, 47, pp. 79-106 (1991)
35. Hirsch, E. D. Jr.: *Cultural Literacy*. New York, NY: Vintage Books 1988
36. Illich, I.: *Deschooling Society*. London, England: Penguin Books 1971
37. Jameson, F.: *The Prison-House of Language: a Critical Account of Structuralism and Russian Formalism*. Princeton, NJ: Princeton University Press 1972
38. Johnson, W. L.: *Intention-Based Diagnosis of Novice Programming Errors*. London: Pitman, and Los Altos, CA: Morgan Kaufmann 1986
39. Johnson, W. L. & Soloway E.: PROUST: Knowledge-Based Program Understanding, Technical Report No. 285, New Haven, CT. Yale University, Computer Science Department 1985
40. Johnson, W. L., Soloway, E., Cutler, B., & Draper, S.: Bug Catalogue I, Technical Report No. 286, New Haven, CT: Yale University, Computer Science Department 1983
41. Labov, W.: *Sociolinguistic Patterns*. Philadelphia: University of Philadelphia Press, and Oxford: Blackwell 1972
42. Larkin, J., McDermott, J., Simon, D. P., & Simon, H. A.: Expert and novice performance in solving physics problems, *Science*, 208, pp. 1335-42 (1980)
43. Latour, B.: *Science in Action: How to Follow Scientists and Engineers Through Society*. Cambridge, MA: Harvard University Press 1987
44. Lave, J. & Wenger, E.: *Situated learning: Legitimate Peripheral Participation*, Cambridge, MA: Cambridge University Press 1991
45. Lodder, C.: *Russian Constructivism*, New Haven, CT: Yale University Press 1983
46. Noble, D. D.: Mental material: the militarization of learning and intelligence in US education. In: *Cyborg Worlds: the Military Information Society*, (L. Levidow & K. Robins, eds.). London: Free Association Books 1989
47. Owens, D.: *None of the Above: Behind the Myth of Scholastic Aptitude*. Boston, MA: Houghton Mifflin Company 1985
48. Papert , S.: *Mindstorms*. New York, NY: Basic Books 1980
49. Project Zero: *Portfolio: The Newsletter of Arts PROPEL, Volume 1, Number 1*, Cambridge, MA: Project Zero, The Harvard Graduate School of Education 1987
50. Resnick, L.: Learning in school and out, *Educational Researcher*, 4, pp. 13-20 (1987)
51. Rich, C.: A formal representation for plans in the programmer's apprentice. Proceedings of the IJCAI, pp. 1044-1052, Los Altos, CA, Morgan Kaufmann, 1981
52. Robinson, A. & Katzman, J.: *The Princeton Review: Cracking the System: The GRE, 1991 Edition*, New York, NY: Villard Books 1990
53. Sack, W.: Knowledge compilation and the language design game. *Proceedings of the 2nd International Conference on Intelligent Tutoring Systems*, Montreal, Quebec (C. Frasson, G. Gauthier & G. McCalla, eds.), pp. 225-233, Lecture Notes in Computer Science, Vol. 608, Berlin: Springer-Verlag 1992
54. Sack, W., Bennett, R., & Soloway, E.: The advanced placement computer science practice and feedback system. In: *Cognitive Models and Intelligent Environments for Learning Programming*, (E. Lemut, B. du Boulay, G. Deltori, eds.), pp. 291-298, NATO ASI Series F, Vol. 111, Berlin: Springer-Verlag 1993
55. Sack, W. & Soloway, E.: From PROUST to CHIRON: Intelligent Tutoring System design as iterative engineering; intermediate results are important!, In: *Computer Assisted Instruction and Intelligent Tutoring Systems: Shared Issues and Complementary Approaches* (J. Larkin, C. Scheftic, & R. Chabay, eds.). Hillsdale, NJ: Lawrence Erlbaum Associates 1991
56. Schank, R. & Abelson, R.: *Scripts, Plans, Goals, and Understanding*. Hillsdale, NJ: Lawrence Erlbaum Associates 1977
57. Simon, H. A.: *The Sciences of the Artificial, 2nd edition*. Cambridge, MA: MIT Press 1981
58. Soloway, E.: Learning to program = learning to construct mechanisms and explanations, *Communications of the ACM*, 29(9), pp. 850-858 (1986)
59. Soloway, E. & Ehrlich, K.: Empirical studies of programming knowledge, *IEEE Transactions on Software Engineering*, SE-10(5), pp. 595-609 (1984)

60. Soloway, E., Guzdial, M., Brade, K., Hohmann, L., Tabak, I., Weingrad, P., & Blumenfeld, P.: Technological Support for the Learning and Doing of Design, unnumbered working paper, Ann Arbor, MI: Highly-Interactive Computing Environments Group, Department of Electrical Engineering and Computer Science, University of Michigan 1991
61. Soloway, E., Lochhead, J., & Clement, J.: Does computer programming enhance problem solving ability? Some positive empirical evidence. In: *Computer Literacy*, (R. Seidel, ed.). New York, NY: Academic Press 1982
62. Soloway, E., Rubin, E., Woolf, B., Bonar, J., & Johnson, W. L.: MENOII: An AI-Based programming tutor, *Journal of Computer-Based Instruction*, 10(1&2), pp. 20-34 (1983)
63. Spohrer, J.: MARCEL: A Generate-Test-and-Debug (GTD) Impasse/Repair Model of Student Programmers, Technical Report No. 687, New Haven, CT: Yale University, Computer Science Department 1989
64. Spohrer, J., Pope, E., Lipman, M., Sack, W., Freiman, S., Littman, D., Johnson, W. L., & Soloway, E.: Bug Catalogue II, III, IV, Technical Report No. 386, New Haven, CT: Yale University, Computer Science Department 1985
65. Spohrer, J., Soloway, E.: Novice mistakes: are the folk wisdoms correct? *Communications of the ACM*, 29(7), pp. 624-632 (1986)
66. Suchman, L.: *Plans and Situated Actions*. Cambridge, UK: Cambridge University Press 1987
67. Tinker, R. F. & Papert, S.: Tools for science education. In: *AETS Yearbook: Information Technology and Science Education*, (J. D. Ellis, ed.). Association for the Education of Teachers in Science 1988
68. Todorov, T. (translator): *Theorie de la literature: textes des formalistes russes reunis*. Paris: Editions du Seuil 1966
69. Turkle, S.: *Psychoanalytic Politics: Freud's French Revolution*, New York, NY: Basic Books 1978
70. Turkle, S.: *The Second Self: Computers and the Human Spirit*. New York, NY: Simon and Schuster 1984
71. Van Dijk, T. A.: *News as Discourse*, Hillsdale, NJ: Lawrence Erlbaum Associates 1988
72. Wenger, E.: *Artificial Intelligence and Tutoring Systems*. Los Altos, CA: Morgan Kaufmann 1987
73. Winnocott, D. W.: *Playing and Reality*, New York, NY: Basic Books 1971
74. Winnocott, D. W.: Transitional objects and transitional phenomena. In: *Essential Papers on Object Relations*, (P. Buckley, ed.). New York, NY: New York University Press 1986
75. Winograd, T. & Flores, F.: *Understanding Computers and Cognition*. Reading, MA: Addison-Wesley 1986
76. Wittgenstein, L.: *Philosophical Investigations*. (G. E. M. Anscombe, translator), New York, NY: Macmillan 1953

# Subject Index

# NATO ASI Series F

Including Special Programmes on Sensory Systems for Robotic Control (ROB) and on Advanced Educational Technology (AET)

# NATO ASI Series F

# NATO ASI Series F

# NATO ASI Series F

# NATO ASI Series F

# NATO ASI Series F